THE
BEST OF
FOOD&WINE
1986 COLLECTION

THE BEST OF FOOD & WINE 1986 COLLECTION

American Express
Publishing Corporation
New York

THE BEST OF FOOD & WINE/1986 COLLECTION
Editor: Kate Slate
Art Director: Elizabeth G. Woodson
Designer: René-Julien Aussoleil

Published by American Express Publishing Corporation
1120 Avenue of the Americas, New York, New York 10036

Manufactured in the United States of America

Library of Congress Cataloging in Publication Data

Main entry under title:

The Best of Food & Wine

Includes index.
I. Cookery, International. I. Food & Wine (New York, N.Y.)
II. American Express Publishing Corporation. III. Title: Best of Food and Wine.
TX725.A1B48232 1986 641.5'14 85-22912

ISBN 0-916103-03-X

10 9 8 7 6 5 4 3 2 1
First Edition

TABLE OF CONTENTS

FOREWORD

Welcome to *The Best of Food & Wine/1986 Collection*, more than 480 recipes and 32 pages of glorious color photographs from issues of our magazine that appeared during the past year. This volume is the third in the series of our very well received *Best of Food & Wine* anthology cookbooks.

Those of you who know our magazine realize how highly we prize the food we present in each issue. Those who do not can rest assured that every recipe in *Food & Wine*, and therefore every recipe in this volume, has been tested and, where necessary, adapted or adjusted for use by home cooks. Two major responsibilities of our Test Kitchen cooks are to create workable recipes filled with flavor, and to simplify food preparation without robbing dishes of their fundamental integrity.

Where do these recipes come from? Some, a higher percentage than in any other American epicurean magazine, are developed by the Test Kitchen staff itself. During the period of time spanned by the contents of this book, our kitchen was directed by Diana Sturgis. Her principal assistants are John Robert Massie and Anne Disrude. The remainder have been created by contributors to the magazine. You will find a list crediting these talented cooks and writers on pages 255-256.

The recipes that we have gathered together represent a balance of foods and of the various courses that make a meal. They also represent what we feel to be a superb sampling of the best of contemporary cooking, delicious and beautiful food equally suitable for your family or for entertaining.

FOOD & WINE'S VINTAGE RATINGS
1974-1984

COMPILED BY ELIN McCOY & JOHN FREDERICK WALKER

	1974	1975	1976	1977	1978
Red Bordeaux	4 No charm. Hard & lightweight. Drink now.	8½ Classic, concentrated. Start drinking. Will last.	7 Soft, full, attractive. Drink now.	4 Lightweight, lacks fruit. Best now.	9 Rich, full, good depth. Wait 1-5 years.
Sauternes	3 Very poor. Avoid.	9 Deep, rich; some classics. Start drinking.	9 Elegant & luscious. Start drinking.	3 Very weak. Avoid.	5 Big, but lacks typical richness. Drink now.
Red Burgundy	4 Light & lean; no depth. Now or never.	3 Thin, weak; most are poor. Avoid.	7 Deep, full, tannic. Drink now.	4 Light, thin, uneven. Drink now.	8 Outstanding; excellent balance. Drink now.
White Burgundy	4 Thin & fading. Most past best.	4 Very light wines. Drink up.	7 Big, soft, rich wines. Drink now.	5 Light, lean, acidic. Drink now.	9 Superb; well-balanced. Wonderful now.
Napa/Sonoma Cabernet Sauvignon	8 Fat, rich, tannic; some overripe. Drink now.	7 Lacks power, but best have elegance. Drink now.	7 Variable. Many heavy and tannic. Drink now.	7½ Variable. Some well-balanced wines. Drink now.	8 Full, rich, balanced. Start drinking; best will keep.
Napa/Sonoma Chardonnay	6 Full-bodied, fast-maturing. Most past it.	8 Intense, well-balanced. Drink now.	6 Big, ripe; some too powerful. Drink up.	7 Uneven. Some attractive. Drink now.	8 Powerful, ripe wines. Drink up.
Piedmont Barolo & Barbaresco	8 Excellent, full & round. Drink now.	5 Light & attractive. Drink now.	6 Light, well-balanced. Drink now.	4 Light, thin wines. Drink now.	9 Classic, concentrated & tannic. Wait 2-4 years; will last.
Chianti	6 Light, pleasant, fading. Drink up.	9 Exceptional. Well-balanced wines. Now ready.	3 Lightweight, disappointing. Now or never.	7 Good to very good; firm, stylish. Drink now.	9 Exceptional; big, solid, tannic. Start drinking; will hold.
Germany	5 Uneven & fading. Drink up.	8 Excellent balance, stylish. Drink now.	9½ Super-rich wines. Enjoy; best balanced will keep.	6 Lightweight, crisp. Drink up.	6 Lightweight, crisp. Drink up.
Vintage Porto	No vintage declared.	6½ Light & stylish. Try in 2-4 years. Some wines fast-maturing.	No vintage declared.	9½ Superlative; ripe & dense. Wait 8-10 years.	5 Not generally declared. Rich, soft. Try in 3-4 years.

The following ratings and comments reflect a variety of opinions, including our own, on the quality and character of various categories of wines from recent vintages. The ratings—0 for the worst, 10 for the best—are averages, and better or worse wine than indicated can be found in each vintage. Assessments of the most current vintages are more predictive and hence less exact than those of older vintages.

Scores are based on a wine's quality at maturity. A lower-rated but mature wine will often be superior to a higher-rated but immature wine. When-to-drink advice is based on how such wines seemed to be developing in mid-1985, and presumes good storage. The earliest date suggested for consumption applies to the lesser wines of the vintage, which will mature faster than the finest examples of that year.

1979	1980	1981	1982	1983	1984
8 Fruity & delicious. Start drinking.	5 Small-scale, lightweight, pleasant. Drink up.	7½ Well-balanced wines. Wait 2 years.	10 Fabulous. Try in 4-8 years.	8 Firm, powerful. Try in 5 years.	7 Small-scale, firm. Wait 4 years.
6 Light but has character. Start drinking.	7 Attractive, small-scale. Start drinking.	7½ Well-balanced wines. Start drinking.	7 Variable. Best are big, powerful wines. Sample now.	9 Very promising, rich, classic wines. Wait 1-2 years.	7 Moderate quality. Some good.
6 Soft, supple, appealing. Drink now.	7 Mostly light wines for early drinking.	6 Variable vintage. Most early maturing.	7 Big, soft wines. Drink now.	9 Some very good, powerful wines. Start sampling.	7 Variable quality.
7 Attractive, fruity wines. Most best now.	5 Variable; the best are attractive.	8 Attractive wines for early drinking.	9 Excellent. Big, rich wines. Start drinking.	8 Good, promising wines. Start drinking.	7 Some fine. Start sampling.
7 Uneven quality; some very good. Start drinking.	8½ Powerful but well-balanced. Will keep.	7½ Variable. Early maturing; try now.	7½ Lighter style; some attractive. Try now.	7 Good, but not particularly promising.	8 Big, soft, promising.
8 Rich, intense, impressive. Drink up.	9 Many have superb balance. Drink now.	7 Soft, ripe wines. Drink now.	8 Many light, some excellent. Drink now.	7 Good moderate year. Drink now.	7½ Good year. Start sampling.
8 Elegant, well-balanced wines. Start drinking; will hold.	6 Uneven. Best are well-balanced, attractive. Start drinking.	7 Firm, solid wines. Start sampling.	8½ Big, powerful wines; very promising. Wait 2-5 years.	7½ Promising vintage.	5½ Light, variable. For early drinking.
7 Attractive, ripe wines. Drink now.	6 Uneven; best are small-scale.	7 Good, firm wines.	8 Attractive but early maturing.	8 Attractive, early maturing.	5 Spotty. For early drinking.
7 Good quality & balance. Drink now.	5 Light & lean. Drink now.	8 Well-balanced, attractive. Drink now.	7 Soft, fruity. Drink now.	9 Excellent year. Marvelous late-harvest wines. Start tasting.	7 Good. For early drinking.
No vintage declared.	7 Light but promising. Sample in 5-8 years.	No vintage declared.	8 Firm, well-balanced. Sample in 6-9 years.	8 Good, solid wines. Sample in 7-10 years.	——

BEVERAGES

SPIRITED CITRUS CUP

MAKES ABOUT 1½ QUARTS

¼ cup honey
½ teaspoon grated orange zest
2 cups orange juice
3 tablespoons fresh lemon juice
6 whole cloves
1¼ cups Cognac or other brandy
2 tablespoons orange liqueur, such as Triple-Sec

1. Place the honey and orange zest in a medium noncorrodible saucepan with 2½ cups of water. Bring to a boil, stirring occasionally, and cook until the honey dissolves completely.

2. Add the orange juice, lemon juice and cloves and return to a boil. Remove from the heat and immediately stir in the Cognac and orange liqueur. Serve in heatproof punch glasses.

—Warren Picower

ICED CRANBERRY AQUAVIT

This peach-colored aperitif is ideal for holiday toasting.

MAKES 2 BOTTLES

2 packages (12 ounces each) fresh cranberries
2 bottles (750 ml each) aquavit
2 tablespoons black peppercorns

1. Divide the cranberries among 3 quart jars. Pour in the aquavit to cover; rinse and reserve the aquavit bottles and caps. Add the peppercorns, dividing equally among the jars. Cover and let steep at room temperature for at least 3 days.

2. Strain through a sieve into a large pitcher; reserve the cranberries (see Note). Pour the aquavit back into the original bottles and store in the freezer.

3. To encase each bottle in a block of ice, rinse out 2 half-gallon milk cartons and cut off the tops. Set each bottle in a ½-gallon milk carton and surround with water. Place in the freezer. When the water is frozen, tear away the carton, shave off the square corners of the ice block with a knife and return to the freezer until ready to serve.

NOTE: The cranberries can be used to make a flavorful sauce or relish. If you do decide to make cranberry sauce, here's a hint for removing the peppercorns: Place the drained cranberries in a large pot of water; the peppercorns will sink, so you can scoop the berries off the surface.

—Anne Disrude

TEQUILA SNAP

A blend of zesty, sweet and bitter flavors. Add more fresh ginger to make the drink even zippier. Don't worry if the drink seems cloudy; no matter how fine the sieve, some ginger fiber will slip through and settle out as the drink stands.

MAKES 4 DRINKS

12 ounces (1½ cups) white tequila
4 ounces (½ cup) Triple-Sec
4 teaspoons coarsely chopped fresh ginger
6 dashes Angostura bitters
4 orange slices, for garnish

1. Place the tequila, Triple-Sec, ginger and bitters in a blender or food processor and puree until smooth.

2. Strain through a very fine sieve or a double thickness of dampened cheesecloth. Pour over ice cubes into large old-fashioned glasses. Garnish each with an orange slice.

—Warren Picower

STONEWALL COCKTAIL

MAKES 2 DRINKS

20 allspice berries
2 cinnamon sticks
2 tablespoons brown sugar
3 ounces (6 tablespoons) applejack
1 ounce (2 tablespoons) light rum
Lemon twists, for garnish

1. In a small saucepan, combine the allspice, cinnamon, brown sugar and ½ cup of water. Bring to a boil, reduce the heat and simmer for 30 minutes.

2. Pour the spices and liquid into a measuring cup and add enough hot water to equal ½ cup. Let cool.

3. Strain into a screw-top container or bottle. Add the applejack and rum. Cap the container and freeze until icy, or, if serving immediately, stir with large ice cubes until chilled through, then strain. Serve in chilled, stemmed cocktail glasses, garnished with a lemon twist.

—Warren Picower

VANILLA THRILLER

Like the traditional Indian *lassi* that inspired this concoction, this is a refreshing thirst quencher during hot weather or a cool accompaniment to spicy hot food any time of year.

MAKES 2 DRINKS

1 cup milk
15 whole cloves
15 cardamom pods
2 cinnamon sticks
1 cup vanilla yogurt
1 tablespoon honey

1. In a small heavy saucepan, combine the milk, cloves, cardamom and cinnamon and scald over moderate heat until a skin forms. Remove the heat and let cool, then refrigerate until chilled through.

2. Strain into a blender; discard the spices. Add the yogurt and honey and blend until smooth. Cover the blender container tightly and refrigerate until ready to use. **(The recipe can be made several hours ahead to this point.)**

3. Just before serving, add 3 to 4 cracked ice cubes per serving to the blender and blend until frothy. Serve in all-purpose wine glasses.

—Warren Picower

ORANGE-VANILLA COFFEE

The choice of orange liqueur used in this recipe will have a distinct effect on the flavor of the drink: Grand Marnier, for instance, gives a strong, rich taste, heady with Cognac, while Cointreau will provide a very pleasant, flowery nuance.

4 SERVINGS

3 cups freshly brewed coffee
¼ cup heavy cream
4 teaspoons sugar
¼ teaspoon vanilla extract
2 tablespoons plus 2 teaspoons orange liqueur
Curls of orange zest, for garnish

1. In a medium saucepan, combine the coffee, cream, sugar and vanilla. Heat until simmering.

2. Meanwhile, pour 2 teaspoons of the orange liqueur into each of four 10-ounce glasses. Place a spoon in each glass to prevent cracking and pour the hot coffee over the orange liqueur. Garnish with a curl of orange zest.

—Warren Picower

CHOCOLATE-CHERRY DEMITASSE

This rich drink is just right for demitasse sipping. If a tall drink is desired, cut the amount of chocolate to 1 ounce and serve the drink in two tall glasses, topped with whipped cream and shaved chocolate.

4 SERVINGS

1½ ounces semisweet chocolate, broken into bits
½ cup milk
¼ cup heavy cream
¼ cup freshly brewed strong coffee
2 teaspoons sugar
¼ teaspoon vanilla extract
⅓ cup kirschwasser (cherry brandy)

1. In a small heavy saucepan, combine the chocolate, milk and cream. Warm over moderate heat, stirring occasionally, until the chocolate melts. Whisk to blend well.

2. Stir in the coffee, sugar and vanilla and heat until simmering.

3. Remove from the heat and stir in the kirsch. Serve in demitasse cups.

—Catherine Fredman

HOT RUM MILK WITH CARDAMOM

Be sure to use whole cardamom pods, not the seeds, for this recipe, or the flavor will be too intense.

4 SERVINGS

1 quart milk
2 heaping teaspoons whole cardamom pods (about 40)
3 tablespoons sugar
½ cup dark rum

1. In a heavy medium saucepan, combine the milk, cardamom and sugar. Heat, stirring to dissolve the sugar, until the milk begins to foam.

2. Meanwhile, divide the rum among four large mugs and 10-ounce glasses with a spoon in them to prevent cracking. Strain the milk into the glasses.

—Anne Disrude

NORMAN HOT TODDY

4 SERVINGS

1 cup milk
⅓ cup heavy cream
1 cinnamon stick
¾ cup Calvados
⅓ cup apricot brandy
Sugar
Freshly grated nutmeg, for garnish
Cinnamon sticks, for garnish

1. In a medium saucepan, combine the milk, cream and cinnamon stick. Bring to a simmer over moderate heat. Reduce the heat to low. Stir in the Calvados and apricot brandy and cook until just warmed through; do not boil.

2. Meanwhile, place a large pinch of sugar in each of four mugs or 8-ounce glasses. Place a spoon in each glass to prevent cracking and pour in the hot toddy. Sprinkle with the nutmeg and garnish with a cinnamon stick.

—Warren Picower

HOT SCOT

4 SERVINGS

1 quart milk
½ cup Scotch whisky
¼ cup Drambuie
4 teaspoons unsalted butter (optional)
4 dashes of aromatic bitters, such as Angostura

1. Place the milk in a medium saucepan and heat until warmed through; do not boil.

2. Meanwhile, into each of four large mugs or 10-ounce glasses with a spoon in them to prevent cracking, place 2 tablespoons of the whisky, 1 tablespoon Drambuie, 1 teaspoon butter and a dash of bitters.

3. Strain the milk into the mugs. Stir gently until the butter melts.

—*Warren Picower*

KEY WEST SUNSET

MAKES ABOUT 2½ CUPS

2 very ripe large bananas, sliced
8 teaspoons frozen orange juice concentrate
1 cup milk
2 tablespoons grenadine syrup
Orange slice or long curl of orange peel, for garnish

In a blender, combine all of the ingredients and blend thoroughly. Sieve. Serve as is or with alcohol. Garnish with the orange slice or peel.

—*W. Peter Prestcott*

GRAPE DEW

MAKES ABOUT 2½ CUPS

1 cup seedless green grapes (see Note)
1 cup white grape juice
1 cup cubed, very ripe honeydew melon
Chilled grapes or slice of melon, for garnish

In a blender, combine all of the ingredients and blend well. Sieve. Serve with or without alcohol, garnished with grapes or a slice of melon.

NOTE: For a frostier, thicker drink, use frozen grapes. Blend and serve at once without sieving.

—*Warren Picower*

ICED IBERIAN

MAKES ABOUT 2½ CUPS

1 medium tomato, chopped
1 medium red bell pepper, seeded and cut into strips
1 Kirby cucumber, peeled and thickly sliced
2 scallion bulbs with just a touch of the green
About 1 cup tomato juice
Juice of ½ large lemon
2 dashes of hot pepper sauce
Leafy celery stalk, cucumber stick, trimmed scallion or lemon slice, for garnish

1. In a blender, combine the chopped tomato, bell pepper, cucumber, scallion bulbs, 1 cup of tomato juice, the lemon juice and hot sauce. Blend to a fine puree. Taste and add more lemon juice or hot sauce to taste.

2. Top with more tomato juice to measure 2½ cups and whirl briefly. Sieve. Serve as is, with seltzer for a spritzer or with vodka or rum. Garnish the glass with one of the garnishes listed above.

—*Warren Picower*

CARIBBEAN MANDARIN

MAKES ABOUT 2½ CUPS

1½ cups chilled orange juice
½ teaspoon grated orange zest
1 cup unsweetened coconut milk
1 tablespoon grenadine syrup
½ cup coarsely chopped ice cubes
Orange slice or long curl of orange peel, for garnish

In a blender, combine all of the ingredients and blend thoroughly. Serve immediately garnished with the orange slice or peel.

—*Warren Picower*

PEACH GLACIER

We used peach and cantaloupe flavors here, but you can use any compatible fruit nectar and sherbet.

MAKES ABOUT 2½ CUPS

1 cup peach nectar
1 cup cantaloupe sherbet
2 tablespoons honey
1 teaspoon almond extract
Juice of 1 lime
Slice of fresh peach, cantaloupe or lime, for garnish

In a blender, combine all of the ingredients and blend thoroughly. Garnish and serve at once.

—*Warren Picower*

ORCHARD FLAVORITE

MAKES ABOUT 2½ CUPS

2 cups apple cider
2 tablespoons finely chopped crystallized ginger
2 teaspoons grenadine syrup
Apple slice or long curl of apple peel, for garnish

In a blender, combine all of the ingredients and blend thoroughly. Serve with seltzer for a spritzer or with vodka or rum. Garnish with the apple slice or peel.

—*Warren Picower*

HOMEMADE GINGER ALE

MAKES ABOUT 1 QUART

1 quart chilled seltzer
¼ cup Ginger Syrup (p. 243)

Pour the seltzer into a pitcher. Stir in the ginger syrup and serve over ice.

—*Diana Sturgis*

APPETIZERS & STARTERS

PEPPERED PECANS

These are delicious with a glass of rich red wine.

MAKES ABOUT 1 CUP

¼ cup sugar
1 tablespoon coarse (kosher) salt
1½ to 2 tablespoons coarsely ground black pepper
1 cup (4 ounces) pecan halves

1. In a small bowl, blend the sugar, salt and 1½ to 2 tablespoons pepper, to taste. Set the seasoning mixture aside.
2. Heat a large, very heavy skillet, preferably cast iron, over high heat until it is hot enough to vaporize a bead of water on contact. Add the pecans and cook, tossing constantly, for 1 minute to bring the nut oil to the surface.
3. Sprinkle the nuts with half the seasoning mixture. Shake the pan vigorously until the sugar melts, about 1 minute. Add the remaining seasoning mixture and continue shaking the pan until the sugar again melts and coats the pecans. Immediately turn the nuts onto a baking sheet, spreading them apart. Let cool; then seal in a plastic bag.

—Barbara Tropp

CURRIED TOASTED ALMONDS

MAKES ABOUT 1½ CUPS

1 tablespoon unsalted butter
½ pound unblanched almonds
1½ tablespoons curry powder
½ teaspoon salt

In a heavy skillet, melt the butter over moderately high heat. Add the almonds and sauté, stirring frequently, until the skins begin to split, about 3 minutes. Sprinkle with the curry powder and salt and toss to coat well.

MARINATED OLIVES LE CHERCHE-MIDI

MAKES ABOUT 1 PINT

½ pound Nyons or other dry-cured black olives
3 small dried hot red peppers
1 teaspoon herbes de Provence
2 garlic cloves, unpeeled and bruised
1 cup extra-virgin olive oil

In a pint jar, combine the olives, hot peppers, herbs and garlic. Add the olive oil and let marinate, loosely covered, in a cool place for 3 days.

VARIATION: Marinate Picholine or other brine-cured green olives in virgin olive oil with several broken dried fennel stalks and strips of lemon zest.

—Sally Scoville, Le Cherche-Midi, New York City

CHEESE TWISTS

While these twists are absolutely delicious when prepared and eaten on the same day, they are also quite acceptable when formed a few days ahead, covered and frozen on flat sheets and baked on the day of the party.

MAKES ABOUT 5 DOZEN

1 to 1¼ pounds prepared puff pastry, such as 1 sheet of Voilà or 2 sheets of Pepperidge Farm, chilled
1 tablespoon Dijon-style mustard
1 egg, beaten
1½ cups grated Gruyère cheese (¼ pound)

1. Cover a large cookie sheet with parchment or waxed paper. Lightly flour the paper and lay a single sheet of puff pastry on top. Brush the pastry with the mustard, then lightly brush with beaten egg. Reserve any remaining egg for glazing.
2. If using a single large sheet of pastry, sprinkle half with the cheese and fold the other half of the pastry over the filling. If using two sheets of pastry, sprinkle the cheese over the mustard-coated sheet and lay the other sheet on top. Roll the pastry into a 12-by-16-inch rectangle and refrigerate for 20 minutes, until well chilled.
3. With a very sharp knife and using clean, decisive strokes, trim away ¼ inch from each pastry edge. Wipe the blade and dip it in a little flour between each cut to prevent pulling or tearing the pastry.
4. Handling the pastry as little as possible, cut the rectangle lengthwise into 32 strips, 16 inches long by ¼ to ⅜ inch wide. Refrigerate for 30 minutes, until well chilled.
5. Preheat the oven to 400°. Without stretching the strips, twist them together in pairs, pinching the ends to seal. Lay the twists 2 to 3 inches apart on ungreased baking sheets. Cover and refrigerate the strips until ready to bake.
6. Brush the twists lightly with the reserved beaten egg and bake in the upper third of the oven for 12 to 20 minutes, until deep golden brown and crisp. Let cool on the baking sheets, then cut into 4-inch lengths.

—Diana Sturgis

GRILLED CHEDDAR CANAPES WITH CORNICHONS

MAKES 32

8 slices of rye bread
2 tablespoons unsalted butter, softened
Cornichons, thinly sliced lengthwise
½ pound Cheddar cheese, grated

1. Preheat the broiler and broil the bread until toasted on one side. Leave the broiler on.

2. Spread the untoasted sides with the butter. Cover with a layer of cornichons and sprinkle with the cheese. Broil until the cheese is melted and bubbling, about 2 minutes.

3. Trim each slice into a square, then quarter diagonally to form 32 triangles. Garnish each with a slice of cornichon.

DUXELLES FINGER SANDWICHES

20 SERVINGS (60 PIECES)

1 ounce dried cèpes
1 ounce dried morels
4 tablespoons unsalted butter
6 large shallots, minced (about ½ cup)
1 pound cultivated mushrooms, minced
1 cup dry Madeira
1 teaspoon salt
¼ teaspoon freshly ground pepper
1 loaf unsliced firm-textured white bread, cut into 24 slices ⅛ inch thick
½ cup clarified butter

1. Combine the cèpes and morels in a bowl and cover with boiling water. Let soak for 30 minutes. Using a slotted spoon, remove the mushrooms from the soaking liquid; reserve the liquid. If the mushrooms are still sandy, carefully wash them under running water. Drain and mince. Strain the soaking liquid through a coffee filter or a double thickness of dampened cheesecloth and reserve 1 cup.

2. In a large skillet, melt the unsalted butter over moderate heat. When the foam subsides, add the shallots and sauté until softened, about 4 minutes. Add the dried and fresh mushrooms and sauté, stirring frequently, until all the liquid has evaporated, about 10 minutes.

3. Add the Madeira, reserved soaking liquid, salt and pepper. Cook, stirring frequently, until the liquid evaporates and the individual pieces of mushroom begin to separate and brown. Taste for seasoning and adjust the salt and pepper if necessary.

4. Spread 8 slices of the bread to within ⅛ inch of the crust with half the duxelles mixture. Lay a slice of bread on top of each and spread with the remaining duxelles. Top with the remaining slices of bread to make 8 triple-layered sandwiches. Place the sandwiches on a baking sheet, cover them with another baking sheet and lightly weigh down with two #2½ cans for about 10 minutes to set the sandwiches.

5. In a large heavy skillet, heat 2 tablespoons of the clarified butter to just below the smoking point. One at a time, brown the sandwiches over moderately high heat, turning once, about 30 seconds on each side. Wipe out the pan between each sandwich and add more clarified butter as necessary. (**The recipe may be prepared to this point 3 hours ahead.** Wrap the sandwiches in foil and set aside. To proceed, place the wrapped sandwiches in a single layer on a baking sheet, weigh down and warm in a 300° oven for 15 minutes.)

6. With a sharp knife, cut the crusts from each sandwich; try not to tear the bread. Cut each sandwich into 8 small triangles or rectangular fingers. Serve warm.

—John Robert Massie

FETA CHEESE WITH THYME

MAKES ABOUT 5 DOZEN

1½ teaspoons thyme
½ cup extra-virgin olive oil
1 pound feta cheese, cut into ¾-inch cubes

In a shallow bowl, combine the thyme and olive oil. Add the cheese cubes and toss to coat well. Serve with toothpicks.

CHORIZO-FILLED DATES WRAPPED IN BACON

Tasty, bite-size and easy to prepare ahead, these sweet-spicy morsels are the perfect tapas.

4 TO 6 SERVINGS

1 small Spanish chorizo sausage, about 2 ounces
24 pitted dates
8 slices of bacon, cut crosswise in thirds

1. Cut off the ends of the chorizo and slice the chorizo crosswise into 3 equal pieces, about ¾ inch long; remove the casing if it is tough. Halve each of these pieces lengthwise; then cut each into 4 lengthwise strips to make a total of 24 small sticks. (If your chorizo is very thick and these pieces are too large for the dates, halve again.)

2. Insert each piece of chorizo into a date and pinch the ends of the dates closed around the sausage. Wrap a strip of bacon around each date. Secure, if necessary, with a toothpick. (**The recipe can be prepared up to a day in advance and refrigerated.**)

3. Place the wrapped dates in a skillet, with the seam side of the bacon down, and sauté, turning, until

the bacon is golden on all sides. Drain on paper towels. Serve hot.

—*Penelope Casas*

BRANDADE-FILLED POTATOES

20 SERVINGS (60 PIECES)

¾ pound dried salt cod
30 small red potatoes (about 2 pounds), 1½ inches or less in diameter
½ cup plus 4 tablespoons fruity olive oil
¼ cup milk
¼ cup heavy cream
Pinch of freshly grated nutmeg
½ teaspoon freshly ground white pepper

1. Soak the salt cod in cold water, changing the water occasionally, for 12 to 24 hours, depending on the level of saltiness.

2. Cut each potato in half. Trim the bottom of each half so the potato will sit flat with the cut side up. Using a melon baller or teaspoon, scoop out the inside of each potato, leaving a ¼-inch shell. Set these aside.

3. Place the potato shells in a large saucepan, cover with cold water and bring to a boil over moderately high heat. Reduce the heat and simmer until tender but still firm, 12 to 15 minutes. Drain the potato shells and gently toss with 2 tablespoons of the olive oil.

4. In a small saucepan, combine ½ cup of the oil, the milk and cream. Bring to a simmer over moderate heat.

5. Drain the salt cod and cut it into 2-inch pieces. Place in a food processor and pulse until the cod is broken up; do not puree.

6. With the machine on, gradually pour the hot oil-milk mixture into the cod. Season with the nutmeg and white pepper and blend briefly until no large pieces of cod remain, but the brandade still has some texture. Taste and adjust the seasoning if necessary. Let the mixture cool until it is slightly thickened. (**The recipe may be prepared to this point one day ahead.** Cover and refrigerate the brandade and potatoes separately. Let return to room temperature before proceeding.)

7. Preheat the broiler. Spoon the brandade into the potatoes or pipe with a #5 plain tip, filling each shell with about 1 tablespoon of brandade. Place the filled shells on a baking sheet and brush the tops lightly with the remaining 2 tablespoons oil. Broil about 5 inches from the heat until lightly browned, about 3 minutes. Serve hot.

—*John Robert Massie*

GUACAMOLE EL NOPALITO

This traditional recipe comes from El Nopalito in Galveston, Texas.

4 SERVINGS

2 very ripe medium avocados, preferably Hass, peeled and pitted
½ teaspoon salt
½ cup minced tomato
¼ cup minced red onion
Corn tortilla chips, as accompaniment

Place the avocado in a bowl. Add the salt and mash with a fork. Stir in the tomato and onion. Serve immediately with corn tortilla chips.

—*Molly O'Neill*

CHOPPED CHICKEN LIVER

Serve this rich chopped liver with shredded lettuce, sliced tomato, radishes and a choice of pumpernickel or rye bread.

MAKES ABOUT 4¼ CUPS

1½ medium onions, coarsely chopped
3 tablespoons rendered chicken fat (see Note)
2 tablespoons peanut oil
2½ pounds chicken livers, well rinsed
3 hard-cooked eggs
1 teaspoon salt
¼ teaspoon freshly ground pepper

1. Preheat the oven to 350°. In a roasting pan, combine the onions, chicken fat and oil. Bake, stirring occasionally, until the onions are lightly browned, about 30 minutes. Add the chicken livers to the roasting pan; stir to coat them with the pan juices. Continue cooking until the livers are hard, about 30 minutes. Cool slightly until the livers can be handled; reserve the pan juices.

2. In a food processor using an on-off technique or in a meat grinder with the coarse disk, grind together the livers, onions, eggs and the reserved pan juices until chopped. Do not puree until smooth; the liver should have a coarse texture. Season with the salt and pepper.

NOTE: Rendered chicken fat is available in many butcher shops and supermarkets. To render the fat yourself, pull off the excess fat from the inside of the chicken and place it in a small saucepan with 2 tablespoons of water. Cook over low heat for 20 to 30 minutes; strain. The fat will keep in a tightly covered jar in the refrigerator for several months.

—*Leo Steiner, Carnegie Delicatessen, New York City*

PORK RILLETTES

MAKES ABOUT 6 CUPS

5 pounds fresh pork fat, cut up
3½ pounds lean pork shoulder, cut into 4-inch chunks

6 large sprigs of fresh thyme or 1 tablespoon dried
4 imported bay leaves
1½ teaspoons salt
1 teaspoon coarsely cracked pepper

1. Put the fat pieces into a large pot, add 2 cups of water and bring to a boil. Reduce the heat and simmer, covered, for about 4 hours, until all the fat is rendered and the pieces are reduced to crisp, brown cracklings. Remove the cracklings and reserve for another use. **(This can be done a week ahead.)**

2. Place the pork chunks in a heavy deep 6-quart saucepan. Tie the thyme and bay leaves in several layers of cheesecloth and add to the pan. Cover with the rendered pork fat and bring to a simmer. Cook, uncovered, skimming off scum as it accumulates and turning the pork occasionally to make sure it is evenly covered with the fat, until the pork is soft and shreds easily, about 4 hours.

3. Remove the pork with a slotted spoon and let stand until cool enough to handle; tear it into fine shreds. Toss with the salt and pepper. Add 1¾ cups of the liquid fat. Mix well and pack into a 2-quart crock. Ladle fat at least ½ inch deep over the top to seal the rillettes. Let cool to room temperature, then cover and refrigerate. Well-sealed rillettes can be refrigerated for 2 weeks or frozen for up to 3 months.

—Anne Disrude

CURED FISH WITH AVOCADO AND ZUCCHINI

MAKES ABOUT 2 DOZEN

8 ounces Herb-Cured Fish (p. 28), sliced and coarsely chopped (about 1 cup)
2 small zucchini, cut crosswise on the diagonal into ⅛-inch ovals
2 tablespoons olive oil
1 tablespoon plus 1 teaspoon fresh lime juice
½ teaspoon minced fresh herb (whatever kind was used in curing the fish)
¼ teaspoon minced fresh hot red pepper or a pinch of crushed hot red pepper
Pinch of salt
Pinch of freshly ground black pepper
½ ripe avocado

1. Mound about 2 teaspoons of the fish on top of each zucchini slice.

2. In a small bowl, whisk together the oil, 1 teaspoon of the lime juice, the herb, hot pepper, salt and black pepper.

3. Cut the avocado into 24 small slices about 1 by ½ by ¼ inch. Drizzle with the remaining 1 tablespoon lime juice to prevent discoloration. Place a piece of avocado on top of each hors d'oeuvre. Drizzle about ¼ teaspoon of dressing over each, stirring the dressing often so that each hors d'oeuvre gets a little hot pepper and herb.

—Anne Disrude

CUCUMBER-WRAPPED SCALLOPS WITH PICKLED GINGER

The inspiration for this dish is seviche, raw fish that is "cooked" by marinating it in fresh lime juice. Wrapped in thin ribbons of cucumber, these scallop rolls are perfect finger food for summer entertaining.

F&W BEVERAGE SUGGESTION
California Fumé Blanc

4 SERVINGS

½ pound bay scallops
2 tablespoons fresh lime juice
1 tablespoon light olive oil
2 European seedless cucumbers, as straight as possible
¼ teaspoon salt
*1 tablespoon minced Japanese pink pickled ginger (shoga)**
**Available at Oriental groceries*

1. Remove and discard the tough connecting muscle from the scallops. In a shallow bowl, toss the scallops with the lime juice and oil. Cover and refrigerate overnight, tossing occasionally, until almost completely white and opaque throughout.

2. Using a swivel-bladed vegetable peeler or a mandoline, cut the cucumbers lengthwise into thin ribbons about 1 inch wide and 10 inches long; avoid slicing ribbons from the central seed core. Discard the skin-covered green slices and the core.

3. Remove the scallops from the refrigerator and drain well. Place a scallop at one end of a strip of cucumber. If the cucumber strips are too wide for the scallop, slice off a thin strip along one edge. Sprinkle very lightly with salt. Tightly roll up the scallop in the cucumber; it will seal itself at the end.

4. Top each with a pinch of pickled ginger. **(The recipe can be made up to 1 hour ahead.** Cover and refrigerate.) Serve slightly chilled.

—Anne Disrude

BAY SCALLOPS WITH TARRAGON SAUCE

MAKES ABOUT 5 DOZEN

1 pound bay scallops
¼ cup bottled clam juice
½ cup sour cream
1 tablespoon heavy cream
1 teaspoon tarragon
1 tablespoon chopped fresh parsley
1 teaspoon fresh lemon juice
¼ teaspoon salt
Pinch of white pepper

1. In a saucepan, cook the scallops in the clam juice over moderately low heat, stirring frequently, until the scallops are almost opaque. Drain and let cool.

2. In a food processor, combine the sour cream, heavy cream, tarragon, parsley, lemon juice, salt and pepper. Blend until smooth and pale green. Taste and add 1 or 2 more teaspoons tarragon if desired.

3. Serve the scallops with toothpicks and the dipping sauce on the side.

SNAILS IN GARLIC BUTTER

20 SERVINGS (72 PIECES)

3 cans (7½ ounces each) "very large" snails (24 snails per can)
2 cups dry white wine
1 medium onion, quartered
1 medium carrot, quartered
1 celery rib, quartered
Bouquet garni: 10 parsley stems, 1 bay leaf, ½ teaspoon thyme and 10 peppercorns tied in several layers of cheesecloth
1½ sticks (¾ cup) unsalted butter, softened
5 garlic cloves, crushed
½ cup chopped parsley
1 tablespoon fresh lemon juice
1 teaspoon salt
¼ teaspoon freshly ground pepper
½ cup coarse dry bread crumbs

1. Preheat the oven to 400°. Drain the snails and rinse under cold running water. Place the snails in a large noncorrodible saucepan. Add the wine, onion, carrot, celery, bouquet garni and 2 cups of water. Bring to a boil over moderately high heat, reduce the heat and simmer for 10 minutes. Drain the snails; discard the vegetables, bouquet garni and liquid.

2. Place the butter, garlic, parsley, lemon juice, salt and pepper in a food processor and puree until smooth, about 1 minute.

3. Place the snails in a large, shallow baking dish. Dot the snails with the garlic butter. Sprinkle the bread crumbs on top. Bake in the center of the oven for 15 minutes, or until piping hot. Serve hot with toothpicks.

—*John Robert Massie*

SARDINES MARINATED WITH LEMONS AND ONIONS

12 SERVINGS

6 cans (3¾ ounces each) sardines in olive oil, drained
2 lemons, thinly sliced
1 large Spanish onion, thinly sliced
1 teaspoon thyme
6 imported bay leaves
¼ teaspoon freshly ground pepper
¾ cup olive oil
4 to 5 heads of Bibb lettuce, separated into leaves

1. In a deep noncorrodible baking dish, carefully arrange one-third of the sardines in a single layer. Top with 6 to 8 slices of the lemon, one-third of the onions, one-third of the thyme and 2 bay leaves. Sprinkle with one-third of the pepper. Repeat 2 more times.

2. Pour the olive oil over the sardines. Cover with plastic wrap and refrigerate for at least 12 hours, or up to several days. Use a bulb baster to remoisten the top layer with the olive oil once a day.

3. Before serving, remove the onion slices and chop coarsely. Squeeze the juice from the lemon slices through a sieve into a small bowl. Transfer the sardines to a platter, arranging them, overlapping slightly, in a fish design.

4. Remove and reserve the bay leaves. Whisk the olive oil remaining in the dish into the lemon juice. Drizzle over the sardines. Garnish with 3 or 4 rows of the chopped onion and the bay leaves.

5. Serve with the lettuce leaves in a bowl on the side. To eat, fill a lettuce leaf with a sardine and a sprinkling of chopped onion.

—*Anne Disrude*

QUESADILLAS (STUFFED CORN TORTILLAS)

Although made with cheese here, *quesadillas* are often stuffed with beef, potatoes or squash blossoms. Sliced avocados drizzled with lime juice are a perfect accompaniment.

8 SERVINGS

8 corn tortillas, preferably homemade (p. 154)
6 ounces quesillo de Oaxaca or Armenian string cheese, torn into fine, short strands
8 large epazote leaves or 4 teaspoons chopped fresh coriander (cilantro)
Vegetable oil, for frying
Salsa Fresca (p. 235) or hot taco sauce

1. If using fresh tortillas, peel off the top sheet of waxed paper from each; use the bottom sheet to help fold them over. Cover half of each tortilla with one-eighth of the cheese, leaving a ½-inch border around the

edge. Place an *epazote* leaf in the center of each portion of cheese or sprinkle each with ½ teaspoon of the chopped coriander. Fold the tortilla over and pinch the edges to seal. (You won't be able to seal prepared corn tortillas, but the *quesadillas* will taste delicious anyway.)

2. In a large skillet, heat ½ inch of oil until shimmering. Adjust the heat as necessary throughout so that the oil is very hot but not smoking. Add half the *quesadillas* and fry until crisp and golden brown on the bottom, about 2 minutes. Turn carefully with a wide slotted spatula and fry until crisp and golden brown all over, 2 to 3 minutes longer. Remove with a spatula and drain on paper towels. Repeat with the remaining *quesadillas*. Serve hot, with Salsa Fresca or hot taco sauce on the side.

—Jim Fobel

SAUTEED EGGPLANT WITH RED PEPPERS

F&W BEVERAGE SUGGESTION
Rosé, such as Souverain Pinot Noir Rosé

4 SERVINGS

3 tablespoons olive oil
1 pound baby eggplant or skinny Japanese eggplant, stems removed and eggplant cut lengthwise into eighths
2 red bell peppers, cut lengthwise into eighths
2 medium garlic cloves, finely chopped
1 small onion, finely chopped
4 plum tomatoes—peeled, seeded and chopped
¼ cup tomato puree
¼ cup red wine
1½ tablespoons cider vinegar
½ teaspoon salt
⅛ teaspoon cayenne pepper
⅛ teaspoon sugar
2 tablespoons pine nuts (pignoli)
2 tablespoons minced fresh basil
1 tablespoon minced fresh parsley

1. In a large heavy noncorrodible skillet, heat 1 tablespoon of the oil until almost smoking. Add half of the eggplant and toss to coat with the oil. Cook over moderately high heat, turning the pieces occasionally, until browned on both sides, about 5 minutes. Remove to a bowl. Add 1 tablespoon oil to the skillet and, when hot, brown the remaining eggplant. Transfer to the bowl.

2. Heat the remaining 1 tablespoon oil in the skillet. Add the peppers and sauté, stirring frequently, until crisp-tender, about 5 minutes.

3. Reduce the heat to moderate and stir in the garlic, onion, tomatoes, tomato puree, wine, vinegar, salt, cayenne and sugar. Cook, uncovered, until bubbling.

4. Add the eggplant and toss to coat with sauce. Cook, tossing frequently, until the vegetables are tender but not mushy, about 15 minutes. If the sauce seems too dry, add 1 tablespoon of water. Sprinkle with the pine nuts, basil and parsley. Serve warm or at room temperature.

—Café Fortuna,
Beverly Hills, California

ROASTED PEPPERS AND CELERY ON TOASTED CROUTONS

Without the bread, this delicious vegetable makes an excellent accompaniment to roasted or grilled meats.

8 SERVINGS

8 bell peppers—halved, cored and deribbed
10 large celery ribs, peeled and cut into 2-by-¼-inch strips
1 teaspoon thyme
⅔ cup extra-virgin olive oil
1 teaspoon grated orange zest
½ teaspoon salt
¼ teaspoon freshly ground black pepper
16 slices Italian bread, cut 1 inch thick

1. Preheat the oven to 350°. Place the peppers in a large roasting pan in a single layer, cut-side down. Distribute the celery around the peppers and sprinkle with the thyme. Drizzle the oil over the vegetables.

2. Roast in the oven until the pepper skins are wrinkled and loose, about 45 minutes. Remove from the oven and let stand until cool enough to handle. (Leave the oven on.) Peel the peppers. Tip the pan and pour the oil and juices into a bowl; reserve.

3. Cut the peppers into 2-by-¼-inch strips. Place the peppers and celery in a bowl. Add the orange zest, salt and black pepper and toss to mix. (**The recipe can be prepared to this point up to 5 days ahead.** Refrigerate, covered. Let return to room temperature before proceeding.)

4. Brush both sides of the bread with the reserved oil and place in the roasting pan. Bake, turning once or twice, until the croutons are golden and crisp, about 20 minutes.

5. Spoon the pepper mixture over the croutons and serve.

—Anne Disrude

RED PEPPER AND EGGPLANT TERRINE

Serve this terrine with shreds of fresh mozzarella tossed with minced basil, cracked black pepper and any remaining pepper juices. The terrine needs to be refrigerated overnight (although it can be made up to three days ahead), so plan accordingly.

8 SERVINGS

Salt
2 medium eggplants (about 1 pound each), peeled and sliced crosswise ⅛ inch thick
8 medium red bell peppers—halved, cored and deribbed
⅓ cup plus 3 tablespoons extra-virgin olive oil

1. Lightly salt the eggplant slices and place in a colander to drain for 30 minutes.

2. Pat the eggplant dry. Layer the slices between paper towels. Cover with a cookie sheet and weigh down with a heavy pot for 1 hour. Preheat the oven to 350°.

3. Meanwhile, place the peppers in a roasting pan in a single layer, cut-side down. Drizzle on ⅓ cup of the oil. Roast the peppers until the skins are wrinkled and loose, 30 to 40 minutes. Remove from the oven and let stand until cool enough to handle. Peel off the skins. Tip the pan and pour the oil and juices into a bowl; reserve.

4. Pour the remaining 3 tablespoons oil into a small bowl. Dip a paper towel into the oil and very lightly grease a large skillet. Add as many of the eggplant slices as will fit in a single layer and fry, over moderately high heat, turning once, until tender and lightly browned, 2 to 3 minutes on each side. Drain on paper towels. Keep the skillet lightly oiled by rubbing it with the oil-dampened towel between batches. It is important not to allow the eggplant to absorb too much oil or the terrine will not hold together. (**The recipe can be prepared to this point up to 2 days ahead.** Refrigerate the peppers and eggplant separately.)

5. To assemble the terrine, preheat the oven to 350°. Lightly coat a noncorrodible 6-by-3-by-2-inch loaf pan with the reserved oil and pepper juices. Line the bottom and sides with slightly overlapping eggplant slices, pressing into the corners to form a rectangular shape. Cover with an even layer of red peppers, pressing into corners and cutting pieces to fit as needed. Continue layering eggplant and peppers until the mold is filled, ending with a layer of eggplant.

6. Bake the terrine for 30 minutes. Use a paper towel to blot any liquid that has accumulated on top of the terrine during baking. Cover the terrine with plastic wrap and weight the top with a loaf pan of the same size filled with pie weights or beans. Let cool to room temperature. If additional oil rises to the surface, blot it with a paper towel. Refrigerate the weighted terrine overnight or for up to 3 days.

7. Unmold the terrine. With a sharp thin knife, cut into 8 equal slices. (If slices become distorted, reform by pressing on the sides with a knife.) To serve, place a slice of the terrine on each of 8 plates and garnish with a small mound of shredded mozzarella if you like.

—Anne Disrude

ASPARAGUS WITH ANISE EGGS

8 TO 10 SERVINGS

*1½ cups soy sauce, preferably mushroom soy**
3 tablespoons rice wine vinegar
2 dried hot red peppers
4 (¼-inch) slices fresh ginger, peeled
*10 star anise pods**
12 hard-cooked eggs, peeled
5 pounds asparagus, trimmed to 7 inches and peeled
2 tablespoons safflower or other light vegetable oil
1 leek or 4 scallions, blanched and cut lengthwise into thin 8-inch-long strips (optional)
**Available at Oriental groceries*

1. In a medium noncorrodible saucepan, combine the soy sauce, vinegar, hot peppers, ginger and star anise with 2 cups of water. Bring to a boil, reduce the heat and simmer for 5 minutes to blend the flavors. Let cool.

2. Place the eggs in a glass or other noncorrodible bowl or jar just large enough to hold them with about ½ inch room at the top. Pour the cooled soy marinade over the eggs. Cover and refrigerate for 2 to 7 days, turning the eggs occasionally so that they color evenly.

3. Bring a stockpot of salted water to a boil. Add the asparagus and simmer until just tender, about 4 minutes. Drain and rinse under cold running water until cool; pat dry.

4. Drain the eggs, reserving ½ cup of the marinade. Whisk together the reserved marinade and the oil.

5. Arrange the asparagus in bundles of 6 spears each. Cut the eggs lengthwise into ¼-inch slices. Lay 2 slices of egg on top of each bundle and loosely tie with 2 strips of blanched leek. Place on a serving plat-

ter and drizzle the sauce on top. For a simpler, more casual presentation, arrange the asparagus on a platter and lay a band of overlapping egg slices or chopped egg across the asparagus. Cut any leftover eggs into small wedges and serve on the side or as an hors d'oeuvre at another time.

—*Anne Disrude*

ARTICHOKE HEARTS WITH RED PEPPER DRESSING

F&W BEVERAGE SUGGESTION
Geyser Peak Chardonnay

2 SERVINGS

2 medium artichokes, stems attached
2½ tablespoons fresh lemon juice
1 red bell pepper, finely chopped
1 tablespoon corn or other vegetable oil
1 teaspoon cider vinegar
¼ teaspoon salt (optional)
Pinch of freshly ground white pepper
Fresh basil and coriander leaves, for garnish

1. Cut off about 2 inches from the top of each artichoke so that the tips of the purple choke show. Break off all of the leaves and trim away the leaf bases to expose the heart. Scoop out the choke with a sharp spoon. With a swivel-bladed vegetable peeler, pare the stem. Trim off the woody bottom of the stem and brush all over with some of the lemon juice.

2. In a medium noncorrodible saucepan of boiling water, place the artichokes and remaining lemon juice and boil until tender, 10 to 12 minutes. Remove from the heat and let the artichokes cool in the liquid.

3. Meanwhile, place the red pepper, oil, vinegar, salt, if desired, and white pepper in a food processor or blender and puree, about 10 seconds. Strain through a fine sieve.

4. Remove the artichokes from the cooking liquid, reserving the liquid. Pare away any remaining fibrous layers. Slice each artichoke in half lengthwise. Cut 3 very thin lengthwise slices from the cut side of each half. Immediately return the slices to the cooking liquid to prevent discoloration. Cut the remaining artichoke into small wedges and immerse in the cooking liquid.

5. To serve, divide the red pepper puree between 2 serving plates and spread to cover. On each plate, arrange 6 large artichoke slices on top of the puree in the shape of a flower, with the stems pointing inward. Mound the wedges in the center. Garnish with basil and coriander leaves.

—*The Ritz-Carlton Hotel, Chicago, Illinois*

CIBREO'S CHICKEN LIVER CROSTINI

This makes a typical Italian first course. The livers must soak for 24 hours, so plan ahead.

F&W BEVERAGE SUGGESTION
Fruity Italian red, such as Dolcetto

4 SERVINGS

1 pound chicken livers
2 cups milk
½ cup olive oil, preferably extra-virgin
3 garlic cloves, coarsely chopped
¾ cup beef stock or canned broth
¼ cup dry red wine
1 teaspoon tomato paste
2 anchovy fillets, finely chopped
¾ teaspoon minced fresh sage or ½ teaspoon crumbled dried
1 tablespoon small capers
¼ teaspoon coarsely cracked pepper
8 slices (about 2 by 4 by ¼ inch) coarse peasant bread
1 tablespoon minced fresh parsley

1. Trim the livers of any connecting membranes and fat. Place in a small bowl, cover with the milk and refrigerate, covered, for 24 hours. Drain the livers and pat dry; finely chop.

2. In a medium skillet, heat ¼ cup of the oil. Add the livers and garlic and cook over moderately high heat, stirring, until lightly browned, about 2 minutes. Add the stock, wine, tomato paste, anchovies and sage. Simmer, uncovered, stirring occasionally, until most of the liquid has evaporated and the mixture is a thick paste, about 30 minutes. Stir in the capers and pepper. Set aside.

3. Brush both sides of the bread slices with the remaining ¼ cup oil. In a large skillet, fry 4 slices at a time over moderate heat, turning once, until golden brown, about 3 minutes on each side. Drain on paper towels.

4. To serve, mound about 2½ heaping tablespoons of the liver mixture onto each crostini. Place 2 crostini on each of 4 warmed plates. Sprinkle with parsley and serve warm.

LA NORMANDE'S TARTE A L'OIGNON

This satisfying onion tart is designed as a first course or appetizer but could easily become an entrée for a brunch or a simple dinner.

4 TO 6 SERVINGS

¾ cup all-purpose flour
Pinch of sugar
½ plus ⅛ teaspoon salt
10 tablespoons cold unsalted butter
1½ to 2 tablespoons ice water
1 large onion, diced
1 small leek (white and 2 inches of green), finely chopped, with white and green kept separate
2 eggs, beaten
¼ cup heavy cream
⅛ teaspoon white pepper

1. In a food processor, combine the flour, sugar and ½ teaspoon salt. Cut 6 tablespoons of the butter into small pieces and add to the flour. Turn the machine on and off quickly until the butter is the size of small peas. With the processor running, drizzle in the water until the dough masses together. Gather the dough into a ball and briefly knead until smooth. Form into a 6-inch disk, cover with waxed paper and refrigerate for 30 minutes.

2. Butter a 9-inch tart pan with a removable bottom and set aside. On a lightly floured surface, roll out the dough to a 10½-inch round, ⅛ inch thick. Fit into the pan, pressing against the sides without stretching; trim off any excess. Cover with plastic wrap and refrigerate for at least 30 minutes. (**The tart shell can be made a day ahead to this point.**)

3. Meanwhile, in a large skillet, melt the remaining 4 tablespoons butter over moderate heat. Add the onion and white of leek and cook, stirring frequently until softened and translucent, about 30 minutes.

4. Add the green of leek and cook until soft, about 2 minutes. Remove from the heat and let cool.

5. Preheat the oven to 400°. Loosely line the tart shell with aluminum foil and fill with pie weights, rice or dried beans. Bake on the bottom rack of the oven for 20 minutes, or until the sides have slightly shrunk away from the pan. Remove the weights and foil and bake for an additional 5 minutes, or until the crust is dry all over.

6. Add the eggs, cream, pepper and the remaining ⅛ teaspoon salt to the cooked onions; stir to blend. Pour into the tart shell. Bake in the middle of the oven for 20 minutes until set.

—La Normande,
Pittsburgh, Pennsylvania

BUCKWHEAT BLINI WITH SMOKED SALMON, SOUR CREAM AND TWO CAVIARS

Serve the blini in a napkin-covered basket surrounded by the accompaniments so that guests can help themselves. Each guest fills a small blini with a few of the accompaniments—caviar, shallots and a squeeze of lemon, for example, or sour cream and salmon—folds it over, then dips it in the melted butter and eats it. This is most definitely finger food, so be sure to provide large napkins.

Although the blini batter takes about four hours—there are two risings—it can be prepared either in the morning or the night before.

F&W BEVERAGE SUGGESTION
Iced vodka or Champagne, such as Bollinger or Pol Roger

8 SERVINGS

1 package (¼ ounce) active dry yeast
1 teaspoon sugar
2½ cups lukewarm (about 110°) buttermilk
1 cup sifted buckwheat flour
1 teaspoon baking soda
1 stick (¼ pound) plus 2 tablespoons unsalted butter, melted and cooled
4 eggs, separated
1 cup sour cream
1½ cups sifted all-purpose flour
1 teaspoon salt
½ cup milk
½ cup vegetable oil

ACCOMPANIMENTS:
2 sticks (½ pound) unsalted butter, clarified
1 cup sour cream
¾ cup minced shallots
½ pound thinly sliced smoked salmon
4 ounces red caviar
4 ounces black caviar
4 lemons, cut into thin wedges

1. Stir the yeast and sugar into ½ cup of the buttermilk and let stand until the yeast begins to bubble, about 5 minutes.

2. In a large bowl, combine the buckwheat flour and the baking soda with the remaining 2 cups buttermilk. Add the yeast liquid, stirring well to dissolve any lumps. Cover the bowl with a kitchen towel and let stand in a warm, draft-free place until the mixture doubles in volume, about 2 hours.

3. In a medium bowl, combine 6 tablespoons of butter with the egg yolks and sour cream. Stir in the flour and salt; mix well to dissolve any lumps. Gradually fold into the buckwheat mixture. Stir in the milk. Cover the bowl and let stand in a warm, draft-free place for 2 hours. (**The recipe may be prepared to this point up to 1 day ahead.** Cover and refrigerate. To continue, let return to room temperature; stir in ¼ to ½ cup water, if the batter has thickened, to return it to its original consistency.)

4. Beat the egg whites until stiff but not dry. Fold gently into the batter. Loosely cover the bowl with plastic wrap and let stand in a warm draft-free place for 30 minutes.

5. Preheat the oven to 250°. Lightly brush one or two heavy skillets or griddles, preferably nonstick, with some of the vegetable oil. Warm over high heat until barely smoking, 1 to 2 minutes.

6. For each pancake, ladle 2 to 3 tablespoons of batter onto the skillets, allowing plenty of room in between, to form pancakes about 3 inches in diameter. Cook over moderately high heat until bubbles break on the surface and the top is almost dry, 2 to 3 minutes. Turn and cook until golden brown on the bottom, 1 to 2 minutes. Lightly brush each blini with a little of the remaining 4 tablespoons butter. Stack on a plate and keep warm in the oven. Brush the skillet with more veg-

etable oil and repeat with the remaining batter. The blini should be served as soon as possible after they are cooked.

7. To serve, place the blini in a napkin-covered basket. Place the melted butter in a small chafing dish or butter warmer and arrange the remaining accompaniments in serving bowls.

—W. Peter Prestcott

CORN CREPE CAKE WITH CHICKEN CHILE FILLING

4 SERVINGS

2 eggs
½ cup milk
½ cup corn kernels, fresh or frozen
½ cup all-pupose flour
¼ cup yellow cornmeal
2 tablespoons corn oil, plus oil for cooking the crêpes
½ teaspoon salt
⅛ teaspoon freshly ground black pepper
2 teaspoons sugar
1 teaspoon ground cumin
2 tablespoons olive oil
½ medium onion, chopped
1 garlic clove, minced
2 plum tomatoes—peeled, seeded and chopped
2 tablespoons chopped fresh coriander
1½ cups finely diced cooked chicken
3 scallions, thinly sliced
1 jalapeño pepper (fresh or pickled)—seeded, deveined and cut into slivers
¼ cup freshly grated aged Monterey Jack or Parmesan cheese
½ cup shredded Monterey Jack cheese
2 tablespoons sour cream, plus sour cream for accompaniment

1. In a blender or food processor, combine the eggs, milk, corn and ½ cup of water. Puree until smooth. Add the flour, cornmeal, 2 tablespoons corn oil, the salt, black pepper, sugar and cumin. Mix until blended. Refrigerate, covered, for about 1 hour before using.

2. Heat a 6- to 7-inch crêpe pan over moderate heat. Brush with a little corn oil. Pour about 3 tablespoons of corn crêpe batter into the center of the pan and swirl to cover the bottom evenly. Cook for about 1 minute, until the bottom of the crêpe is lightly browned. Turn and cook for about 10 seconds, until dry and spotted brown on the other side. Repeat until the batter is used up, stacking the finished crêpes between sheets of paper towels.

3. Preheat the oven to 400°. In a medium skillet, heat the olive oil. Add the onion and garlic and sauté over moderate heat until the onion is translucent, about 3 minutes.

4. Add the tomatoes and coriander and cook, stirring occasionally, until the sauce thickens, about 10 minutes. Remove from the heat and stir in the chicken, scallions and jalapeño.

5. To assemble, use 6 crêpes. (Freeze any extras for another use.) Mix together the grated and shredded cheeses. Place one crêpe on a lightly oiled baking sheet. Spread about a fifth of the chicken mixture evenly over the crêpe. Sprinkle with 2 tablespoons of the cheese. Place another crêpe on top and lightly press to flatten. Repeat with remaining filling, cheese and crêpes. Spread 2 tablespoons of sour cream on top and sprinkle on the remaining cheese.

6. Bake for 10 to 15 minutes, until the cheese melts and the crêpes and filling are heated through. Let rest for 5 minutes. Use a large spatula to transfer the "cake" to a serving platter. Cut into wedges and pass a bowl of sour cream on the side.

—Jeanette Ferrary & Louise Fiszer

SHRIMP WITH VERMOUTH AND SUN-DRIED TOMATOES

F&W BEVERAGE SUGGESTION
Italian white, such as Galestro

6 SERVINGS

¼ cup olive oil
2 pounds large shrimp, shelled and deveined
1 medium shallot, minced
1 large garlic clove, minced
½ cup sun-dried tomatoes packed in oil, drained and cut into thin strips
½ cup dry vermouth
1 cup heavy cream
½ teaspoon salt
¼ teaspoon freshly ground pepper
3 tablespoons chopped fresh mint

1. In a large heavy skillet, heat the oil. Add the shrimp and sauté over moderately high heat, tossing, until they begin to curl and turn pink, about 2 minutes. Quickly remove with a slotted spoon and set aside.

2. Add the shallot, garlic and sun-dried tomatoes to the skillet and sauté over moderate heat until the shallots and garlic are softened but not browned, about 3 minutes.

3. Pour in the vermouth, increase the heat to high and boil until the mixture is syrupy, about 3 minutes.

4. Pour in the cream and cook, stirring frequently, until the sauce thickens slightly, about 5 minutes. Season with the salt and pepper. Return the shrimp to the sauce. Cook until heated and cooked through, about 1 minute. Serve hot, sprinkled with the chopped mint.

—Jeanette Ferrary & Louise Fiszer

SHRIMP WITH CUCUMBER AND MINT

8 SERVINGS

1½ pounds medium shrimp
¼ cup plus 2 tablespoons olive oil
2 tablespoons minced fresh mint
¾ teaspoon salt
¼ teaspoon freshly ground pepper
2 tablespoons dry white wine
8-inch section of unwaxed European cucumber—halved lengthwise, seeded and cut into 2-by-¼-inch matchsticks
1 large scallion, cut into 2-inch-long julienne strips
Sprigs of mint, for garnish

1. Cut the shrimp shells down the back with a pair of scissors and remove the veins; do not shell. Toss the shrimp in 2 tablespoons of the olive oil. Heat a heavy skillet, preferably cast iron, until smoking. Working in 3 batches, cook the shrimp, turning once, until opaque, about 2 minutes on each side. Remove to a bowl to cool.

2. Shell the shrimp, reserving the shells. Place the shrimp in a bowl and toss with 1 tablespoon of the mint and half the salt and pepper.

3. Place the shells in a medium heavy saucepan. Add the wine and the remaining ¼ cup olive oil and bring to a boil. Cover partially, reduce the heat and simmer for 10 minutes to infuse the oil with the flavors of the shells. Return to a boil and cook, uncovered, until steam is no longer emitted from the oil, about 5 minutes. Cool slightly, then strain the oil. Measure out 2 tablespoons of oil; reserve the remainder for another use. **(The recipe may be prepared 1 hour ahead to this point.)**

4. In a large skillet, warm the flavored oil over moderate heat. Add the cucumbers and toss for 1 minute. Add the shrimp and toss for 1 minute longer. Add the scallion, the remaining 1 tablespoon mint and the remaining salt and pepper and toss briefly until warmed through, about 30 seconds.

5. To serve, divide among 8 small plates and garnish each with a small mint sprig.

—*Anne Disrude*

MUSSELS WITH CHILI VINAIGRETTE

6 SERVINGS

½ cup olive oil, preferably extra-virgin
2 tablespoons minced red bell pepper
2 teaspoons minced jalapeño pepper
¼ cup cider vinegar
4 small shallots, minced
½ teaspoon Dijon-style mustard
½ teaspoon Worcestershire sauce
2 tablespooons minced fresh coriander
1½ teaspoons minced fresh parsley
⅛ teaspoon coarsely cracked black pepper
Pinch of salt
1 cup dry white wine
3 small bay leaves
1 teaspoon whole black peppercorns
3 pounds large mussels, scrubbed and debearded
4 ounces spinach, stemmed and shredded (2 cups)
Sprigs of fresh coriander, for garnish

1. In a small skillet, warm 1 tablespoon of the oil over moderately high heat. Add the red peppers and jalapeño and sauté, stirring frequently, until softened, 3 to 4 minutes. Scrape into a medium bowl and let cool.

2. Add the vinegar, half of the shallots, the mustard, Worcestershire sauce, coriander, parsley, cracked black pepper and salt to the cooled peppers. Whisk in the remaining 7 tablespoons oil and let stand at room temperature for 1 hour.

3. In a large noncorrodible pot, combine the wine, bay leaves, remaining shallots and peppercorns. Cover and simmer for 5 minutes.

4. Add the mussels, increase the heat to high, cover and cook, stirring occasionally, until the mussels open, about 5 minutes. Remove the mussels from their shells, reserving half the shells; discard any that have not opened. Toss the mussels with 1 tablespoon of the dressing.

5. Scrub the shells and arrange on a large platter or individual plates. Line each shell with a small amount of shredded spinach. Place a mussel in each shell. Stir the vinaigrette to blend the seasonings and drizzle 1 teaspoon over each mussel. Garnish with coriander sprigs. Serve chilled or at room temperature.

—*John Downey, Downey's, Santa Barbara, California*

ARUGULA AND SCALLOP SALAD

2 SERVINGS

1 small bunch of arugula
2 tablespoons olive oil, preferably extra-virgin
Salt and freshly ground black pepper
2 garlic cloves, minced
½ pound bay scallops, trimmed of connecting muscle
1 small or ½ large red or yellow bell pepper, cut into thin lengthwise strips
1 small jicama (about 3 ounces), peeled and cut lengthwise into thin strips
½ small fennel bulb—trimmed, cored and cut into thin lengthwise strips
1 tablespoon minced chives
2 teaspoons minced fresh tarragon or ½ teaspoon dried
2 teaspoons minced fresh parsley

1. Toss the arugula with ½ tablespoon of the olive oil and divide between 2 plates. Season lightly with salt and black pepper.

2. In a large skillet, heat the remaining 1½ tablespoons olive oil. Add the garlic and sauté over moderately high heat for 30 seconds. Add the scallops and continue to cook, tossing, for 1 minute.

3. Add the bell pepper, jicama and fennel. Cook, tossing, until the scallops are opaque throughout and the vegetables are warmed through. Add the chives, tarragon, parsley, ½ teaspoon salt and ⅛ teaspoon black pepper. Toss well and arrange over the arugula.

—Anne Disrude

SCALLOPS WITH BEURRE BLANC

4 SERVINGS

2 medium shallots, chopped
1 cup dry vermouth
16 sea scallops, with the coral attached if available
1 cup heavy cream
1 stick (¼ pound) unsalted butter
½ teaspoon salt
¼ teaspoon freshly ground pepper

1. Preheat the broiler. In a large skillet, combine the shallots and vermouth. Cook over moderate heat until the shallots are slightly softened, about 2 minutes. Add the scallops and the coral, if you have it. Increase the heat to moderately high and cook until the scallops are almost opaque, about 1½ minutes on each side. With a slotted spoon, transfer to a bowl.

2. Increase the heat to high and bring the vermouth to a boil. Cook until reduced to 1 tablespoon, about 5 minutes. Add the cream and boil until reduced by half, about 4 minutes.

3. Reduce the heat to low and whisk in the butter, 1 tablespoon at a time. Add the salt, pepper and any liquid rendered by the scallops. Strain the sauce through a fine-mesh sieve.

4. Set 4 scallop shells on a baking sheet and divide the scallops and coral among them. Spoon on the sauce and broil 4 inches from the heat until lightly browned, about 45 seconds.

—Ostaù de Baumanière,
Les Baux-de-Provence, France

PEPPER-CURED SABLEFISH

A creation of San Francisco chef Barton Levinson, this is a delicious, peppery cured fish, ideal sliced paper thin and served with light pumpernickel or Scandinavian *limpa* bread, cold radishes, lemon wedges and iced vodka.

Sablefish, the commercial name for black cod, is extra special, though sea bass, halibut or pompano may be used. Whatever the fish, it must be absolutely fresh. The fish is cured for two days before serving, so plan accordingly.

F&W BEVERAGE SUGGESTION
California Fumé Blanc, such as Dry Creek

4 TO 6 SERVINGS

2½ teaspoons fruity black peppercorns, such as Tellicherry
4 whole cloves
⅓ cup plus 1 teaspoon sugar
2 tablespoons soy sauce
2 tablespoons vodka
2½ teaspoons grated lemon zest
2 teaspoons fresh lemon juice
1½ pounds fresh black cod fillet (or sea bass, halibut or pompano), skinned and small bones removed

1. Finely grind the pepper and cloves together. In a small noncorrodible saucepan, combine the sugar, soy sauce, vodka, lemon zest, lemon juice and pepper and cloves. Bring to a simmer and cook until it is the consistency of liquid honey, about 10 minutes. Set aside until completely cool.

2. Rinse the fish with cool water and pat dry. Place the fish in the center of a clean, lint-free towel (the towel will be stained by the soy). Rub the syrup over both sides of the fillets.

3. Wrap the fish and place on a large dinner plate. Place a second plate on top and weigh down with a heavy jar or can. Refrigerate for 24 hours.

4. Turn the wrapped fish over, replace the plate and weight and refrigerate for another 24 hours.

5. Unwrap the fish, discarding any excess juices on the plate, and slice paper thin for serving. Leftovers can be rewrapped in the curing cloth and refrigerated for 1 to 2 days longer. Serve the fish raw or sauté the slices briefly in butter over low heat until just opaque.

—Barbara Tropp

SAUTEED HERB-CURED FISH WITH SNOW PEAS AND CARROTS

4 SERVINGS

1 tablespoon plus ½ teaspoon unsalted butter
¾ pound Herb-Cured Fish (recipe follows), sliced
½ teaspoon hazelnut, walnut or sesame oil
⅛ teaspoon grated lemon zest
1 medium carrot, peeled, cut into 1/16-by-1½-inch julienne strips (1 cup)
2 ounces snow peas, strings removed, cut into 1/16-by-1½-inch julienne strips
1 small scallion, white and green, cut into 1/16-by-1½-inch julienne strips

¼ teaspoon fresh lemon juice
⅛ teaspoon salt
Pinch of freshly ground pepper

1. In a large skillet, melt 1 tablespoon of the butter over moderate heat. Add the slices of fish in batches and cook for about 30 seconds on each side, until opaque. Cover loosely with foil to keep warm while cooking the remaining slices.
2. In a medium skillet, combine the hazelnut oil, remaining ½ teaspoon butter, the lemon zest and 2 tablespoons of water. Boil over high heat for 1 minute. Add the carrot. Reduce the heat to moderate, cover and cook for 1 minute. Add the snow peas and stir-fry for 30 seconds. Stir in the scallion, lemon juice, salt and pepper.
3. To serve, divide the fish among four warmed dinner plates. Garnish with the vegetables.

—Anne Disrude

HERB-CURED FISH

For best results, use small fillets of no more than six ounces each.

8 SERVINGS

1½ pounds lean fish fillets, skin on (4 to 6 ounces each)
1½ tablespoons coarse (kosher) salt
1½ tablespoons sugar
1 cup coarsely chopped fresh basil, dill, coriander or tarragon (1½ ounces)

1. Remove the line of bones from each fillet using needle-nose pliers or flat tweezers. Trim away any fatty pieces and connective tissue.
2. In a small bowl, mix the salt and sugar. Sprinkle this curing mixture over the flesh side of the fillets; gently press to adhere.
3. Place half of the fillets skin-side down in a single layer in a shallow glass or ceramic dish of a size to just fit. Sprinkle the herbs over the top. Sandwich the remaining fillets on top, skin-side up, thick end against thick, thin against thin, to reconstruct the fish.
4. Cover the dish tightly with plastic wrap and refrigerate for 24 hours. Pour off any liquid that has accumulated in the dish, cover and refrigerate for 24 hours longer.
5. Check for "doneness" by cutting a thin slice on the diagonal. It should be firm and translucent.
6. Gently scrape the herbs from the fillets with the back of a knife. Pat the fillets dry. Cut crosswise on the diagonal into very thin slices. Re-cover and refrigerate for up to 4 hours until ready to serve.

—Anne Disrude

SMOKED TROUT TIMBALES WITH SHERRY BEURRE BLANC

12 SERVINGS

1 pound sole fillets
1 pound smoked trout fillets
6 egg whites, chilled
1½ cups heavy cream, chilled
1 tablespoon prepared white horseradish, well drained
1 teaspoon salt
½ teaspoon freshly ground white pepper
Sherry Vinegar Beurre Blanc (p. 233)
3 tablespoons grated lemon zest

1. Preheat the oven to 350°. Place the sole and trout fillets in a processor and coarsely puree. Place the bowl in the freezer for 10 minutes to chill the fish.
2. With the machine on, gradually add the egg whites through the feed tube. Process for 1 minute; place in the freezer for 5 minutes.
3. With the machine on, gradually add the heavy cream. Add the horseradish, salt and white pepper and process for 1 minute. Place in the freezer for 5 minutes.
4. Butter twelve ½-cup ramekins. Fill them two-thirds full with the fish mixture. Loosely cover each with a buttered round of parchment or waxed paper.
5. Set the ramekins in a roasting pan. Place the pan in the oven and pour in enough boiling water to reach halfway up the ramekins.
6. Bake the timbales until they puff and a cake tester inserted into the center comes out clean, about 30 minutes.
7. Dry the ramekins and unmold two timbales onto each plate. Spoon a little Sherry Vinegar Beurre Blanc over each one and sprinkle with the lemon zest.

—W. Peter Prestcott

WILD LEEK AND SEAFOOD TIMBALES WITH LIME SABAYON SAUCE

This is an elegant presentation, lovely for the first course of a spring dinner party. Although the dish requires time for its preparation, it can be almost entirely made ahead and is not difficult.

F&W BEVERAGE SUGGESTION
California Sauvignon Blanc, such as Inglenook Reserve

8 SERVINGS

2 bunches of small wild leeks (ramps), about 3 dozen (¾ pound)
1½ tablespoons unsalted butter
¾ pound shrimp, in the shell, chilled
1½ teaspoons tomato paste
½ pound scallops, chilled

½ teaspoon salt
3 whole eggs, chilled
½ cup heavy cream, chilled
1 egg yolk
1½ tablespoons fresh lime juice
About 1 tablespoon minced fresh mint
Mint sprigs, for garnish

1. Trim off the roots from the ramps. Cut apart the leaves and bulb/stem sections, leaving no stem on the leaves. Wash the leaves and bulbs well. In a large skillet of simmering, salted water, place the leaves flat and simmer for 2 minutes. Drain and refresh in cold water; spread on a towel.

2. Peel the first layer from the bulbs. Pick 8 of the prettiest, tiniest bulbs and drop them into the simmering water. Boil until barely tender, about 1 minute. Drain and refresh in cold water.

3. Slice the remaining bulbs. In a skillet, melt the butter over moderately low heat. Add the sliced ramps and 1 tablespoon of water and cook gently until very tender, about 15 minutes. Cool, then cover and refrigerate.

4. Peel the shrimp, placing the shells in a small saucepan. Add 2 cups of water to the shrimp shells and simmer, partly covered, for 20 minutes. Uncover and boil until the liquid is reduced to about ⅓ cup. Strain out the shells, pressing hard. Add the tomato paste and boil until reduced to ¼ cup. **(The recipe can be prepared ahead to this point.** Let the sauce come to room temperature; cover and refrigerate.)

5. Butter eight 6-ounce custard cups. Line these with the ramp leaves, overlapping the leaves slightly, allowing them to overhang the edges of the cups. Cut large and broad leaves in half crosswise to fit the cups. Preheat the oven to 350°.

6. In a food processor, combine the shrimp, scallops (halved if large) and ¼ teaspoon of the salt; puree. Add 1 whole egg and 1 egg white, then process for about 10 seconds. Scrape down the sides and process for about 5 seconds. Add the cooked ramps and process to blend. With the machine on, pour in the cream.

7. Divide the mousse mixture among the custard cups. With wet hands even the mixture and tap the dishes to settle it. Fold over the leaves. Set the dishes on a rack in a large roasting pan. **(The recipe can be prepared ahead to this point.** Cover with foil and refrigerate until about 20 minutes before serving time.)

8. Pour boiling water into the pan to come about halfway up the custard cups. Set in the center of the oven and bake, uncovered, for 15 minutes.

9. Meanwhile, in the top of a double boiler, beat the remaining whole egg and 2 egg yolks with the lime juice and remaining ¼ teaspoon salt until light and fluffy. Heat the reserved shrimp stock and beat into the sauce in the double boiler. Set over barely simmering water and beat until hot and slightly thickened. Add more lime juice and salt to taste. Fold in about 1 tablespoon of minced mint or to taste.

10. Divide the sauce among 8 warmed plates. Unmold a timbale onto each. Garnish with the reserved ramp bulbs and mint sprigs. Serve hot.

—Elizabeth Schneider

MACEDOINE OF MONKFISH

F&W BEVERAGE SUGGESTION
California Sauvignon Blanc, such as Konocti

2 SERVINGS

½ pound monkfish, tough outer membrane removed
½ cup shelled fresh peas
1 medium carrot, cut into ¼-inch dice
1 medium tomato, seeded and chopped
2 scallions, thinly sliced
2 tablespoons sherry wine vinegar
¼ cup mayonnaise, preferably homemade
2 tablespoons chopped fresh parsley
1 tablespoon capers, rinsed and drained
½ teaspoon salt
¼ teaspoon freshly ground black pepper
Dash of hot pepper sauce
1 ripe avocado, halved

1. In a small saucepan of simmering salted water, poach the monkfish over moderate heat until firm and white, about 8 minutes. Drain, let cool and cut into ½-inch dice.

2. In another small saucepan of salted boiling water, blanch the peas until tender, 3 to 5 minutes. Remove with a skimmer, drain and let cool.

3. Add the carrots to the same saucepan and boil until tender, about 3 minutes. Drain and cool.

4. In a medium bowl, combine the monkfish, peas, carrot, tomato and scallions. Add the vinegar and toss to coat. Cover and refrigerate until chilled, at least 1 hour. **(The recipe can be prepared to this point up to 1 day ahead.)**

5. In a small bowl, combine the mayonnaise, parsley, capers, salt, black pepper and hot sauce. Blend well. Add to the salad and toss to mix. Spoon into the avocado halves. Serve slightly chilled.

—Jeanette Ferrary & Louise Fiszer

SALMON-STUDDED SCALLOP MOUSSE WITH GREEN MAYONNAISE

This elegant mousse, served with a vibrant herbed mayonnaise, makes an impressive first-course or buffet presentation. It could precede either a dressy stew or a good roast.

F&W BEVERAGE SUGGESTION
Bordeaux white, such as Chevalier de Védrines

12 TO 16 SERVINGS

1½ pounds sea scallops
2 egg whites
1⅛ teaspoons salt
⅛ teaspoon cayenne pepper
3 teaspoons fresh lemon juice
2 cups heavy cream
½ pound salmon fillet
Green Mayonnaise (p. 233)

1. In a food processor, chop the scallops. Add 1 of the egg whites, 1 teaspoon of the salt, the cayenne and 2 teaspoons of the lemon juice. Puree until smooth. Scrape down the sides of the bowl, add the second egg white and mix until well blended. Add 1 cup of the cream and let the machine run for 1 minute. Remove the lid, cover the processor bowl with plastic wrap and place in the freezer for 15 minutes. Preheat the oven to 350°.

2. Meanwhile, cut the salmon into ½-inch cubes. In a small bowl, toss with the remaining ⅛ teaspoon salt and 1 teaspoon lemon juice.

3. Return the bowl of scallop puree to the processor, turn the machine on and slowly pour the remaining 1 cup cream through the feed tube. Scrape down the sides of the bowl and mix again for a full 30 seconds.

4. Turn the mousse into a large bowl. Add the salmon cubes and fold to distribute evenly. Pack into a lightly oiled 8-cup loaf pan or decorative mold, preferably nonstick. Cover the pan with lightly oiled aluminum foil.

5. Place the loaf pan in a larger roasting pan and set in the oven. Pour in enough boiling water to reach about halfway up the loaf pan. Bake for 1 hour, or until the top feels springy and a skewer inserted in the center comes out clean. Let cool, then refrigerate, covered, for at least 6 hours or overnight. Serve chilled, with Green Mayonnaise.

—*Susan Wyler*

BOUDIN DE FRUITS DE MER (SEAFOOD SAUSAGE)

This delightful dish can be prepared ahead and is simple to make with a food processor. Chop the shrimp, scallops and crab in the machine before pureeing the fish; no need to wash the bowl in between. The sausages can be cooked an hour before serving. Although delicious paired with a classic beurre blanc sauce, a mousseline (hollandaise sauce with whipped cream) is just as good and holds longer without breaking. Garnish the plate with briefly sautéed spinach if desired.

8 SERVINGS

¾ pound red snapper fillets, cut into chunks, chilled
1⅓ cups heavy cream, chilled
¼ pound shrimp—shelled, deveined and finely chopped
¼ pound scallops, finely chopped
¼ pound fresh lump crabmeat, picked over and shredded
Salt and freshly ground white pepper
2 teaspoons minced fresh chives
1 teaspoon minced fresh parsley
Pinch of cayenne pepper
3 egg yolks
2 sticks (½ pound) unsalted butter, melted and cooled until tepid
1 tablespoon fresh lemon juice
1 large plum tomato—peeled, seeded and diced, for garnish

1. In a food processor, puree the fish. With the machine on, add ½ cup of the cream through the feed tube and process for 30 to 60 seconds, until the fish masses together around the blade.

2. For finer results, pass the puree through the fine blade of a food mill or rub through a fine mesh sieve into a medium bowl.

3. Whip ½ cup of the cream until soft peaks form. Working quickly, fold the cream, shrimp, scallops, crab, ¼ teaspoon salt, ⅛ teaspoon white pepper, the herbs and the cayenne into the fish puree. Cover and refrigerate for about 1 hour, until chilled.

4. In a heavy, medium noncorrodible saucepan, whisk the egg yolks with 1 tablespoon of water and a pinch of salt and white pepper over very low heat until just thick enough to leave a trail when the whisk is drawn across the bottom of the pan.

5. Immediately remove from the heat and begin whisking in the butter by droplets. When the sauce begins to thicken, whisk in the remaining butter in a thin stream; do not add the milky residue at the bottom of the pan.

6. Beat in the lemon juice. Season with salt and white pepper to taste. **(The sauce may be held over hot—not simmering—water or in a thermos rinsed with hot water for 1 hour.)** Whip the remaining ⅓ cup heavy cream until stiff peaks form. Cover and refrigerate.

7. Cut out eight 9-inch squares of aluminum foil and butter one side of each. Spoon ⅓ cup of the chilled seafood mixture in a 4-inch-long log along one edge of the buttered side of a square of foil. Roll into a sausage shape and pinch the ends of the foil to

seal the package. Repeat with the remaining 7 squares of foil.

8. Place the seafood sausages in a single layer in a large heavy pot of cold water and weigh down with a plate so that they remain submerged. Over high heat, bring the water to just below a simmer (190°); do not let boil. Remove from the heat, cover tightly and set aside for 20 minutes. (The wrapped sausages may be held in warm water for up to 1 hour.)

9. Just before serving, fold the reserved whipped cream into the hollandaise sauce. Spoon about ¼ cup of the sauce onto each warmed plate. Unwrap the seafood sausages and place one on each plate. Sprinkle with the tomato.

—Patrick Clark,
Café Luxembourg, New York City

ROQUEFORT CREAM AND WALNUTS IN PUFF PASTRY

4 SERVINGS

4 ounces frozen puff pastry
4 ounces Roquefort cheese
2 tablespoons unsalted butter, softened
½ cup tawny port
½ cup chicken stock or canned broth
1 cup crème fraîche
1 cup walnut pieces
2 tablespoons minced chives, for garnish

1. Cut 4 rectangles measuring 3 by 1½ by ⅛ inch from the puff pastry; reserve the remainder. Bake according to package directions; remove from the oven. Before the pastry cases cool, cut the tops off and set aside. Leave the oven on.

2. Meanwhile, crumble about 2 tablespoons of Roquefort into a small bowl. Add the butter and mash until blended to make Roquefort butter. Refrigerate until ready to use.

3. In a small noncorrodible saucepan, reduce the port to a syrupy consistency over moderately high heat. Stir in the chicken stock and crème fraîche and continue boiling until reduced to about ½ cup. Off the heat, stir in the Roquefort butter. Set aside; keep warm.

4. Thinly slice the remaining Roquefort and place on top of the pastry cases. Put the cases in the oven for 1 minute until the cheese begins to melt.

5. Remove from the oven and put one case on each of 4 plates. Sprinkle each case with walnut pieces. Dividing evenly, ladle the sauce over each. Sprinkle a pinch of chives on each and top with the pastry lids. Serve warm.

—Chef Hubert,
Le Bistro d'Hubert, Paris, France

PUFF PASTRY CASES

These crisp flaky containers will hold your favorite seafood or chicken filling for a truly elegant first course.

MAKES 6

All-purpose flour
1-pound sheet of puff pastry, chilled
1 egg lightly beaten with 1 teaspoon water, to make an egg glaze

1. Cut a sheet of parchment paper or aluminum foil into a 16-inch square. Dust lightly with flour. Place the pastry on top and with a lightly floured rolling pin, roll into a 16-by-12-inch rectangle. Slide the paper and pastry onto a cookie sheet and refrigerate until chilled through, at least 15 minutes.

2. Flour the edge of a 3¾-inch round cookie cutter and cut out 12 circles. Flour the edge of a 2½-inch round cookie cutter and cut out circles from 6 of the larger circles. Separate the outer rings and small circles. Refrigerate on the cookie sheet until chilled through, at least 15 minutes.

3. Preheat the oven to 400°. Line a cookie sheet with parchment paper or aluminum foil. With a metal spatula, transfer the 5 large, whole circles to the cookie sheet, flipping them over to their other side. Lightly dampen a 1-inch border around the edge of each pastry with water.

4. With a metal spatula, invert the pastry rings on top of the large circles. Transfer the small pastry circles to the cookie sheet, to be used as lids for the cases or as separate canapé bases. Brush the rings and the lids with the egg glaze. Crosshatch the lids with a sharp knife or prick with a fork to form a decorative pattern.

5. Bake in the center of the oven for 20 minutes, or until golden. Check and remove the lids if they are becoming too brown. Bake the containers for 5 minutes longer, until golden brown. Transfer to a wire rack.

6. While still warm, remove any soft flakes of pastry from the center of each case with a small fork to form a shell. Let cool before filling.

NOTE: Bite-size pastry cases, called *bouchées*, can be served as hors d'oeuvre with hot or cold fillings. Roll out the pastry ⅛-inch thick. Use a 2-inch cookie cutter to cut out the large circles. With a 1-inch round cookie cutter, press a circle halfway through each *bouchée*. Bake for 20 minutes. Transfer to a wire rack. With a small knife, lift off the center circle and use as a lid. Scoop out the soft flakes of pastry in the center to make a cavity.

—Diana Sturgis

MIXED GAME PATE

Though most game is no longer truly wild nor particularly abundant, it is available and worth seeking out. With the exception of venison (to order in better butcher shops or by mail, see Sources, below), all the meats called for are available in the average supermarket. Once you have located the ingredients, it is almost as simple to make as the familiar meat loaf, and since the completed pâté needs at least three days of refrigerated aging to develop full flavor, it can be prepared well in advance of serving.

10 TO 12 SERVINGS

1 duckling (4½ to 5 pounds), liver reserved
⅓ cup bourbon
2 teaspoons salt
1¼ teaspoons freshly ground pepper
½ domestic rabbit (or see Substitutions, below)
4 tablespoons unsalted butter
2 medium onions, finely chopped
1 pound venison, trimmed of fat and sinews, cut into large cubes (or see Substitutions, below)
⅓ pound lean pork, cut into large cubes
¾ pound fresh pork fat
3 garlic cloves, peeled
1 teaspoon thyme
½ teaspoon marjoram
½ teaspoon nutmeg
¼ teaspoon cinnamon
1 egg, beaten
1 pound sliced bacon
2 bay leaves
3 whole allspice berries
Cranberry-Bourbon Relish (p. 240), for garnish

1. Skin the duckling. Remove the breast meat in two whole pieces and transfer them to a small bowl. Add the bourbon, ½ teaspoon of the salt, ¼ teaspoon of the pepper and let marinate at room temperature, turning occasionally, for 1 hour. Cut the remaining meat off the duck and trim away any fat or tendons. Reserve along with the duck liver.

2. Bone the rabbit loin (it may be in two pieces) and add it to the marinating duck breast. Reserve the rest of the rabbit half for another use.

3. In a medium skillet, melt the butter over moderate heat until foaming. Add the onions, cover, reduce the heat to moderately low and cook until very soft but not browned, about 15 minutes. Remove from the heat and let cool slightly.

4. In a meat grinder, grind together the cubed venison, pork, pork fat, reserved duck (*not* the marinating breast meat) and duck liver, garlic and onions, including the butter in which they cooked. (If you use a food processor, grind using quick on-off motions, leaving plenty of texture; do not overprocess.)

5. Transfer the ground meats to a large mixing bowl. Add the thyme, marjoram, nutmeg, cinnamon and egg. Drain the bourbon marinade into the ground meats. Cut the duck breast and rabbit loin into ½-inch cubes. Add to the ground meats and stir to mix. Add the remaining 1½ teaspoons salt and 1 teaspoon pepper and mix well.

6. In a small skillet, fry a small patty of the pâté mixture over moderate heat, turning once or twice, until lightly browned and fully cooked. As soon as the meat is cooled, taste and correct the seasoning of the pâté if necessary. (Salt liberally as the pâté is served slightly chilled.)

7. Preheat the oven to 350°. Line a 9-by-5-by-3-inch (8-cup) loaf pan with the bacon strips, leaving enough overhang to completely enclose the pâté. Spoon the pâté mixture into the lined pan, mounding it slightly. Fold the overhanging strips of bacon over to enclose the pâté mixture and press the bay leaves and allspice berries into the bacon in a decorative pattern.

8. Wrap the filled pan completely in foil and set it in a larger baking dish at least 4 inches deep. Place in the oven and add boiling water to reach about three-quarters of the way up the sides of the loaf pan. Bake for 2½ to 3 hours, or until an instant-reading thermometer inserted into the center of the pâté registers 170°.

9. Cut a square of cardboard that will just fit inside the top of the loaf pan. Wrap the cardboard in foil. Remove the pâté from the hot water bath, remove the foil wrapping and set in a larger pan to catch any juices. Place the foil-covered cardboard on top of the pâté and weigh it down with one or two cans or other heavy objects. Let cool to room temperature. Remove the weights, wrap the pâté well and refrigerate for at least 3 days before serving.

10. Run a knife around the edges, then dip the pan briefly in warm water to melt the fat; unmold the pâté. Wipe away jellied cooking juices. Thinly slice the pâté and serve garnished with the Cranberry-Bourbon Relish.

SOURCES: *Venison* is available by mail from Enzed Traders, P.O. Box 7108, Ann Arbor, MI 48107; (313) 663-6987.

SUBSTITUTIONS: A nationally available brand of frozen *rabbit* is sold, packed in halves, in many supermarkets. If you cannot find rabbit, buy a second duck, marinate the breast meat of both and grind the leg meat of both. Include both livers.

If you cannot get *venison*, buy an additional pound of lean pork; the effect will be much less gamy, but you will still have a delicious pâté.

—Michael McLaughlin

Appetizers to complement aperitifs (left to right: Grilled Cheddar Canapés with Cornichons (p. 16), Curried Toasted Almonds (p. 16) and Marinated Olives Le Cherche-Midi (p. 16).

Left, Spicy Cucumber and Fruit Salad (p. 167) and Cucumber-Wrapped Scallops with Pickled Ginger (p. 19). Above, Mixed Greens with Polenta Croutons and Gorgonzola (p. 162).

RUM-MARINATED RABBIT TERRINE

Flecked with white rabbit meat and layered with the dark-hued liver, this makes a beautiful presentation. Have your butcher cut half the fatback into thin slices to be used for lining the terrine mold. The terrine needs to be refrigerated one day before serving, so plan accordingly. Accompany the terrine with Sweet and Sour Prunes (p. 238).

10 TO 12 SERVINGS

5- to 6-pound rabbit, cut up, with liver reserved
3 chicken livers
½ pound pork shoulder, cut into ½-inch cubes
1 pound unsalted pork fatback—half thinly sliced, half cut into ½-inch cubes
¾ cup light rum
2 garlic cloves
2 shallots, halved
2 tablespoons dried summer savory
1 egg
2½ teaspoons salt
¾ teaspoon freshly ground pepper
⅛ teaspoon ground cloves
¾ cup minced fresh chives
6 ounces smoked slab bacon, cut into ¼-inch dice
Pinch of freshly grated nutmeg

1. In a large noncorrodible bowl, combine the rabbit and liver, the chicken livers, pork shoulder, cubed fatback, the rum, garlic, shallots and 1 tablespoon of the summer savory. Toss to mix. Cover and refrigerate for 12 hours or overnight, or let stand at room temperature for 3 hours, to marinate.

2. Remove the meat from the marinade, scraping off as much of the herbs as possible. Strain the marinade, reserving 1 garlic clove and 2 shallot halves.

3. Remove the loin fillets and other meaty parts from the rabbit. Cut the meat into ¼-inch cubes. Place the rabbit cubes in a small bowl and cover with the marinade.

4. With a sharp boning knife, cut away all the remaining bits of rabbit meat from the carcass. Pick the pork shoulder cubes and fatback cubes out of the liver mixture. Place in a food processor fitted with the steel blade and add the rabbit bits. Process until finely minced, 2 to 3 minutes. Add the reserved garlic and shallot, the egg, 2 teaspoons of the salt, ½ teaspoon of the pepper, the cloves, and ½ cup of the minced chives. Puree until very smooth, about 1 minute. Transfer to a large bowl.

5. Preheat the oven to 350°. Bring water to a boil in a medium saucepan and blanch the cubes of bacon for 30 seconds to remove excess saltiness; drain and rinse under cold water. Pat dry and add to the rabbit and marinade mixture. Add the remaining ¼ cup of chives and 2 teaspoons of the savory.

6. In a food processor, combine the reserved rabbit and chicken livers, the remaining 1 teaspoon savory, ½ teaspoon salt, ¼ teaspoon pepper and the nutmeg, and puree until very smooth, about 1 minute.

7. Evenly line the bottom and sides of an 8- to 10-cup terrine with the sheets of fatback, leaving enough excess hanging over the sides to wrap over the top of the mold when it is filled.

8. Spoon half of the ground rabbit and pork into the lined terrine; press to fill the corners. Sprinkle with one-third of the rabbit and bacon cubes. Add a layer of the liver mixture. Sprinkle with half the remaining rabbit and bacon cubes. Cover with the remaining liver mixture, then the remaining rabbit and bacon cubes and finally the remaining ground meat. Fold over the extra pork fatback to cover the top.

9. Set the terrine in a shallow baking dish, place the baking dish in the oven and pour in enough boiling water to reach halfway up the sides of the terrine. Bake for 1½ to 2 hours, or until a metal skewer inserted in the center of the terrine comes out very hot to the touch and the juices run clear.

10. Remove from the water bath and let stand until slightly cooled. Place in a baking dish to catch any excess fat. Put another baking sheet directly on top of the terrine and anchor it down with at least 5 pounds of weight, such as two #2½ cans. Let the terrine stand until it reaches room temperature, 3 to 4 hours. When cool, remove the weights, cover the terrine and refrigerate for at least one day before serving.

11. To unmold the terrine, set the mold in hot water for 5 minutes to loosen the fat. Invert to unmold. With a large sharp knife, cut into slices to serve.

—Patricia Wells

Pepper-Cured Sablefish (p. 27).

THAI MEE KROB

4 TO 6 SERVINGS

2 tablespoons plus 2 teaspoons fresh lemon juice
*¼ cup rice wine vinegar**
6 tablespoons plus 2 teaspoons sugar
*6 tablespoons nuoc nam (Vietnamese fish sauce)**
*2 tablespoons miso (soybean paste)**
Vegetable oil, for deep-frying
*½ pound rice stick noodles**
4 large garlic cloves, chopped
2 large onions, chopped
½ pound lean pork, cut into 2-inch julienne strips
1 skinless, boneless chicken breast (about 1 pound), cut into 2-inch julienne strips
2 tablespoons coarsely chopped fresh coriander (cilantro)
3 cups (about ¾ pound) bean sprouts
2 small hot green chilies, chopped, or 2 tablespoons chopped canned hot chiles
Grated zest of 1 large orange
**Available at Oriental markets*

1. In a small bowl, stir together the lemon juice, vinegar, sugar, *nuoc nam* and *miso* until the sugar is dissolved and the sauce is smooth.

2. In a wok, deep-fryer or large heavy saucepan, heat about 3 inches of oil to 375°. (To test, break off a piece of the rice stick noodles and drop into the oil. The noodles should sink down and then very quickly rise to the surface, puffed and browned.)

3. When the oil is at the correct temperature, break off a handful of the noodles and drop into the oil. (Fry only one handful at a time, as they puff up.) When the noodles are light gold, after about 30 seconds, turn and brown them on the other side. Remove and drain the noodle clusters on paper towels. Fry the remaining noodles in the same manner.

4. In a wok or large skillet, heat 2 tablespoons of the oil used to fry the noodles. Add the garlic and onion and stir-fry over moderately low heat until the onion is soft but not browned, about 15 minutes. Add the pork, increase the heat to moderate and stir-fry until the pork is no longer pink, about 1 minute. Add the chicken and continue to stir-fry until the chicken and pork are cooked through, about 2 minutes longer. Add the sauce, reduce the heat to moderately low and simmer for 3 minutes.

5. To serve, arrange the noodles on a large serving platter. Top with the meats and sauce and sprinkle with the chopped coriander. Garnish the platter with piles of bean sprouts and sprinkle the chopped chile pepper and orange zest on the sprouts.

—Susan Grodnick

SOUPS

CHILLED AVOCADO SOUP WITH FRESH CORIANDER

Sour cream enhances the flavor of the avocado and insures that the soup will hold its green color for up to two hours.

4 SERVINGS

1 medium avocado, preferably Hass, peeled and pitted
1 garlic clove
1 scallion, chopped
¼ cup fresh coriander sprigs
1 cup sour cream
2 cups chilled chicken stock or canned broth
½ teaspoon salt, or more to taste
Dash of hot pepper sauce
Minced scallion and/or whole coriander leaves, for garnish

1. In a blender or food processor, combine the avocado, garlic, chopped scallion, coriander, sour cream, chicken stock, salt and hot sauce. Puree until smooth, about 3 minutes.

2. Refrigerate, covered, for up to 2 hours, until chilled. Serve garnished with minced scallion or coriander.

—Molly O'Neill

JERUSALEM ARTICHOKE SOUP

Jerusalem artichokes—sometimes labeled sunchokes—are available in specialty produce stores, many supermarkets and some health food shops.

8 SERVINGS

Juice of 2 lemons
3 pounds Jerusalem artichokes (sunchokes)
6 tablespoons unsalted butter
2 medium onions, finely chopped
2 large carrots, finely chopped
2 large leeks (white part only), finely chopped
6 sprigs of Italian flat-leaf parsley
1 teaspoon thyme
5 cups chicken stock or canned broth
Salt and freshly ground white pepper
6 to 8 tablespoons heavy cream
8 sprigs of watercress, for garnish

1. Fill a large bowl halfway with cold water and add the lemon juice. Peel the Jerusalem artichokes and drop them into the acidulated water to prevent discoloration.

2. In a large saucepan, melt the butter over moderate heat until foaming. Add the onions, carrots, leeks, parsley and thyme. Cover and reduce the heat to moderately low. Cook, stirring occasionally, until the vegetables are tender and lightly colored, about 15 minutes.

3. Add the chicken stock, increase the heat and bring to a boil. Partially cover, reduce the heat to a simmer and cook for 25 minutes. Let cool slightly; then strain, discarding the solids. Return the liquid to the pan.

4. Drain the Jerusalem artichokes and cut them into 1-inch chunks. Add to the liquid in the pan, season lightly with salt and white pepper and bring to a boil. Partially cover, reduce the heat to a simmer and cook, stirring occasionally, until the artichokes are very tender, about 45 minutes.

5. Force the soup through the fine disk of a food mill or puree in batches in a food processor. (**The soup can be prepared to this point several days in advance of serving.** Let cool to room temperature; cover and refrigerate.)

6. To serve, reheat the soup gently, stirring often. Thin to desired consistency with the cream. Correct the seasoning and serve hot. Garnish each bowl with a sprig of watercress.

—Michael McLaughlin

CREAM OF ASPARAGUS AND MOREL SOUP

Asparagus and morels complement each other, and they represent springtime at its best. I made this soup with morels from Oregon during May and June. Substitute various mushrooms in subsequent months, since asparagus now is widely available throughout the year.

8 SERVINGS

2¼ pounds asparagus
5 tablespoons unsalted butter
3 tablespoons all-purpose flour
6 cups chicken stock, preferably homemade
½ pound fresh morels or other wild mushrooms, well washed
1¼ cups crème fraîche or heavy cream
Salt and freshly ground pepper

1. Snap off the tough end of each asparagus spear and peel the stalk. Bring a large pot or 2 skillets of salted water to a boil. Add the asparagus and cook until just tender, 3 to 5 minutes. Drain and rinse under cold running water to refresh. Cut off 16 asparagus tips and reserve. Coarsely chop the remaining asparagus.

2. In a large heavy saucepan or flameproof casserole, melt 3 tablespoons of the butter over moderate heat. Add the flour and cook, stirring, for 1 minute. Whisk in the chicken stock and bring to a boil, stirring occasionally. Add the chopped asparagus and morels, reserving the 8 smallest morels for garnish. Reduce the heat, cover and simmer for 30 minutes.

3. With a slotted spoon, transfer the asparagus and morels to a food processor. Add 1 cup of the stock and puree until smooth. Blend the puree

and the remaining stock and pass the soup through a fine-mesh sieve to remove any tough fibers.

4. In a small saucepan, heat the remaining 2 tablespoons butter and ¼ cup of the crème fraîche until simmering. Add the 8 reserved morels and cook over moderately low heat for 10 minutes. Add the reserved asparagus tips and cook for 2 minutes longer.

5. To serve, reheat the soup if necessary. Whisk in the remaining 1 cup crème fraîche. Season with salt and pepper to taste. Add the morels and asparagus tips with their liquid. Serve very hot, garnishing each bowl with 1 morel and a couple of asparagus tips.

—Lydie Marshall

ZUPPA DI CASTAGNE (CHESTNUT SOUP)

For an intense chestnut flavor (and a few less calories), omit the cream.

6 TO 8 SERVINGS

1 stick (¼ pound) unsalted butter
1 large onion, coarsely chopped
2 medium carrots, coarsely chopped
¼ cup all-purpose flour
2 quarts chicken stock or canned broth
1 pound peeled, cooked chestnuts, fresh or jarred
½ teaspoon salt
¼ teaspoon freshly ground white pepper
2 cups heavy cream (optional)

1. In a large heavy saucepan, melt the butter over moderate heat. Add the onion and carrots and sauté, stirring occasionally, until the onion is softened and translucent, about 5 minutes.

2. Sprinkle on the flour and stir to coat the vegetables. Cook, stirring, for 2 minutes.

3. Whisk in the chicken stock, 1 cup at a time. Add the chestnuts and season with the salt and pepper. Simmer, uncovered, until the soup is slightly thickened, about 30 minutes.

4. Puree the soup in batches in a blender or food processor until completely smooth. Add the cream, if desired, and reheat until warmed through. Serve hot.

—John Virella, Villa Virella, Blakeslee, Pennsylvania

POTATO SOUP WITH GREENS AND CRISP POTATO SKIN CROUTONS

8 TO 10 SERVINGS

3 russet or other baking potatoes
¼ pound smoked slab bacon with rind
1 medium onion, coarsely chopped
2 garlic cloves, coarsely chopped
½ pound kale, large stems removed, coarsely chopped (about 8 cups)
2 cups chicken stock or canned broth
3 tablespoons olive oil
1 teaspoon salt
¼ teaspoon freshly ground pepper
1 bunch of watercress, coarsely chopped
2 tablespoons unsalted butter (optional)

1. Preheat the oven to 400°. Pierce the potatoes several times with a fork. Bake for about 50 minutes, or until tender when pierced with a fork.

2. Meanwhile, remove the rind from the bacon in one piece and reserve. Slice the bacon into ¼-inch-thick slices and then slice crosswise into ¼-inch-wide matchsticks. In a stockpot, fry the bacon over moderate heat until browned. Remove with a slotted spoon and drain on paper towels; reserve the bacon for garnish.

3. Pour off all but 2 tablespoons of the bacon fat. Add the onion and garlic to the pan. Cover and cook over low heat until softened but not browned, about 5 minutes.

4. Add the kale, chicken stock, reserved bacon rind and 4 cups of water. Bring to a simmer and cook, partially covered, for 1 hour. Remove and discard the bacon rind.

5. When the potatoes are done, cut them in half and scoop out the insides; set aside. Halve each potato skin lengthwise. Brush liberally on both sides with the oil. Place on a baking sheet and bake at 400°, turning once, for 15 minutes, until browned and crisp. Remove from the oven and sprinkle with ½ teaspoon salt. Chop into bite-size croutons.

6. Mash half of the reserved potato pulp and stir into the soup. Break the remainder into small pieces and drop into the soup. Simmer until warmed through, about 10 minutes. Season with the remaining ½ teaspoon salt and the pepper.

7. Stir the watercress into the soup. Swirl in the butter. Ladle the soup into individual soup bowls and sprinkle the potato skin croutons and bacon on top.

—Anne Disrude

MUSHROOM-BARLEY SOUP

Some variations on this recipe call for beaten egg yolks to be added to the soup just before serving to thicken it; if you do, remember not to boil the soup, or the egg will coagulate.

8 SERVINGS

1 pound fresh mushrooms, sliced
1 small tomato, quartered
2 medium carrots—peeled and either shredded or coarsely chopped
1 medium onion, coarsely chopped
2 celery ribs, coarsely chopped
4 sprigs of parsley, finely chopped
½ cup barley
½ teaspoon salt

1. In a large saucepan, combine the mushrooms, tomato, carrots, onion, celery, parsley, barley and salt; add 1 quart of water.

2. Bring to a boil, then reduce to a simmer; cover and cook for 1 hour. Adjust seasoning to taste before serving. This soup can be held and reheated before serving.

—Diana Sturgis

COUNTRY LENTIL SOUP

6 SERVINGS

1½ cups lentils
8 cups beef stock or water
1 onion, peeled and stuck with a clove
1 carrot
1 celery rib
Bouquet garni: 1 large sprig of parsley, 6 peppercorns and 1 teaspoon thyme tied in a double thickness of cheesecloth
1 pound smoked ham hocks or ham steak
2 tablespoons unsalted butter
¼ cup plus 1 tablespoon olive oil
2 medium shallots, minced
2 garlic cloves, minced, plus 1 garlic clove, halved
1 teaspoon ground cumin
Pinch of ground coriander
1 cup heavy cream
Salt and freshly ground pepper
12 slices of French bread, cut ½ inch thick
Minced fresh parsley, for garnish

1. In a large saucepan, combine the lentils with the beef stock, onion, carrot, celery, bouquet garni and ham hocks. Bring to a boil, reduce the heat and simmer, covered, for about 45 minutes, or until the lentils are soft.

2. Remove and discard the onion, carrot, celery and bouquet garni. Remove the ham hocks and set aside to cool. With a slotted spoon, remove 1½ cups of the lentils and set aside. Puree the remaining soup in a blender or food processor until smooth.

3. In a large saucepan, melt the butter in 1 tablespoon of the oil. Add the shallots and minced garlic and cook over low heat until softened but not browned. Add the cumin and coriander and cook for 1 minute longer.

4. Add the pureed soup, the reserved lentils and the heavy cream. Bring the soup to a simmer, skimming off the foam that rises to the top. Season with salt and pepper to taste.

5. Remove the meat from the ham hocks. Cut into fine dice and add to the soup. (**The recipe can be made a day ahead up to this point.** Cover and refrigerate. Reheat the soup before proceeding.)

6. Before serving, rub the bread slices with the cut garlic clove. In a large skillet, heat the remaining ¼ cup olive oil. Add the bread slices and sauté over moderate heat, turning, until browned on both sides, about 2 minutes. Drain the croutons on a double layer of paper towels and reserve.

7. Ladle the soup into individual bowls. Garnish each serving with a crouton and a sprinkling of parsley. Serve the remaining garlic croutons on the side.

—Perla Meyers

WILD RICE SOUP

6 SERVINGS

½ cup wild rice
3 thick slices hickory-smoked bacon, diced
½ cup finely chopped onion
½ cup finely chopped celery
½ cup finely chopped carrot
5 cups chicken stock or canned broth
1 cup heavy cream
¼ teaspoon salt
¼ teaspoon white pepper
2 tablespoons minced parsley

1. Rinse the wild rice and drain well. In a large heavy pot, cook the bacon over moderate heat until crisp. Add the onion, celery, carrot and rice and cook, stirring occasionally, until the onions are translucent, 3 to 4 minutes.

2. Add the chicken stock and bring to a boil. Reduce the heat to low, cover and simmer until the rice is tender, 45 minutes to 1 hour.

3. Add the cream, stirring to combine. Season with the salt and pepper. To serve, garnish with the parsley.

—Rowe Inn, Ellsworth, Michigan

THE POLO'S MUSHROOM SOUP

This is a rich soup, but it's worth every drop of cream. The truffle juice is a necessary ingredient and enhances the taste of the mushrooms.

4 SERVINGS

3 tablespoons unsalted butter
1 pound mushrooms, minced
4 cups heavy cream
1 tablespoon truffle juice (see Note)
1 teaspoon salt
¼ teaspoon freshly ground pepper
4 slices of truffle or 4 sprigs of Italian flat-leaf parsley, for garnish

1. In a large saucepan, melt the butter over moderately high heat. Add the mushrooms and sauté, stirring occasionally, until all the liquid is evaporated, about 10 minutes.

2. Add the cream, reduce the heat to moderate and simmer, stirring occasionally, for 20 minutes to blend the flavors.

3. Puree the soup in a blender or food processor. Strain through a sieve for a creamier texture. (**The recipe can**

be prepared to this point up to a day ahead. Cool quickly in iced water, then cover and refrigerate. Bring to a simmer, stirring, before proceeding.)

4. Add the truffle juice and season with the salt and pepper. Ladle into individual serving bowls and garnish with a slice of truffle or a sprig of parsley.

NOTE: Truffle juice is available in specialty food stores or by mail order from Maison Glace, 52 E. 58th St., New York, NY 10022. Although truffle juice sells for about $3.25 an ounce, a little goes a long way; use it to complement *any* mushroom dish and in meat or cream sauces for pasta.

—Patrice Boely, The Polo, Westbury Hotel, New York City

HAM AND LIMA BEAN SOUP

This soup puts the ham bone left over from a baked ham to good use.

MAKES ABOUT 4 QUARTS

1 pound dried baby lima beans
1 meaty ham bone (about 2½ pounds)
1 medium onion, chopped
2 large carrots, thinly sliced
3 celery ribs, cut into ¼-inch dice
1 sprig of fresh thyme or ¼ teaspoon dried
1 bay leaf
3 quarts unsalted chicken stock or water
2 cups cooked ham, cut into ⅜-inch dice
¼ cup chopped fresh parsley

1. Place the lima beans in a large saucepan or flameproof casserole. Add cold water to cover by 2 inches. Bring to a boil over high heat and boil uncovered for 2 minutes. Remove from the heat, cover and let stand for 1 hour. Drain and return the beans to the pan.

2. Add the ham bone, onion, carrots, celery, thyme, bay leaf and stock. Bring to a boil over high heat, reduce the heat to moderately low and simmer, partially covered, for 1 to 1½ hours until the beans are tender. Remove and discard the ham bone. **(The soup can be prepared 1 day ahead up to this point.** Let cool; then refrigerate. Skim the fat and rewarm before proceeding.)

3. With a slotted spoon, dip out 2 cups of beans and vegetables and place in a blender or food processor. Add a little of the liquid and puree. Return the puree to the pan and gently reheat the soup. Stir in the ham and parsley.

—Diana Sturgis

REAL HOT AND SOUR SOUP

One of China's most memorable contributions to the corpus of "barbarian pepper" recipes, this dish is the place to use a sharp and zesty peppercorn—and plenty of it! Some of the ingredients are best if marinated or soaked overnight, so if you have the time, plan accordingly. This soup reheats beautifully and freezes well.

4 TO 6 SERVINGS

6 ounces well-trimmed boneless pork loin
2 tablespoons plus 2 teaspoons soy sauce
2 teaspoons Chinese rice wine or dry sherry
¼ teaspoon sugar
3 tablespoons plus 1 teaspoon cornstarch
1¼ teaspoons Oriental sesame oil
*3 tablespoons tree ears**
*25 lily buds**
*6 medium Chinese dried black mushrooms**
*2 cakes (½ pound) firm Chinese tofu**
4¼ cups rich unsalted chicken or pork and chicken stock
*¼ cup Japanese rice vinegar**
¾ teaspoon freshly ground black pepper
¼ teaspoon freshly ground white pepper
1 egg, lightly beaten
3 scallions, thinly sliced
**Available at Oriental groceries*

1. Cut the meat into thin julienne strips (partial freezing makes slicing easier). Mix 2 teaspoons of the soy, the wine, sugar, 1 teaspoon of the cornstarch and ¼ teaspoon of the sesame oil until smooth. Pour over the pork and toss to coat. Set aside at room temperature for at least 30 minutes or, preferably, refrigerate overnight. Let return to room temperature before cooking.

2. In 3 small bowls, cover the tree ears, lily buds and dried mushrooms with a generous amount of cool water. Let soak until flexible, about 30 minutes (or if you have time, soak them overnight, which will give better flavor and texture).

3. Drain the tree ears, rinse well to remove any grit and pinch off the hard "eyes." Break into quarter-size pieces if large. Drain the lily buds, remove any hard stems if present and shred the buds lengthwise or simply cut crosswise in two. Drain the mushrooms, rinse well under cold running water, then remove and discard the stems. Shred the caps into ⅛-inch slivers.

4. Cut the tofu horizontally into slabs ¼ inch thick, then cut crosswise into ¼-inch-wide strips.

5. Mix the remaining 2 tablespoons soy sauce and 3 tablespoons cornstarch with ¼ cup cold stock.

6. In a large noncorrodible saucepan, bring the remaining 4 cups stock to a simmer over moderate heat. Add the tree ears, lily buds, mushrooms and tofu. Stir gently to combine.

7. Increase the heat to high and bring the soup to a boil. Stir in the pork, separating the pieces. Reduce the heat to moderate; simmer for 2 minutes.

8. Stir the cornstarch mixture, then add it to the soup, stirring until the soup turns glassy, 15 to 20 seconds. Add the vinegar and the black and white peppers. Stir to mix, then remove from the heat.

9. Pour the beaten egg into the soup in a thin stream, from about 5 inches above the pot, stirring slowly so that it rises to the surface in thin wisps.

10. Taste and add more pepper if zest demands. Then stir in the remaining 1 teaspoon sesame oil. Serve garnished with scallion rings.

—Barbara Tropp

MUSHROOM HAZELNUT SOUP

4 TO 6 SERVINGS

1/3 cup hazelnuts (about 2 ounces)
4 tablespoons unsalted butter
1 large onion, chopped
1 pound mushrooms, coarsely chopped
About 4 cups chicken stock, preferably homemade
Salt and freshly ground pepper
1 to 2 tablespoons minced Italian flat-leaf parsley

1. Preheat the oven to 350°. Place the hazelnuts on a baking sheet and toast until golden brown, 8 to 10 minutes. Place the hot nuts in a sieve and rub with a dish towel to remove as much skin as possible. Let the nuts cool to room temperature. Grind the nuts in a nut grater or food processor.

2. In a large saucepan, melt the butter over moderately high heat. Add the onion and sauté until softened and translucent, about 5 minutes. Add the mushrooms and cook, stirring frequently, for 5 minutes. Add 4 cups of stock and bring to a boil; reduce the heat and simmer for 5 minutes.

3. Working in batches, transfer the solids and a small amount of the liquid from the soup to a blender. Add some of the hazelnuts to each batch and puree until smooth. Pour into a large saucepan. Cook over moderate heat until warmed through, about 5 minutes. Season with salt and pepper to taste. Thin with more stock if desired. Pour into a warm tureen or individual soup bowls and garnish with a sprinkling of parsley.

—Joyce Goldstein, Square One Restaurant, San Francisco, California

NARSAI'S MUSHROOM-CLAM VELOUTÉ

This flavorful, creamy soup is simple to prepare, especially if you mince the mushrooms in a food processor.

F&W BEVERAGE SUGGESTION
Meursault, such as Joseph Drouhin

6 SERVINGS

2 tablespoons unsalted butter
1/4 cup all-purpose flour
2 cups fresh clam liquor or bottled clam juice
10 ounces fresh mushrooms, minced
1 cup heavy cream
1/2 teaspoon freshly ground pepper
Salt

1. In a heavy medium saucepan, cook the butter and flour together over moderate heat, stirring constantly, until the roux becomes nut brown, 6 to 10 minutes.

2. Add the clam liquor, mushrooms and 2/3 cup of water and stir briskly to combine. Bring to a boil, reduce the heat and simmer, stirring occasionally, for 15 minutes to blend the flavors.

3. Whisk in the cream and pepper and simmer for 5 minutes. Season with salt to taste.

—Narsai David

CREAM OF MUSSEL SOUP WITH SAFFRON

Chef Jean-Louis Palladin makes this soup with a sauce of lobster cooked in cream. This version for home kitchens is not as rich but emphasizes the taste of the mussels.

6 SERVINGS

2½ pounds (about 40) mussels, scrubbed and debearded
2 cups fish stock or bottled clam juice
3/4 cup dry white wine
1 tablespoon black peppercorns
1 small imported bay leaf
1 large leek (white and tender green), rinsed well
2 celery ribs
2 large carrots
1 quart heavy cream
Pinch of saffron threads

1. In a large stockpot or flameproof casserole, place the mussels, stock, wine, peppercorns and bay leaf. Cover and cook over high heat, shaking the pot occasionally, until the mussels open, about 5 minutes after the liquid begins to boil. Remove from the heat.

2. Remove the mussels from their shells, discarding the shells and any mussels that haven't opened. Cover and set aside. Strain the cooking liquid through a double thickness of dampened cheesecloth and set aside.

3. Cut enough of the pale green part of the leek into 2-inch julienne strips to measure 1/4 cup; coarsely chop the remaining green and white parts. Cut enough celery into 2-inch julienne strips to measure 1/4 cup; coarsely chop the remainder. Cut the carrot in the same manner. Combine the julienned vegetables.

4. In a large heavy saucepan, combine the chopped vegetables. Add the heavy cream and saffron and bring to a boil over moderately high heat. Reduce the heat and simmer until the

liquid is reduced by one-fourth, about 30 minutes.

5. Strain out the vegetables; return the cream to the saucepan. Add the reserved mussel liquid. Bring to a boil, reduce the heat and simmer until the liquid is reduced by one-fourth, about 10 minutes.

6. Meanwhile, in a medium saucepan of lightly salted boiling water, blanch the julienned vegetables for 30 seconds. Drain and rinse under cold running water; drain well. (**The recipe can be prepared to this point about 5 hours in advance.** Cover and refrigerate the soup, vegetables and mussels separately. Return the cream soup base to a simmer before proceeding.)

7. Divide the mussels among 6 heated bowls. Pour the hot soup on top. Garnish each soup with the julienned vegetables.

—Jean-Louis Palladin,
Jean-Louis, Washington, D.C.

MUSSEL AND CORN CHOWDER

12 TO 16 SERVINGS

6 pounds mussels, scrubbed and debearded
¾ pound lean salt pork, cut into ¼-inch dice
2 medium onions, coarsely chopped
Kernels from 3 ears of fresh corn or 1 package (10 ounces) frozen corn or 1 can (12 ounces) vacuum-packed corn niblets
4 cups heavy cream

1. In a large stockpot, put the mussels with ¼ cup water. Place over high heat and cook, shaking the pot and stirring several times, until the mussels open, about 5 to 7 minutes. When they are cool enough to handle, remove the mussels from their shells. Reserve the broth for another use if desired.

2. In a large flameproof casserole, sauté the salt pork over moderately high heat until the fat renders out and the pork is brown and crisp, 6 to 8 minutes. With a slotted spoon, remove the pork and drain on paper towels.

3. Pour off and discard all but 2 tablespoons of the rendered pork fat. Add the chopped onion and cook over low heat until very soft and translucent, about 40 minutes. (This long cooking develops the flavor.)

4. Add the mussels, corn and salt pork to the onions. Pour in the cream, increase the heat to high and bring to a boil. Reduce the heat to low and simmer for 1 hour. Serve hot.

—Stephanie Sidell & Bob Sasse

BOSTON'S BEST CLAM CHOWDER

6 SERVINGS

2 ounces salt pork, cut into ⅛-inch dice (⅓ cup)
3 ounces slab bacon, cut into ¼-inch dice (½ cup)
2 medium onions, cut into ¼-inch dice
1 small garlic clove, minced
2 cups shucked quahog clams (about 3 dozen), minced
2 cups strained clam juice, preferably fresh
½ pound baking potatoes, peeled and cut into ¼-inch dice
1 small bay leaf
2 cups heavy cream
1 small leek (white and tender green), cut into 1½-inch julienne strips
¼ teaspoon freshly ground white pepper
Pinch of cayenne pepper
Salt

1. In a small saucepan of boiling water, blanch the salt pork for 1 minute. Drain.

2. In a large saucepan, sauté the blanched salt pork and the bacon over moderate heat until browned, about 10 minutes. Drain off all but 2 tablespoons of fat. Add the onions and garlic and sauté until softened, about 5 minutes.

3. Add the clams, clam juice, potatoes and bay leaf. Cover and simmer over moderately low heat until the potatoes and clams are tender, about 20 minutes.

4. Meanwhile, in a separate saucepan, bring the cream to a boil. Lower the heat and simmer until reduced by one quarter, about 20 minutes.

5. When the potatoes are tender, add the leek and cook until softened, 3 to 4 minutes. Add the reduced heavy cream. Season with the white pepper, cayenne and salt to taste.

—Massachusetts Bay Company,
Boston, Massachusetts

SMOKY CORN CHOWDER

To cut corn from the cob, prop the ear at a 90-degree angle on a counter or cutting board and use a sharp knife to remove the kernels.

6 SERVINGS

2 slices of bacon, minced
1 small onion, minced
4 cups of sweet corn kernels (from about 6 ears of corn) or 2 packages (12 ounces each) frozen niblets, defrosted
4 cups (1 quart) milk
2 cups (1 pint) heavy cream
½ teaspoon salt
½ teaspoon freshly ground black pepper
Dash of hot pepper sauce

¼ cup minced sun-dried tomatoes packed in olive oil (about 4 halves)
2 scallions, minced

1. In a large saucepan, cook the bacon and onion over low heat until the onion is softened and the bacon has rendered its fat, 5 to 10 minutes.

2. Add the corn, milk, cream, salt, black pepper and hot sauce. Simmer for 10 minutes. Add the sun-dried tomatoes and scallions. Serve hot.

—Molly O'Neill

CURED FISH CHOWDER WITH TOMATOES AND SPINACH

2 SERVINGS

8 plum tomatoes
1 tablespoon olive oil
2 shallots, chopped
1 large garlic clove, chopped
6 ounces Herb-Cured Fish (p. 28), thinly sliced on the diagonal, plus 4 to 6 skins from the cured fish
⅓ cup herb reserved from Herb-Cured Fish
¼ cup tomato puree
1 cup bottled clam juice
2 to 3 waxy potatoes, peeled and cut into ¼-inch dice
¼ pound fresh spinach, stemmed and shredded
⅛ teaspoon freshly ground pepper
1½ to 2 tablespoons unsalted butter, softened
1 teaspoon minced fresh basil, dill, coriander or tarragon, depending on what was used to cure the fish

1. Chop 4 of the tomatoes, reserving as much of the juice as you can. Peel and seed the remaining 4 tomatoes and cut them into ½-inch dice.

2. In a large noncorrodible saucepan, heat the oil. Add the shallots and garlic and sauté over moderate heat, stirring, until they are softened, 2 to 3 minutes.

3. Add the 4 chopped unpeeled tomatoes with their juices, the fish skins, the curing herb, tomato puree, clam juice and ½ cup of water. Cover and simmer for 30 minutes.

4. Strain into a bowl pressing on the solids. Return the liquid to the pan. Bring to a boil and add the potatoes. Cover and cook until the potatoes are tender, about 10 minutes.

5. Add the diced tomatoes, spinach and pepper. Bring to a boil, remove from the heat and stir in the butter. Add the sliced fish. Press with a spoon to submerge, cover the pot and let stand for 1 minute.

6. Ladle into warm soup plates and sprinkle with the minced fresh herb and serve hot.

—Anne Disrude

LOBSTER PLATE CHOWDER

F&W BEVERAGE SUGGESTION
California Pinot Blanc, such as Jekel

4 SERVINGS

4 live lobsters, 1½ pounds each
1½ pounds red potatoes, peeled and cut into ¼-inch dice
1 cup heavy cream
½ teaspoon salt
6 tablespoons unsalted butter
1 medium red onion, thinly sliced
Minced fresh chives and cayenne pepper

1. Bring a large stock pot of water to a boil. Fill a large bowl with ice water and set aside. Drop 2 lobsters head first into the boiling water, cover and cook for 3 minutes. With tongs, transfer the lobsters to the ice water and let soak until cool enough to handle. Repeat with the remaining two lobsters.

2. Break off the tail and claws from each lobster. Remove the meat from the claws and knuckles. Split the tails lengthwise in half, leaving the meat in the shell. Remove the light green tomalley from the body, pass through a fine-mesh sieve and set aside.

3. Remove and discard any dark green matter from the bodies. Coarsely chop the carcasses and place in a large saucepan. Add water to cover. Bring to a boil over high heat, reduce the heat and simmer until the liquid is reduced to 1 cup, about 30 minutes. Strain the liquid through a fine-mesh sieve into a medium saucepan, then set the lobster stock aside.

4. Meanwhile, place the diced potatoes in a medium saucepan and add cold water to cover by at least 1 inch. Bring to a boil over high heat and cook for about 3 minutes; the potatoes should still be very firm. Drain and rinse under cold water; drain well and set aside.

5. Add the cream and salt to the reserved lobster stock. Simmer over moderate heat for 5 minutes. Whisk in 4 tablespoons of the butter, 1 tablespoon at a time. Remove from the heat.

6. In a large skillet or saucepan, melt the remaining 2 tablespoons butter over moderate heat. Add the onion and cook until softened and translucent, about 2 minutes. Add the potatoes and cook, tossing, for 1 minute. Pour in the cream sauce and add the reserved lobster meat and tail halves. Simmer until the lobster is cooked through, about 3 minutes; do not overcook. Spoon the chowder into individual soup plates. Add a spoonful of the sieved tomalley to the sauce in each bowl. Garnish each with a pinch of chives and a dash of cayenne.

—Bruce Frankel, Panache Restaurant, Cambridge, Massachusetts

FISH AND VEGETABLE CHOWDER

This lovely soup is elegant, with its fine julienne of carrot and leek and colorful nuggets of corn and sun-dried tomatoes. Serve as a substantial first course or use as the focus of a luncheon or supper.

For a sit-down dinner, this rich, complex chowder could appropriately precede a simple meat, such as a roast beef or leg of lamb. Because there are corn and potatoes in the soup, offer only a vegetable or two with the main course; no starch is needed. If you are centering the meal around the chowder, begin with a salad of mixed greens garnished with mushrooms or follow with a salad topped with rounds of baked goat cheese. In either case, the choice of dessert will affect the tone of the meal. I'd pick chocolate as a flavor and would serve a large bowl of mousse for the more formal dinner or warmed brownies topped with vanilla ice cream and fudge sauce for an informal party.

MAKES ABOUT 5 QUARTS

4 tablespoons unsalted butter
2 tablespoons olive oil
2 large onions, cut into ⅜-inch dice
2 celery ribs with leafy tops, cut into ¼-inch dice
1 large leek—white part cut into ⅜-inch dice; green cut into thin julienne strips
¼ pound Black Forest or baked ham, cut into ¼-inch dice
¼ cup all-purpose flour
1 cup dry white wine
2 quarts milk
1½ teaspoons salt
1 teaspoon Worcestershire sauce
½ teaspoon hot pepper sauce
¼ teaspoon freshly ground black pepper
2 imported bay leaves
1 pound red potatoes, cut into ½-inch dice
1 large carrot, cut into thin julienne strips
2 pounds cod or scrod fillet, cut into 1-inch pieces
1 can (17 ounces) corn kernels, preferably vacuum packed
2 ounces sun-dried tomatoes (6 to 8 halves), cut into ¼-inch dice (optional)
1 tablespoon fresh lemon juice

1. In a stockpot or very large flameproof casserole, melt the butter in the oil over moderate heat. Add the onions, celery and white of leek. Cook, stirring occasionally, until softened and translucent, 3 to 5 minutes. Add the ham and cook until the vegetables are just beginning to color, about 2 minutes longer.

2. Add the flour and cook, stirring, for 1 to 2 minutes without browning. Add the wine and cook, stirring, until it boils and thickens. Pour in the milk and 1 cup of water. Season with the salt, Worcestershire sauce, hot sauce, pepper and bay leaves. Bring to a boil over moderately high heat, stirring occasionally.

3. Add the potatoes, reduce the heat to moderate and boil, partially covered, until the potatoes are barely tender, 10 to 15 minutes.

4. Add the carrot, cod, corn, sun-dried tomatoes, lemon juice and julienned leek green. Reduce the heat to moderately low and simmer until the fish is opaque throughout, 5 to 7 minutes. Serve hot.

—*Susan Wyler*

PORTUGUESE CHORIZO AND KALE SOUP

This soup is even better made a day ahead and reheated.

16 SERVINGS

¾ pound dried red kidney beans
2 tablespoons olive oil
5 pounds shin beef with bones
2 medium onions, chopped
2 garlic cloves, crushed through a press
1 medium carrot, cut in half
1 bay leaf
2 teaspoons salt
2 pounds kale, tough ribs removed, leaves torn into 1-inch pieces
1 pound red potatoes, unpeeled, cut into 1-inch cubes
1 pound chorizo, cut into ¼-inch rounds
½ teaspoon crushed hot red pepper

1. In a large saucepan, cover the beans with 3 cups of cold water. Bring to a boil over high heat, remove from the heat, cover and set aside for 1 hour; drain the beans.

2. Meanwhile, in a stockpot or large flameproof casserole, heat the oil. Add the beef shins and sauté over moderate heat, turning until browned on all sides, about 15 minutes. Remove the beef and set aside.

3. Add the onions to the pot and cook over moderately low heat, stirring frequently, until softened and translucent, about 10 minutes. Add the garlic.

4. Return the beef to the pot. Add the carrot, bay leaf, salt and enough cold water to cover by 1 inch. Simmer for 2½ hours, skimming frequently.

5. Remove the beef from the pot. As soon as it is cool enough to handle, remove the meat from the bone and cut into ¾-inch dice, discarding any gristle.

6. Return the beef to the soup. Add the kidney beans. Cook until the beans are tender, 45 to 60 minutes.

7. Add the kale, potatoes, chorizo and hot pepper. Cook for 1 hour longer.

—*Stephanie Sidell & Bob Sasse*

COCIDO OAXAQUENO (OAXACA-STYLE COMBINATION SOUP)

This soup, a favorite in Oaxaca, takes advantage of the abundance of high-quality livestock and produce that thrive in the region. The chayote (a squashlike vegetable) can be omitted, and any other squash—pattypan, summer squash or zucchini—can be substituted.

12 SERVINGS

8 ounces (about 1 cup) dried garbanzo beans (chick-peas)
½ pound boneless pork shoulder, cut into ¾-inch cubes
½ pound boneless beef chuck, cut into ¾-inch cubes
½ pound boneless lamb shoulder, cut into ¾-inch cubes
1 pound chicken thighs—skinned, boned and cut into ¾-inch pieces
1 medium onion, coarsely chopped
3 garlic cloves, crushed through a press
5 large sprigs of fresh mint
5 large sprigs of fresh coriander (cilantro)
2 quarts chicken stock or canned broth
½ pound cabbage (¼ of a small head)
4 medium carrots, cut into ¾-inch lengths
2 large red potatoes, peeled and cut into ¾-inch cubes
½ pound green beans, cut into ¾-inch lengths
2 medium chayote (about ¾ pound), pattypan, summer squash or zucchini, cut into ¾-inch cubes
Salt and freshly ground pepper
2 limes, cut into wedges

1. Rinse the garbanzo beans and place them in a large pot with 3 quarts of cold water. Bring to a boil, remove from the heat and let stand, covered, for 1 hour; or soak the beans in cold water overnight. Bring to a boil, reduce the heat and simmer for 30 minutes. Drain and rinse under cold water.

2. Meanwhile, in a large saucepan or flameproof casserole, combine the pork, beef, lamb, chicken, onion, garlic, 4 sprigs of the mint and 4 sprigs of the coriander. Add the chicken stock and 2 quarts of cold water. Bring to a boil over moderate heat, skimming occasionally. Reduce the heat and simmer, partially covered, for 30 minutes.

3. Add the garbanzo beans and simmer for 1 hour longer, or until the meat and beans are very tender.

4. Meanwhile, place the wedge of cabbage in a medium saucepan with 6 cups of cold water. Bring to a boil over moderately high heat, reduce the heat and boil gently until the cabbage is tender when pierced with a fork, about 10 minutes. Drain the cabbage and chop coarsely.

5. Add the carrots and potatoes to the soup and simmer for 15 minutes.

6. Add the chopped cabbage, green beans, chayote and remaining sprigs of mint and coriander. Simmer for 10 to 15 minutes, or until the vegetables are just tender. Season with salt and pepper to taste. Serve hot, with lime wedges to squeeze into the soup.

—Jim Fobel

INDONESIAN NOODLE SOUP WITH MEATBALLS

This soup makes a lovely first course for an omelet supper. The flavors are familiar, yet the overall effect is rather exotic.

4 TO 6 SERVINGS

1 tablespoon plus 2 teaspoons vegetable oil
1 small onion, minced, plus 1 large onion, thinly sliced
1 garlic clove, minced, plus 2 garlic cloves, sliced
½ pound ground beef chuck
1 egg white
1 tablespoon cornstarch
½ teaspoon salt
⅛ teaspoon freshly ground pepper
¼ pound fresh thin Chinese egg noodles
1 tablespoon minced fresh ginger
2 carrots, thinly sliced
2 scallions, thinly sliced
¼ pound Chinese cabbage, shredded (2 cups)
5 cups beef stock or canned broth
2 tablespoons soy sauce

1. In a small skillet, heat 1 teaspoon of the oil over low heat. Add the minced onion and minced garlic and sauté until softened, about 5 minutes.

2. In a medium bowl, mix the ground chuck, egg white, cornstarch, salt, pepper and sautéed onion-garlic mixture until well combined. Shape the mixture into balls about 1 inch in diameter.

3. In a large pot of simmering water, cook the meatballs until no longer pink inside, about 3 minutes. With a slotted spoon, transfer the meatballs to a bowl. Bring the water to a boil and add the noodles. Cook until tender but still firm, about 2 minutes. Drain and toss with 1 teaspoon of the oil.

4. In a large saucepan, heat the remaining 1 tablespoon oil over low heat. Add the sliced onion and garlic and sauté until golden, about 7 minutes. Add the ginger, carrots, scallions and cabbage and sauté until softened, about 4 minutes.

5. Add the stock, soy sauce and more pepper to taste. Bring to a boil, reduce the heat to moderately low and simmer the soup until the carrots are barely tender, about 5 minutes. Add the noodles and meatballs and simmer until heated through, about 5 minutes.

—Susan Grodnick

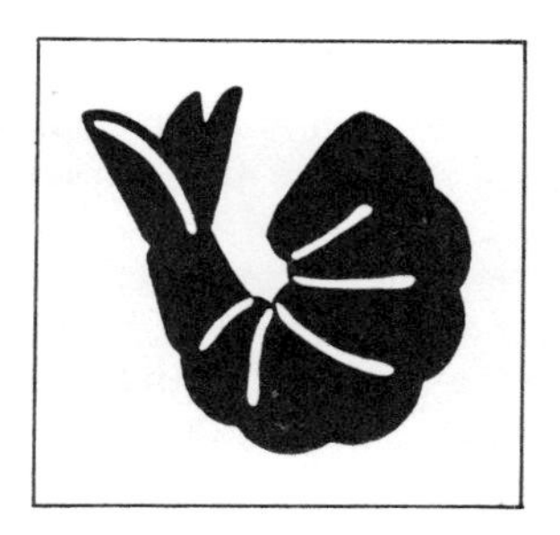

FISH & SHELLFISH

GRILLED MARINATED SWORDFISH WITH CORIANDER BUTTER

F&W BEVERAGE SUGGESTION
California Chardonnay, such as Simi

4 SERVINGS

1 cup plus 2 tablespoons soy sauce
¼ cup Oriental sesame oil
3 tablespoons minced fresh ginger
8 medium garlic cloves, minced
½ teaspoon freshly ground pepper
4 swordfish steaks (about 8 ounces each), cut 1 inch thick
½ cup dry white wine
2 tablespoons rice wine vinegar
½ cup packed fresh coriander leaves
1 teaspoon grated lemon zest
2 anchovy fillets
1 stick (½ cup) unsalted butter, cut into pieces and softened
3 tablespoons fresh lemon juice
1 tablespoon dry sherry
½ teaspoon salt

1. In a shallow noncorrodible dish just large enough to hold the swordfish steaks in one layer, combine 1 cup of the soy sauce, the sesame oil, 2 tablespoons of the ginger, half of the garlic and ¼ teaspoon of the pepper. Add the swordfish steaks and turn to coat. Let marinate at room temperature, turning occasionally, for 1 hour.

2. Meanwhile, make the sauce. In a small noncorrodible saucepan, combine the wine, vinegar and remaining 2 tablespoons soy sauce. Bring to a boil over high heat and boil until reduced to ½ cup, about 3 minutes. Remove from the heat.

3. In a food processor or blender, combine the remaining garlic, 1 tablespoon ginger and ¼ teaspoon pepper and the coriander, lemon zest and anchovy fillets. Puree to a paste. Add the butter, lemon juice, sherry and salt and puree until smooth.

4. Light the grill or preheat the broiler. Grill or broil the swordfish about 4 inches from the heat, turning once, for 5 to 6 minutes on each side, until barely opaque throughout and still juicy.

5. Meanwhile, bring the wine-soy reduction to a boil over high heat. Reduce the heat to low and whisk in the coriander butter, 1 tablespoon at a time. Serve the sauce over the fish.

—Cindy Black, Sheppard's, San Diego, California

GRILLED SWORDFISH WITH MUSTARD-SHALLOT BUTTER

F&W BEVERAGE SUGGESTION
California Chardonnay, such as Joseph Phelps

4 SERVINGS

4 tablespoons unsalted butter, at room temperature
1 tablespoon grainy mustard, such as Pommery
1 large shallot, minced
¼ teaspoon salt
¼ teaspoon white pepper
4 swordfish steaks, 6 ounces each, about 1 inch thick
2 tablespoons vegetable oil

1. Preheat the broiler and broiler pan. In a small bowl, cream together the butter, mustard, shallot, salt and pepper until well blended.

2. Pat the fish dry and brush both sides lightly with half the oil. Brush the hot broiler pan with the remaining oil. Broil the fish about 4 inches from the heat, turning once, until just opaque throughout and slightly crusty on top, about 3 minutes on each side.

3. Place 1 heaping tablespoon of the mustard butter on each piece of fish. Run under the broiler for about 20 seconds to start the butter melting. Serve the fish immediately.

—St. Botolph, Boston, Massachusetts

BAKED REDFISH EN PAPILLOTE

F&W BEVERAGE SUGGESTION
California Sauvignon Blanc, such as Sterling Vineyards

6 SERVINGS

6 tablespoons unsalted butter, melted
6 redfish fillets (8 ounces each), or substitute red snapper or bluefish
1 tablespoon Creole Seafood Seasoning (p. 238)
2 cups Creole Sauce (p. 234)
3 scallions, thinly sliced
6 sprigs of Italian flat-leaf parsley, torn apart

1. Preheat the oven to 400°. Cut out 6 heart-shaped pieces of butcher's paper or foil measuring 12-by 12-inches at their longest points.

2. Working with one piece of paper at a time, brush 1 tablespoon of butter over the unwaxed surface. Place one fillet diagonally over one half of each paper.

3. Sprinkle each fillet with ½ teaspoon of Creole Fish Seasoning.

4. Ladle ⅓ cup of the Creole Sauce over each fillet. Sprinkle the scallions and parsley on top.

5. Fold the paper over to cover the fillet and seal with a series of tight overlapping folds. (**The recipe can be prepared several hours ahead to this point**. Refrigerate the papillotes and return to room temperature before continuing.)

6. Transfer to two baking sheets or 6 individual ovenproof plates, place in the oven and bake for about 15 minutes (10 to 12 minutes for red snapper or bluefish), until the papillotes are puffed. Cut the papillotes open at the table.

—Emeril Lagasse, Commander's Palace, New Orleans, Louisiana

SEA BASS WITH SWEET PEPPERS

F&W BEVERAGE SUGGESTION
White Graves, such as Château de Fieuzal

4 SERVINGS

3 tablespoons olive oil
1/4 cup very coarse dry bread crumbs, preferably from peasant or sourdough bread
4 tablespoons unsalted butter
1/2 medium red bell pepper, cut into 1/4-inch dice
2 tablespoons capers
3/4 teaspoon grated lemon zest
1/2 teaspoon salt
1/4 teaspoon freshly ground black pepper
1 pound sea bass fillets (2 large), cut into 8 even pieces

1. In a small skillet, heat 2 tablespoons of the oil. Add the bread crumbs and toss to coat well. Fry the crumbs over moderate heat, tossing frequently, until browned and crunchy, about 10 minutes. Remove to a small bowl; wipe out the skillet.

2. In the same skillet, melt the butter over moderately high heat. When it begins to brown and smell faintly nutty, add the red pepper and cook until slightly softened, about 3 minutes. Add the capers and cook briefly until warm, about 20 seconds. Add the lemon zest and half the salt and pepper. (**The recipe may be prepared to this point 3 hours ahead.**)

3. Preheat the oven to 450°. Paint a baking pan with the remaining 1 tablespoon oil. Place the fish pieces in the pan and sprinkle with the remaining salt and pepper. Bake on the bottom rack of the oven for 3 minutes, or until the fish is opaque throughout. Remove to a warmed platter or individual plates.

4. Quickly reheat the peppers and capers. Toss with the bread crumbs until warmed through. Spoon over the fish.

—Anne Disrude

BROILED SALMON STEAKS WITH FRESH OYSTER SAUCE

F&W BEVERAGE SUGGESTION
Fumé Blanc

4 SERVINGS

2 tablespoons olive oil
2 tablespoons fresh lemon juice
Pinch of paprika
4 center-cut salmon steaks, 1 inch thick
1/2 pint shucked oysters (about 10), with their liquor
2 tablespoons unsalted butter
1 small shallot, finely chopped
2 tablespoons minced fresh chives
1/2 cup heavy cream
1/4 teaspoon Pernod
Salt and freshly ground pepper

1. In a small bowl, whisk the olive oil, lemon juice and paprika until blended. Pat the salmon steaks dry with paper towels and place them on a platter. Brush the steaks on both sides with the oil marinade.

2. Drain the oysters into a fine sieve set over a bowl; reserve the oyster liquor (1/2 to 3/4 cup).

3. In a heavy medium saucepan, melt 1 tablespoon of the butter over moderately low heat. Add the shallot, cover and cook until soft but not brown, about 5 minutes. Add the oysters, cover and cook, turning, until firm but still tender, about 2 minutes. Add 1 tablespoon of the chives and the oyster liquor. Simmer for 5 minutes longer.

4. In a blender or food processor, puree the oyster mixture until completely smooth, about 2 minutes. Pour the oyster sauce back into the saucepan and bring to a boil over high heat. Cook, stirring occasionally, until reduced by about one-fourth, about 10 minutes. Meanwhile, preheat the broiler with the broiling pan set about 4 inches from the heat.

5. Stir in the cream and continue to cook until the sauce is thick enough to coat the back of a spoon heavily, about 10 minutes. Whisk in the remaining 1 tablespoon butter and the Pernod. Season with salt and pepper to taste. Remove from the heat and cover the sauce to keep warm.

6. Lightly oil the hot broiling pan and arrange the salmon steaks on it; reserve any marinade remaining on the platter. Cook the salmon for 4 minutes. Brush the steaks with the reserved marinade and, without turning, return to the broiler. Cook for 2 to 3 minutes, or until the salmon is just slightly translucent at the center.

7. To serve, spoon the sauce onto 4 warm plates. Arrange the salmon in the center and sprinkle the remaining 1 tablespoon chives over the fish.

—Thorvald G. Lauritsen

BARBECUED SALMON

F&W BEVERAGE SUGGESTION
Washington Chardonnay, such as Château Ste. Michelle

8 TO 10 SERVINGS

3/4 cup fresh apple cider
6 tablespoons soy sauce

2 tablespoons unsalted butter
1 large garlic clove, crushed through a press
2 salmon fillets, 2½ to 3 pounds each, or 4 to 5 pounds salmon steaks, cut about 1 inch thick
Sprigs of fresh parsley or coriander and lemon slices, for garnish

1. In a small noncorrodible saucepan, combine the cider and soy sauce. Bring to a boil over high heat, reduce the heat to moderate and simmer for 3 minutes. Add the butter and garlic and continue cooking, stirring occasionally, until the liquid thickens enough to coat the back of a spoon, about 20 minutes. Remove the marinade from the heat. Let cool to room temperature.

2. Pat the salmon fillets dry and place them skin-side down on a rack. Brush the marinade evenly over the salmon. Let stand at room temperature for 30 minutes.

3. **To cook the salmon outdoors:** Light the grill. When the coals are hot, oil the rack and place the salmon skin-side down on the grill. Tent with aluminum foil and "bake" until the flesh is still slightly translucent in the thickest part; roughly 15 to 20 minutes, depending on the heat of the grill. You can turn the fish once during cooking, but you run the risk of breaking the fillet.

To cook the salmon indoors: Preheat the broiler. Place the salmon, skin-side down, on a well-oiled broiler rack and broil about 6 inches from the heat until the top is glazed and the fish is still slightly translucent in the center, 12 to 15 minutes. Serve garnished with parsley and lemon slices.

—Lila Gault

SALMON BAKED IN PARCHMENT WITH HERBS AND VEGETABLES

F&W BEVERAGE SUGGESTION
Clinton Vineyards Seyval Blanc

4 SERVINGS

1 celery rib, peeled and cut into thin julienne strips
1 medium carrot, peeled and cut into thin julienne strips
1 medium leek (white and tender green), cut into thin julienne strips
Vegetable oil
8 salmon fillets (about 3 ounces each)
4 teaspoons dry white wine
4 teaspoons fresh lemon juice
4 teaspoons bottled clam juice
1 medium tomato—peeled, seeded and diced
8 sprigs of fresh tarragon or a pinch of dried
1 tablespoon minced fresh chervil or parsley
Freshly ground pepper

1. Preheat the oven to 375°. In a medium pot of boiling water, cook the celery, carrot and leek until crisp-tender, about 1 minute. Drain and rinse under cold running water; drain and dry on paper towels.

2. Cut 4 sheets of parchment or butcher's paper into 20-inch-wide heart shapes. Lightly brush with oil. Spread one-fourth of the julienned vegetables over half of each papillote. Place 2 salmon fillets on each bed of vegetables.

3. In a small bowl, combine the wine, lemon juice and clam juice. Pour 1 tablespoon over each portion of fish.

4. Sprinkle about 1 tablespoon of diced tomato over each. Mince 4 of the tarragon sprigs. Combine the minced or dried tarragon and the chervil and sprinkle evenly over each portion. Season with pepper to taste and top each with a sprig of the remaining tarragon.

5. Fold the other half of the heart over the salmon and, with a series of tight, overlapping folds, seal the papillotes. Place on a large baking sheet. Bake in the center of the oven for 10 minutes, or until the bags are puffed up. Serve at once, letting each guest cut the papillote open at table.

—Tim Ryan, American Bounty, Hyde Park, New York

SALMON STEAKS WITH CRUSHED FENNEL SEED

F&W BEVERAGE SUGGESTION
Château Talbot

4 SERVINGS

3 tablespoons grape seed oil (see Note) or safflower oil
4 salmon steaks, cut 1 inch thick (about 8 ounces each)
¼ teaspoon salt
⅛ teaspoon freshly ground pepper
1 teaspoon fennel seed, finely crushed

1. Put a large heavy skillet, preferably cast iron, over high heat. When the skillet is quite hot, after about 1 minute, pour in the oil. Tilt the pan to coat the bottom evenly. Heat the oil for another minute; then add the salmon steaks. Season with half of the salt and pepper. Cook the salmon for 3 minutes; then turn each steak carefully. Season the second sides with the remaining salt and pepper. Cook for 3 minutes longer, or until the steaks are slightly resistant to the touch. (They should be rare inside but crisp and brown outside.)

2. Remove the steaks from the skillet. Sprinkle each with the fennel and serve.

NOTE: Grape seed oil can be heated to very high temperatures without burning, making it particularly appro-

priate for recipes like this one that require high-temperature searing.

—*John Robert Massie*

ROAST SALMON WITH RED WINE SAUCE AND MEDITERRANEAN EGGPLANT

Here is an unexpected marriage: densely rich salmon tempered by a red wine sauce, complemented in turn by a sweet eggplant caviar and soothing slices of beef marrow.

The caul fat bastes the salmon, keeping it moist, and gives added flavor. The resulting taste is unforgettable. After the salmon is roasted, the sauce is thickened with some of the eggplant, which "darkens" the taste and color. The marrow brings all the tastes and textures together.

F&W BEVERAGE SUGGESTION
Bordeaux, such as Château Cos d'Estournel

4 TO 6 SERVINGS

1¼ cups full-bodied red wine, such as Petite Sirah, California Zinfandel, hearty Burgundy or Côtes du Rhône
¼ cup sliced shallots
½ cup unsalted fish stock boiled until reduced to 2 tablespoons or 2 tablespoons frozen concentrate of fish and lobster (see Sources, below)
2 cups meat or poultry stock, degreased and boiled until reduced to ½ cup
Mediterranean Eggplant (p. 128)
Salt and freshly ground pepper
A few drops of fresh lemon juice
¼ pound caul fat, about 1 foot square*
1 tablespoon distilled white vinegar
2 pounds center-cut fresh salmon, boned into 2 fillets with the skin on
2 tablespoons olive oil
1 large imported bay leaf, broken into 4 pieces
32 slices of marrow (see Note), cut ¼ inch thick
4 tablespoons unsalted butter
1½ tablespoons minced chives
**Available at French, Italian and Chinese meat markets and at specialty butcher shops*

1. In a medium noncorrodible saucepan, bring the wine to a boil. Add the shallots and simmer over moderately low heat until reduced to a glaze, about 30 minutes.

2. Add the reduced fish and meat stocks and 2 tablespoons of the Mediterranean Eggplant. Simmer for 5 minutes to blend flavors. Strain into a small saucepan, pressing down on the solids. Season to taste with salt, pepper and a few drops of lemon juice. Set aside. **(The sauce can be made to this point several hours ahead.)**

3. Place the caul fat in a small bowl. Add the vinegar and cold water to cover. Let soak for 15 minutes. Rinse under cold running water and drain well.

4. Season the salmon, top and bottom fillets, lightly with salt and pepper on both sides. Sprinkle with 2 teaspoons of the olive oil. Place one fillet on top of the other, arranging a fat side against a thin side so that the fish will cook evenly. Set the pieces of bay leaf on top. Wrap the entire fish in caul fat and brush the top with the remaining olive oil. Set into a shallow medium baking dish. **(The salmon can be prepared ahead to this point up to 8 hours in advance and kept refrigerated, covered.)**

5. In a large heavy skillet of barely simmering lightly salted water, cook the marrow slices over moderately low heat for 4 to 5 minutes until they are translucent throughout. Remove with a slotted spoon, drain on a kitchen towel and set aside. **(The marrow can be poached up to 1 hour ahead of time, but do not refrigerate.)**

6. About 30 minutes before serving, preheat the oven to 500° and remove the salmon fillets from the refrigerator.

7. About 15 minutes before serving, roast the salmon for 7 minutes. Meanwhile, reheat the red wine sauce. Whisk in the butter, 1 tablespoon at a time, just until incorporated. Add the chives, correct the seasoning and keep warm over very low heat. (There should be about ⅔ cup sauce.)

8. Remove the salmon from the oven. Increase the heat to broil. As soon as the fish is cool enough to handle, unwrap and peel off the caul fat and skin. (The center of the fish will be slightly undercooked.)

9. In a shallow medium baking dish, spread the remaining eggplant over an area large enough to hold both fillets. Put the fillets on the eggplant, inner-sides up. Drizzle with 2 tablespoons of the fat from the pan to moisten. Broil for 1 to 2 minutes, or until the fish is almost opaque throughout.

10. Divide the salmon and eggplant among warmed plates. Fold the marrow into the red wine sauce and let warm for about 30 seconds. Pour over the salmon and serve at once.

SUBSTITUTIONS: If caul fat is unavailable, steam the salmon as follows. Cut each fillet into 4 equal parts. Season the fish with salt and pepper and a dab of unsalted butter. Tightly wrap 2 pieces of the salmon, fat side over thin, in heatproof plastic wrap. Repeat to make 4 packets. Steam for 4 minutes, turn over and steam for 3 minutes longer. Open the packages immediately after cooking to avoid any bacterial buildup. (You can steam the salmon up to 20 minutes before serving, unwrap and keep warm.) Reheat the Mediterranean Eggplant and proceed to Step 10 (above).

SOURCES: Four-ounce packages of Saucier frozen concentrate of lobster and fish essence are sold nationally in specialty food shops and some supermarkets for about $3. Alternatively, a frozen concentrate of fish essence called Glace de Poisson is available by mail order through Maison Glass, 52 E. 58th St., New York, NY 10022; 212-755-3316. The minimum order is two jars (7 ounces each) and the cost, including shipping, is $25.90.

NOTE: To obtain this amount of marrow, buy about 12 inches of marrow bone cut into 2-inch lengths. Poach in simmering water for 1 minute; then gently push out the marrow in whole pieces. Soak overnight in 2 or 3 changes of cold salted water before slicing into ¼-inch rounds.

—Paula Wolfert

STUFFED SALMON WITH TWO SAUCES

4 SERVINGS

2 small whole salmon, about 1 pound each, boned, with head and tail on
Salt and freshly ground pepper
1 recipe Basic Fish Mousseline (p. 55)
Beurre Blanc (p. 233)
Watercress Beurre Blanc (p. 234)

1. Season the interior of the fish with salt and pepper. Stuff the cavity of each fish with the mousseline; smooth with a spatula.

2. Wrap each fish securely in plastic wrap or aluminum foil and place in a single layer in a large skillet, fish poacher or shallow roasting pan. Pour in enough boiling water to reach halfway up the fish. Cover and simmer over moderate heat for 20 to 30 minutes, until the mousseline is firm.

3. Unwrap and drain the fish. Place on a warmed platter. Leaving the skin on the head, carefully peel the skin from the exposed side of the body. To serve, spoon the Beurre Blanc around the fish on half of the platter. Spoon the Watercress Beurre Blanc around the other half.

—Richard Grausman

SAUTEED WHITEFISH WITH CRISP CRUMB TOPPING

F&W BEVERAGE SUGGESTION
Sonoma Valley Chardonnay

4 SERVINGS

1¼ pounds whitefish or scrod fillets
½ teaspoon salt
¼ teaspoon freshly ground pepper
2 tablespoons unsalted butter
¼ cup olive oil
3 medium garlic cloves, minced
1 medium red bell pepper—roasted, peeled, seeded and diced—or ¼ cup diced canned roasted red pepper
2 tablespoons minced fresh parsley
2 tablespoons chopped capers
¼ cup dry bread crumbs
Lemon wedges, for garnish

1. Preheat the broiler. Pat the whitefish fillets dry with paper towels and season both sides with the salt and pepper. Fold the thinner ends under in order to make the fillets an even thickness.

2. In a large ovenproof skillet or flameproof gratin dish, melt the butter in the oil over moderate heat. Add the garlic and cook until golden, about 3 minutes. Increase the heat to moderately high and arrange the fillets in a single layer. Sauté without turning until the fillets are partially cooked (they will still be translucent in the center), about 4 minutes. Remove from the heat.

3. In a small bowl, combine the roasted red pepper, parsley and capers; toss to mix. Sprinkle this mixture evenly over the fillets. Scatter the bread crumbs on top. Drizzle some of the melted butter from the skillet over the bread crumbs.

4. Transfer to the broiler and cook about 4 inches from the heat for 1 to 2 minutes, until the crumbs are toasted. Serve garnished with lemon wedges.

—Silvia Hendricks

CATFISH FILLETS WITH ROSEMARY

As an accompaniment to this dish, try sautéed spinach and steamed buttered turnips.

F&W BEVERAGE SUGGESTION
California Sauvignon Blanc, such as Robert Mondavi Fumé Blanc

6 SERVINGS

1½ cups dry white wine
½ cup fish stock or bottled clam juice
2 tablespoons sherry wine vinegar
2 large shallots, minced
2½ teaspoons minced rosemary
2 sticks (½ pound) unsalted butter
¼ teaspoon plus a pinch of white pepper
¼ teaspoon plus a pinch of salt
Pinch of cayenne pepper
1 cup finely ground yellow cornmeal
12 catfish fillets (about 3 ounces each)
½ cup vegetable oil, preferably peanut
6 lemon wedges

1. In a medium noncorrodible saucepan, combine the wine, fish stock, vinegar, shallots and rosemary. Bring to a boil over high heat, and boil until reduced to ½ cup, about 10 minutes.

2. Cut 1½ sticks of the butter into small pieces. Reduce the heat under

the sauce to low. Whisk in the butter 1 piece at a time, allowing each piece to be incorporated before adding the next. Strain the sauce through a fine sieve into a double boiler. Season with a pinch each of white pepper, salt and cayenne. Keep warm over barely simmering water, whisking occasionally.

3. Preheat the oven to low. Cover a platter with paper towels and set in the oven to warm. Mix the cornmeal with the remaining ¼ teaspoon each of salt and pepper. Dredge the catfish fillets in the cornmeal; shake off any excess and set on a rack.

4. In a large skillet, melt the remaining 4 tablespoons butter in the oil over moderately high heat. When the foam subsides, add as many of the fillets as will comfortably fit without crowding. Cook until golden on the bottom, about 2 minutes. Turn and cook for an additional 1 to 2 minutes until golden on both sides. Transfer to the platter with a slotted spatula. Keep warm, uncovered, in the oven. Cook the remaining catfish in the same way.

5. To serve, place 2 fillets on each plate. Pour about 3 tablespoons of the sauce over the catfish. Garnish each serving with a lemon wedge.

—*Tom J. McCombie, Chez T.J., Mountain View, California*

CHINESE FISH IN WINE SAUCE

F&W BEVERAGE SUGGESTION
California Chenin Blanc, such as Simi

2 TO 4 SERVINGS

2½ tablespoons cornstarch
1¼ teaspoons salt
⅛ teaspoon white pepper
½ cup Chinese rice wine or dry sherry
3 tablespoons vegetable oil
1 egg white
1 pound flounder fillets, cut into 2-inch squares
*2 tablespoons dried tree or wood ears (Chinese black fungus)**
1 tablespoon sugar
1¼ teaspoons minced fresh ginger
1 medium garlic clove, minced
¼ cup slivered smoked ham
¼ cup slivered snow peas
**Available at Oriental markets*

1. In a medium bowl, combine 1½ tablespoons of the cornstarch, ½ teaspoon of the salt, the pepper, 1 tablespoon of the rice wine and 1 tablespoon of the oil; mix until smooth. Beat the egg white until soft peaks form and fold into the cornstarch mixture. Add the flounder pieces and toss briefly to coat. Cover and refrigerate for 2 to 4 hours.

2. In a small bowl, soak the tree ears in hot water to cover until softened, about 15 minutes. Drain, pat dry on paper towels and trim off any hard bits.

3. In a medium bowl, dissolve the remaining 1 tablespoon cornstarch, ¾ teaspoon salt and the sugar in the remaining rice wine. Add 1¼ cups of cold water and stir until smooth. Set this sauce aside.

4. In a large saucepan of simmering water, cook the flounder pieces, stirring gently, until opaque throughout, about 1½ minutes. Drain the flounder into a colander and rinse off any extraneous bits of egg white.

5. Heat a wok or large heavy skillet over high heat for 1 minute. Pour in the remaining 2 tablespoons oil. When the oil is almost smoking, add the ginger and garlic and stir-fry for 30 seconds. Reduce the heat to moderate and add the tree ears, ham and snow peas; stir-fry for 10 seconds longer. Stir in the reserved sauce and bring to a boil. Cook, stirring, for 1 minute. Place the flounder in a warm deep platter and pour the sauce over the fish. Serve hot, with plain boiled rice.

—*Anne Disrude*

BASIC FISH MOUSSELINE

This mixture may be used as part of another dish—such as the individual Mousselines with Scallops (p. 56), the Shellfish Savarin or the Stuffed Salmon (p. 54)—or by itself. If you choose to use this recipe by itself, double it and bake in a water bath in a large loaf pan or in individual molds. Serve cold with an herb mayonnaise or hot with a simple hollandaise or Beurre Blanc (p. 233), Watercress Beurre Blanc (p. 234), Tomato-Basil Coulis (p. 235) or Saffron Sauce (p. 236).

MAKES ABOUT 3 CUPS

½ pound cod, sole or flounder fillets
½ pound shrimp, shelled and deveined
2 egg whites
1 to 1¼ cups chilled heavy cream
½ teaspoon salt
⅛ teaspoon freshly ground black pepper
Pinch of nutmeg

1. Cut the cod and the shrimp into 1-inch pieces and place in a food processor fitted with a plastic blade and puree until smooth.

2. Add the egg whites one at a time, processing until well blended.

3. With the machine on, pour in ¾ cup of the cream and mix until just incorporated. Pass the mixture through the medium disk of a food mill into a metal bowl set in a larger bowl filled with ice and water. Let stand for 20 to 30 minutes, until completely chilled; the mousseline will

firm, allowing absorption of more cream.

4. Using a wooden spatula or spoon, gradually stir in as much of the remaining cream as the mousseline will absorb without becoming runny.

5. Beat in the salt, pepper and nutmeg. Test for seasoning by shaping a tablespoon of the mousseline into a ball and poaching it in simmering water for 1 minute. Adjust the salt, pepper and nutmeg if necessary.

—*Richard Grausman*

MOUSSELINES WITH SCALLOPS AND TOMATO-BASIL COULIS

4 SERVINGS

8 bay scallops
1 recipe Basic Fish Mousseline (above)
Tomato-Basil Coulis (p. 235)
Fresh basil leaves, for garnish

1. In a medium saucepan of simmering water or fish stock, poach the scallops for 15 seconds. Drain immediately and set aside. (This prevents shrinkage within the mousseline.)

2. Preheat the oven to 350°. Butter eight ¾-cup ramekins and divide the mousseline equally among them. Bury a scallop in the center of each portion. Cover each ramekin with a round of buttered parchment or aluminum foil.

3. Place the ramekins in a baking pan. Pour in enough boiling water to reach halfway up the sides of the ramekins. Bake for 15 to 20 minutes, or until firm.

4. To serve, spoon about ¼ cup of the tomato coulis onto individual warmed plates. Unmold the mousselines onto paper towels and place in the center of the coulis. Garnish with fresh basil leaves.

—*Richard Grausman*

SHELLFISH SAVARIN WITH SAFFRON SAUCE

F&W BEVERAGE SUGGESTION
Beringer Fumé Blanc Reserve

8 TO 10 SERVINGS

Saffron Sauce (p. 236)
Double recipe Basic Fish Mousseline (p. 55)
2 tablespoons unsalted butter
2 medium shallots, finely chopped
2 pounds mussels in the shell, cleaned and debearded
½ cup dry white wine
½ pound medium shrimp, shelled and deveined
½ pound bay scallops
1 tablespoon minced fresh chives
Pinch of saffron threads, for garnish

1. Make the Saffron Sauce and set aside.

2. Preheat the oven to 350°. Butter a 1½-quart savarin or ring mold. Fill with the mousseline and smooth the surface with a spatula. Place the mold in a baking pan. Pour in enough boiling water to reach halfway up the mold and bake for 30 to 40 minutes, until the top is springy to the touch and a cake tester inserted in the center comes out clean and warm.

3. In a medium saucepan, melt 2 tablespoons of the butter over moderate heat. Add the shallots and cook until softened and translucent, about 2 minutes. Add the mussels and wine. Cover, increase the heat to high and steam for about 1 minute, or until the mussels open. Working over a large bowl, remove the mussels from the shells and set aside; discard any that have not opened. Strain the mussel liquor through a sieve lined with several layers of dampened cheesecloth. Add to the saffron sauce.

4. Bring a large saucepan of water to a boil over high heat. Drop in the shrimp and scallops. When the water returns to the boil, drain immediately and rinse under cold running water; set aside.

5. Heat the saffron sauce in a large saucepan over low heat. Add the scallops, shrimp and mussels to the sauce. Cook, stirring occasionally, until the sauce begins to simmer; do not boil.

6. To assemble, unmold the savarin onto a large warmed serving platter. With a slotted spoon or skimmer, transfer the shellfish to the center of the savarin. Pour the sauce over the shellfish and around the sides of the mold. Garnish with the chives and sprinkle with the saffron threads.

—*Richard Grausman*

SHRIMP WITH GARLIC AND GINGER

F&W BEVERAGE SUGGESTION
California Fumé Blanc, such as Chateau St. Jean, La Petite Etoile

6 SERVINGS

2 tablespoons Oriental sesame oil
2 pounds medium shrimp, peeled and deveined, shells reserved
2 medium garlic cloves, minced
½ teaspoon minced fresh ginger
1 small shallot, minced
1 tablespoon soy sauce
½ cup dry white wine
½ cup heavy cream
1 tablespoon julienned sunchokes, white of leek or water chestnuts
1 tablespoon julienned scallion
1 tablespoon julienned carrot
¼ teaspoon fresh lemon juice
Salt and freshly ground pepper

1. In a large skillet, warm the oil over moderately high heat. Add the

shrimp and sauté, tossing frequently, until only half-cooked and loosely curled, about 2 minutes. Remove with a slotted spoon and set aside.

2. Add the garlic, ginger, shallot and reserved shrimp shells and sauté to release the flavors, about 10 seconds. Add the soy sauce and wine, increase the heat and boil until reduced by half, about 5 minutes. Add the heavy cream and boil until reduced by one-third, about 5 minutes.

3. Strain the sauce, pressing to extract all the liquid. Return to the skillet. Reduce the heat to moderate and add the shrimp, sunchokes, scallion and carrot. Cook until the shrimp are warmed through and opaque throughout, about 1 minute.

4. Add the lemon juice and season with salt and pepper to taste. Divide the shrimp among warmed plates. Spoon the sauce and vegetables on top.

—*Sanford D'Amato, John Byron, Milwaukee, Wisconsin*

SKEWERED PEPPER SHRIMP

This is a wonderful treatment for truly fresh shrimp in their shells, simple and delicious hot or tepid. Note the marinating times. You may want to start this recipe a day or more ahead.

F&W BEVERAGE SUGGESTION
Well-chilled Sauvignon Blanc, such as Preston

4 SERVINGS

¾ cup corn or peanut oil
¼ cup Oriental sesame oil
5 quarter-size slices of peeled fresh ginger
3 large scallions, cut into 2-inch lengths
1 tablespoon coarsely cracked black pepper
1 tablespoon finely chopped orange or tangerine zest
2 tablespoons soy sauce
½ teaspoon crushed dried hot red pepper (optional)
2 pounds fresh large shrimp in their shells

1. In a small heavy saucepan, heat the corn and sesame oils over moderate heat until they are hot enough so that a bit of ginger will foam on contact. Remove from the heat. Smash the ginger and scallion pieces with the broad side of a cleaver or chef's knife to release juices and add them to the hot oil. Add the black pepper, orange zest, soy sauce and hot pepper. Let stand until it is cool, overnight if desired. Strain, pressing on the solids to extract the flavor.

2. Rinse the shrimp in cold water and pat dry. Using a small scissors, cut along the top of the shell and remove the vein; leave the shell and tail intact.

3. Toss the shrimp with the seasoned oil. Seal tightly and refrigerate for 12 to 24 hours, stirring once or twice. Let the shrimp return to room temperature before cooking.

4. Soak about sixteen 8-inch-long thin bamboo skewers in warm water for 1 to 2 hours to prevent them from burning during cooking. Thread the shrimp on pairs of skewers set about 1½ inches apart to hold the shrimp in place and make turning easy.

5. Grill on an oiled rack over medium-hot coals, turning and basting occasionally with the seasoned oil, for about 5 minutes, depending on size. Or broil 6 inches from the heat in a preheated broiler for 5 to 6 minutes, turning and basting once, halfway through. Serve hot or warm.

—*Barbara Tropp*

SOLE AND SHRIMP WITH SHRIMP SAUCE

F&W BEVERAGE SUGGESTION
Spanish White, such as C.U.N.E. Monopole

2 SERVINGS

3 sole fillets (about 4 ounces each), halved lengthwise
¼ teaspoon salt
⅛ teaspoon freshly ground pepper
1 teaspoon unsalted butter
1 shallot, minced
¼ pound small shrimp, shelled, shells reserved
⅓ cup dry white wine
½ teaspoon Shrimp Powder (p. 237; optional)
½ cup heavy cream
1 teaspoon fresh lemon juice
1 tablespoon minced fresh chives, basil or parsley

1. Flatten the strips of sole slightly with a heavy knife. Lay out smooth-side up and sprinkle lightly with the salt and pepper. Starting at the narrower, tail end, roll up the strips and set aside.

2. Rub the inside of a small noncorrodible skillet with the butter. Sprinkle the shallot over the bottom and add the fish rolls and shrimp. Scatter the reserved shrimp shells around. Pour in the wine and ⅓ cup of water.

3. Bring to a boil, then reduce the heat to low, cover and poach for 3 minutes, turning the shrimp and fish to cook them evenly. Poach until the fish and shrimp are almost opaque throughout, about 2 minutes longer. With a slotted spoon, remove the shrimp and fish to a plate and cover loosely with foil to keep warm.

4. Add the shrimp powder to the liquid and shells in the skillet. Increase the heat to high and boil to reduce the liquid to about 2 table-

spoons, 3 to 4 minutes. Add the heavy cream and boil to reduce to a creamy consistency, another 5 minutes. Add any juices that have accumulated on the plate holding the fish. Boil until the sauce is thick enough to coat the back of a spoon. Add the lemon juice. Taste and add a pinch of salt and pepper if necessary.

5. Strain the sauce into a small bowl, pressing on the solids to extract as much juice as possible. Stir in the chives.

6. Place three fish rolls on each of 2 warmed plates. Divide the shrimp between the plates. Pour the sauce over each and serve.

—*Anne Disrude*

POTATO AND PEPPER FISH STEW

F&W BEVERAGE SUGGESTION
Spanish white, such as Bodegas Olarra

4 SERVINGS

3 tablespoons unsalted butter
3 Italian frying peppers, or small green bell peppers, cut into ¼-inch strips
1 medium onion, halved and thinly sliced
1 small carrot, cut into ¼-inch dice
1 small celery rib, cut into ¼-inch dice
1 large garlic clove, minced
2 plum tomatoes, coarsely chopped
3 tablespoons minced fresh parsley
1 tablespoon minced fresh tarragon or 1 teaspoon dried thyme
¼ teaspoon crushed hot red pepper
1 cup fish stock or bottled clam juice
½ cup dry white wine
½ pound waxy (boiling) potatoes, cut into slices ½ inch thick
½ teaspoon salt
½ teaspoon freshly ground black pepper
1 pound gray sole fillets, cut into 3-by-1½-inch pieces

1. In a large heavy saucepan, melt the butter over moderate heat. Add the frying peppers, onion, carrot, celery and garlic. Stir to coat with the butter, cover and cook until the onions are soft and translucent, about 10 minutes.

2. Add the tomatoes, parsley, tarragon, hot pepper, fish stock and wine. Lay the potatoes on top of the other vegetables and sprinkle with half the salt and black pepper. Bring to a boil, reduce to a simmer, cover and cook until the potatoes are fork-tender, about 10 minutes.

3. Lay the fish on top of the potatoes. Sprinkle with the remaining salt and black pepper. Cover and simmer until the fish is barely opaque, about 2 minutes.

4. Remove the fish to a plate. Ladle the vegetables and liquid into 4 soup dishes. Arrange the fish on top.

—*Anne Disrude*

SAUTEED SHRIMP WITH ROASTED TOMATOES AND POBLANO AND CHIPOTLE CHILES

Accompanying this fiery, intensely flavored dish with rice and warm flour tortillas, followed by a cooling salad.

F&W BEVERAGE SUGGESTION
Full-bodied California Chardonnay, such as Fetzer Barrel Select or Perret Vineyards

6 SERVINGS

6 large tomatoes, cored
4 fresh poblano chiles
Zest of ½ orange, cut into fine julienne strips
¼ cup olive oil
6 medium garlic cloves, minced
¼ cup fish stock or bottled clam juice
1 cup fresh orange juice
¼ teaspoon salt
¼ teaspoon freshly ground black pepper
3 or 4 dried chipotle chiles (reconstituted in hot water) or canned chipotle chiles
2 pounds large shrimp, peeled and deveined
¼ cup orange liqueur or orange mezcal
¼ cup chopped fresh coriander

1. Roast the tomatoes and poblano chiles under a broiler flame or over a gas flame, turning, until charred all over (the tomatoes will take less time than the peppers, so be sure to remove them as they char). As soon as the tomatoes are cool enough to handle, slip off the skins, halve and remove the seeds. Coarsely chop the tomatoes and set aside. When the peppers are blackened, seal them in a paper bag for 10 minutes. Remove the skins; seed and devein. Cut the peppers into thin strips and set aside.

2. In a small saucepan of boiling water, blanch the orange zest for 2 minutes. Drain and set aside.

3. In a large noncorrodible skillet or flameproof casserole, heat 2 tablespoons of the oil over moderate heat. Add the garlic and sauté until softened but not browned, about 2 minutes. Add the chopped tomatoes, fish stock, orange juice, blanched orange zest, salt and black pepper. Simmer over low heat until the sauce is thickened, about 30 minutes. Season with additional salt and pepper to taste. **(The recipe can be prepared ahead to this point.)**

4. Puree the chipotle chiles with ½ cup of the tomato sauce. Depending on the hotness desired, add from half to all of the chile puree to the remaining tomato sauce. Keep warm over low heat.

5. Heat the remaining 2 tablespoons olive oil in a large skillet over high heat until almost smoking. Add the shrimp and sauté, tossing, until

they are almost opaque but still slightly translucent, about 4 minutes. Add the orange liqueur and ignite. When the flames subside, add the shrimp to the tomato sauce and toss to coat. Serve, garnished with the poblano chile strips and fresh coriander.

—Mark Miller, Fourth Street Grill, Berkeley, California

GINGERED SHRIMP

3 TO 4 SERVINGS

1 garlic clove, smashed, plus 1 garlic clove, minced
⅓ cup corn oil
1 pound medium shrimp—shelled, deveined and patted dry
1½ tablespoons minced, peeled fresh ginger
¼ cup thinly sliced scallions
½ teaspoon salt
1 tablespoon fresh lemon juice

1. In a large skillet or wok, place the smashed garlic clove and oil. Warm over low heat until the garlic sizzles, 3 to 5 minutes. Stir briefly to flavor the oil; remove and discard the garlic before it browns.

2. Increase the heat to high and add the shrimp in a single layer. Cook for 30 seconds, turn them and cook for 30 seconds longer. They should be opaque but not browned; do not overcook. With a slotted spoon, transfer the shrimp to paper towels to drain.

3. Pour off all but 1 tablespoon of oil from the skillet. Add the minced garlic and the ginger and scallions to the pan and sauté over moderate heat for 1 minute. Return the shrimp to the pan, sprinkle with the salt and toss until coated with the ginger mixture and hot, about 15 seconds. Remove the shrimp from the heat and stir in the lemon juice. Serve hot or at room temperature.

—Diana Sturgis

SHRIMP CREOLE

This piquant dish can be served by itself over steamed rice or as an accompaniment to Jambalaya (p. 60).

4 SERVINGS

2 tablespoons vegetable oil
1½ pounds medium shrimp, shelled and deveined
2 teaspoons Creole Seafood Seasoning (p. 238)
3 cups Creole Sauce (p. 234)

1. In a large skillet, heat the oil over moderately high heat. Add the shrimp, sprinkle with the Creole Seafood Seasoning and cook over moderately high heat for about 30 seconds on each side, until slightly pink.

2. Pour in the Creole Sauce, stir and cook over moderate heat until the shrimp are pink and curled, 2 to 3 minutes.

—Emeril Lagasse, Commander's Palace, New Orleans, Louisiana

SHRIMP BALL CURRY

4 SERVINGS

1 pound raw shrimp—peeled, deveined and finely chopped
2 garlic cloves, minced
1 teaspoon finely chopped fresh ginger
1 teaspoon cornstarch
1 teaspoon salt
1 tablespoon corn or peanut oil
2 tablespoons thinly sliced onion (½ small onion)
1 teaspoon crushed hot red pepper
½ teaspoon turmeric
¼ cup chopped tomato (fresh or canned)
1 teaspoon Oriental fish sauce
¼ cup coarsely chopped fresh coriander

1. In a bowl, combine the shrimp, half the garlic, the ginger, cornstarch and ½ teaspoon of the salt. Mix until well blended. Shape heaping teaspoons into round balls.

2. In a medium noncorrodible saucepan, heat the oil. Add the onion, hot pepper, turmeric and remaining garlic. Stir-fry over moderate heat until the onion is softened but not browned, about 2 minutes. Add the tomato and 1½ cups of water. Bring to a boil, then simmer, uncovered, for 5 minutes.

3. Stir in the fish sauce and remaining ½ teaspoon salt. Add the shrimp balls; they will not be completely submerged. Cook, uncovered, over moderately low heat for 10 minutes. Stir in the coriander and continue cooking, uncovered, for 5 minutes longer. Serve as an entrée with boiled rice or as an appetizer.

—Copeland Marks

SEAFOOD STEAMED IN BANANA LEAVES (MARISCOS MARIMBA)

6 SERVINGS

4 tablespoons unsalted butter
¾ cup finely chopped scallions
2 medium garlic cloves, minced
6 large tomatoes, coarsely chopped
1 canned chipotle chile, minced (about 2 teaspoons)
1 teaspoon oregano, preferably Mexican
Salt and freshly ground black pepper
7 banana leaves, 18 by 15 inches each (see Note)
1 pound bay scallops or quartered sea scallops
1 pound medium shrimp, peeled and deveined
2 bottles Mexican dark beer, such as Dos Equis

1. In a medium skillet, melt the butter over moderate heat. Add the

scallions and garlic and sauté until translucent, about 1 minute. Add the tomatoes and cook, stirring, for 2 minutes. Add the chipotle and oregano and cook, uncovered, until the sauce has thickened and is no longer runny, about 5 minutes. Season with salt and pepper to taste. Remove from the heat and let cool to room temperature.

2. Rinse the banana leaves and pat dry. Tear one banana leaf lengthwise into 12 strips, ¼ inch wide. Tie pairs of the strips together to make 6 long ties. Set aside.

3. Combine the scallops and shrimp. Spread a banana leaf flat. Spoon about ⅓ cup of the sauce onto the center and spread into a 6-inch square. Place about one-sixth of the seafood mixture in a single layer on top of the sauce. Season lightly with salt and pepper.

4. Fold one short edge of the banana leaf over to cover the shellfish. Fold up the other short edge and then the top and bottom to form a 6-inch square packet. Tie with a banana leaf strip. Repeat with the remaining banana leaves, tomato sauce and seafood mixture.

5. Preheat the oven to low. In a steamer large enough to fit half the packets in a single layer or in a large roasting pan, pour in enough beer to cover the bottom by at least 1 inch. Bring to a boil over high heat. Set the rack in place and arrange 3 packets, folded sides up, in a single layer. Cover and steam for 6 minutes. Remove to the oven to keep warm and steam the remaining 3 packets.

6. To serve, cut the ties holding the packets and fold back the leaves to partially expose the filling.

NOTE: If banana leaves are not available, parchment or butcher's paper may be substituted, although it will not impart the same flavor as the banana leaf. Fold the parchment in the same manner as the banana leaves and tie with kitchen string.

—Zarela Martinez, Café Marimba, New York City

JAMBALAYA

F&W BEVERAGE SUGGESTION
California Sauvignon Blanc, such as Concannon

6 TO 8 SERVINGS

1 tablespoon unsalted butter
1 pound boneless chicken (breast and/or leg and thigh meat), cut into 1½-inch chunks
½ pound andouille sausage or chorizo, cut into ¼-inch rounds
½ pound smoked ham, cut into ½-inch cubes
12 medium shrimp—shelled, deveined and cut into 1-inch pieces
1 medium onion, chopped
1 medium green bell pepper, chopped
2 medium celery ribs, chopped
5 garlic cloves, finely chopped
1 tablespoon Creole Meat Seasoning (p. 238)
1 can (28 ounces) Italian peeled tomatoes, with their juices
1 cup chicken stock or canned broth
5 imported bay leaves
2 tablespoons Worcestershire sauce
1 tablespoon Louisiana Red Hot Sauce or other hot pepper sauce
½ teaspoon paprika, preferably hot
½ teaspoon salt
3 cups converted long-grain rice
2 scallions, thinly sliced
Shrimp Creole (p. 59)

1. Melt the butter in a large flameproof casserole over moderately high heat. Add the chicken and sauté, stirring occasionally, for 1 minute. Add the sausage and ham and cook for 1 minute longer.

2. Add the shrimp, onion, bell pepper, celery and garlic and cook, stirring occasionally, for 1 minute.

3. Stir in the Creole Meat Seasoning and the tomatoes with their juices and cook for 1 minute.

4. Add the chicken stock, bay leaves, Worcestershire sauce, hot sauce, paprika and salt. Bring to a boil, reduce the heat and simmer for 5 minutes.

5. Stir in the rice and bring to a boil. Reduce the heat to moderately low. Stir in the scallions. Cook, uncovered, stirring occasionally, for 12 minutes. Cover, remove from the heat and let stand, stirring occasionally, for about 10 minutes, or until the rice is tender. Serve the Jambalaya accompanied with Shrimp Creole.

—Emeril Lagasse, Commander's Palace, New Orleans, Louisiana

SEA SCALLOPS WITH SAUVIGNON BLANC CREAM SAUCE

F&W BEVERAGE SUGGESTION
California Fumé Blanc, such as Chateau St. Jean

4 SERVINGS

4 tablespoons clarified butter
1½ pounds medium sea scallops
¼ teaspoon salt
⅛ teaspoon freshly ground white pepper
¼ cup Cognac or brandy
¾ cup Sauvignon Blanc or other dry white wine
1 cup heavy cream
1 tablespoon fresh tarragon leaves or ½ teaspoon dried

1. In a large skillet, warm the butter over moderately high heat. When it begins to shimmer, add the scallops, season with the salt and pepper and sauté, tossing occasionally, until opaque, about 1 minute.

2. Add the Cognac, swirl to warm it, then ignite with a match. When the flames subside, add the wine, cream and tarragon and bring to a boil. Using a slotted spoon, remove the cooked scallops to a warm dish, cover and set aside. Boil the sauce until it is thick enough to coat the back of a spoon, about 5 minutes. (**The recipe may be prepared to this point 2 hours in advance.** Hold the scallops in the refrigerator. Return the scallops to room temperature and warm the sauce before proceeding.)

3. Return the scallops and any accumulated juices to the pan. Stir briefly to warm and serve.

—John Robert Massie

SHERRY-MARINATED FLOUNDER AND SCALLOP BROCHETTES

Broiled or grilled, these seafood brochettes are simple and delicious. Serve them with rice pilaf sprinkled with toasted sliced almonds for an elegant entrée.

F&W BEVERAGE SUGGESTION
Gewürztraminer

4 TO 6 SERVINGS

1 pound flounder filets, cut into 1- to 1½-inch squares
1 pound sea scallops
½ pound lean sliced bacon
1 cup dry sherry
Lemon wedges

1. In a shallow noncorrodible container, place the flounder and scallops in an even layer. Arrange the bacon strips on top and pour on the sherry. Cover with plastic wrap and marinate in the refrigerator for at least 3 hours.

2. Preheat the broiler. Drain off the marinade. Thread the bacon, scallops and flounder on metal skewers, intertwining the bacon around the seafood and alternating the scallops and flounder.

3. Broil about 4 inches from the heat, turning once, until the bacon is cooked and the seafood is opaque, 10 to 15 minutes. Serve hot with the lemon wedges.

—David Jordan, Virginia Museum of Fine Arts, Richmond, Virginia

STEAMED SCALLOPS WITH FETTUCCINE AND ROSY BUTTER SAUCE

Although this dish was created with tomato fettuccine in mind, if you can't find any, green spinach fettuccine adds a festive touch. Likewise, if fresh basil is unavailable, substitute two tablespoons of julienned steamed or blanched leek green for garnish.

F&W BEVERAGE SUGGESTION
Meursault, such as Joseph Drouhin

4 SERVINGS

1 tablespoon plus ¼ teaspoon salt
1 teaspoon olive oil
2 medium tomatoes—peeled, seeded and coarsely chopped
1 tablespoon tomato paste
¼ cup dry white wine
2 tablespoons white wine vinegar
2 tablespoons chopped shallots (about 2 medium)
¼ teaspoon freshly ground white pepper
1 tablespoon heavy cream
2 sticks (½ pound) plus 2 tablespoons unsalted butter, cut into tablespoons
½ pound fresh egg fettuccine
½ pound fresh tomato fettuccine
24 sea scallops (about 1¼ pounds)
8 large basil leaves, julienned, for garnish

1. Set a large pot with 6 quarts of water to boil for the pasta. Add 1 tablespoon of the salt.

2. Meanwhile, in a small saucepan, heat the olive oil until warm but not smoking. Stir in ¼ cup of the chopped tomatoes and the tomato paste. Cook over moderate heat, stirring occasionally, until the excess liquid has evaporated, about 5 minutes. Pass through a fine-meshed sieve set over a bowl; reserve the tomato puree.

3. In a small noncorrodible saucepan, combine the wine, vinegar, shallots and pepper. Bring to a boil over moderately high heat and reduce to a syrupy glaze, about 1 tablespoon of liquid. Reduce the heat to low and stir in the cream.

4. Whisk in 2 sticks of the butter, 2 tablespoons at a time, adding each just before the previous addition is completely incorporated. The goal is to create an emulsified butter sauce; do not let the butter melt completely. Whisk in the reserved tomato puree. Add ¼ teaspoon of the salt. Keep the sauce warm in a pan of hot—not boiling—water; the sauce will hold for up to 1 hour.

5. When the pasta water boils, add the egg and tomato fettuccine. Cook until just tender to the bite, 2 to 3 minutes. Drain well. In a large bowl, toss the hot pasta with the remaining 2 tablespoons butter. Cover to keep warm.

6. Meanwhile, in a large steam basket, steam the scallops in a single layer until opaque, about 2 minutes.

7. To assemble, mound the pasta in the center of 4 warmed large plates. Surround each serving with about ⅓ cup of the sauce. Arrange six scallops on top of the sauce around each mound of pasta. Garnish with the remaining chopped tomato and basil.

—Christian Delouvrier, The Maurice, New York City

SCALLOPS WITH LEMON PESTO IN A VEGETABLE NEST

This beautiful dish from the spa at the Sonoma Mission Inn is both light and elegant. If you are not on a low-sodium diet, you might want to season the sauce with salt to taste when you add the pepper in Step 5.

4 SERVINGS

1 teaspoon olive oil
1 pound bay scallops
1 tablespoon minced shallot
*1 tablespoon Vegit seasoning**
½ cup fish stock or dry white wine
3 tablespoons Low-Calorie Lemon Pesto (p. 235)
1½ tablespoons fresh lemon juice
1 medium carrot
2 medium zucchini
2 medium yellow squash
2 tablespoons chopped fresh dill
2 small cucumbers—peeled, seeded and coarsely shredded
½ teaspoon cornstarch
1 tablespoon dry sherry
⅛ teaspoon freshly ground pepper
1 medium tomato—peeled, seeded and diced
1½ teaspoons minced fresh chives
**Available in health food stores*

1. In a medium skillet, warm the olive oil over moderate heat. Add the scallops and cook, tossing frequently, for 1 minute (the scallops will finish cooking later). With a slotted spoon, transfer the scallops to a bowl. Add the shallot to the skillet and cook until softened, about 1 minute. Add the Vegit, fish stock, pesto and lemon juice. Simmer over moderate heat for 5 minutes. Remove the sauce from the heat and set aside.

2. With a mandoline or other vegetable cutter, cut the carrot the entire length of the vegetable into very thin julienne strips. Set aside separately. Cut the zucchini and squash in the same way.

3. In a large saucepan, bring ⅔ cup of water to a boil over high heat. Add the carrot and cook, covered, for 30 seconds. With tongs, transfer to a colander. Add the zucchini and squash to the pan, cover and cook until just tender but still resistant to the bite, about 30 seconds. Drain in the colander, tossing to remove as much water as possible. Return the vegetables to the warm pan. Add the dill and toss lightly to mix.

4. Divide the vegetables among 4 warmed large plates. With your hands, quickly form them into nests, leaving a 3-inch center. Place the shredded cucumber in the center of the nests.

5. Reheat the sauce. Mix the cornstarch with the sherry until smooth. Stir into the sauce. Bring to a boil, stirring, until thickened. Add the pepper. Add the scallops to the sauce and cook over moderately low heat until warmed through and opaque throughout, about 1 minute. Mound the scallops on top of the cucumber. Pour the remaining sauce over the scallops. Garnish with the tomato and chives.

—Christian Chavanne,
Sonoma Mission Inn and Spa,
Boyes Hot Springs, California

LOBSTER SOUFFLE IN THE SHELL

F&W BEVERAGE SUGGESTION
California Chardonnay, such as Matanzas Creek

4 SERVINGS

3 tablespoons plus ½ teaspoon salt
2 live lobsters, 1¼ pounds each
3 tablespoons unsalted butter
2½ tablespoons all-purpose flour
1 cup milk
¼ teaspoon freshly ground pepper
3 whole eggs, separated
1 egg white
2 tablespoons freshly grated Parmesan cheese

1. Preheat the oven to 375°. Bring a large pot of water to a boil over high heat. Add 3 tablespoons of the salt and drop in the lobsters head first. Cover tightly and cook for about 10 minutes, until the lobsters are bright red. Remove the lobsters from the water, drain and let stand until cool enough to handle.

2. With a large heavy knife, split the lobsters lengthwise in half, cutting through cleanly from the head to the tail. Remove the tail meat and any bits of meat from the body. Remove and reserve any tomally and roe; discard the intestines. Separate the claws from the body of the lobsters and working carefully with a nut cracker and kitchen shears, remove the meat from each in one piece. Remove and reserve the meat from the claw joints. Discard the claw shells.

3. Using kitchen shears, carefully cut away and discard the sand sac in the head and any innards in the body so that the inside of each shell is cleaned out. Try to leave the small legs intact. Wash out the 4 half shells and dry them well.

4. Set aside the whole meat from the claws. Finely chop all the rest of the lobster meat.

5. In a heavy medium saucepan, melt the butter over moderate heat. Add the flour and cook, stirring, for 3 minutes without allowing to color to make a roux.

6. Meanwhile, in a medium saucepan, scald the milk over moderately high heat. Gradually whisk the hot milk into the roux. Bring to a boil, whisking constantly. Cook, stirring, until the béchamel thickens, about 2 minutes.

7. Add the chopped lobster and season with the remaining ½ teaspoon salt and the pepper. Pass the mixture through the medium disk of a food mill or puree in a food processor.

8. Return to a large saucepan. Bring the pureed lobster mixture to a boil over moderately high heat. Remove from the heat and beat in the 3 egg yolks, one at a time. Set aside to cool slightly.

9. Beat the 4 egg whites until stiff but not dry. Stir one-fourth of the beaten whites into the lobster base to lighten it. Quickly fold the lightened soufflé base into the remaining egg whites.

10. Place the lobster shells on a large baking sheet. Spoon the soufflé mixture into the 4 shells. Bake in the lower third of the oven for 15 minutes, until well puffed and golden, but still slightly soft. Sprinkle each serving with ½ tablespoon of Parmesan cheese and bake for 5 minutes longer, or until the cheese is melted.

11. Just before the soufflé is done, rewarm the claws by steaming them or by heating them in a microwave oven until warmed through. Serve the soufflés as soon as they are cooked, garnishing each lobster half with a whole piece of claw meat.

—John Robert Massie

CHILLED CORN AND CRAB FLAN

Leftover corn is happy in this light luncheon or supper flan, which is served with a tangy tomato vinaigrette.

4 SERVINGS

5 eggs
¾ cup milk
½ cup heavy cream
¼ cup fresh bread crumbs
½ teaspoon salt
¼ teaspoon freshly ground black pepper
Dash of cayenne pepper
Dash of freshly grated nutmeg
3 cups of corn kernels (from 4 to 5 ears of corn) or 1 package (12 ounces) frozen niblets, defrosted
8 ounces lump crabmeat
Spicy Tomato Vinaigrette (p. 237)

1. Preheat the oven to 325°. In a large bowl, beat together the eggs, milk, cream, bread crumbs, salt, black pepper, cayenne and nutmeg until blended. Stir in the corn and crabmeat. Pour into a well-buttered, shallow 2-quart baking dish and cover with aluminum foil. Place the baking dish in a larger roasting pan and pour in enough hot water to reach about two-thirds up the sides of the dish. Bake for 35 to 40 minutes, until the flan is firm.

2. Remove the flan from the water bath and let cool slightly. Unmold onto a large platter, cover and refrigerate overnight. Serve chilled, cut into wedges, accompanied with the tomato vinaigrette.

—Molly O'Neill

CRAB CAKES WITH ORANGE ZEST

MAKES 8 CAKES

2 tablespoons unsalted butter
3 large shallots, minced (about ¼ cup)
2 eggs, beaten
¼ cup crème fraîche or heavy cream
2½ teaspoons grated orange zest
¾ teaspoon salt
¼ teaspoon freshly ground pepper
1 pound fresh lump crab meat, picked over and shredded
4 cups coarse fresh bread crumbs, preferably from sourdough bread
1½ cups clarified butter or vegetable oil
Orange wedges, for garnish

1. In a small skillet, melt the unsalted butter over moderate heat. Add the shallots and cook, stirring occasionally, until soft, 3 to 4 minutes. Remove to a large bowl and let cool to room temperature.

2. Add the eggs, crème fraîche, orange zest, salt and pepper to the shallots and stir to mix. Add the crab and stir gently until incorporated.

3. Divide the crab mixture into 8 portions and form into 1-inch thick patties. Coat evenly with the bread crumbs, pressing so that they will adhere. Place the cakes on a rack and refrigerate until very firm, about 1 hour.

4. Pour the oil and clarified butter into a heavy skillet to a depth of ½ inch. Heat to 375° or until the fat begins to shimmer. Working in 2 batches, fry 4 of the crab cakes, turning once, until well browned, about 4 minutes for each side. Remove and drain on paper towels. Repeat with the 4 remaining cakes. (**The crab cakes can be held at room temperature for up to 3 hours.** Reheat in a 325° oven for 15 minutes before serving.) Garnish with the orange wedges and serve hot.

—Lauren Berdy

GOLDEN CLAM CAKES

MAKES ABOUT 36 CAKES

5 cups all-purpose flour
1¾ tablespoons baking powder
1 teaspoon salt
4 eggs, beaten
1 cup chopped quahog or cherrystone clams, drained, with their liquor reserved (about 1 dozen medium clams)
Vegetable oil, for deep-frying

1. In a large bowl, combine the flour, baking powder and salt. Combine the beaten eggs with the chopped clams and stir into the flour mixture until thoroughly combined.

2. Strain the reserved clam liquor through several thicknesses of dampened cheesecloth and measure. Add enough water to equal 1½ cups. Gradually stir into the clam mixture to form a slightly thick batter that will fall easily from a spoon.

3. Heat about 1 inch of oil in a deep fryer or large heavy saucepan to 350°. Scoop up about 2 tablespoons of the batter and drop into the hot oil. Fry for about 5 minutes, turning occasionally, until golden. Drain on paper towels. Repeat with the remaining batter.

—Dovecrest Indian Restaurant, Exeter, Rhode Island

LITTLENECK CLAMS STEAMED IN BEER

8 TO 10 SERVINGS

6 pounds littleneck clams (about 7 dozen)
1 cup cornmeal (optional)
2 cups zesty pilsner-style beer or light ale
2 celery ribs, broken in half
1 large onion, coarsely chopped
2 large garlic cloves, coarsely chopped
2 teaspoons freshly ground pepper
½ teaspoon thyme
¼ teaspoon ground cloves

1. If the clams have been purchased at a seafood market, simply rinse in cool fresh water to remove any sand remaining on the shells. If they have been dug at a local beach, place them in a bucket filled with bay, ocean or fresh water. Add the cornmeal and let them soak overnight so that any sand inside the shells will be thoroughly discharged.

2. Pour 4½ cups of water and the beer into a large stockpot. Add the celery, onion, garlic, pepper, thyme and cloves. Bring to a boil over moderately high heat and cook for 3 minutes, stirring occasionally.

3. Add the clams, cover the pot and cook for 10 to 12 minutes, stirring occasionally to promote even steaming, until the clams open. Remove the celery and serve the clams at once with the cooking broth.

—Lila Gault

SAUTEED SNAILS WITH SCALLIONS, GARLIC AND COUNTRY HAM ON CAPELLINI

Chef Marcel Desaulniers serves this dish with garlic-flavored capellini as an appetizer. We think it's so good, though, that we've increased the amounts to the size of an entrée.

F&W BEVERAGE SUGGESTION
White Burgundy, such as Mâcon-Viré

6 SERVINGS

12 tablespoons (1½ sticks) unsalted butter
6 medium shallots, minced
4 medium garlic cloves, minced
½ cup dry white wine
¼ cup Cognac or brandy
3 to 4 dozen canned snails, drained and washed
¾ teaspoon salt
¼ teaspoon freshly ground pepper
2 teaspoons fresh lemon juice
8 plum tomatoes—peeled, seeded and coarsely chopped (2 cups)
3 scallions, cut into 1½-inch julienne strips
6 ounces smoked ham, such as Black Forest, cut into 1½-inch-long julienne strips
2 teaspoons chopped fresh parsley
1 pound capellini

1. In a large skillet, melt 2 tablespoons of the butter over moderately low heat. Add the shallots and garlic and cook until softened and translucent, 4 to 5 minutes. Add the wine, Cognac, snails and half of the salt and pepper. Bring to a simmer and cook, uncovered, stirring occasionally, until all of the liquid has evaporated, about 15 minutes.

2. Cut 8 tablespoons of butter into small pieces. Add the butter and the lemon juice to the snails. Cook, stirring, over moderate heat until the butter is melted and incorporated into the sauce. Set aside. (**The recipe can be prepared to this point several hours ahead.** Cover and set aside at room temperature.)

3. Bring a large pot of salted water to boil for the pasta. Reheat the snails in the garlic butter over moderate heat until warmed through, about 5 minutes. Add the tomatoes and scallions and cook for 2 minutes. Add the ham and parsley and cook until warmed through, about 1 minute.

4. Meanwhile, cook the pasta in the boiling water until tender but still firm to the bite, 2 to 4 minutes for fresh pasta, 5 to 8 minutes for dried.

5. Drain the pasta and toss with the remaining 2 tablespoons butter and remaining salt and pepper. Divide among 6 warmed plates. Spoon the snails and sauce on top.

—Marcel Desaulniers, The Trellis, Williamsburg, Virginia

POULTRY

CHICKEN ROASTED WITH MORELS

6 SERVINGS

¾ pound fresh morels
4 tablespoons unsalted butter
3½-pound whole chicken, liver and heart reserved and finely chopped
1 teaspoon salt
Large pinch of cinnamon
⅛ teaspoon freshly ground pepper
1 cup veal or beef stock
Watercress, for garnish

1. Trim the morels. Cut off and chop the bases. If the morels are small, halve them lengthwise; if medium, cut them across into ¼-inch rounds; if large, first cut them in half lengthwise then into half-rounds. Place the morels in a sieve and rinse vigorously under running water, then dry on a towel.

2. In a large skillet, melt 2 tablespoons butter. Stir in the morels and sauté over high heat until the liquid has evaporated. Add the chicken liver and heart and sauté for 30 seconds. Transfer the mixture to a dish and toss with ¼ teaspoon of the salt, the cinnamon and pepper. Let cool.

3. Remove the large pieces of fat from the chicken. Wipe it dry and set on a rack. Let stand at room temperature until the stuffing is cool.

4. Preheat the oven to 325°. Slip 1 tablespoon butter under the breast skin and smooth to distribute. Fill the cavity with the morel mixture. Sew the cavity closed and truss the chicken. Rub the remaining tablespoon butter all over the chicken.

5. Set the chicken, breast-side down, on a rack in a roasting pan. Roast for 45 minutes. Baste with the butter in the pan, sprinkle with half the remaining salt, then gently turn breast-side up. Sprinkle with the remaining ¾ teaspoon salt and return to the oven for 45 minutes, basting occasionally. Increase the oven temperature to 400° and roast the bird until it is golden, about 15 minutes longer.

6. Remove the chicken and let stand for 5 minutes. Meanwhile, pour the stock into the roasting pan, bring to a boil and simmer until reduced by half.

7. Carve the chicken into serving pieces and transfer the morel stuffing to the reduced stock. Bring the stock and morels to a simmer to heat through.

8. Arrange the chicken on a bed of watercress on a serving platter. Pour the morels into a bowl and serve on the side.

—Elizabeth Schneider

ROAST CHICKEN WITH GOAT CHEESE, HONEY AND THYME

4 SERVINGS

3-pound whole chicken, rinsed and dried
1 teaspoon coarse (kosher) salt
½ teaspoon coarsely cracked black pepper
12 large sprigs of fresh thyme or 2 teaspoons dried
1 head of garlic, cloves separated but unpeeled
1 tart green apple, such as Granny Smith—peeled, quartered and cored
1 onion, peeled and quartered
4 whole shallots, unpeeled
4 tablespoons unsalted butter
¼ cup honey
¼ cup cider vinegar
1 cup dry white wine
2 ounces mild goat cheese, such as Montrachet
¼ cup heavy cream

1. Preheat the oven to 450°. Sprinkle the cavity of the chicken with ¼ teaspoon each of the salt and pepper. Place half the thyme and half the garlic cloves in the cavity. Truss the chicken. Rub the skin with the remaining salt and pepper.

2. Place the chicken breast-side up in a roasting pan. Surround with the apple, onion, shallots and remaining garlic cloves. Roast for 30 minutes.

3. Meanwhile, in a small heavy saucepan, combine the butter, honey and vinegar. Cook over moderate heat, stirring frequently, until the butter is melted, to make a basting sauce.

4. Baste the chicken every 5 to 10 minutes as it roasts for about 30 minutes longer, or until the juices run clear when the thigh is pricked to the bone. Turn the vegetables occasionally to coat with drippings so that they will be evenly caramelized.

5. Turn off the oven. Remove the chicken, shallots and garlic cloves to a heatproof platter, cover loosely with foil and return to the oven to keep warm.

6. Place the roasting pan on top of the stove. Add the wine and bring to a boil, scraping up any browned bits from the bottom and sides of the pan and mashing the apples and onion into the sauce.

7. Strain the sauce into a medium saucepan and return to a boil. Strip the leaves from the remaining thyme and mince. Stir the thyme, goat cheese and cream into the sauce. Boil until slightly thickened, about 5 minutes.

8. To serve, remove the thyme and garlic from inside the chicken and discard. Carve the chicken into serving pieces and arrange on a platter. Surround with the caramelized garlic and shallots. Pass the sauce separately.

—Robert Del Grande, Café Annie, Houston, Texas

THREE-PEPPER CHICKEN

2 TO 4 SERVINGS

1 chicken (2½ to 3 pounds)
1½ tablespoons sweet Hungarian paprika
½ tablespoon coarsely ground black pepper
½ tablespoon Szechuan peppercorns, bruised
1 tablespoon plus 1 teaspoon olive oil
¼ teaspoon salt

1. Preheat the oven to 425°. Split the chicken in half. Remove any excess fat and cut out the backbone. Press flat with a meat pounder or cleaver and cut several slits through the skin to the thigh bones to facilitate even cooking.

2. Mix the paprika, black pepper and Szechuan peppercorns in a shallow bowl. Coat the chicken, inside and out, with the pepper mixture.

3. Grease the inside of a small roasting pan with 1 tablespoon of the oil. Place the chicken in the pan, skin-side up. Press any remaining pepper mixture into the skin. Drizzle the remaining 1 teaspoon oil over the chicken and sprinkle with the salt.

4. Bake in the center of the oven for 25 to 30 minutes, or until the juices run clear when a thigh is pierced. Do not turn.

—*William Rice*

CHICKEN BAKED WITH QUINCES

F&W BEVERAGE SUGGESTION
Simi Chenin Blanc

4 SERVINGS

4 medium quinces (about 2 pounds)—quartered, peeled and cored
1 cup apple juice
1 cup fruity white wine, such as Chenin Blanc
2 tablespoons light brown sugar
¼ cup all-purpose flour
½ teaspoon salt
3- to 3½-pound chicken, cut into 8 serving pieces
2 tablespoons unsalted butter
1 tablespoon vegetable oil
2 teaspoons ground coriander
¼ teaspoon white pepper

1. In a noncorrodible medium saucepan, combine the quinces with the apple juice and wine and simmer, covered, until tender (timing varies, but 30 to 40 minutes is average).

2. Add the brown sugar and simmer, uncovered, until the liquid is reduced to 1 cup, 5 to 10 minutes.

3. Meanwhile, mix together the flour and salt. Dredge the chicken pieces in the seasoned flour.

4. Preheat the oven to 375°. In a large skillet, melt the butter in the oil. Add the chicken and sauté over high heat until browned on all sides, 8 to 10 minutes.

5. Pour off all the fat from the pan. Sprinkle the chicken with 1 teaspoon of the coriander. Turn the pieces over and sprinkle with the remaining 1 teaspoon coriander. Place the chicken, skin-side up, in a shallow baking dish and sprinkle with the white pepper.

6. With a slotted spoon, transfer the quinces to the baking dish. Pour the quince liquid left in the saucepan into the skillet in which you browned the chicken and bring to a boil, stirring. Pour over the chicken pieces.

7. Bake, covered, in the upper third of the oven for 15 minutes. Baste thoroughly, then return to the oven, uncovered, for about 15 minutes, basting every 5 minutes until golden and glazed.

—*Elizabeth Schneider*

COQ AU RIESLING

F&W BEVERAGE SUGGESTION:
California Johannisberg Riesling, such as Jekel

6 TO 8 SERVINGS

½ pound lean slab bacon, thickly sliced and cut crosswise into ¼-inch-thick matchsticks (lardons)
8 tablespoons (1 stick) unsalted butter, softened
2 chickens (2½ to 3 pounds each), quartered
1 medium onion, coarsely chopped
1 large garlic clove, coarsely chopped
1 medium carrot, coarsely chopped
3 cups dry Riesling wine
1 cup chicken stock or canned broth
2 pounds mushrooms, quartered
¼ cup Cognac or brandy
½ teaspoon fresh lemon juice
Salt and freshly ground pepper
2 tablespoons all-purpose flour
1 tablespoon minced fresh parsley, for garnish

1. In a large flameproof casserole, cook the bacon over moderate heat, stirring occasionally, until golden, about 3 minutes. Drain on paper towels and set aside. Pour off the fat from the pan, reserving 2 tablespoons.

2. Heat 4 tablespoons of the butter and 1 tablespoon of the reserved bacon fat in the same casserole. Working in 2 batches, sauté the chicken over moderately high heat, turning once, until golden on both sides, about 10 minutes per batch. As it cooks, transfer the chicken to a large platter.

3. Add the onion, garlic and carrot to the pan and sauté over moderate heat until the carrot is soft, 10 to 15 minutes.

4. Preheat the oven to 200°. Add the wine and stock to the sautéed vegetables and bring to a boil, scraping up any browned bits from the bottom of the pan. Reduce the heat to moder-

ately low, return the chicken to the pan, cover and simmer for about 15 minutes, until the breast meat is just cooked through. Remove the breasts to a heatproof platter and keep warm in the oven. Continue cooking the dark meat for 10 minutes longer, or until the juices run clear. Add to the platter in the oven. Cover the pan and continue to simmer the sauce for 5 minutes.

5. Meanwhile, in a large heavy skillet, melt 2 tablespoons of the butter in the remaining 1 tablespoon bacon fat over moderately high heat. Add the mushrooms and sauté until they are soft and have absorbed all of the liquid in the skillet, about 5 minutes. Pour in the Cognac and ignite with a match, shaking the skillet until the flames subside. Season with the lemon juice and salt and pepper to taste. Spoon the mushrooms around the chicken. Pour the juices on top.

6. In a small bowl, mash the remaining 2 tablespoons butter into the flour until smooth to form a beurre manié. Gradually stir the beurre manié into the simmering sauce ½ teaspoon at a time until the sauce thickens slightly. Simmer for 3 minutes longer.

7. To serve, sprinkle the bacon over the chicken. Pour the sauce on top and garnish with the minced parsley.

—*Anne Disrude*

CHICKEN BREASTS STUFFED WITH MORELS

Boned chicken breasts stuffed with morels are a classic combination. In the following recipe, imported dried black morels have been used for the stuffing. The soaking liquid from the morels is used in the sauce.

F&W BEVERAGE SUGGESTION
California Cabernet Sauvignon such as Clos du Val

4 SERVINGS

½ ounce imported dried black morels
4 skinless, boneless chicken breast halves
½ teaspoon salt
¼ teaspoon freshly ground pepper
11 tablespoons unsalted butter
4 medium shallots, minced
½ cup crème fraîche or heavy cream
½ pound fresh black morels, or dried, reconstituted
1 teaspoon fresh lemon juice
1½ tablespoons all-purpose flour
1 cup chicken stock, preferably homemade
4 sprigs of fresh tarragon or ¼ teaspoon dried

1. In a medium bowl, soak the dried morels in 1 cup of warm water for 30 minutes, until softened.

2. Meanwhile, remove the small fillets from each breast half; reserve. Using a sharp knife, cut a pocket in the thickest part of each breast half. Sprinkle with ¼ teaspoon of the salt and ⅛ teaspoon of the pepper and set aside.

3. Preheat the oven to 400°. Using a slotted spoon, lift the morels from the soaking liquid; reserve the soaking liquid. Rinse the morels carefully under running water to remove any sand and grit. Dry and chop them.

4. In a heavy medium skillet, melt 2 tablespoons of the butter over moderate heat. Add the shallots and sauté until softened and translucent, 2 to 3 minutes. Add the chopped morels, a pinch of salt and pepper, ¼ cup of the crème fraîche and simmer, covered, for 10 minutes, or until tender. Set aside to cool.

5. Strain the reserved soaking liquid through a coffee filter paper or double thickness of dampened cheesecloth and set aside.

6. Stuff the shallot-morel mixture into the pockets of the 4 pieces of chicken. Stuff the reserved fillets into the opening of each pocket to close them.

7. Trim the stems from the fresh morels. Rinse them quickly in water and drain. Split or quarter them depending on their size. In a medium skillet, melt 3 tablespoons of the butter over moderate heat. Add 1 tablespoon of the morel soaking liquid, a pinch of salt and pepper and the fresh morels. Cover and braise for 15 minutes, stirring occasionally, until tender.

8. Meanwhile, melt 4 tablespoons of the butter and pour it into a medium baking dish. Arrange the stuffed chicken breasts in the dish in a single layer. Sprinkle with the lemon juice and 2 tablespoons of the morel soaking liquid. Cover with foil and bake for 10 minutes.

9. Meanwhile, prepare the sauce. In a small saucepan, melt the remaining 2 tablespoons butter over moderate heat. Add the flour and cook, stirring, for 2 minutes without coloring to make a roux. Whisk in the stock, the remaining morel liquid, the remaining crème fraîche and the tarragon. Bring to a boil, whisking constantly. Reduce the heat to moderately low and simmer for 15 minutes. Remove the tarragon sprigs. Season the sauce with the remaining ¼ teaspoon salt and ⅛ teaspoon pepper. Add the braised morels to the sauce and heat through.

10. Remove the chicken from the oven. Arrange the chicken on a platter and strain the cooking juices from the dish into the sauce. Pour the sauce over the chicken.

—*Lydie Marshall*

Grilled Chicken Santa Fe Style (p. 77).

Rosé Blanquette of Cornish Hen (p. 86) with Wild Mushroom and Scallion Pilaf (p. 150) and Miniature Vegetables with Lime and Basil (p. 136).

Pineapple Chutney (p. 240) is a spicy and colorful complement to a simple baked ham.

Above: top, Skirt Steak with Soy and Ginger Marinade (p. 96); bottom, Grilled Marinated Swordfish with Coriander Butter (p. 50). Right, Pepper-Lavender Steak (p. 96).

Beef Stew in Red Wine (p. 98).

GRILLED CHICKEN SANTA FE STYLE

F&W BEVERAGE SUGGESTION
Cold beer or California Chardonnay

4 SERVINGS

4 small whole chicken breasts, bones removed, skin on
1/3 cup fresh lime juice
3 tablespoons olive oil
1/2 teaspoon salt
1/4 teaspoon freshly ground black pepper
1 1/2 cups canned whole peeled tomatillos (1 1/2 cans, 13 ounces each), drained and rinsed*
1/2 cup heavy cream
5 plum tomatoes—peeled, seeded and cut into 1/4-inch dice
1 small onion, cut into 1/4-inch dice
1 fresh jalapeño pepper—seeded, deribbed and minced*
*1/4 cup minced fresh coriander**
2 tablespoons red wine vinegar
**Available in Latin American markets and some supermarkets*

1. Preheat the broiler with the broiling pan set about 4 inches from the heat, or light the charcoal. Pat the chicken breasts dry with paper towels. With a sharp paring knife, lightly score the skin in a cross-hatch pattern.

2. In a small bowl, whisk together the lime juice, olive oil, 1/4 teaspoon of the salt and the black pepper until blended. Brush the marinade on both sides of the chicken.

3. In a blender or food processor, process the *tomatillos* until finely chopped. Pour into a medium noncorrodible saucepan and stir in the cream. Bring to a simmer over moderately high heat and cook, stirring occasionally, until slightly reduced and thickened, about 5 minutes. Season with the remaining 1/4 teaspoon salt. Remove from the heat and cover the sauce to keep it warm.

4. To cook the chicken, arrange the breasts skin-side down on the grill or broiling pan. Cook, turning once, for 5 to 7 minutes on each side, until no longer pink but still moist.

5. Meanwhile, in a medium bowl, combine the tomatoes, onion, jalapeño pepper, coriander and vinegar until mixed to make a *salsa.*

6. To serve, spoon the *tomatillo* sauce onto 4 warmed plates. Arrange the chicken in the center and mound a heaping tablespoon of the *salsa* on top of each serving. Pass extra *salsa* at the table.

—Jean Cooper

Top to bottom: Minted Ginger Cantaloupe (p. 226) and Ginger Beef Stir-Fry (p. 98).

BREAST OF CHICKEN PECAN

F&W BEVERAGE SUGGESTION
Cabernet Sauvignon such as Jordan

2 SERVINGS

1/2 cup all-purpose flour
1/2 teaspoon salt
1/4 teaspoon freshly ground pepper
1 egg white, beaten until frothy
3 tablespoons grainy mustard, such as Pommery
1/2 cup finely ground pecans
1/2 cup fresh bread crumbs
2 skinless, boneless chicken breast halves, 6 ounces each
2 tablespoons unsalted butter
1/4 cup heavy cream

1. In a shallow bowl, combine the flour, salt and pepper. In a second shallow bowl, blend the egg white with 2 tablespoons of the mustard. In a third shallow bowl, combine the pecans and bread crumbs.

2. One at a time, dredge each chicken breast in the flour and shake off the excess. Next, dip in the egg white mixture to coat. Finally, dip into the pecan-bread crumb mixture, pressing so the coating adheres to both sides. Set aside on a rack. (**The recipe can be prepared to this point 2 hours ahead.** Place the rack of chicken, uncovered, in the refrigerator.)

3. In a medium skillet, melt the butter over moderately high heat. When the foam subsides, add the chicken breasts. Cook on one side until crisp and brown, about 3 minutes. Then turn, reduce the heat to moderately low and cook until the chicken has just lost its pinkness inside, about 5 minutes.

4. Meanwhile, in a small saucepan, warm the cream over moderate heat. Add the remaining 1 tablespoon mustard and a pinch of pepper; cook until warmed through, 3 to 5 minutes.

5. To serve, slice the breasts on the diagonal and fan out decoratively on 2 warmed serving plates. Pass the sauce on the side.

—Steve Christianson, The Lion's Rock, New York City

BREAST OF CHICKEN WITH LEEKS, COMTE CHEESE AND PINK PEPPERCORNS

This dish is a beautifully orchestrated and unexpected blending of flavors and textures. If you can't find Comté cheese, substitute a Swiss Gruyère.

F&W BEVERAGE SUGGESTION
Italian white, such as Antinori Galestro

4 SERVINGS

7 tablespoons unsalted butter
4 medium leeks, white and tender green, cut crosswise into 1/2-inch slices

¾ cup crème fraîche
¾ teaspoon salt
Freshly ground black pepper
4 skinless, boneless chicken breast halves
¼ cup Cognac
1 cup chicken stock or canned broth
1 tablespoon chopped fresh tarragon or 1 teaspoon dried
2 tablespoons pink peppercorns
½ cup grated Comté cheese
1 tablespoon minced chives, for garnish

1. In a large skillet or sauté pan with a lid, melt 3 tablespoons of the butter over moderate heat. Add the leeks, cover the pan and reduce the heat to moderately low. Cook, stirring occasionally, until the leeks are tender, about 15 minutes.

2. Stir in 3 tablespoons of the crème fraîche, ¼ teaspoon of the salt and a pinch of black pepper. Set aside and keep warm.

3. Remove the fillet from each chicken breast half. Cut each breast diagonally into strips approximately the same size as the fillets. Season the chicken with ½ teaspoon of the salt and ¼ teaspoon of black pepper.

4. In a large skillet, melt 3 tablespoons of the butter over moderate heat. Working in two batches, add the chicken and cook over moderate heat, turning occasionally, until the pieces are browned but still springy to the touch, about 3 minutes. Remove from the pan and drain on paper towels. Cover loosely with foil and return to a low oven to keep warm.

5. Pour off the fat from the pan and return it to moderate heat. Add the Cognac and bring to a boil, scraping up any brown bits from the bottom of the pan. Pour in the stock and the remaining crème fraîche. Increase the heat to high and boil until the mixture is slightly thickened, about 4 minutes.

6. Stir in the tarragon, the pink peppercorns and ¼ cup of the cheese. Cook, stirring, until the cheese is melted. Off the heat, stir in the remaining 1 tablespoon butter. Taste the sauce and adjust seasonings if necessary.

7. To serve, make a bed of leeks on each of four dinner plates. Arrange one-fourth of the chicken on top of each. Pour the sauce over each and garnish each plate with some of the remaining cheese and the chives.

—*Chef Hubert, Le Bistro d'Hubert, Paris, France*

CHICKEN BREASTS WITH GINGER AND LEMON

The chicken for this elegant ginger dish needs to marinate overnight, so plan your time accordingly.

F&W BEVERAGE SUGGESTION
Alsace Riesling, such as Hugel or Faller Frères, or Ockfener Bockstein

4 SERVINGS

1¾ cups diagonally sliced scallions
⅓ cup chopped unpeeled fresh ginger, or ½ cup fresh ginger peelings, plus 1½ teaspoons grated, peeled fresh ginger
2 garlic cloves, chopped
Zest of 1 lemon, removed with a vegetable peeler in 1-inch-wide strips
½ teaspoon salt
½ teaspoon freshly ground pepper
4 skinless, boneless chicken breast halves (about 1¼ pounds)
1 cup chicken stock or canned broth
½ cup dry white wine
¼ cup Stone's Original Ginger-Flavored Currant Wine or sweet white wine*
1 stick (¼ pound) cold unsalted butter, cut into 12 pieces, plus 1 tablespoon butter, melted
2 tablespoons fresh lemon juice
**Available in most liquor stores*

1. In a shallow baking pan, toss together 1 cup of the scallions, the chopped unpeeled ginger, the garlic, lemon zest, salt and pepper.

2. Pat the chicken dry with paper towels; add to the scallion mixture, turning to season both sides. Cover tightly with plastic wrap and refrigerate overnight.

3. Pick out the lemon zest and blanch it in 1 cup of boiling water for 3 minutes. Drain and rinse under cold, running water. Cut the zest into long, thin strips.

4. Scrape the seasonings from the chicken and the baking pan into a small noncorrodible saucepan. Place the chicken back in the baking pan, cover and set aside.

5. Add the chicken stock, dry white wine and ginger-currant wine to the saucepan. Bring to a boil over high heat, reduce the heat to low, cover and simmer for 20 minutes. Pour through a strainer into a small bowl, pressing on the solids. Pour the liquid into a clean small saucepan; there will be about 1¼ cups. Bring to a boil and continue to cook over high heat until the liquid is reduced to ¼ cup, about 10 minutes.

6. Remove from the heat and whisk in the cold butter, 1 piece at a time, adding each piece just as the previous one is almost incorporated. (If necessary, return to low heat briefly, whisking to produce a creamy emulsion; do not let the butter melt completely or the sauce will separate.)

7. Stir the remaining ¾ cup scallions, the lemon zest, lemon juice and grated peeled ginger into the sauce.

Season with additional salt and pepper to taste.

8. Lightly brush the chicken breasts on both sides with the melted butter. Transfer to a broiler rack lined with foil and broil about 6 inches from the heat, for 4 to 5 minutes per side, or until just cooked through, moist with no trace of pink. Transfer to serving plates or a platter.

9. Gently reheat the sauce, if necessary, and spoon over the chicken.

—*Jane Helsel Joseph*

CHICKEN WITH VERMOUTH

This low-calorie (247 per serving), low-sodium (155 mg per serving) chicken dish is from the Ambassador Grill's Menu Manhattan.

F&W BEVERAGE SUGGESTION
Chateau Bouchaine Alexander Valley Chardonnay

4 SERVINGS

Vegetable cooking spray, such as Pam
4 skinless, boneless chicken breast halves, 7 ounces each
¾ teaspoon freshly ground white pepper
1 medium carrot, peeled and cut into 2-inch julienne strips
1 celery rib, peeled and cut into 2-inch julienne strips
1 medium leek (white and tender green), cut into 2-inch julienne strips
½ cup unsalted chicken stock or low-sodium canned broth
3 tablespoons dry vermouth

1. Put a large skillet over moderately high heat. Coat lightly with the cooking spray. Season the chicken breasts with ½ teaspoon of the white pepper. Add to the skillet and sauté, turning once, until browned on the outside and opaque throughout, about 10 minutes. Remove and set aside.

2. Add the carrot, celery and leek to the skillet. Season with the remaining ¼ teaspoon pepper and cook for 1 minute. Pour in the stock and vermouth, partly cover and simmer until the vegetables are tender and the liquid thickens to the consistency of light syrup, about 10 minutes.

3. Return the chicken to the skillet and cook until heated through, 3 to 5 minutes.

—*Ambassador Grill, New York City*

FARM-STAND DINNER IN A PACKET

4 SERVINGS

6 small links of spicy, dried sausage such as chorizo, cut into ¼-inch slices
4 small zucchini, stem ends trimmed
4 small ears of sweet corn, shucked
4 small tomatoes
4 skinless, boneless chicken breast halves (about 6 ounces each), lightly pounded
½ cup dry white wine
4 tablespoons unsalted butter, cut into small pieces
1 tablespoon coarse (kosher) salt
2 teaspoons freshly ground pepper
4 sprigs of fresh rosemary

1. Preheat the oven to 450°. Cut out 4 pieces of aluminum foil, 14 by 20 inches each. Lay slices of 1 sausage in the center of each piece of foil. Arrange the zucchini, corn and tomato on top of the sausage. Place the chicken breast over the vegetables. Top with the remaining sausage. Sprinkle the meat and vegetables with the wine, dot with the butter and season generously with the salt and pepper. Top each with a sprig of rosemary.

2. Fold up to seal each pouch tightly, but allowing room for steam to form as it cooks. Bake in the preheated oven for 25 minutes. Serve at once.

—*Molly O'Neill*

ONION-CHARRED CHICKEN

4 SERVINGS

1 tablespoon Charred Onion Powder (p. 237)
*½ teaspoon Chinese 5-spice powder**
¼ teaspoon salt
¼ teaspoon freshly ground pepper
¼ cup honey
2 tablespoons soy sauce
4 large skinless, boneless chicken breast halves, pounded ¼ inch thick
1 to 2 teaspoons vegetable oil
**Available at Oriental groceries*

1. In a small bowl, combine the onion powder, 5-spice powder, salt, pepper, honey and soy sauce. Spread the mixture on both sides of the chicken breasts and let marinate for 30 minutes, turning several times.

2. Heat a nonstick skillet over moderate heat for 2 to 3 minutes. Wipe the skillet with the vegetable oil. Add the chicken breasts smooth-side down. Press them lightly with a spatula to encourage even browning. Cook for 3 minutes, until a mahogany glaze forms. Reduce the heat and cook on the other side for 3 to 4 minutes. Serve hot or at room temperature.

—*Anne Disrude*

DEVILED CHICKEN PAILLARDE WITH ZUCCHINI

F&W BEVERAGE SUGGESTION:
Rosé, such as Château de Selle

2 SERVINGS

2 large skinless, boneless chicken breast halves, about 7 ounces each
2 tablespoons olive oil
½ teaspoon thyme
½ teaspoon coarsely cracked pepper
1 medium zucchini, cut into 24 thin slices

2 large tomatoes, halved lengthwise and cut into 24 thin half-moon slices
1 medium onion, halved lengthwise and cut into 24 thin half-moon slices
½ teaspoon ground coriander
½ teaspoon salt
2 tablespoons plus ½ teaspoon dry white wine
¼ teaspoon powdered mustard
1 teaspoon Dijon-style mustard
2 tablespoons coarse white bread crumbs

1. Preheat the oven to 375°. Between two layers of plastic wrap, pound each chicken breast to a ¼ inch thickness. In a small bowl, combine 1 tablespoon of the olive oil, the thyme and ¼ teaspoon of the pepper. Paint both sides of each breast with the seasoned oil and set aside.

2. On a baking sheet with sides, arrange overlapping slices of the zucchini, tomato and onion in 4 rows, alternating the vegetables so that each row contains 6 slices each of zucchini, tomato and onion. Sprinkle with the remaining ¼ teaspoon pepper, the coriander and ¼ teaspoon of the salt. Paint with the remaining 1 tablespoon oil. Sprinkle with 2 tablespoons of the wine.

3. Bake for 15 minutes, basting twice with the pan juices, until the onion is softened. Remove from the oven and cover with aluminum foil to keep warm.

4. Preheat the broiler and set the broiler pan about 4 inches from the heat. In a bowl, combine the powdered mustard with the remaining ½ teaspoon wine; stir until smooth. Blend in the Dijon-style mustard.

5. Oil the hot broiler pan. Lay the chicken breasts on it and broil, turning once, for 1 minute on each side. Remove the chicken from the broiler; leave the heat on. Brush the mustard sauce on both sides of the breasts. Return the chicken to the pan and sprinkle one side with the remaining ¼ teaspoon salt and the bread crumbs. Return the chicken to the broiler and cook until the bread crumbs are browned, 1 to 2 minutes.

6. To serve, place each chicken breast in the center of a warmed plate. Lay a row of the baked vegetables on either side of the breast.

—Alain Sailhac, Le Cirque, New York City

CHICKEN CUTLETS WITH CURRIED CREAM SAUCE

Here is a simply sauced chicken sauté that is easily made within 30 minutes.

2 SERVINGS

2 skinless, boneless chicken breast halves, pounded ¼ inch thick
½ teaspoon salt
3 tablespoons unsalted butter
¼ pound mushrooms, quartered
⅓ cup half-and-half
¼ teaspoon curry powder
⅛ teaspoon paprika
⅛ teaspoon freshly ground pepper
1 tablespoon chopped parsley
Lemon wedges, for garnish

1. Season the chicken breast halves on both sides with the salt.

2. In a medium heavy skillet, warm 2 tablespoons of the butter over moderately high heat until sizzling. Add the chicken breasts and sauté, turning once, until lightly colored, about 1 minute per side (the chicken will finish cooking later). Transfer to a warm platter and cover with foil.

3. Add the remaining 1 tablespoon butter and heat until sizzling. Add the mushrooms and sauté, stirring, until softened, 1 to 2 minutes. Increase the heat to high and add the half-and-half, curry powder, paprika and pepper. Boil, uncovered, until reduced to about ¼ cup, 3 to 5 minutes.

4. Reduce the heat to low and return the chicken breasts to the skillet, along with any meat juices from the platter. Simmer until the chicken is hot and cooked through, about 2 minutes. Transfer to the platter and pour the sauce with the mushrooms on top. Sprinkle the chopped parsley on top and serve with lemon wedges.

CHICKEN WITH GARLIC, CAPERS AND PARMESAN CHEESE

F&W BEVERAGE SUGGESTION
A light red, such as Valpolicella

3 TO 4 SERVINGS

¼ cup olive oil
6 large garlic cloves, sliced
6 chicken thighs
2 teaspoons thyme
2 teaspoons coarsely cracked pepper
½ teaspoon salt
1 tablespoon capers, chopped
¼ cup freshly grated Parmesan cheese

1. Preheat the oven to 350°. In a large heavy skillet, warm the oil over moderate heat until shimmering. Add the garlic and sauté, stirring, until golden, about 3 minutes. Remove from the oil with a slotted spoon and finely chop.

2. Season the chicken thighs on both sides with the thyme and pepper. Reheat the oil in the skillet over moderate heat until rippling. Add the chicken and sauté until golden, about 10 minutes on each side. Remove from the heat and drain briefly on paper towels. Season with the salt.

3. Combine the capers and chopped garlic and spread on top of the chicken thighs. Sprinkle with the cheese and arrange on a baking sheet. Bake until the cheese melts and the chicken is cooked through, about 15 minutes.

—Anne Disrude

FRIED CHICKEN WITH MOROCCAN SALAD

This is an adaptation of the Spanish-Moroccan dish, *criadillas*—lamb sweetbreads marinated in olive oil, garlic and lemon juice, then cooked in a highly unorthodox way: dipped *first* in bread crumbs, *second* in beaten eggs and then deep fried. As soon as the meat hits the hot oil, a thin lacy web of egg seals around it, keeping the chicken juicy and tender and, when it comes out of the oil, almost grease free. The preserved lemons for the salad need to ripen for a week, so plan accordingly.

F&W BEVERAGE SUGGESTION
Chilled lager beer

4 TO 5 SERVINGS

8 small chicken legs with thighs (2 pounds total), separated into 2 pieces and boned
3 tablespoons olive oil
3 tablespoons fresh lemon juice
3 garlic cloves, thinly sliced
1½ tablespoons chopped parsley
Pinch of ground ginger
Pinch of cinnamon
½ teaspoon salt
½ teaspoon freshly ground pepper
About 1 quart vegetable oil, for deep frying
3 eggs
1½ tablespoons milk
1½ cups fine dry bread crumbs
1 cup bite-size pieces of butter lettuce, such as Boston
3 lemons, cut into wedges
Moroccan olives, for garnish
Coarse (kosher) salt
Moroccan Tomato, Red Pepper and Preserved Lemon Salad (p. 166)

1. Pound each chicken piece ¼ inch thick. Trim away any fat and gristle. Put the chicken in a bowl.

2. In a small bowl, whisk together the oil, lemon juice, garlic, parsley, ginger, cinnamon, salt and pepper. Pour over the chicken. Let marinate for at least 1 hour at room temperature, tossing occasionally, or in the refrigerator for no more than 4 hours.

3. In a deep fryer or large heavy saucepan, heat at least 3 inches of oil to 360°.

4. In a small bowl, beat the eggs and milk until well blended. Drain the chicken pieces, but do not pat dry; discard the marinade. Dip the moist chicken in the bread crumbs and arrange the pieces side by side on a large tray or baking sheet.

5. Dip 3 or 4 pieces of breaded chicken at a time (enough to fit in the fryer without crowding) into the beaten eggs and add one at a time to the hot oil. Fry until the pieces float to the surface and turn golden brown, 2 to 3 minutes. Turn and fry until the second side is golden, 2 to 3 minutes. Remove with a slotted spoon and drain on paper towels. Repeat with the remaining chicken pieces.

6. Cover a large platter with the lettuce. Arrange the chicken on top. Decorate with lemon wedges and olives. Sprinkle with coarse salt. Serve the chicken warm or at room temperature with the Moroccan Tomato, Red Pepper and Preserved Lemon Salad.

—*Paula Wolfert*

ARROZ CON POLLO WITH SHRIMP AND ARTICHOKES

All this hearty dish needs beforehand is a small selection of nibbles—some olives and toasted almonds, perhaps. Sliced hard sausage or prosciutto would not be amiss, and you might enjoy trying some of the Spanish cheeses that have recently been imported, such as the rich blue-veined Cabrales, which often comes wrapped in grape leaves.

For a simple but striking cool dessert, try a scoop of good-quality mango sherbet doused with Grande Passion, a light passion fruit liqueur.

F&W BEVERAGE SUGGESTION
Spanish white, such as Marqués de Cáceres

10 TO 12 SERVINGS

3 large artichokes (see Note)
2 tablespoons fresh lemon juice
12 chicken thighs (about 3½ pounds), trimmed of excess fat
2¾ teaspoons salt
¾ teaspooons freshly ground black pepper
4 tablespoons olive oil
3 medium onions, chopped
1½ pounds chorizo or hot Italian sausage, cut into 1-inch lengths
3 garlic cloves, finely chopped
1 can (35 ounces) Italian peeled tomatoes, with their juice
1½ bottles (12 ounces each) lager beer, such as Budweiser
1 can (13¾ ounces) chicken broth
2 imported bay leaves
1½ teaspoons oregano
½ teaspoon crushed hot red pepper
½ teaspoon (loosely packed) saffron threads (.2 grams)
3 cups converted rice
1½ pounds medium shrimp, shelled and deveined
1 package (10 ounces) frozen peas, thawed
Strips of roasted red pepper, preferably homemade, for garnish

1. Trim the stems off the artichokes. Cut off two-thirds of the top to leave about 1½ inches of artichoke. Bend back and pull off all the tough outer dark green leaves. As each artichoke is trimmed, drop into a bowl of

cold water with 1 tablespoon of the lemon juice to prevent discoloration.

2. In a large saucepan of boiling salted water with the remaining 1 tablespoon lemon juice, cook the artichokes until tender, 15 to 20 minutes. Drain and rinse under cold running water. (**The artichokes can be cooked a day ahead.**) Remove the chokes and cut each artichoke into 8 to 12 wedges.

3. Preheat the oven to 350°. Season the chicken with ¾ teaspoon of the salt and ¼ teaspoon of the pepper. In a very large (8-quart) flameproof casserole, heat 3 tablespoons of the oil. Add as many thighs as will fit in a single layer and fry over moderately high heat, turning once, until lightly browned, 3 to 5 minutes on each side. Transfer to a plate and repeat with the remaining thighs. Set the chicken aside. (If you do not have a big enough casserole, all the ingredients can be sautéed in a large skillet and transferred to a large covered turkey roaster for baking.)

4. Remove all but 3 to 4 tablespoons of fat from the casserole. Add the onions and sauté over moderate heat until softened and beginning to brown, about 10 minutes.

5. Meanwhile, in a large skillet, heat the remaining 1 tablespoon oil. Add the chorizo and cook over moderate heat, turning occasionally, until lightly browned, 5 to 10 minutes.

6. Add the garlic to the onions and sauté until fragrant, about 2 minutes. Add the tomatoes and their juice, the beer, chicken broth, bay leaves, oregano, hot pepper, saffron and the remaining 2 teaspoons salt and ½ teaspoon pepper. Bring to a boil over high heat. Stir in the rice. With a slotted spoon, transfer the chorizo or sausages to the casserole. Add the chicken and any juices that have collected on the plate.

7. Cover the casserole tightly and bake for 25 minutes, or until the rice has absorbed most of the liquid.

8. Add the shrimp and stir to bury in the rice. Bake for 5 minutes. Add the peas and artichokes and bake for 5 to 10 minutes longer, until the shrimp are pink and loosely curled. Serve on a large deep platter, garnished with strips of roasted pepper.

NOTE: To save time, you can substitute 1 package (10 ounces) frozen artichoke hearts, thawed. Skip Steps 1 and 2 and add the artichokes with the shrimp at the beginning of Step 8.

—Susan Wyler

STIR-FRY OF CHICKEN, RED PEPPERS, ARUGULA AND PROSCIUTTO

The marinating and precooking techniques used in this recipe can also be used for any poultry, fish or shellfish stir-fry.

Remember that except for the final cooking, all of the chopping, shredding, julienning and marinating can be done in advance. To make the final frying easier, have all the prepared ingredients for one category in a single bowl. This way adding them all at once is fast and simple.

F&W BEVERAGE SUGGESTION
California Sauvignon Blanc, such as Kendall-Jackson

2 SERVINGS

MARINADE: ½ egg white (see Note), 1½ teaspoons dry vermouth, 1½ teaspoons cornstarch, ½ teaspoon coarse (kosher) salt
½ pound skinless, boneless chicken breast, cut into 1-inch squares
1 teaspoon vegetable oil
2 tablespoons olive oil
AROMATICS: 1 tablespoon minced fresh parsley; 1 tablespoon minced onion; 2 medium garlic cloves, minced; pinch of crushed hot red pepper
1 large red bell pepper, cut into ¼-inch-wide strips or ¾-inch squares (about 1¼ cups)
¼ teaspoon salt
Pinch of sugar
1 cup shredded arugula
SEASONINGS: 1 tablespoon finely chopped prosciutto, ¼ teaspoon oregano, freshly ground black pepper to taste

1. In a medium bowl, whisk together the MARINADE ingredients. Add the chicken and toss to mix well. Cover and refrigerate for at least 1 and up to 12 hours.

2. Add the vegetable oil to a large pot of simmering water. Add the chicken and cook, stirring gently, until almost cooked through but still pink in the center, about 1 minute. Drain and rinse off any excess cornstarch under cold running water; pat dry and set aside. (**The recipe can be prepared up to 3 hours ahead to this point.** Refrigerate, covered. Let the precooked chicken pieces return to room temperature before proceeding.)

3. Warm a wok or large heavy skillet over high heat until a drop of water evaporates on contact. Pour in the olive oil in a thin stream around the edge; it will smoke immediately.

4. Add the AROMATICS (parsley, onion, garlic and crushed hot red pepper) all at once. Cook, stirring, until fragrant, about 10 seconds; do not let the garlic brown.

5. Add the red bell pepper to the wok. Sprinkle with the salt and sugar and toss until almost crisp-tender, 1½ to 2 minutes. (If the vegetable begins to dry out or burn, add 1 tablespoon of water.)

6. Add the precooked chicken to

the wok and toss over heat until warmed through, about 30 seconds.

7. Add the arugula and SEASONINGS (prosciutto, oregano and black pepper) and toss to blend the flavors, about 20 seconds. Remove from the heat and season to taste with more salt and pepper if desired.

NOTE: To obtain ½ egg white, lightly beat 1 whole egg white and measure out 1 tablespoon.

—Anne Disrude

THAI CHICKEN AND FRESH BASIL

This version of a popular Thai dish takes up an entire plate. It is served on a bed of shredded cabbage with bowls of rice.

4 SERVINGS

2 tablespoons peanut oil
8 to 10 small red or green hot peppers, seeded and minced
2 tablespoons dried chopped lemon grass tied in a cheesecloth bag or 2 teaspoons grated lemon zest*
½ cup canned unsweetened coconut milk
4 large skinless, boneless chicken breast halves (about 2 pounds), cut crosswise into ½-inch strips
*3 tablespoons Oriental fish sauce**
2 tablespoons minced fresh basil or 1½ tablespoons minced fresh coriander
2 cups finely shredded cabbage
**Available in Southeast Asian and many Chinese groceries*

1. In a large skillet, warm the oil over moderate heat until shimmering. Add the hot peppers and sauté, stirring, for 3 minutes.

2. Add the lemon grass and coconut milk, increase the heat to high and boil until the sauce is slightly thickened, about 2 minutes.

3. Reduce the heat to moderate. Add the chicken and cook, stirring occasionally, until opaque throughout, about 5 minutes. Stir in the fish sauce and basil. Discard the lemon grass.

4. To serve, make a bed of cabbage on a large platter. Pour the chicken and sauce on top.

—Keo Sananikone, Keo's Thai Cuisine, Honolulu, Hawaii

POACHED CAPON WITH SPRING HERB SAUCE

With so few ingredients, make sure they are of the best quality. Canned chicken broth will not be satisfactory for this recipe.

F&W BEVERAGE SUGGESTION
White Zinfandel or Rosé of Cabernet

8 TO 10 SERVINGS

1 capon, 8 to 10 pounds
4 quarts Chicken Stock (p. 231)
Bouquet garni: 10 parsley stems, 1 bay leaf, 10 peppercorns and ½ teaspoon thyme tied in cheesecloth
Spring Herb Sauce (p. 236)

1. Put the capon, breast-side up, in a large stockpot. Pour the chicken stock over the bird. Add the bouquet garni. Cover and bring to a boil over moderately high heat. Reduce the heat and simmer for 2 hours (see Note).

2. Carefully remove the bird from the stock, draining the liquid from its cavity. Cover loosely with foil and set aside to cool to room temperature. Discard the bouquet garni. Reserve the stock for the Spring Herb Sauce (p. 236).

3. Serve the capon at room temperature with a sauce boat of warm or hot Spring Herb Sauce on the side.

NOTE: If the stock does not cover the bird completely, turn the bird after 1 hour to ensure even cooking.

—John Robert Massie

ROASTED DUCKLING WITH RHUBARB

Rhubarb suffers from an identity crisis. Although technically a vegetable, it is used almost exclusively as a fruit, usually as pie filling. So often is this the case that old cookbooks refer to it as pie-plant. Crisp, sweetly spiced duckling and smooth, tart rhubarb sauce make a surprisingly complementary pair.

F&W BEVERAGE SUGGESTION
California Zinfandel, such as Ridge San Luis Obispo

4 SERVINGS

5-pound duckling with giblets
1 celery rib with leaves, cut into pieces
1 teaspoon allspice
1 teaspoon basil, finely crumbled
1 teaspoon salt
1 teaspoon sugar
½ teaspoon freshly ground pepper
¼ teaspoon cinnamon
1 pound rhubarb
Honey
Red wine vinegar
Watercress, for garnish

1. Cut off the wing tips from the duck and place them in a heavy medium saucepan with the celery, the duck neck and gizzard and 1 quart of water. (Wrap the liver and heart and reserve for another use.) Bring to a simmer, skimming. Simmer, partially covered, for at least 2 hours, adding water as needed to keep the solids covered. Strain and return the liquid to the saucepan. Boil until reduced to 1 cup. (**The stock can be made a day ahead.** Alternatively, you can make

the stock after Step 2, while the duck is coming to room temperature.)

2. Cut off loose interior fat from the duck and discard. Rinse the duck and pat dry. Combine the allspice, basil, salt, sugar, pepper and cinnamon in a small dish. Sprinkle one-third of the mixture evenly inside the duck's cavity and rub in. Rub the remainder evenly into the skin on all sides. Set on a rack in a roasting pan and refrigerate, uncovered, for up to 36 hours, turning once or twice.

3. Remove the duck from the refrigerator about 2 hours before roasting to allow it to come to room temperature. Preheat the oven to 300°.

4. Rinse the rhubarb and cut into ¼- to ½-inch slices. Place 1 cup of the rhubarb in the duck, then sew up the openings tightly. Pat the duck dry and set on its side on the rack in the pan.

5. Roast for 30 minutes. With a needle, prick the duck on all its uppermost fatty parts, holding the needle at a shallow angle to avoid piercing the meat. With paper towels, hold the legs and turn the duck onto its other side. Increase the heat to 350° and roast the duck for 30 minutes. Prick the fatty parts on the upturned side. Turn the duck onto its breast and roast for 30 minutes.

6. Prick the uppermost side of the duck, then turn it breast upward. Raise the heat to 400° and roast the duck for about 20 minutes, until it is richly browned.

7. While the duck is finishing, combine the reserved stock and remaining rhubarb slices in a heavy, medium, noncorrodible saucepan and simmer until the mixture forms a coarse puree when stirred, 10 to 15 minutes.

8. Open the duck cavity and scrape the contents into the pot of rhubarb. Stir well to combine, cooking briefly if necessary. Season with honey, vinegar, salt and pepper to taste.

9. With a cleaver or heavy knife, cut the duck into small serving pieces, keeping the shiny skin intact. Arrange the duck on a bed of watercress on a serving platter. Serve hot or warm. Pass the rhubarb sauce separately.

—Elizabeth Schneider

ROAST FRESH TURKEY WITH MADEIRA GRAVY

8 SERVINGS

10-pound fresh turkey, at room temperature
8 tablespoons (1 stick) unsalted butter, softened
Salt and freshly ground pepper
¼ cup vegetable oil
½ cup chicken stock or canned broth

1. Preheat the oven to 325°. Cut off the first joint of each wing and reserve, along with the neck, heart and gizzard, for use in the Madeira Gravy (recipe follows). Reserve the liver for another use.

2. Rub the breast with 2 tablespoons of the butter. Season the breast and the main cavity lightly with salt and pepper. Truss the turkey if you wish, although this step is unnecessary if the bird is unstuffed.

3. Set the turkey breast-side up in a shallow roasting pan just large enough to hold it comfortably. Dampen a 10-by-20-inch square of cheesecloth, double it and drape it over the turkey breast. About 3½ hours before you wish to eat, set the turkey in to roast.

4. In a small saucepan, melt the remaining 6 tablespoons butter in the oil and chicken stock over low heat. When the turkey has baked for 30 minutes, baste it liberally through the cheesecloth with half the butter mixture. Baste again with the remaining butter mixture after another 30 minutes. After another 15 minutes, baste the turkey with the accumulated juices from the roasting pan and repeat every 15 minutes until the turkey is done (when an instant-reading thermometer in the thickest part of the breast registers 160°). Begin checking the turkey for doneness after 2 hours and 15 minutes.

5. With a bulb baster remove the cooking juices from the roaster and reserve for basting a stuffing if you're making one. (Be sure to include any juices that have accumulated in the turkey cavity.) Wrap the turkey well in foil and set aside until ready to carve.

—Michael McLaughlin

MADEIRA GRAVY

This recipe for Roast Fresh Turkey with Madeira Gravy was designed to be paired with the Country Ham and Wild Mushroom Stuffing (p. 158). If you elect to make the stuffing, save the mushroom soaking liquid and add to the Madeira and chicken stock in Step 2 below.

MAKES ABOUT 3 CUPS

6 tablespoons unsalted butter, at room temperature
1 tablespoon vegetable oil
Turkey necks, giblets and wing tips reserved from Roast Fresh Turkey (p. 84)
2 medium onions, chopped
2 leeks (white part only), chopped
3 carrots, chopped
1 teaspoon thyme
1 bay leaf
Stems from 1 bunch of parsley
1 cup dry (Sercial) Madeira

About 5 cups chicken stock or canned broth
¼ cup all-purpose flour
Salt and freshly ground pepper

1. In a medium saucepan, melt 2 tablespoons of the butter in the oil over moderate heat until foaming. Add the turkey giblets, neck and wing tips and cook, stirring often, until brown, about 20 minutes. Add the onions, leeks, carrots, thyme, bay leaf and parsley stems; cover, reduce the heat and cook, stirring occasionally, until the vegetables are tender and lightly colored, about 20 minutes.

2. Combine the Madeira with enough chicken stock to equal 6 cups; add to the pan. Bring to a boil, partially cover, reduce the heat and simmer for 30 minutes, skimming.

3. Let cool slightly; then strain, discarding the solids. You should have about 5 cups of stock.

4. Wipe out the pan and return the liquid to it. Bring to a boil and cook, uncovered, until reduced to 3 cups, about 30 minutes. (**The gravy can be prepared to this point 24 hours in advance.** Let cool to room temperature, then cover and refrigerate. Reheat slowly until simmering before proceeding.)

5. In a small bowl, mash the remaining 4 tablespoons butter with the flour to form a smooth, thick paste (beurre manié). Reduce the heat under the gravy to very low and whisk the beurre manié into it, 1 tablespoon at a time. Increase the heat to moderate and simmer, stirring, for 5 minutes. Season with salt and pepper to taste before serving.

—*Michael McLaughlin*

L'ESPERANCE'S SALMI DE PIGEON

F&W BEVERAGE SUGGESTION
California Merlot, such as Rutherford Hill

4 SERVINGS

1 bunch of watercress
4 squab or Cornish game hens, cut in half
Salt and freshly ground pepper
5 tablespoons unsalted butter
2 tablespoons peanut or other vegetable oil
2 medium shallots, minced
¼ cup white wine vinegar
1 teaspoon Dijon-style mustard
1 cup heavy cream

1. Set aside 4 watercress sprigs for garnish. Strip the leaves from the remaining watercress and place in a blender. Add ¼ cup of water and puree until smooth. Scrape the puree into a fine-mesh sieve and drain, pressing out as much moisture as possible. Discard the liquid and reserve the puree.

2. Sprinkle the squab on both sides with a pinch of the salt and pepper. In a large noncorrodible skillet, melt 3 tablespoons of the butter in the oil over high heat. When the foam subsides, add the squab, skin-side down. Cook, turning occasionally, until browned, 6 to 8 minutes. Remove to a plate and cover loosely with foil to keep warm.

3. Pour off the excess fat from the skillet. Add the shallots and sauté over moderate heat until softened and lightly browned, 4 to 5 minutes.

4. Add the vinegar and boil, scraping up the browned bits on the bottom of the skillet. Stir in the mustard, cream and the reserved watercress puree. Increase the heat and bring the mixture to a boil. Reduce to simmer and cook until slightly thickened, 3 to 4 minutes. Swirl in the remaining 2 tablespoons butter and season with salt and pepper to taste.

5. Return the squab to the skillet and simmer for 3 to 4 minutes for rare, 6 to 8 minutes for medium; if using Cornish game hens, cook for 20 minutes. Remove the squab to serving plates. Strain the sauce through a fine-mesh sieve. Pool the sauce around the squab. Garnish with sprigs of watercress.

—*Marc Meneau, l'Espérance, Vézelay, France*

PIGEON WITH GARLIC

Don't panic at the thought of 40 cloves of garlic. In fact, garlic lovers may even double the number of cloves used in this recipe, for here garlic is used as a vegetable, not simply a seasoning. Blanching the garlic softens it and reduces its intensity.

F&W BEVERAGE SUGGESTION
California Merlot, such as Clos du Val

4 SERVINGS

40 garlic cloves, peeled (from about 4 heads)
1 stick (¼ pound) unsalted butter
1 medium shallot, minced
4 chicken livers
4 pigeons (8 to 12 ounces each), with livers reserved
1 tablespoon Cognac or brandy
½ teaspoon salt
¼ teaspoon freshly ground pepper
1 cup chicken stock or canned broth
8 slices French bread (about ½ inch thick), toasted, with crusts removed
Watercress, for garnish

1. In a large saucepan of boiling water, blanch the garlic cloves for 3 minutes; then drain. Preheat the oven to 450°.

2. In a small saucepan, melt 2 tablespoons of the butter over moderately high heat. Add the shallot, chicken livers and pigeon livers and sauté for 2 minutes, until the livers are just pink inside. In a blender or food processor, combine the liver mixture, the Cognac, ¼ teaspoon of the salt and ⅛ teaspoon of the pepper and process until smooth. Set aside.

3. Season the pigeons inside and out with the remaining ¼ teaspoon salt and ⅛ teaspoon pepper. In a large ovenproof skillet, melt the remaining 6 tablespoons butter over moderately high heat. Add the pigeons and sauté, turning, for a total of 6 minutes—2 minutes on each side and 2 minutes on the back. Distribute the garlic cloves over the pigeons and roast in the oven for 12 minutes, turning the garlic cloves after 5 minutes so that they do not burn.

4. Remove the skillet from the oven. Transfer the pigeons and garlic to a warmed platter and cover with foil to keep warm. Preheat the broiler.

5. Meanwhile, make the sauce. Pour off the excess fat from the skillet. Add the chicken stock and bring to a boil over high heat, scraping up any brown bits from the bottom. Boil until the mixture is reduced to a syrupy glaze, about 5 minutes. Season with salt and pepper to taste.

6. Working quickly, spread the liver paste on the toasted French bread slices. Place the croutons on a baking sheet and run under the preheated broiler for 1 minute.

7. To serve, arrange 2 croutons on each of 4 warmed plates. Cut the pigeons in half and place next to the croutons. Garnish with the garlic cloves and the watercress. Spoon the sauce over the pigeons.

—Patricia Wells

ROSE BLANQUETTE OF CORNISH HEN

F&W BEVERAGE SUGGESTION
Bordeaux, such as Château d'Angludet

6 TO 8 SERVINGS

1 onion, peeled and stuck with 2 cloves
1 carrot, quartered
1 celery rib, halved
Bouquet garni: 6 parsley stems, 2 large bay leaves, 1 teaspoon peppercorns and 1 tablespoon thyme tied in cheesecloth
6 cups chicken stock or canned broth
1 stick plus 3 tablespoons unsalted butter
¼ cup olive oil, preferably extra-virgin
6 Cornish game hens, quartered
1½ pounds small mushrooms, stemmed (stems reserved for another use)
1½ pounds small white boiling onions, trimmed and peeled
1 tablespoon sugar
¼ cup all-purpose flour
¼ cup tomato paste
1 cup minced dry sun-dried tomatoes
4 egg yolks
1 cup crème fraîche
3 tablespoons minced fresh parsley, for garnish

1. In a medium stockpot, combine the onion, carrot, celery, bouquet garni and chicken stock. Bring to a boil over high heat. Reduce the heat to a simmer.

2. In a large heavy skillet, melt 4 tablespoons of the butter in 2 tablespoons of the oil over high heat. Sauté the hen pieces in batches, turning until golden brown, about 3 minutes per side.

3. When the hen pieces are browned, add them to the stock. Simmer until tender, about 20 minutes. With a slotted spoon, transfer the hens to an ovenproof platter. Cover loosely with foil.

4. Strain the stock through a fine-mesh sieve set over a medium saucepan. Press on the vegetables to extract as much liquid as possible. Bring the stock to a boil over high heat. Add the mushroom caps and cook for 5 minutes. With a wire skimmer or slotted spoon, transfer the caps to a small bowl. Continue boiling the stock until reduced to 4 cups, about 15 minutes.

5. Meanwhile, in a large ovenproof skillet, melt 2 tablespoons of the butter in the remaining 2 tablespoons oil over moderate heat. Add the onions and sugar. Sauté, shaking the pan from time to time, until the onions are golden and tender, about 15 minutes.

6. Preheat the oven to 300°. In a medium saucepan, melt the remaining 5 tablespoons butter over moderately high heat. Add the flour and cook, whisking, for about 2 minutes without coloring. Gradually whisk in the stock and bring to a boil. Stir in the tomato paste, sun-dried tomatoes and mushroom caps. Reduce the heat to low and simmer for 10 minutes. (**The recipe can be prepared ahead to this point.** Reheat the sauce before proceeding.)

7. Place the hens and onions in the oven to reheat.

8. In a medium bowl, whisk together the egg yolks and crème fraîche. Slowly stir in ½ cup of the hot sauce. Gradually whisk this mixture back into the sauce. Remove from the heat.

9. To serve, ladle the sauce over the hens. Arrange the onions around the platter and sprinkle with the parsley.

—W. Peter Prestcott

GUINEA HENS WITH SHERRY VINEGAR

2 SERVINGS

2 guinea hens or Cornish game hens (about 1 pound each)
½ teaspoon salt
¼ teaspoon freshly ground pepper
4 tablespoons unsalted butter
¼ cup Armagnac or other brandy
½ cup sherry wine vinegar
½ cup veal or chicken stock, preferably homemade
1½ ounces prosciutto, chopped
1 tablespoon chopped fresh tarragon or 1 teaspoon dried
1 tablespoon chopped fresh basil or 1 teaspoon dried

1. Preheat the oven to 400°. Season the hens inside and out with half the salt and pepper. Truss them.

2. In a large flameproof noncorrodible casserole, melt 2 tablespoons of the butter over moderately high heat. Add the hens and cook, turning, until browned on all sides, 5 to 8 minutes.

3. Pour off the fat, add the Armagnac and ignite. When the flames subside, pour in the vinegar and bring to a boil. Add the stock, prosciutto, tarragon and basil. Cover the casserole and cook the hens in the hot oven until the juices run clear when the thighs are pierced with a fork, about 30 minutes.

4. Remove the trussing strings, cut each hen in half and place on serving plates. Strain the sauce. Add the remaining 2 tablespoons butter, ¼ teaspoon salt and ⅛ teaspoon pepper and spoon the sauce over the hens.

—Ostaù de Baumanière, Les Baux-de-Provence, France

STUFFED QUAIL WITH PORK, ROSEMARY AND SAGE

This is a spectacular dish, especially when served atop a bed of fresh pasta or watercress. It may also be served chilled, sliced, like a terrine. In that case, garnish with cornichons and sprigs of watercress.

Ask your butcher to bone the quail, or do it yourself with the help of our simple directions.

F&W BEVERAGE SUGGESTION
California Pinot Noir, such as Acacia "Winery Lake Vineyard"

4 SERVINGS

1 slice firm-textured white bread
2 tablespoons ruby port
5 juniper berries
5 peppercorns
½ teaspoon sweet paprika
½ teaspoon rosemary
½ teaspoon sage
½ pound pork shoulder, cubed, with any trimmings reserved
3 ounces smoked bacon, coarsely chopped
4 quail, boned (see Note)—bones, gizzards, livers and hearts reserved
3 ounces calf's liver, cut in 4 strips
4 sheets of barding fat, about 4 by 8 inches each*
3 sprigs of parsley
1 medium onion, sliced
3 garlic cloves, crushed
**Available at butcher shops*

1. Preheat the oven to 400°. Place the bread in a shallow dish and soak with the port.

2. With a mortar and pestle or in a spice grinder, combine the juniper berries, peppercorns, paprika, rosemary and sage and grind coarsely. Drain the soaked bread.

3. In a food processor or meat grinder, combine the pork shoulder, bacon and the reserved quail gizzards, livers and hearts with the ground seasonings and the bread. Finely grind.

4. Divide the stuffing mixture into 4 equal portions. Bury a piece of calf's liver in the center of each mound of stuffing, surrounding it completely. Stuff each quail with 1 portion.

5. Tie the legs of each bird together with butcher's twine. Wrap each quail in a piece of barding fat and secure the fat with butcher's twine.

6. In a large roasting pan, place the reserved bones, any reserved pork trimmings, the parsley, onion and garlic. Roast for about 20 minutes, until browned.

7. Place the stuffed quail on top of the bones and roast for 40 minutes, until the juices run clear when pierced with a fork. To serve, remove the barding fat and twine and serve with some of the pan drippings spooned over the quail. Accompany with a bed of fresh pasta or watercress.

NOTE: Quail are tiny, and although boning them requires a bit of dexterity and patience, it is a simple technique that can easily be mastered. First, pull back the flap of skin covering the neck opening of the bird. Turn the flap inside out and using a very sharp small knife, cut away the V-shaped first bone, or wishbone. Now turn the entire bird inside out. Using your fingers, slowly separate the carcass from the meat until most of the carcass can be removed in one piece. Do not attempt to bone out the tiny legs or wings; they are too small, and removing them will damage the shape of the bird. Turn the quail right-side out again, and stuff as directed.

—Patricia Wells

CONFIT OF QUAIL AND SPARERIBS

This preserved garniture for choucroute (see Holiday Choucroute, p. 104) owes its inspiration and success to Paula Wolfert, whose book *The Cooking of South-West France* provides wonderfully detailed instructions for making *confit*.

12 SERVINGS

3 tablespoons plus 1 teaspoon coarse (kosher) salt
1 tablespoon plus 1 teaspoon thyme
2 teaspoons ground juniper berries
2 teaspoons ground allspice
1½ teaspoons finely crumbled imported bay leaves
1 teaspoon coarsely cracked black pepper
12 quail (2¾ to 3 pounds total), rinsed and dried (see Note)
2 slabs of pork spareribs (6 pounds), halved lengthwise (ask your butcher to do this)
8 to 10 cups fresh rendered pork and goose fat (see Sources)
4 garlic cloves, peeled

1. In a small bowl, combine the salt, thyme, juniper berries, allspice, bay leaves and pepper to make a seasoning mixture. Place the quail in a large baking dish.

2. Trim and discard the fat from the ribs. Trim each strip of ribs into a long, even rectangle (see Note). Place the strips of ribs in a single layer in another baking dish.

3. Sprinkle half the seasoning mixture over and inside the quail. Sprinkle the remainder over both sides of the ribs. Cover with plastic wrap and refrigerate overnight.

4. Rinse the seasonings from the quail and ribs under cold running water; dry well with paper towels. Truss the quail. Separate the ribs into individual pieces and set aside.

5. In a large heavy pot, melt 8 cups of the fat over low heat until clear, about 15 minutes. Add the garlic and the quail. If they are not completely covered with fat, add some of the remaining 2 cups of fat.

6. Over moderately low heat, slowly heat the fat to 160°. Cook the quail until firm to the touch, about 1 hour.

7. Remove from the heat and let the quail cool in the fat for 1 hour. With a slotted spoon, transfer the birds to a platter. Cover loosely with foil and set aside.

8. Place the ribs in the fat, adding more fat if necessary to cover the ribs. Over moderately low heat, cook the ribs for 2 hours, until the meat can be easily pierced with a fork; do not let the temperature exceed 160°.

9. Remove from the heat and let cool in the fat for 1 hour. With a slotted spoon, transfer the ribs to a platter and cover loosely with foil. Remove the garlic from the fat and discard.

10. Bring the fat to a simmer, skimming frequently, over moderately high heat. Let bubble until the steam from the evaporating moisture stops, about 10 minutes. Remove from the heat and let cool for 15 minutes.

11. Place the ribs and quail in a deep container (large enough to hold all the meat with 2 to 3 inches of head space). Strain the warm fat over the meat. Let cool to room temperature, then cover with plastic wrap and refrigerate. If the ribs and quail are not completely submerged, let the fat harden overnight, then pour on a layer of vegetable oil to completely cover. Replace the plastic wrap and refrigerate for at least 4 days or up to 1 week.

12. Four or 5 hours before serving, remove the *confit* from the refrigerator and pour off any vegetable oil, reserving it for another use. Let the *confit* slowly return to room temperature. Remove the ribs and quail from the fat and place on a baking rack set over a large baking pan. Place in the oven and turn the heat to 250°. Bake until the fat has run off the meat, about 30 minutes. Remove the ribs and quail and set aside.

13. Place the quail in a large skillet over moderate heat and sauté, turning occasionally, until evenly browned, about 10 minutes. Drain on paper towels and cover loosely with foil until ready to serve. Sauté the ribs in the same manner until evenly browned; cover and keep warm for up to 1 hour until ready to serve.

SOURCES: If you haven't cooked a goose recently, *rendered goose fat* is available by mail order in 24-ounce tins for $6.95 plus postage and handling from Maison E.H. Glass, Mail Order Dept., 52 E. 58th St., New York, NY 10022; 212-755-3316.

Fresh rendered pork fat is available from most butcher shops. If fresh rendered pork fat is unavailable, do not use commercial lards; use all goose fat instead.

NOTE: If you are making this confit to go with the Holiday Choucroute (p. 104), reserve the quail necks and gizzards, and the trimmings from the spareribs (Step 2), for the Pork Stock (p. 232). In addition, reserve ¼ cup of the rendered fat at the end of Step 12 for the potatoes in the choucroute.

—*Anne Disrude*

MEAT

GRILLED VEAL WITH SUN-DRIED TOMATOES, OLIVES AND SAGE

F&W BEVERAGE SUGGESTION
Oaky Chardonnay, such as Far Niente Estate-Bottled or Chalone

4 SERVINGS

1½ cups dry white wine
*1½ cups chicken, beef or veal stock or canned unsalted chicken broth**
10 oil-cured black olives, halved and pitted
1½ pounds boneless veal loin, cut into 4 pieces and lightly pounded or 4 rib veal chops, 1 inch thick—boned, trimmed and lightly pounded
½ cup all-purpose flour
¼ cup olive oil, preferably extra-virgin
2 large shallots, finely chopped
2 ounces sun-dried tomatoes packed in olive oil—rinsed, dried and julienned
2 teaspoons minced fresh sage or ¾ teaspoon crumbled dried
2 teaspoons unsalted butter
½ teaspoon fresh lemon juice
Freshly ground black pepper
Sprigs of fresh sage or parsley, for garnish
**Available at health food stores*

1. In a medium noncorrodible saucepan, boil the wine until it is reduced by half, about 10 minutes. Add the stock and continue to boil until the liquid is reduced to 1 cup, 10 to 15 minutes longer. **(This step can be done ahead.)**

2. Soak the olives in warm water to cover until slightly softened, about 10 minutes. Drain and pat dry. Chop coarsely.

3. Preheat the oven to 250°. Dredge the veal in the flour, shaking off the excess. In a large heavy skillet, heat the oil until it shimmers. Add the veal to the skillet and cook over moderately high heat until lightly browned on one side, about 4 minutes. Turn, reduce the heat to moderate and cook for 4 minutes, for medium-rare.

4. Remove the veal to a platter. Cover loosely with foil and keep warm in the oven. Add the shallots to the skillet and sauté until softened, about 30 seconds. Add the reduced wine-stock mixture, sun-dried tomatoes and minced sage. Increase the heat and boil, scraping up any browned bits from the bottom of the pan, until the liquid is reduced by one-fourth to ¾ cup, 2 to 3 minutes.

5. Add the olives and return the veal and any accumulated juices to the skillet. Turn the veal to coat with the sauce, then place on warmed plates. Remove the skillet from the heat and swirl the butter into the sauce. Season with the lemon juice and pepper to taste. Spoon the sauce over the veal and garnish with a sprig of fresh sage.

—Sanford D'Amato, John Byron, Milwaukee, Wisconsin

VEAL SCALLOPS WITH WILD MUSHROOMS

Follow this dish with a simple green salad and a light vinaigrette dressing. We also suggest a good crusty bread on the side to mop up the rich, tasty sauce.

F&W BEVERAGE SUGGESTION
St. Emilion, such as Château Pavie

4 SERVINGS

8 veal scallops, 2 ounces each (1 pound total)
⅓ cup all-purpose flour
5 tablespoons unsalted butter
1 medium garlic clove, minced
¼ pound assorted fresh wild mushrooms (such as shiitakes, tree oysters, morels and/or chanterelles), trimmed and washed
¼ cup Cognac
1½ cups heavy cream
2 sprigs of fresh thyme or ¼ teaspoon dried
1 tablespoon fresh lemon juice
⅛ teaspoon salt
⅛ teaspoon freshly ground white pepper

1. Pound the veal scallops between two sheets of waxed paper until ⅛ inch thick. Dredge in the flour, shaking off the excess. Preheat the oven to 200°.

2. In a large deep skillet or flameproof casserole, melt 2 tablespoons of the butter over moderately high heat. When the foam subsides, add half the scallops and sauté, turning once, until lightly browned on both sides, about 2 minutes. Remove to a heatproof platter, cover loosely with foil and keep warm in the oven. Wipe out the skillet with paper towels. Repeat with 2 tablespoons of butter and the remaining 4 scallops.

3. Melt the remaining tablespoon butter in the skillet. When the foam subsides, add the garlic and mushrooms. Sauté until the mushrooms are just tender, about 4 minutes. Pour off any excess liquid.

4. Add the Cognac and swirl to warm. Carefully ignite with a match; shake the pan occasionally until the flames subside.

5. Stir in the cream and the thyme. Cook over moderately high heat, decreasing the heat if necessary to prevent the cream from boiling over, until reduced by half, about 6 minutes. Season with the lemon juice, salt and pepper. Remove the sprigs of thyme.

6. To serve, spoon the mushrooms and the sauce over the warm veal scallops.

—Jack Leone, Café Giovanni, Denver, Colorado

VEAL MARSALA

F&W BEVERAGE SUGGESTION
Chianti, such as Ruffino Riserva Ducale

4 SERVINGS

1¼ pounds veal scallops, pounded ¼ inch thick
2 to 3 tablespoons vegetable oil
½ teaspoon salt
¼ teaspoon freshly ground pepper
1 cup dry Marsala
1 tablespoon unsalted butter
2 teaspoons chopped parsley, for garnish

1. Pat the veal scallops dry with paper towels.

2. In a large heavy skillet, heat 1½ tablespoons of oil until almost smoking. Add as many veal scallops as will fit in a single layer without crowding and sauté over high heat until brown on the bottom, about 2 minutes. Turn and cook until brown on the second side, about 30 seconds. Transfer to a serving platter and cover loosely to keep warm. Repeat with the remaining scallops, adding additional oil to coat the bottom of the skillet as needed. Season the cooked veal with half the salt and pepper.

3. Blot the skillet with paper towels to remove excess oil. Pour in the Marsala. Boil over high heat, scraping up any brown bits from the bottom of the pan, until the wine is reduced slightly. Pour in any accumulated meat juices from the platter and continue cooking until the sauce is reduced to a thin syrup, about 8 minutes.

4. Whisk in the butter just until incorporated. Return the meat to the skillet and turn to coat with the sauce. Arrange on the platter, spooning extra sauce on top. Garnish with the parsley.

—Anne Disrude

VEAL CHOPS WITH PROSCIUTTO AND BASIL CREAM SAUCE

F&W BEVERAGE SUGGESTION
Puligny-Montrachet, such as Clavoillons

4 SERVINGS

1 tablespoon unsalted butter
1 small shallot, minced
1 medium garlic clove, minced
1 large plum tomato, finely chopped
Bouquet garni: 4 peppercorns, 2 sprigs of parsley, ¼ teaspoon thyme and 1 small bay leaf tied in cheesecloth
1 cup plus 2 tablespoons veal or chicken stock, preferably homemade
½ cup dry white wine
1 cup heavy cream
4 veal rib chops, cut 1 inch thick
1 cup all-purpose flour
2 tablespoons olive oil
1 tablespoon dry Marsala
Salt and freshly ground pepper
1 cup minced fresh basil
4 slices of prosciutto, at room temperature
2 tablespoons toasted pine nuts

1. In a medium saucepan, melt the butter over moderate heat. Add the shallot and garlic and sauté until soft and translucent, about 1 minute. Add the tomato, bouquet garni, 1 cup of the stock and the wine. Bring to a boil and cook, uncovered, until reduced to ¼ cup, 10 to 15 minutes.

2. Add the cream and boil until the sauce is reduced by one-fourth and is thick enough to coat a spoon, 5 to 10 minutes. Strain through a fine sieve, pressing to extract as much liquid as possible. **(The recipe can be made to this point up to 2 hours ahead.)**

3. Pat the veal chops dry and dredge in the flour; shake off any excess. In each of two skillets, heat 1 tablespoon of the oil until almost shimmering. Place two chops in each skillet and cook over moderately high heat until well browned on one side, 3 to 4 minutes. Turn and brown the second side, about 2 minutes. Reduce the heat to moderate and cook for an additional 2 minutes on each side, until only slightly pink inside. Remove to a warmed plate and cover loosely with foil.

4. Pour off the fat from both skillets. Pour ¼ cup of water into one skillet and boil over high heat, scraping any browned bits from the sides and bottom of the skillet, for 1 minute. Scrape into the second skillet.

5. Add the Marsala and the remaining 2 tablespoons stock to the second skillet. Boil over high heat, scraping any browned bits from the sides and bottom of the skillet, for 1 minute. Add the reserved cream sauce and bring to a boil, stirring occasionally. Season with salt and pepper to taste. Add any accumulated meat juices from the veal to the sauce. Stir in the basil.

6. To serve, ladle about ¼ cup sauce onto each of 4 warmed plates. Place a veal chop on top. Fold the prosciutto slices and place one on top of each chop. Sprinkle with toasted pine nuts.

—Claire Owens, Les Survivants, Annapolis, Maryland

BROILED VEAL CHOPS WITH CHILE-LIME BUTTER

Serve these delectable veal chops with roasted baby onions or glazed shallots.

F&W BEVERAGE SUGGESTION
California dry Chenin Blanc, such as Kenwood

4 SERVINGS

4 to 6 fresh green serrano chiles, finely chopped (about 2 tablespoons)
8 tablespoons fresh lime juice

¼ cup white wine vinegar
3 tablespoons finely chopped shallots
1 medium mango, peeled and pitted
1½ sticks plus 6 tablespoons unsalted butter
1 tablespoon vegetable oil
4 thick veal chops, cut 1 inch thick (about 2½ pounds total)
¾ teaspoon salt
¼ teaspoon freshly ground black pepper
Sprigs of watercress, sliced mango and slices of fresh red serrano chile, for garnish

1. In a noncorrodible medium skillet, place the chopped chiles, 6 tablespoons of the lime juice, the vinegar, shallots and ¼ cup of water. Bring to a boil over high heat and boil until the liquid is reduced to 2½ tablespoons, about 5 minutes. Remove the skillet from the heat and set aside.

2. Puree the mango in a food processor or food mill and set aside.

3. In a small saucepan, melt 6 tablespoons of the butter. Skim off the white foam to clarify it and pour the clear butterfat into a small bowl, leaving the white solids in the bottom of the pan. Mix in the remaining 2 tablespoons lime juice.

4. Preheat the broiler with the rack set about 4 inches from the heat. Grease the hot broiling rack lightly with the oil and place the chops on the rack. Brush them with the lime butter, sprinkle with ¼ teaspoon of the salt and ⅛ teaspoon of the black pepper. Broil the chops for 3 minutes. Turn, brush with lime butter and sprinkle with another ¼ teaspoon salt and ⅛ teaspoon pepper. Broil for 3 minutes. Lower the rack to 6 inches from the heat and cook the chops for an additional 4 to 6 minutes per side, brushing each side again with the lime butter. The chops should be nicely browned outside and rosy pink near the bone. Remove from the heat, cover loosely with foil and set aside while you finish the sauce.

5. Add the pan drippings to the reserved chile-vinegar reduction. Bring to a boil, reduce the heat to moderately low and cook for 30 seconds. Whisk in the remaining 1½ sticks butter, 1 tablespoon at a time, adding each as the previous one is just incorporated. Strain the sauce into a medium noncorrodible saucepan. Whisk in the reserved mango puree and the remaining ¼ teaspoon salt; reheat briefly over low heat. Do not allow the sauce to boil.

6. Serve the chops with the sauce on the side, garnished with watercress, some mango and a few slices of fresh hot red pepper if desired.

—*Anne Lindsay Greer*

TRADITIONAL OSSO BUCO WITH GREMOLATA

F&W BEVERAGE SUGGESTION
Antinori Tignanello

8 SERVINGS

2 tablespoons unsalted butter
2 tablespoons olive oil
5 pounds veal shanks, cut into 2-inch pieces and tied with string around their circumference
1 cup all-purpose flour
2 medium onions, coarsely chopped
1 large carrot, coarsely chopped
1 medium celery rib, coarsely chopped
3 garlic cloves, crushed
½ teaspoon marjoram
½ teaspoon basil
½ teaspoon thyme
1 can (28 ounces) Italian peeled tomatoes, drained and coarsely chopped
2½ tablespoons tomato paste
2 cups dry white wine or dry vermouth
1 cup chicken stock or canned broth
3 strips of lemon zest, about 2 inches long
1 large bay leaf
4 sprigs of parsley

GREMOLATA:
½ cup minced parsley
3 medium garlic cloves, minced
1 tablespoon grated lemon zest

1. In a large flameproof casserole, melt the butter in the oil over moderate heat.

2. Dredge the veal in the flour and shake off any excess. Working in batches, sauté the veal on all sides until golden brown. Do not crowd the pan. Remove to a bowl.

3. Add the onions, carrot, celery and garlic. Cover and cook until tender, about 15 minutes.

4. Place the veal on top of the vegetables, making sure the bones are upright. Sprinkle the marjoram, basil and thyme on top. Add the tomatoes, tomato paste, white wine, chicken stock, strips of lemon zest, bay leaf and parsley sprigs. If necessary, add enough water to cover the shanks.

5. Bring to a boil, reduce the heat to low and simmer, covered, until the meat is tender, about 2 hours. (**The recipe may be prepared to this point up to 3 days ahead.** Let cool; cover and refrigerate. Warm through before proceeding.)

6. Transfer the veal shanks to a heated platter; remove the strings and cover with foil to keep warm. Increase the heat to high and boil, stirring frequently, until the sauce is reduced by half, about 20 minutes. Pour the sauce over the meat.

7. Just before serving, combine the parsley, garlic and lemon zest to make the *gremolata*. Sprinkle on top.

—*W. Peter Prestcott*

VEAL SHANKS WITH ORANGE, ROSEMARY AND ONIONS

F&W BEVERAGE SUGGESTION
Chianti Classico, such as Frescobaldi

6 SERVINGS

2 meaty veal hindshanks (about 3 pounds each), cut crosswise into 2½-inch pieces
1¼ teaspoons salt
2 tablespoons all-purpose flour
3 tablespoons unsalted butter
1 tablespoon vegetable oil
¼ teaspoon freshly ground pepper
1 large onion, chopped
1 large garlic clove, minced
1½ cups veal or beef stock or canned beef broth
1 cup fresh orange juice
¼ cup fresh lemon juice
1 teaspoon crumbled rosemary
18 small white boiling onions
2 tablespoons plus 1 teaspoon sugar
1 tablespoon cider vinegar
1 teaspoon grated orange zest

1. Preheat the oven to 300°. Cut a slit in the membrane that surrounds each shank. Tie a string around the center of the meat to help keep it in shape. Sprinkle one side of the pieces of meat with ¼ teaspoon of the salt and 1 tablespoon of the flour; turn over and repeat on the other side.

2. In a large skillet, melt 2 tablespoons of the butter in the oil. Sauté the shanks until well browned. Transfer the pieces to a large flameproof casserole with the wide bone ends facing up (to prevent the marrow from slipping out). Add the pepper.

3. Add the chopped onion and garlic to the skillet and sauté until lightly browned. Add the stock, orange and lemon juices, rosemary and ½ teaspoon of the salt. Bring to a boil, stirring. Pour over the veal in the casserole, bring to a simmer and cover.

4. Bake for about 2 hours, until the veal is fork-tender.

5. Meanwhile, blanch the white onions in boiling water for 30 seconds. Drain, rinse and peel.

6. In a large skillet, combine the white onions with the remaining 1 tablespoon butter, ¼ teaspoon of the salt, 1 teaspoon of the sugar and ¼ cup of water. Cover and simmer until the onions are barely tender, 5 to 7 minutes. Uncover and cook over high heat, tossing, until the water evaporates and the onions are browned. Remove from the heat and set aside in the skillet.

7. Increase the oven temperature to 400°. With a wide spatula, carefully transfer the veal to a heatproof serving dish large enough to hold the pieces closely in a single layer. Remove the strings. Skim off any fat from the liquid in the casserole. Boil until the liquid is reduced to a slightly syrupy consistency, about 1¾ cups.

8. In a small heavy saucepan, dissolve the remaining 2 tablespoons sugar in 1 tablespoon of water over high heat. Stir until the syrup turns deep amber. Immediately remove from the heat and stir in the vinegar. Stir in a few tablespoons of the sauce. Then stir all the caramel mixture into the remaining sauce. Add the orange zest.

9. Reheat the onions and scatter over the veal. Pour the sauce on top and bake in the upper third of the oven until the sauce lightly glazes the veal and onions, 4 to 5 minutes.

—Elizabeth Schneider

LA FINANZIERA

F&W BEVERAGE SUGGESTION
Barolo

6 TO 8 SERVINGS

1 pound boneless veal shoulder, cut into 1-inch cubes, chilled
2 ounces prosciutto, coarsely chopped (about ¼ cup)
1 large shallot, coarsely chopped
⅓ cup fresh bread crumbs, preferably from Italian or French bread
2 tablespoons minced fresh parsley
½ teaspoon salt
½ teaspoon freshly ground pepper
Pinch of freshly grated nutmeg
1 egg, lightly beaten
1 tablespoon distilled white vinegar or fresh lemon juice
1 pound veal sweetbreads
1 veal kidney
½ pound chicken livers
¾ pound skinless, boneless chicken breast
1 cup chicken or beef stock or canned broth
⅓ cup all-purpose flour
4 tablespoons unsalted butter
4 tablespoons olive oil
½ cup red wine vinegar
*6 ounces Italian prepared mushrooms in vinegar or mushrooms in oil (about 1 cup)**
*3 ounces cornichons (French gherkin pickles) sliced lengthwise (about ½ cup)**
⅓ cup dry Marsala
**Available in specialty food shops*

1. Grind the veal, prosciutto and shallot in a meat grinder, or chop in a food processor, turning the machine on and off quickly, until the mixture is minced but not pureed. Scrape into a bowl. Add the bread crumbs, parsley, salt, pepper, nutmeg and egg. Mix well to combine. Shape into 1-inch balls.

2. Bring a medium noncorrodible saucepan of water to a boil. Reduce to a simmer, add the vinegar and sweetbreads and blanch the sweetbreads for 5 minutes, or until lightened in color. Rinse under cold running water until cool. Peel off the outer membrane covering the sweetbreads and trim away any connective tissue. Cut into 1-inch chunks.

3. Halve the kidney lengthwise and trim away any fat, connective tissue and tubules. Cut into 1-inch chunks. Trim the chicken livers and separate the lobes. Cut the chicken breast into 2-by-½-inch strips. Keep the meats separate.

4. In a large saucepan, bring the stock to a simmer. Keep partially covered to prevent evaporation.

5. Dredge the meatballs and each of the meats separately in the flour; shake off any excess and set aside. In a large skillet, melt 2 tablespoons of the butter in 2 tablespoons of the oil over high heat. Add the chicken breast strips and sauté 2 minutes. Remove with a slotted spoon and set aside.

6. Reduce the heat to moderate and add 1 tablespoon each of butter and oil to the skillet. When the foam subsides, add the meatballs and sauté until browned, 4 to 5 minutes. Remove with a slotted spoon and transfer to the simmering broth.

7. Heat the remaining 1 tablespoon each of butter and oil in the skillet. Add the sweetbread chunks and sauté, tossing, until lightly browned, about 4 minutes. Remove with a slotted spoon and transfer to the broth.

8. Add the kidney chunks to the skillet and sauté, tossing, until lightly browned, about 6 minutes. With a slotted spoon, transfer to the broth.

9. Add the chicken livers to the skillet and sauté, turning, until browned, about 4 minutes. Remove with a slotted spoon and transfer to the broth. Add the reserved chicken strips and any juices to the broth.

10. Pour any fat from the skillet. Add ¼ cup of the vinegar and deglaze the skillet over moderately high heat, scraping any browned bits from the sides and bottom of the pan. Scrape into the saucepan with the meats. Stir in the mushrooms and cornichons.

11. Cover the meats and simmer for 10 minutes longer.

12. Stir in the remaining ¼ cup vinegar and the Marsala. Simmer, uncovered, for 5 minutes to allow the flavors to blend.

—Diane Darrow & Tom Maresca

BREAST OF VEAL WITH BULGUR, MUSHROOM AND SWEET RED PEPPER STUFFING

For this dish, ask the butcher to give you the wide rectangular plate end of the breast, about 6 ribs wide (about 4½ pounds). This should then be boned (bones reserved) and trimmed, the trimmings ground for the stuffing.

F&W BEVERAGE SUGGESTION
Bordeaux Rouge, such as Chevalier de Védrines

4 TO 6 SERVINGS

1 ounce dried wild mushrooms, such as cèpes, porcini or Polish mushrooms
1 tablespoon walnut oil
½ cup medium bulgur (precooked cracked wheat)
¼ pound slab bacon, cut into ¼-inch dice
1 medium onion, minced, plus 1 medium onion, sliced
1 medium red bell pepper, cut into ¼-inch dice
1 tablespoon cornstarch
1 egg, lightly beaten
Ground veal trimmings (½ to ¾ cup)
½ teaspoon freshly grated nutmeg
½ teaspoon salt
¼ teaspoon freshly ground black pepper
4½ pounds veal breast, boned and trimmed
Veal rib bones (reserved from the trimmed breast), cut into individual ribs
1 carrot, sliced
½ cup dry white wine or dry vermouth

1. Soak the mushrooms in a small bowl with the walnut oil and 1 cup of hot water until softened, about 30 minutes. Soak the bulgur in 1 cup of hot water for 30 minutes.

2. Meanwhile, in a medium skillet, cook the bacon over moderate heat until browned and crisp, about 10 minutes. Remove the bacon with a slotted spoon; pour off and reserve the fat.

3. Heat 2 tablespoons of the reserved bacon fat in the same skillet. Add the minced onion and sauté until lightly browned, about 5 minutes. Add the red pepper and sauté until slightly softened, about 3 minutes. Transfer the onion-pepper mixture to a large bowl.

4. Drain the mushrooms, reserving the soaking liquid. Rinse the mushrooms quickly; then chop and add to the bowl. Strain the liquid through a coffee filter or paper towel.

5. Drain the bulgur and toss in the sieve to remove some of the moisture. Add the bulgur to the stuffing.

6. In a medium bowl, dissolve the cornstarch in 1 tablespoon of water. Mix in the egg, veal trimmings, bacon, nutmeg, salt and black pepper. Add to the stuffing mixture and blend well. (**The recipe can be made several hours ahead to this point.** Let cool; then refrigerate, covered.)

7. Place the veal breast on a work surface with the boned-side facing up. Spoon the stuffing down the center from one long end to the other. Pack the stuffing into a tight, neat cylinder.

Fold the meat up and over the stuffing and temporarily secure the two open ends closed with skewers. Then loosely sew up the long seam to enclose the stuffing. Remove the skewers and sew the two ends closed.

8. Preheat the oven to 300°. In a large flameproof casserole, preferably oval, heat 1 tablespoon of the reserved bacon fat. Add the rib bones and brown well. Remove the bones to a plate. Pour out the fat and add 2 more tablespoons of the bacon fat. Add the stuffed breast of veal and cook, turning, until evenly browned. With a bulb baster, remove the fat. Add the sliced onion and carrot and brown lightly.

9. Arrange the bones around the breast. Pour in the reserved mushroom soaking liquid and the wine. Bring to a simmer. Cover the casserole and bake, basting every 30 minutes, until the veal is tender, about 2 hours.

10. Transfer the veal to a carving board and let rest for 15 minutes. Remove the strings and carve into even slices; arrange on a warm platter.

11. Meanwhile, skim off any surface fat from the juices remaining in the casserole. Strain through a fine sieve. Pass the juices separately with the veal.

—*Elizabeth Schneider*

BRISKET OF BEEF

Serve this brisket with sliced carrots and broccoli or green beans and plenty of boiled potatoes or Kasha Varnishkes (p. 152) to soak up the gravy.

F&W BEVERAGE SUGGESTION
Hearty red, such as Louis M. Martini Barbera

8 TO 10 SERVINGS

6-pound brisket of beef, cut in half
2 medium onions, chopped
2 tablespoons vegetable oil
4 tablespoons garlic powder
3 tablespoons ketchup

1. Trim the meat, leaving only a small amount of fat. Wash the meat and pat it dry with paper towels.

2. In a large flameproof casserole, sauté the onions in the vegetable oil over moderate heat, until golden, about 8 minutes. Remove the onions with a slotted spoon and set aside.

3. Add one piece of meat to the casserole, increase the heat to moderately high and brown on both sides, about 10 to 12 minutes. Set aside. Repeat with the other piece of meat. Return the onions to the casserole. Put both pieces of meat back on top of the onions.

4. Sprinkle the meat with 2 tablespoons of the garlic powder. Spread the ketchup on top. Add ½ cup of water.

5. Cover and cook over moderately low heat for 30 minutes. Turn the meat and sprinkle with the remaining 2 tablespoons garlic powder. Cover and continue to cook, turning occasionally, until tender, about 2½ hours. (**The recipe may be made a day ahead to this point.** Cover and refrigerate. Spoon off the excess fat from the drippings before reheating.)

6. Remove the meat from the pot and let sit for 30 minutes; reserve the pan drippings and spoon off any excess fat. With a sharp knife, slice the meat against the grain into ¼-inch slices. Return the slices to the pot, and tip to cover with the gravy. Reheat, covered, over very low heat until ready to serve.

—*Nell Picower*

ENTRECOTE A LA BORDELAISE

F&W BEVERAGE SUGGESTION
Saint-Julien, such as Château Brunaire

8 SERVINGS

2 boneless beef rib steaks, cut 3 inches thick (2 to 2½ pounds each)
1 teaspoon salt
½ teaspoon freshly ground pepper
2 tablespoons grape seed oil (see Note) or clarified butter
1 large beef marrow bone, cut crosswise into 2-inch sections
3 medium shallots, minced
1 cup red Bordeaux wine, preferably from Saint-Julien
1 cup rich beef stock or canned broth
1 tablespoon unsalted butter, softened
1 tablespoon all-purpose flour
1 tablespoon chopped parsley

1. Preheat the oven to 400°. Season the steaks with ½ teaspoon of the salt and ¼ teaspoon of the pepper. In a large noncorrodible skillet, heat the oil. Add the steaks and sauté over high heat, turning, until well browned all over, about 8 minutes. (The steaks should be crisp, almost charred outside.) Transfer the steaks to a roasting pan; set the skillet aside.

2. Roast the steaks until the internal temperature reaches 140° to 150°, about 15 minutes.

3. Meanwhile, individually wrap the marrow bones in aluminum foil. Simmer in a saucepan of water for 2 minutes. Remove the bones, unwrap and gently push the marrow out of each bone. Carefully slice each marrow section crosswise into ¼-inch slices.

4. Return the skillet to moderately high heat. Add the shallots and cook, stirring occasionally, until softened, about 5 minutes. Add the wine, beef stock and remaining ½ teaspoon salt

and 1/4 teaspoon pepper. Bring to a boil, scraping up any brown bits from the bottom of the pan. Reduce the heat and simmer for 5 minutes.

5. Mash together the softened butter and flour until well blended to make a beurre manié. Whisk by bits into the sauce. Simmer, stirring occasionally, until thickened, about 5 minutes. Season with salt and pepper to taste.

6. To serve, put the steaks on a large platter; nap with some of the *bordelaise* sauce. Garnish each steak with slices of bone marrow and sprinkle with the parsley. At table, carve each steak straight down into 1/4-inch-thick slices. Serve the remaining sauce on the side.

NOTE: Grape seed oil can be heated to very high temperatures without burning, making it particularly appropriate for recipes like this one that require high-temperature searing.

—John Robert Massie

HERBED STEAK WITH STEVE'S MUSTARD SAUCE

This dish can also be prepared with butterflied leg of lamb. Serve with side dishes of sautéed zucchini and yellow squash or a mixture of brown and wild rices.

6 SERVINGS

1/2 cup Dijon-style mustard
3/4 teaspoon Worcestershire sauce
1/2 teaspoon grated fresh ginger
1 small garlic clove, minced
1/2 teaspoon basil
1/2 teaspoon oregano
1/2 teaspoon rosemary, crumbled
1/2 teaspoon tarragon
1/4 teaspoon coarsely ground pepper
Vegetable oil
2 1/2- to 3-pound sirloin or porterhouse steak, cut 1 1/2 to 2 inches thick

1. In a small bowl, blend the mustard, Worcestershire, ginger and garlic. Cover and let stand at room temperature for 1 hour.

2. Preheat the broiler. Combine the basil, oregano, rosemary, tarragon and pepper. Lightly brush vegetable oil over both sides of the steak. Sprinkle the herb mixture over both sides, pressing to adhere.

3. Brush the broiler pan with oil. Broil the steak 4 inches from the heat, turning once, for about 10 minutes for rare, 15 for medium-rare.

4. Remove to a platter, cover loosely with foil and let rest for 10 minutes.

5. Stir any meat juices that have accumulated on the platter into the mustard sauce. Slice the meat and pour any additional juices into the sauce. Pass the sauce separately.

—Stephen Schimoler, The Terrace Restaurant, Locust Valley, New York

SKIRT STEAK WITH SOY AND GINGER MARINADE

These skirt steaks are best when grilled over a charcoal or wood fire, although a broiler can also be used.

F&W BEVERAGE SUGGESTION
California Merlot, such as Stephen Zellerbach

6 SERVINGS

6 garlic cloves, coarsely chopped
3 ounces fresh ginger, peeled and coarsely chopped (about 2/3 cup)
1/4 cup soy sauce, preferably dark
1/4 cup dry sherry
1/4 cup rice wine vinegar
1/4 cup olive oil
2 tablespoons Oriental sesame oil
6 skirt steaks, 8 ounces each, trimmed of fat

1. In a noncorrodible container large enough to hold all of the steaks, combine the garlic, ginger, soy sauce, sherry, vinegar, olive oil and sesame oil.

2. Add the steaks; turn to coat with the marinade. Cover and marinate for at least 1 hour at room temperature or up to 8 hours in the refrigerator. (**The recipe can be prepared ahead to this point.** Let the meat return to room temperature before cooking.)

3. Light the grill or preheat the broiler. Scrape the ginger and garlic off the steaks and pat dry with paper towels. Grill or broil the steaks about 4 inches from the heat, turning once, for about 3 minutes on each side for rare, 4 for medium-rare.

4. Remove from the heat and let rest, loosely covered, for about 10 minutes. Cut on the diagonal into thin slices.

—Cindy Pawlcyn, Mustards Grill, Napa, California

PEPPER-LAVENDER STEAK

F&W BEVERAGE SUGGESTION
California Zinfandel, such as Clos du Val

4 SERVINGS

4 rib-eye steaks (8 to 10 ounces each), trimmed of most exterior fat
1 teaspoon coarse (kosher) salt
2 tablespoons black peppercorns, preferably Tellicherry, coarsely ground
2 tablespoons fennel seeds, coarsely ground
1 tablespoon white peppercorns, coarsely ground
1 teaspoon dried lavender, ground to a powder
3 tablespoons light olive oil

1. Sprinkle both sides of the steaks with the salt and set aside for about 10 minutes.

2. In a baking dish or large flat plate, mix the black pepper, fennel, white pepper and lavender. Press both sides of the steaks into the mixture to form a spice crust.

3. Heat 2 large heavy skillets, preferably cast iron, over high heat. Add 1½ tablespoons of oil to each skillet. When the oil is almost smoking, add the steaks carefully so as not to disturb their crusts. Immediately reduce the heat to moderate. Cook the first side until the bottom crust browns, about 4 minutes. Turn and finish cooking the steaks to the desired doneness (3 minutes for medium-rare).

—Barbara Tropp

FILLET STEAKS STUFFED WITH POBLANO CHILES AND CHEESE (TAPADO TLAXCOLA)

Chef Zarela Martinez serves this flavorful entrée with both Rice with Sour Cream and Chiles (p. 149) and Cheese and Chile Corn Bread (p. 155) accompanied with Jicama Relish (p. 239).

F&W BEVERAGE SUGGESTION
California Zinfandel, such as Louis M. Martini

6 SERVINGS

3 fresh poblano or long green chiles
1 trimmed fillet of beef (3 to 4 pounds), cut into 6 steaks about 2½ inches thick
¼ cup lard
3 medium onions, chopped
8 garlic cloves, minced
1½ teaspoons salt
1 teaspoon freshly ground black pepper
6 ounces white Cheddar cheese, shredded (about 1½ cups)

1. Roast the poblano chiles directly over a gas flame or broil 4 inches from the heat, turning with tongs, until the skin is blackened and blistered all over, about 10 minutes. Seal in a bag and let steam to loosen the skin, about 10 minutes. Peel under cold running water; pat dry. Stem and seed the chiles and finely chop.

2. Place a fillet steak on its edge and with a sharp knife, cut through the middle across the grain to within 1 inch of the bottom edge. Spread the steak open and, with your hand or a meat pounder, flatten to an even ¾-inch thickness. Butterfly the remaining steaks in the same manner. Cover with plastic wrap to prevent drying out and set aside. (**The recipe can be prepared to this point up to a day ahead.** Wrap the steaks and chiles separately and refrigerate. Let them both return to room temperature before proceeding.)

3. In a large skillet, melt the lard over moderately high heat. Add the chiles, onions and garlic and sauté until the onions are softened and translucent, about 5 minutes. Remove from the heat; let cool to room temperature.

4. Preheat the broiler. Season the inside of the butterflied steaks with salt and black pepper. Divide the chiles and onions among the steaks, spreading the mixture over half of each. Sprinkle the cheese over the chile-onion mixture. Fold over the steaks to enclose the filling. Season on both sides with salt and pepper.

5. Grill over hot coals or broil 4 inches from the heat, turning once, for about 8 minutes for rare, 10 to 12 for medium. Serve with Jicama Relish, Rice with Sour Cream and Chiles, and Cheese and Chile Corn Bread.

—Zarela Martinez, Café Marimba, New York City

BEEF SHANK IN CHILI SAUCE

6 SERVINGS

6 large (6-inch) dried New Mexican chiles—stemmed, seeded and torn into large pieces*
1 teaspoon cumin seed
1 can (16 ounces) peeled tomatoes, drained
3 large garlic cloves, minced
1½ teaspoons salt
3 pounds beef shank with bones, cut crosswise into 1½-inch-thick pieces
¼ cup minced fresh coriander
**Available in Latin American groceries*

1. Preheat the oven to 325°. In a food processor or blender, combine the chiles with the cumin seed and 2½ cups of boiling water. Cover and let stand until the chiles soften, about 30 minutes. Puree and pour into a baking dish large enough to hold the meat in one layer.

2. In the processor, puree the tomatoes with the garlic and salt. Add to the chile mixture and stir to blend well. Add the meat, turning to coat with sauce. Tightly cover the dish with foil.

3. Bake, turning the meat after 1½ hours, until the meat is tender, about 3 hours. Uncover and bake, basting several times, until the meat is fork-tender and the sauce is slightly thickened, 30 to 45 minutes longer. (If the sauce still seems too thin, the beef shanks can be cooked longer. If you're short on time, however, you can pour the sauce off into a saucepan and reduce it to the desired consistency on stovetop while you keep the beef shanks warm in the turned-off oven.)

4. Pull the meat from the bones in large chunks and transfer to an ovenproof baking/serving dish. Pour the

sauce over the meat and reheat to bubbling. Sprinkle the coriander on top and serve.

—Elizabeth Schneider

DEVILED OXTAIL WITH RUTABAGA PUREE

3 SERVINGS

2½ pounds disjointed oxtail
1 medium onion
4 whole cloves
1 teaspoon thyme
3 tablespoons cider vinegar
1¼ teaspoons salt
½ teaspoon freshly ground pepper
1½ pounds rutabaga, peeled and thinly sliced
1½ tablespoons rice
1 cup fine dry bread crumbs
2 eggs
3 tablespoons sharp mustard

1. In a large heavy saucepan, cover the oxtail with 2 quarts of water. Simmer, skimming, for 3 to 4 minutes. Stick the onion with the cloves. Add the onion, ¾ teaspoon of the thyme and the vinegar to the saucepan. Cover and simmer until the meat is tender, 1½ to 2½ hours.

2. Remove the oxtail and season with ¼ teaspoon each of the salt and pepper. Skim off and reserve any fat from the stock. Strain the stock and then return it to the saucepan and bring to a simmer.

3. Add the rutabaga, ½ teaspoon of the salt and the rice and cook, covered, until the rutabaga is tender, 40 to 50 minutes. Drain and puree through the medium disk of a food mill. Season with the remaining ½ teaspoon salt and ¼ teaspoon pepper.

4. Preheat the oven to 450°. In a shallow dish, mix the remaining ¼ teaspoon thyme with the bread crumbs. In a small bowl, lightly beat the eggs with 2 teaspoons of water. One at a time, heavily paint the oxtail pieces all over with the mustard, then roll lightly in the bread crumbs. Dip into the beaten eggs, then roll again in the crumbs until well coated. Arrange on a baking sheet and drizzle evenly with 2 tablespoons of the reserved fat.

5. Bake in the upper third of the oven, without turning, for 25 minutes, or until crisp and well browned. To serve, reheat the rutabaga puree in the oven. Scoop onto a platter and surround with oxtail pieces.

—Elizabeth Schneider

GINGER BEEF STIR-FRY

Ginger is used as a vegetable here. It adds a pleasing crunchy texture as well as a full but not overpowering ginger flavor. Boiled rice makes a good accompaniment.

F&W BEVERAGE SUGGESTION
Rosé of Cabernet Sauvignon, such as Simi

3 TO 4 SERVINGS

1 pound trimmed, boneless sirloin steak, cut ½ inch thick
1 teaspoon cornstarch
2 tablespoons soy sauce, preferably dark
2 tablespoons dry sherry
½ cup peanut oil
2½ ounces fresh ginger, peeled and cut into fine 2-inch shreds (about ½ cup)
1 bunch of watercress, tough stems removed

1. Slice the steak crosswise on the diagonal into very thin strips, about 2 by ½ by ¼ inch. Place in a bowl and sprinkle with the cornstarch. Toss to coat evenly. Stir in the soy sauce and sherry. Set aside for 5 minutes.

2. In a wok or large skillet, heat the oil—a piece of meat should sizzle loudly on contact. Add the meat, reserving the marinade in the bowl. Stir-fry over high heat until the meat loses most of its pinkness, about 1 minute. With a slotted spoon, transfer to paper towels to drain.

3. Pour off all but 1 tablespoon oil from the wok. Add the ginger and stir-fry over high heat for 15 seconds. Add the watercress and the cooked steak and stir-fry for 5 seconds. Pour in the reserved marinade and toss for 10 seconds. Transfer the mixture to a warmed platter. Serve hot with plain boiled rice.

—Diana Sturgis

BEEF STEW IN RED WINE

F&W BEVERAGE SUGGESTION
California Zinfandel, such as Dry Creek

6 SERVINGS

2 pounds lean beef chuck, cut into 1½-inch cubes
1 teaspoon freshly ground pepper
¼ cup all-purpose flour
¼ cup corn oil
1 large onion, chopped
3 medium carrots, thinly sliced
1 cup dry red wine, preferably Zinfandel
½ cup beef stock or canned broth
1 bay leaf
1 teaspoon thyme
Salt

1. Sprinkle the meat cubes with the pepper. Lightly dredge them in the flour; shake off any excess.

2. In a large flameproof casserole, warm the oil over high heat until shimmering. Add one-fourth of the meat cubes and cook, stirring occasionally, until brown on all sides, about 3 minutes. Remove with tongs

and place on a plate; set aside. Repeat with the remaining meat, cooking in 3 more batches. Drain off all but about 1 tablespoon of the oil.

3. Reduce the heat to moderate and sauté the onion and carrots, stirring, until slightly softened, 2 to 3 minutes. Return the meat to the casserole and stir in the red wine, stock, bay leaf and thyme. Increase the heat to high and bring the stew to a boil.

4. Reduce the heat to low, cover and simmer until the meat is tender, about 2 hours. Season with salt and additional pepper to taste.

—*Diana Sturgis*

CHILAQUILES DE ESTUDIANTE (TORTILLA AND BEEF CASSEROLE, STUDENT STYLE)

Originally created to make use of stale corn tortillas, *chilaquiles* (broken-up old sombreros) is so popular in Oaxaca, Mexico, that the home cook usually begins with fresh tortillas and lets them air-dry while preparing the chile sauce and beef filling. Flavored with mild *ancho* chiles, the casserole is a substantial home-style dish that typifies traditional Mexican cooking. A mixed green salad is all that needs to be added for a complete meal.

F&W BEVERAGE SUGGESTION
Mexican beer such as Carta Blanca

8 TO 12 SERVINGS

1 pound corn tortillas (about 1½ dozen), cut into ½-inch-wide strips
4 ounces dried ancho chiles (about 10)
2 large onions, cut into ¼-inch-thick slices
12 unpeeled garlic cloves
¾ cup whole blanched almonds
2 tablespoons sesame seeds
1 can (28 ounces) Italian peeled tomatoes, with their juices
1½ tablespoons sugar
7 peppercorns
3 whole cloves
½ teaspoon ground cinnamon
1 teaspoon salt
½ cup plus 2 tablespoons vegetable oil
2½ cups chicken stock or canned broth
1½ pounds lean ground beef
1 jar (3 ounces) pimiento-stuffed green olives, drained and sliced
¼ cup (packed) raisins
2 tablespoons cider vinegar
1 cup (about 4 ounces) coarsely shredded queso fresco, or farmer cheese tossed with ½ teaspoon salt
2 cups sour cream, lime wedges, minced fresh coriander, chopped onion, for garnish

1. Spread the tortilla strips on a baking sheet or tray and let them dry out while you prepare the chile sauce and beef filling that follow.

2. To make the chile sauce, pull out and discard the stem from each chile. Cut the chiles in half and seed and devein them. Working with several chile halves at a time, toast them on an ungreased griddle or cast-iron skillet, turning, until they begin to blister, 30 seconds to 1 minute.

3. Bring 6 cups of water to a simmer in a medium saucepan. Add the toasted chiles and simmer over low heat for 15 minutes; drain.

4. Grease a large heavy griddle or skillet. Place over moderate heat, add the sliced onions and garlic in a single layer and cook, turning occasionally with a spatula, until the onions are soft and charred, about 20 minutes, and the garlic cloves are soft and deep golden brown, about 10 minutes.

5. Place the almonds in a small heavy skillet over moderate heat. Toast, shaking the pan frequently, until they are deep golden brown, 3 to 5 minutes. Remove ½ cup of the almonds and set aside for the sauce. Reserve the remaining ¼ cup almonds for the beef filling. Add the sesame seeds to the pan and toast over moderate heat until golden, about 3 minutes. Remove from the heat.

6. In a blender or food processor, puree the tomatoes with their juice. Pour it out to measure it: you should have 3 cups; if you have less, add water to make 3 cups.

7. Place the drained chiles in the blender or food processor. Add 1½ cups of the tomato puree, half of the grilled onion slices, the ½ cup toasted almonds and the sesame seeds.

8. Peel 8 of the garlic cloves and add them to the blender along with 1 tablespoon of the sugar, the peppercorns, 2 of the cloves, ¼ teaspoon of the cinnamon and ½ teaspoon of the salt. Puree the mixture until smooth, about 1 minute.

9. Heat 2 tablespoons of the vegetable oil in a medium noncorrodible saucepan. Scrape the contents of the blender into the pan and cook over moderate heat, stirring occasionally, for 3 minutes. Add the chicken stock, reduce the heat, and simmer for 15 minutes, or until the sauce is slightly thicker than heavy cream.

10. Remove from the heat and set aside. (**The sauce can be made up to 3 days ahead.** Refrigerate in a tightly closed container or freeze for up to 6 months.)

11. To make the beef filling, combine the remaining 1½ cups tomato puree and remaining grilled onion slices in a blender or food processor. Peel the remaining 4 cloves garlic and add them along with the remaining 1 whole clove, ¼ teaspoon cinnamon and ½ teaspoon salt. Puree until smooth.

12. Crumble the ground beef into a heavy medium saucepan and cook over moderate heat, stirring occasionally to break up the lumps of meat, until browned. Add the pureed tomato mixture, the olives, raisins, vinegar, remaining ½ tablespoon sugar and ½ cup of water. Chop the reserved ¼ cup almonds and add to the pan. Bring the mixture to a boil, reduce the heat and simmer, stirring occasionally, until the liquid evaporates, 30 to 40 minutes. Remove from the heat. (**The beef filling can be prepared a day ahead**. Refrigerate, tightly covered. Let return to room temperature before Step 14.)

13. Preheat the oven to 325°. In a large heavy skillet, heat the remaining ½ cup oil until almost smoking. Working in batches, fry the tortilla strips, over moderately high heat, turning them once with tongs, until they are crisp and light golden brown, about 2 minutes. Drain on several layers of paper towels. (The tortilla strips can be fried up to 3 hours before assembling the dish.)

14. Arrange half of the tortilla strips in the bottom of a 13-by-9-inch baking pan. Top with all of the beef filling and then the remaining tortilla strips. Reheat the chile sauce, if necessary, and pour evenly over the top. Sprinkle the cheese on top. Bake, uncovered, until hot, about 30 minutes. Serve accompanied with bowls of sour cream, lime wedges, chopped fresh coriander and chopped onion on the side.

—Jim Fobel

NEW MEXICAN CHILI

This recipe was originally designed, with six pounds of meat, to serve 16 to 18 people. After all, good restaurants consider a cup a respectable portion, especially with a variety of accompaniments, and one-third pound of meat per person, plus beans, should be plenty. Nonetheless, when we taste-tested this chili, it was wolfed down by less than a dozen hungry editors. Therefore it is recommended that this dish serve a mere 10 to 12 and that you make two pots if you are having a really large crowd. Leftover chili will freeze beautifully.

F&W BEVERAGE SUGGESTION
Amber beer, such as Dos Equis or New Amsterdam

10 TO 12 SERVINGS

⅓ cup corn oil
3 large or 5 medium onions, chopped
5 large garlic cloves, chopped
5 tablespoons mild ground chiles, preferably New Mexican
1 teaspoon hot ground chiles or cayenne pepper, or more to taste (see Note)
2 tablespoons ground cumin
1 pound lean ground pork
5 pounds boneless beef chuck, trimmed of excess fat and cut into ½- to ¾-inch cubes
2 teaspoons oregano
2½ teaspoons salt
½ teaspoon freshly ground black pepper
1 can (28 ounces) Italian peeled tomatoes, with their juice
2 bottles (12 ounces each) amber beer, such as Dos Equis or New Amsterdam
1 can (13¾ ounces) beef broth
2 imported bay leaves
2 cans (17 ounces each) kidney beans
Accompaniments: steamed white rice, sour cream, grated Cheddar cheese, thinly sliced scallions and corn tortilla chips

1. In a very large flameproof casserole or stockpot, heat the oil. Add the onions, cover and cook over moderate heat for 5 minutes. Uncover, increase the heat to moderately high and cook, stirring frequently, until the onions begin to brown, 5 to 10 minutes.

2. Add the garlic and cook until fragrant, 1 to 2 minutes. Add the mild and hot ground chiles and the cumin and cook, stirring, for 1 minute to toast the spices. Add the pork and cook, mashing and stirring, until the meat browns and begins to separate.

3. Add the beef, oregano, salt and pepper. Increase the heat to high and cook, stirring frequently, until the meat loses most of its redness, 10 to 15 minutes.

4. Add the tomatoes and their liquid, the beer, beef broth and bay leaves. Bring to a boil, partially cover and reduce the heat to moderate. Cook until the beef is very tender and the sauce is reduced to a chili-like consistency, 1½ to 2 hours.

5. In a medium saucepan, heat the beans in the liquid from the can; drain. Either add them to the chili or serve, as I do, in a separate bowl on the side, along with the other accompaniments: steamed rice, sour cream, grated Cheddar cheese, thinly sliced scallions and corn tortilla chips.

NOTE: It is hard to specify exactly how much hot ground chiles you'll need, as the piquancy of "mild" ground chiles varies from brand to brand. So, for that matter, does the hotness of the hot. I suggest you begin with 1 teaspoon, as in the recipe, and if that is not flaming enough for you, add more, ¼ teaspoon at a time. Remember, you can always make it hotter, but if you overdo the spiciness, there's no reliable way to cool it down.

—Susan Wyler

GLAZED LOIN OF PORK STUFFED WITH CHORIZO AND PINE NUTS

Serve this luscious hearty dish with tiny red potatoes and small green beans in a salsa vinaigrette.

F&W BEVERAGE SUGGESTION
California Zinfandel, such as Buehler

6 TO 8 SERVINGS

1 boneless loin of pork (3½ to 4 pounds), butterflied, with the rack of bones reserved
¼ teaspoon salt
1 pound chorizos, preferably Mexican, or substitute hot Italian sausages and 1 teaspoon cumin
½ cup pine nuts (about 2 ounces)
1 jar (8 ounces) jalapeño jelly (hot or mild depending on your taste preference)

1. Lay the pork roast flat, fatty-side down. Sprinkle with the salt.

2. Remove the sausage casings and crumble the meat, adding the cumin if you are using Italian sausage. Chop in a food processor for 30 seconds, or until evenly ground. Transfer to a bowl and mix in the pine nuts.

3. Lay the chorizo mixture down the center of the roast in a long roll. Bring up the two long sides of the pork around the chorizo mixture. Tie at 1-inch intervals with kitchen twine.

4. Place the rack of bones in a roasting pan. Lay the pork, seam-side down, on top of the bones. Place in a cold oven and turn the temperature to 350°. Roast uncovered for 1 hour.

5. Remove from the oven and spread the jalapeño jelly over the outside of the roast. Return to the oven and roast for 1 hour longer, basting with the pan juices every 15 minutes.

6. Transfer the roast to a carving board and cover loosely with foil; let stand for 15 minutes.

7. Meanwhile, degrease the pan drippings. Reheat the brown juices if necessary. Remove the strings from the roast and cut into ¾-inch slices. Pass the pan drippings separately.

—*Jane Butel*

TENDERLOIN OF PORK "KOBE" STYLE

4 SERVINGS

1 cup soy sauce
3-inch piece of fresh unpeeled ginger, thinly sliced and crushed
3 garlic cloves, unpeeled and lightly crushed
4 navel oranges
1½ to 2 pounds eye of pork loin, well trimmed
½ cup mirin (sweet rice wine)*
½ cup unsalted chicken stock or canned broth
2 tablespoons sugar
1 tablespoon cornstarch dissolved in 1 tablespoon water
1 whole star anise
¼ cup honey
2 tablespoons unhulled sesame seeds
**Available at Japanese groceries*

1. In a noncorrodible dish just large enough to hold the pork, combine ½ cup of the soy sauce, half of the ginger and 2 garlic cloves. With a vegetable peeler, strip the zest from 1 orange. Add the zest and squeeze the juice into the dish. Marinate the pork in this mixture for 2 hours at room temperature, turning occasionally.

2. Preheat the oven to 425°. In a medium noncorrodible saucepan, combine the remaining ½ cup soy sauce, ginger and garlic. Add the mirin, chicken stock, sugar, cornstarch, star anise and the juice of 1 orange. Bring to a boil over high heat, reduce to a simmer and cook uncovered for 10 minutes. Set the sauce aside.

3. Remove the pork from the marinade and pat dry. Place on a rack set over a foil-lined baking sheet. Spread the honey evenly over the pork and sprinkle with the sesame seeds. Roast the pork until the internal temperature registers 140°, about 30 minutes.

4. Remove from the oven and cover loosely with foil to keep warm. Let rest for 10 to 15 minutes. Meanwhile, peel the remaining 2 oranges; halve lengthwise and slice crosswise. Reheat the sauce.

5. Thinly slice the pork against the grain on the diagonal. Arrange on a serving platter and garnish with the orange slices. Strain the sauce into a sauceboat and pass separately.

—*John Ash, John Ash & Co., Santa Rosa, California*

TUSCAN ROAST LOIN OF PORK

F&W BEVERAGE SUGGESTION
Vino Nobile di Montepulciano or Tignanello

6 TO 8 SERVINGS

15 medium garlic cloves, peeled
4 tablespoons fresh rosemary or 3 tablespoons dried
2 tablespoons salt
1½ tablespoons freshly ground pepper
2 tablespoons olive oil
5-pound pork loin, bone in

1. In a food processor or blender, mince the garlic and rosemary with the salt and pepper. With the machine on, drizzle in the olive oil. Process to a thick paste, scraping down the sides of the bowl as necessary.

2. Place the meat, bone-side down, on a rack. Rub the paste all over the meat. Let stand for 2 to 3 hours at room temperature.

3. Preheat the oven to 325°. Place the meat, on the rack, in a roasting pan. Bake for 1½ hours or until the internal temperature reaches 150° on an instant-reading thermometer. Increase the heat to 400° and roast for 10 to 15 minutes longer, until lightly browned.

4. Remove the roast to a carving board. Loosely cover with aluminum foil and let rest for 20 to 30 minutes before serving.

—Diane Darrow & Tom Maresca

PORK MEDALLIONS WITH GINGER SAUCE

Accompany with steamed snow peas with sesame seeds and buttered rice. Follow with tossed endive, romaine and watercress salad with lemon vinaigrette dressing, and fresh mango sherbet with honey wafers.

F&W BEVERAGE SUGGESTION
California Chardonnay

4 SERVINGS

1¼ pounds boneless pork loin, cut into 8 slices about ½ inch thick
½ cup all-purpose flour
6 tablespoons unsalted butter
2 tablespoons minced shallots
2 tablespoons minced fresh ginger
2 tablespoons sherry vinegar
⅔ cup canned chicken broth
2 tablespoons finely chopped parsley
Salt and freshly ground pepper
Sprigs of parsley, for garnish

1. Pat the pork medallions dry with paper towels. Lightly dredge them in the flour; shake off any excess.

2. In a large heavy skillet, melt 2 tablespoons of the butter over moderately high heat until foaming. Add half the pork and sauté until browned on the bottom, 4 to 5 minutes. Turn and cook until browned on the second side, 4 to 5 minutes. Transfer to a serving platter, cover loosely with foil and place in a warm oven. Add the remaining pork to the skillet and sauté in the same way; transfer to the platter.

3. Pour off the excess fat in the skillet. Add the shallots and ginger and stir-fry until the shallots are softened but not browned, 1 to 2 minutes. Add the vinegar and bring to a boil, scraping up any brown bits from the bottom of the skillet. Boil until the sauce is reduced to a glaze, about 3 minutes. Add the chicken broth, increase the heat to high and continue to cook until the liquid is reduced to ⅓ cup, about 4 minutes.

4. Remove the skillet from the heat and whisk in the remaining 4 tablespoons butter, 1 tablespoon at a time. Pour in any meat juices on the platter. Strain the sauce through a fine sieve and stir in the parsley. Season with salt and pepper to taste.

5. To serve, pour the sauce over the pork and garnish with parsley sprigs.

—Diana Steinberg

ONION-CHARRED RIBS

2 TO 4 SERVINGS

3 medium garlic cloves, minced
½ teaspoon coarsely cracked pepper
2 tablespoons Charred Onion Powder (p. 237)
1 tablespoon vegetable oil
2 tablespoons soy sauce
2 teaspoons honey
1 slab (2½ to 3 pounds) pork ribs, cracked

1. In a small bowl, combine all of the ingredients except the ribs. Mix to form a paste. Smear the paste evenly over both sides of the ribs. Cover and let the meat marinate for 1 hour at room temperature or overnight in the refrigerator.

2. Preheat the oven to 350°. Roast the ribs on a rack set over a baking pan, filled with about 1 inch of water, for 1 to 1½ hours until no longer pink.

3. Increase the oven to broil. Place the ribs in the broiler and cook each side 2 to 3 minutes to glaze slightly.

—Anne Disrude

STIR-FRY OF PORK, FENNEL, SPINACH AND SUN-DRIED TOMATOES

The marinating and precooking techniques used for this dish can also be used for any other meat stir-fry. As with all stir-fries, having ingredients prepared and measured out into small bowls helps make the operation fast and efficient.

F&W BEVERAGE SUGGESTION
Alsace Gewürztraminer, such as Willm

2 SERVINGS

½ pound pork shoulder, trimmed of fat
MARINADE: ½ teaspoon tomato paste, ½ teaspoon brown sugar, ½ teaspoon coarse (kosher) salt
¼ cup vegetable oil
2 tablespoons olive oil
AROMATICS: 1 tablespoon minced fresh parsley; 1 tablespoon minced onion; 2 medium garlic cloves, minced; pinch of crushed hot red pepper
1 large fennel bulb, thinly sliced and cut into 1-inch-long matchsticks (about 1¼ cups)
¼ teaspoon salt
Pinch of sugar
1 cup shredded spinach

SEASONINGS: 1 tablespoon drained, finely chopped sun-dried tomatoes packed in olive oil, 1/4 teaspoon fennel seed, freshly ground black pepper to taste

1. Freeze the pork until it is firm enough to slice easily, about 30 minutes. Slice across the grain into thin slices, then cut into 1-by-2-inch pieces.

2. In a medium bowl, combine the pork with the MARINADE ingredients; toss to mix well. Cover and refrigerate for at least 1 and up to 12 hours.

3. In a wok or large skillet, heat the vegetable oil until shimmering. Add the pork with its marinade and stir-fry until it starts to brown, about 3 minutes. Drain in a colander and set aside. (**The recipe can be prepared up to 3 hours ahead to this point.** Cover and refrigerate. Let return to room temperature before proceeding.)

4. Warm a wok or large heavy skillet over high heat until a drop of water evaporates on contact. Pour in the olive oil in a thin stream around the edge; it will smoke immediately.

5. Add the AROMATICS (parsley, onion, garlic and crushed hot red pepper) all at once. Cook, stirring, until fragrant, about 10 seconds.

6. Add the fennel to the wok. Sprinkle with the salt and sugar and toss until almost crisp-tender, 1½ to 2 minutes. (If the vegetable begins to dry out or burn, add 1 tablespoon of water.)

7. Return the precooked pork to the wok and toss over heat until warmed through, about 30 seconds.

8. Add the spinach and SEASONINGS (sun-dried tomatoes, fennel seed and black pepper) and toss to blend the flavors, about 20 seconds. Remove from the heat and season to taste with more salt and pepper.

—*Anne Disrude*

GRILLED PORK SAUSAGE WITH PEPPER, CORIANDER AND LEMON

If you don't feel like stuffing sausage casings, this tasty meat mixture is also delicious formed into patties and pan-fried. The sausage mixture must be prepared a day ahead of time, so plan accordingly.

4 TO 6 SERVINGS

6 ounces fresh pork fat, cut into thick strips, well chilled
1½ pounds fresh pork butt, cut into thick strips, well chilled
4 slices of bread
2 teaspoons salt
2 teaspoons coarsely ground black pepper, preferably Tellicherry
1½ teaspoons grated lemon zest
⅓ cup chopped fresh coriander or flat-leaf Italian parsley
2 yards hog casings packed in salt
1 tablespoon corn or peanut oil
Chopped fresh coriander and grated lemon zest, for garnish

1. Grind the pork fat and then the meat, using the largest grinding plate. Follow with 2 slices of bread to force all the meat through. Discard the bread.

2. Repeat the process using the fine grinding plate.

3. Put the sausage in a medium bowl and add the salt, pepper, lemon zest and coriander. Mix with a fork until the seasonings, fat and lean are evenly distributed. Seal tightly with plastic wrap pressed directly on the surface of the meat. Refrigerate overnight to allow the flavors to develop.

4. Soak the hog casings in tepid water for 30 minutes. Drain and cut into manageable 2- to 3-foot lengths. Flush the casings with cool water to rinse. Cut or tie off any holes in the casings.

5. In a small heavy skillet, fry 1 tablespoon of the pork mixture over moderate heat, turning once, until gray throughout, about 30 seconds. Taste and adjust the seasonings (which should be zesty) if needed.

6. Make a knot at the end of a casing length, slip over a well-oiled stuffing horn and feed the pork mixture into the casing; take care not to overstuff. Knot or tie the open end. Prick the casing with a needle to remove any air bubbles and tie or reverse twist the casing to form 4- to 5-inch links. Repeat with the remaining sausage meat and casings.

7. In a large shallow pan, poach the links in gently simmering water for 10 minutes. Drain, then chill in cold water until cool, 15 minutes. (**The recipe can be prepared to this point 1 or 2 days ahead.** Drain the sausages, pat dry and refrigerate. Let return to room temperature before grilling.)

8. Before grilling, prick the casings all over with a needle, rub them with the oil and grill 3 inches from medium-hot coals, turning until browned, about 10 to 15 minutes. Or pan-fry in a heavy skillet, turning, until browned. Sprinkle with chopped coriander and grated lemon zest, for garnish. Serve with mustard if desired.

—*Barbara Tropp*

SAUSAGE AND FALL VEGETABLE RAGOUT

6 SERVINGS

1 large eggplant, cut into 1-inch cubes
2 teaspoons salt
1 medium head of garlic, separated into unpeeled cloves, plus 2 large garlic cloves, peeled and minced

¾ cup plus 1 tablespoon olive oil, preferably extra-virgin
¼ teaspoon freshly ground black pepper
1½ teaspoons thyme
8 plum tomatoes—peeled, quartered and seeded—or 1 can (14 ounces) Italian peeled tomatoes, drained and quartered
2 small dried hot red peppers, broken in half
¾ pound sweet Italian sausage, separated into links
2 medium zucchini, cut into ¾-inch-thick slices
2 large red onions, quartered and thinly sliced
1 large red bell pepper, thinly sliced
1 large yellow bell pepper, thinly sliced
1 teaspoon oregano
3 tablespoons minced flat-leaf parsley

1. In a colander placed over a bowl, toss the eggplant cubes with 1½ teaspoons of the salt. Set aside to drain for at least 2 and up to 4 hours. Drain the eggplant thoroughly and pat dry on paper towels.

2. Preheat the oven to 375°. Put the unpeeled garlic cloves in a small ovenproof dish. Drizzle on 2 tablespoons of the oil and sprinkle with ¼ teaspoon of the salt, ⅛ teaspoon of the black pepper and ½ teaspoon of the thyme. Roast in the oven, turning once, until soft, about 25 minutes. Let cool; then peel.

3. Toss the tomatoes in a medium bowl with 1 tablespoon of the oil.

4. In a large heavy skillet, heat 2 tablespoons of the oil. Add 1 of the hot peppers and cook over moderate heat until darkened. Remove and discard the pepper. Add the sausages and sauté until nicely browned outside but still pink inside. Set the sausages aside. Pour off the sausage cooking fat, reserving 2 tablespoons in a small bowl.

5. Add 3 tablespoons of the oil to the skillet placed over moderately high heat. Add half the eggplant to the hot oil and sauté quickly, turning and tossing, until evenly browned on all sides. Drain on paper towels. Add 3 more tablespoons of olive oil to the skillet and repeat with the remaining eggplant.

6. Add 1 tablespoon of the oil to the skillet. Add the zucchini and sauté over moderately high heat, tossing, until browned evenly on both sides. Drain on paper towels.

7. Add the remaining 1 tablespoon oil to the skillet. Add the minced garlic, the onions, red and yellow peppers, the second hot pepper and the remaining ¼ teaspoon salt and ⅛ teaspoon black pepper. Reduce the heat to moderately low and cook, partially covered, until the onions are soft and browned, about 35 minutes.

8. Add the sautéed eggplant and zucchini, the oregano, remaining 1 teaspoon thyme, the sausages and the reserved sausage cooking fat. Cook, partially covered, for 10 minutes.

9. Add the whole roasted garlic cloves to the skillet, along with the tomatoes. Cook, tossing gently, until heated through, about 5 minutes. Transfer to a warmed serving dish and garnish with the parsley. **(The recipe can be prepared a day ahead;** reheat until warmed through.)

—Perla Meyers

HOLIDAY CHOUCROUTE

This is a robust and spectacular wintertime dish. As befits the centerpiece of a festive meal, our recipe calls for a superb and delicious Confit of Quail and Spareribs. However the dish will be equally rewarding with only the sausage garnish. Simply skip Steps 1, 5 and 9; in Step 6, roast the new potatoes in ¼ cup fresh rendered pork or goose fat.

F&W BEVERAGE SUGGESTION
Alsatian Riesling, such as Trimbach, or chilled lager beer

10 TO 12 SERVINGS

Confit of Quail and Spareribs (p. 88)
2 tablespoons fresh rendered pork or goose fat
2 large Spanish onions (2½ pounds), thinly sliced
Pork Stock (p. 232)
6 pounds fresh sauerkraut, rinsed and squeezed dry
1 pound double-smoked slab bacon, cut crosswise into 3 pieces
2 cups dry white wine
6 imported bay leaves
1 teaspoon thyme
10 juniper berries
5 garlic cloves, peeled
*8 ounces dried pears, cut into thin strips**
36 small red potatoes (about 4 pounds)
1 pound bratwurst
½ pound Polish sausage
1 pound weisswurst
1 pound knockwurst
½ pound cocktail franks
Kale, for garnish
**Available at natural food stores*

1. Make the Confit of Quail and Spareribs through Step 11 up to a week before you plan to serve the choucroute.

2. In a large flameproof casserole, melt the fat over moderate heat. Add the onions and cook, stirring frequently, until caramelized to a deep golden brown, about 1 hour.

3. Add the pork stock, sauerkraut, bacon, wine, bay leaves, thyme, juniper berries, garlic and pears. Place

over moderately low heat and simmer, partially covered, for 3 hours, stirring occasionally. (Add water ½ cup at a time if the sauerkraut begins to stick.)

4. Let cool to room temperature, cover and refrigerate at least overnight or for up to 1 week to let the flavors mellow.

5. Four or 5 hours before the choucroute is to be served, return the *confit* to room temperature and bake to remove excess fat as directed in Step 12 of the *confit* recipe.

6. Increase the oven temperature to 375°. Pour off all but ¼ cup of the fat accumulated in the baking pan with the *confit*, add the potatoes and toss to coat with the fat. Roast the potatoes for about 30 minutes, or until fork tender. (When the potatoes are done, reduce the oven temperature to 150°.)

7. Meanwhile, warm the sauerkraut slowly over moderate heat until simmering. Add the bratwurst and Polish sausage, burying them in the sauerkraut. Simmer until the bratwurst is no longer pink inside, 30 to 35 minutes. Wrap the meats in foil and keep warm in the oven.

8. Bury the weisswurst and knockwurst in the sauerkraut and simmer until plumped, about 20 minutes. During the last 10 minutes of cooking, add the cocktail franks to the sauerkraut. Wrap the weisswurst, knockwurst and cocktail franks in foil and keep warm in the oven until ready to serve.

9. Meanwhile, complete Step 13 of the *confit* recipe.

10. To serve, garnish the rim of a very large platter with kale. Mound the sauerkraut on the platter. Slice the sausages and arrange them on top, along with the *confit* of quail and spareribs.

—Anne Disrude

BAKED HAM WITH APRICOTS

A 12- to 14-pound ham may seem large for 10 people, and it is. We chose a large ham so that you would have an ample spread, yet still have enough leftovers to try the recipe for Sautéed Ham with Marsala Orange Sauce (recipe follows). The ham bone can also be used to good effect in a soup, such as Ham and Lima Bean Soup (p. 43).

F&W BEVERAGE SUGGESTION
Fruity white wine, such as White Zinfandel or German Riesling, Kabinett

8 TO 10 SERVINGS

1 smoked skinless, shankless ham, 12 to 14 pounds (partially boned)
½ pound dried apricots
2 tablespoons Dijon-style mustard
1 tablespoon cider vinegar
2 cans (8 ounces each) apricot nectar
¼ cup strained apricot preserves

1. Preheat the oven to 325°. Place the ham, fat-side up, on a rack in a roasting pan. With a 2-inch round cookie cutter, mark a row of semicircles in the fat along the cut edge of the ham. Outline each semicircle with a sharp paring knife and slide the knife into the fat at a slight angle to make a pocket 1 inch deep at the center. Make another row of pockets about 2 inches behind the first row. Continue until all of the fat is cut into pockets.

2. Slip an apricot into each pocket so that the edge peeps out. In a small bowl, combine the mustard and vinegar. Lightly brush over the ham and apricots. Insert toothpicks into the pockets to anchor the apricots during cooking. Pour 1½ cups of water into the roasting pan. Tent the ham loosely with foil.

3. Bake the ham for 1 hour. Remove the foil. Baste the ham with the apricot nectar every 20 minutes until the fat is colored, 10 to 12 minutes per pound or about 2 to 2¾ hours.

4. Remove the ham from the oven and place on a serving platter or carving board. Remove the toothpicks. Combine the apricot preserves with 1 tablespoon of the basting liquid from the pan. Brush the ham with the glaze and serve it warm or at room temperature.

—Diana Sturgis

SAUTEED HAM WITH MARSALA ORANGE SAUCE

F&W BEVERAGE SUGGESTION
California Pinot Noir Blanc, such as Sebastiani

4 SERVINGS

7 tablespoons unsalted butter
8 slices of lean cooked ham, ¼-inch-thick (about 1½ pounds)
2 tablespoons minced shallots
⅓ cup dry Marsala
¼ cup fresh orange juice
1 teaspoon freshly grated orange zest

1. Preheat the oven to 250° and set a serving platter in to warm. In a large skillet, melt 2 tablespoons of the butter. Add 4 slices of the ham and sauté, turning once, until browned on the edges, about 1 minute on each side. Arrange the ham slices overlapping on the warmed platter, cover loosely with foil and keep warm in the oven. Add 1 more tablespoon butter to the pan and sauté the remaining 4 slices of ham.

2. Add the shallots to the same skillet and sauté over moderate heat until softened but not browned, about 2 minutes. Add the Marsala and orange juice and cook, stirring to scrape up any browned bits from the bottom and sides of the pan, until the sauce is slightly thickened, about 1 minute.

3. Reduce the heat and stir in ¼ teaspoon of the orange zest and the remaining 4 tablespoons butter, 1 tablespoon at a time. Strain the sauce through a sieve into a warm bowl.

4. Wipe any grease from the ham platter with paper towels. Spoon the warm sauce over the meat. Sprinkle the remaining ¾ teaspoon orange zest on top and serve hot.

—Diana Sturgis

LEG OF LAMB STUFFED WITH LAMB KIDNEYS

6 TO 8 SERVINGS

4 lamb kidneys
1 cup milk
4 tablespoons unsalted butter, softened
¼ cup dry Madeira
1 small leg of lamb, shank half only (preferably under 5 pounds), boned but not butterflied
1 teaspoon salt
½ teaspoon freshly ground black pepper
1 teaspoon minced fresh thyme or a pinch of dried
½ teaspoon minced fresh rosemary or ⅛ teaspoon dried
2 cups lamb or chicken stock, preferably homemade
1 cup crème fraîche
1 tablespoon minced fresh basil or 1 teaspoon dried
1 tablespoon minced fresh tarragon or 1 teaspoon dried
1 teaspoon green peppercorns, drained
1 teaspoon herb mustard

1. Slice the kidneys in half lengthwise and cut away the tough fibers and the fatty cores. Put the kidneys in a small shallow bowl and pour in the milk. Let stand for 1 hour, turning occasionally.

2. Preheat the oven to 500°. Drain the kidneys and pat them dry on paper towels. Cut into ¼-inch dice.

3. In a medium noncorrodible skillet, melt 2 tablespoons of the butter over moderately high heat. When the foam subsides, add the kidneys, season with a pinch of salt and pepper and sauté, tossing frequently, until the kidneys are lightly browned outside but still quite rare, about 1 minute. Using a slotted spoon, transfer to a plate.

4. Pour off the fat and set the skillet over moderately high heat. Pour in the Madeira and bring to a boil, scraping up any brown bits from the bottom of the pan. Cook until reduced to 1 tablespoon, about 1 minute. Off heat, return the kidneys to the skillet and toss to coat with the Madeira. Set aside to cool.

5. Season the boned leg cavity with ¼ teaspoon each of the salt and pepper and the thyme and rosemary. Stuff with the kidneys. Using a trussing needle and string, sew up the lamb, maintaining the leg shape. Spread the remaining 2 tablespoons butter over the leg and season with ½ teaspoon of the salt and the remaining pepper.

6. Put the lamb on a rack in a shallow roasting pan and sear in the hot oven for 15 minutes. Remove from the oven and let rest for 15 minutes. Reduce the oven temperature to 350°.

7. Return the lamb to the oven and roast until the internal temperature reaches 140°, about 45 minutes (10 minutes per pound) for medium-rare. Remove from the oven and cover loosely with foil.

8. Pour off the fat from the roasting pan. Add the stock and boil over moderately high heat until reduced to 1½ cups, about 5 minutes. Add the crème fraîche, basil, tarragon, green peppercorns and mustard. Boil until reduced to 2 cups, about 5 minutes. Strain the sauce through a fine-mesh sieve and season with the remaining ¼ teaspoon salt. To serve, carve the lamb and pass the sauce separately.

—Ostaù de Baumanière, Les Baux-de-Provence, France

ROAST RACK OF LAMB WITH MUSTARD PERSILLADE

F&W BEVERAGE SUGGESTION
Château Lafite or Ducru-Beaucaillou

8 SERVINGS

2 or 3 racks of lamb (about 2 pounds or 8 chops each), trimmed and frenched and chine bones cracked
¼ cup olive oil
1½ cups fresh bread crumbs
½ cup finely chopped parsley
3 tablespoons rosemary, crushed
2 tablespoons grated lemon zest
2 medium garlic cloves, minced
½ cup Dijon-style mustard
1 stick (¼ pound) unsalted butter, melted

1. Preheat the oven to 425°. Lightly brush the lamb with the olive oil. Place the racks, meaty-side up, in a large roasting pan. Roast in the center of the oven for 30 minutes to an internal temperature of 125° on an instant-reading thermometer for rare; 40 minutes and an internal temperature of 135° for medium-rare.

2. Meanwhile, in a large bowl, combine the bread crumbs, parsley, rosemary, lemon zest and garlic, tossing well.

3. Remove the lamb from the oven, cover loosely with foil and let stand for 10 minutes. Leave the oven on and turn to broil.

4. Brush the mustard thickly over the meaty part of the rack. Sprinkle the bread crumb mixture over the mustard, pressing gently so that the

crumbs adhere. Lightly baste the meat with the melted butter.

5. Broil the lamb 6 inches from the heat, leaving the broiler door ajar, for 2 minutes, until the bread crumbs are golden and toasted. Serve hot.

—W. Peter Prestcott

SLICED LOIN OF LAMB WITH GARLIC CREAM

F&W BEVERAGE SUGGESTION
Cru classé Bordeaux, such as 1976 Cos d'Estournel

4 SERVINGS

1 cup heavy cream
8 large garlic cloves, crushed
4 egg yolks
½ teaspoon salt
Pinch of freshly ground white pepper
1 stick (¼ pound) unsalted butter
4 tablespoons olive oil
4 slices French bread (1 inch thick)
2 boneless loins of lamb (about 1 pound)
⅛ teaspoon freshly ground black pepper
1 teaspoon thyme
1 pound plum tomatoes, peeled and thinly sliced
1 pound zucchini, thinly sliced

1. Preheat the oven to 350°. In a small saucepan, bring the cream and the garlic almost to the boil over moderately high heat. Reduce the heat to low and simmer until the garlic is tender, about 40 minutes.

2. Pour the cream and garlic into a food processor or blender and puree until smooth. With the machine on, add the egg yolks, ¼ teaspoon of the salt and the white pepper.

3. Lightly butter a 2-cup soufflé dish or heatproof bowl. Strain the mixture into the dish. Cover directly with a round of buttered parchment or waxed paper. Place in a larger pan of hot water and bake for about 35 minutes, until the custard is set. **(This may be made ahead and held for 2 or 3 hours at room temperature.** Reheat in a gentle water bath.)

4. Meanwhile, make the croutons. In a medium skillet, melt 2 tablespoons of the butter with 1 tablespoon of the olive oil over moderate heat. When the foam subsides, add the slices of bread and sauté, turning once, until golden, about 1 minute on each side. Drain on paper towels and set aside.

5. Preheat the oven to 400°. Rub the 2 loins of lamb with the remaining ¼ teaspoon salt, the black pepper and the thyme. In a skillet, melt 3 tablespoons of the butter with 1 tablespoon of the oil over moderately high heat. Add the loins and sauté, turning, until browned on all sides, about 5 minutes. Transfer to a roasting pan and roast for about 15 minutes, until rare.

6. Meanwhile, in a large skillet, melt 1½ tablespoons of the butter with 1 tablespoon of the oil over moderate heat. Add the tomatoes and sauté, turning gently, until heated through, about 1 minute. Remove to a side dish and cover loosely to keep warm.

7. Melt the remaining 1½ tablespoons butter with the remaining 1 tablespoon oil in the same skillet over moderately high heat. Add the zucchini and sauté, tossing, until tender, about 2 minutes.

8. Remove the lamb from the oven. Let rest for 10 minutes before carving crosswise into thin diagonal slices.

9. To serve, place a crouton on each of 4 warmed dinner plates. Mound one-fourth of the custard on top of each crouton. Overlap several slices of lamb over and around custard. Alternate slices of tomato and zucchini around the lamb.

—Emile Tabourdiau, Le Bristol, Paris, France

LAMB NOISETTES WITH GARLIC FLANS AND RED PEPPER AND BLACK OLIVE PUREES

Lamb noisettes are delicate rounds of meat cut from loin or rib chops. Have the butcher trim them of almost all fat and tie them with string to help hold the shape when the meat is sautéed.

F&W BEVERAGE SUGGESTION
California Zinfandel, such as Louis M. Martini

6 SERVINGS

RED PEPPER PUREE:
2 large red bell peppers, cut into 1-inch pieces
½ cup heavy cream
⅔ cup beef or veal stock
2 teaspoons fresh lemon juice

BLACK OLIVE PUREE:
4 ounces mild oil-cured black olives (about 3 dozen small)
2 garlic cloves
½ teaspoon crushed hot red pepper
6 flat anchovy fillets
Large pinch of powdered mustard
6 tablespoons unsalted butter
2 teaspoons fresh lemon juice, or more to taste

LAMB NOISETTES AND ASSEMBLY:
12 rib lamb chops, 1 inch thick—boned, trimmed and tied
3 medium garlic cloves, halved and lightly crushed
½ teaspoon coarse (kosher) salt
1 teaspoon thyme
½ teaspoon rosemary
6 tablespoons olive oil
4 tablespoons beef or veal stock

Salt and freshly ground black pepper
Garlic Flans (recipe follows)

1. *Prepare the red pepper puree:* Combine the red pepper, cream and stock in a small heavy saucepan. Bring to a boil, reduce the heat to moderate, cover and simmer over low heat, stirring occasionally, until the peppers are very soft, about 15 minutes. Uncover and boil, stirring frequently to prevent scorching, until all the liquid evaporates, about 10 minutes.

2. Transfer the pepper mixture to a food processor and puree until smooth. Blend in the lemon juice. Press through a fine sieve and set aside to cool to room temperature. **(The pepper puree can be made up to 2 days ahead and refrigerated, covered.)**

3. *Make the black olive puree:* Soak the olives in water to cover for 10 minutes; drain, halve and pit them. In a small heavy saucepan, combine the olives, garlic and crushed hot red pepper with 1 cup of water. Bring to a boil over high heat, reduce the heat to moderate and cook, uncovered, stirring frequently, until most of the liquid evaporates and the mixture forms a thick mass and the olives are very soft, about 15 minutes.

4. Transfer the olive mixture to a food processor. Add the anchovies, mustard and butter. Puree until smooth. Press through a fine sieve and mix in the lemon juice. **(The olive puree can be made up to 2 days ahead and refrigerated, covered.)**

5. *Marinate the lamb:* Rub the lamb on both sides with the garlic, salt, thyme and rosemary. Coat with 5 tablespoons of the olive oil, cover loosely with plastic wrap and refrigerate for at least 1 and up to 8 hours.

6. About 30 minutes before serving, remove the lamb from the refrigerator and pat dry with paper towels. Gently reheat the red pepper puree and olive puree in separate small saucepans. Stir 2 tablespoons of stock into each. Season with salt and pepper to taste and keep warm over very low heat.

7. About 10 minutes before serving, warm the remaining 1 tablespoon oil in a large heavy skillet over high heat (or use an extra tablespoon of oil and two skillets). Add the lamb and sauté, pressing the meat with a metal spatula once or twice to encourage formation of a brown crust, 2 minutes for rare, 4 for medium-rare. Turn the meat, sear for 1 minute and reduce the heat to moderately low. Sauté for an additional 3 minutes for rare, 5 minutes for medium-rare. Remove the lamb to a wire rack; pat dry with paper towels and remove the strings.

8. To serve, unmold a garlic flan onto each of 6 warmed plates. Arrange 2 lamb noisettes with a dollop of pepper puree and olive puree on either side.

—Paula Wolfert

GARLIC FLANS

6 SERVINGS

½ pound heads of garlic, cloves separated but unpeeled
1 cup chicken stock, preferably homemade
1 teaspoon unsalted butter
2 pinches of sugar
½ teaspoon white wine vinegar
½ teaspoon salt
¼ teaspoon freshly ground white pepper
2 whole eggs, at room temperature
1 egg yolk, at room temperature
⅔ cup heavy cream, warmed
1 cup milk, warmed

1. In a medium noncorrodible saucepan, place the garlic cloves with cold water to cover. Bring to a boil, cook for 2 minutes and drain. Again cover the cloves with cold water, bring to a boil and cook for 2 minutes. Drain and peel the cloves.

2. Return the garlic to the saucepan. Add the chicken stock, butter, sugar, vinegar, salt and white pepper and simmer, uncovered, until the liquid is reduced to a golden glaze and the garlic is very soft, about 30 minutes. Mash the garlic with the back of a fork to make a puree. Scrape into a bowl.

3. Preheat the oven to 300°. Whisk the whole eggs, egg yolk, cream and milk into the garlic until well blended. Press through a sieve to form a smooth puree. Ladle the garlic custard into 6 small (about 3-ounce) buttered porcelain ramekins or molds (see Note). Place the ramekins in a baking pan in the middle of the oven. Pour enough boiling water into the pan to reach halfway up the sides of the molds. Cook for 30 to 35 minutes, until the flans just puff slightly and the surface barely shudders. Let stand in the hot water for 10 minutes before unmolding. (**The flans can be made 2 hours ahead.** Reheat in their molds in a warm oven for about 5 minutes before unmolding.)

NOTE: If metal molds are used, line the baking pan with 2 or 3 layers of newspaper to act as an insulator.

—Paula Wolfert

Red Pepper and Eggplant Terrine (p. 22).

At left (left to right): Fettuccine with Gorgonzola, Bell Peppers and Basil (p. 139); Goat Cheese and Spinach Tart (p. 120), and Ragout of Lamb with White Beans Provençale (p. 113). Above, Nutted Persimmon Halves (p. 228).

CRUSTY BREAST OF LAMB WITH POTATO-CAULIFLOWER PUREE

This dish is crispy, crunchy, rich and messy. When you poach the meat first, as here, you reduce the fat and have the bonus of a lovely stock in which to cook the vegetables. Have the lamb well trimmed and remind the butcher to crack through the heavy end of the ribs for easy slicing.

F&W BEVERAGE SUGGESTION
California Zinfandel, such as Fetzer

2 TO 3 SERVINGS

2 well-trimmed lamb breasts, about 1¼ pounds each
¾ teaspoon salt
½ teaspoon freshly ground pepper
¾ cup fresh bread crumbs
4 tablespoons minced fresh dill
1 large garlic clove, minced
1 tablespoon olive oil
2 teaspoons fresh lemon juice
1 pound all-purpose potatoes, thinly sliced
½ small head of cauliflower (about ½ pound), cut into florets (about 2 cups)

1. In a large flameproof casserole, combine the lamb breasts with ¼ teaspoon of the salt and 2 quarts of water. Bring to a simmer, skimming; continue skimming for 2 to 3 minutes. Cover and simmer until tender, about 1 hour, turning the lamb breasts once.

2. Preheat the oven to 425°. Transfer the lamb breasts, bony-sides down, to a roasting pan. Season with ¼ teaspoon each of the salt and the pepper. Roast for 15 minutes.

3. In a small bowl, toss the bread crumbs with 2 tablespoons of the dill, the garlic, oil and lemon juice until blended.

4. Remove the lamb from the oven. With a rubber spatula, spread the seasoned bread crumb mixture evenly over the meaty top sides of the lamb breasts, pressing to apply firmly. Roast the lamb for about 20 minutes longer, until the crust is browned and very crisp.

5. Meanwhile, skim off any surface fat from the reserved cooking stock. Add the potatoes and cauliflower and boil until tender, 15 to 20 minutes.

6. Drain the vegetables; then puree through the medium disk of a food mill into a warmed serving dish. Season with the remaining ¼ teaspoon each salt and pepper. Sprinkle the lamb with the remaining 2 tablespoons dill and serve hot with the puree.

—Elizabeth Schneider

An array of fresh homemade cheeses, including Yogurt Cream Cheese (p. 122), Sweet and Savory Whole-Milk Cheeses (p. 121) and Fresh Goat Cheese (p. 120).

LAMB SHANKS BRAISED WITH GARLIC AND TURNIPS

F&W BEVERAGE SUGGESTION
Hearty red wine, such as Inglenook Charbono

4 SERVINGS

4 trimmed lamb shanks (see Note)
1 head of garlic, separated into unpeeled whole cloves
½ cup dry vermouth
½ teaspoon thyme
½ teaspoon salt
¼ teaspoon freshly ground pepper
8 medium turnips (about 1½ pounds), peeled and halved

1. Arrange the lamb on a broiler pan and broil, turning frequently, until well browned on all sides, 20 to 30 minutes.

2. Reduce the oven temperature to 300°. Transfer the shanks to a large flameproof casserole. Add the garlic, vermouth, thyme, salt, pepper and ½ cup of water. Bring to a simmer.

3. Bake, covered, for 45 minutes, or until the lamb is tender. Add the turnips and bake for 30 minutes longer.

4. Stir, then bake for 30 minutes, or until the turnips are tender.

5. With a slotted spoon, transfer the lamb and turnips to a shallow heatproof serving dish. Remove the strings from the lamb; remove the meat from the bones, if you prefer. Keep warm in the turned-off oven.

6. Press the pan juices with the garlic cloves through a sieve or the fine disk of a food mill. Season with additional salt and pepper to taste and pour over the lamb and turnips.

NOTE: Ask the butcher to halve the lamb shanks crosswise, then detach the flaps of breast meat from the wider, more meaty upper shank halves and secure them with string to the narrower, less meaty lower shank halves.

—Elizabeth Schneider

RAGOUT OF LAMB WITH WHITE BEANS PROVENCALE

After cooking, the lamb is allowed to rest overnight, so plan accordingly.

F&W BEVERAGE SUGGESTION
California Zinfandel, such as Sebastiani or Fetzer

6 TO 8 SERVINGS

5 to 6 tablespoons unsalted butter
5 to 7 tablespoons olive oil, preferably extra-virgin
⅓ cup minced shallots
4 large garlic cloves, minced
1 can (35 ounces) Italian peeled tomatoes, drained and cut crosswise into slices
½ teaspoon thyme
¾ teaspoon salt
½ teaspoon freshly ground black pepper
3 to 4 pounds boneless lamb shoulder, trimmed and cut into 1½-inch cubes
Large pinch of sugar
1 tablespoon all-purpose flour

¾ cup dry white wine
Bouquet garni: 1 large sprig of parsley, 1 teaspoon thyme and 1 bay leaf tied in a double thickness of cheesecloth
2 cups beef stock or canned broth
1 large red bell pepper, cut into ½-inch dice
White Beans (p. 124)
½ cup minced fresh parsley
6 anchovy fillets, minced

1. In a medium saucepan, melt 2 tablespoons of the butter in 2 tablespoons of the oil over moderate heat. Add the shallots and half of the garlic and cook for 1 minute without browning. Add the tomatoes and cook, stirring frequently, for 5 minutes. Add the thyme, salt and black pepper.

2. Reduce the heat to low, partially cover and simmer, stirring frequently, until the juices evaporate and the tomato mixture thickens, 20 to 30 minutes. Remove from the heat and set aside.

3. Preheat the oven to 350°. Dry the lamb thoroughly on paper towels. In a large heavy skillet, melt 1 tablespoon of the butter in 2 tablespoons of the oil over high heat. Working in batches, add the lamb cubes without crowding and sauté, turning, until browned on all sides, about 10 minutes. Remove the lamb with a slotted spoon to a side dish. Season with salt and pepper. Add additional butter and oil with the second or third batch if the meat begins to stick.

4. Discard the fat from the skillet. Add 2 tablespoons of the butter and melt over moderate heat. Return the lamb to the skillet. Sprinkle the lamb with the sugar and flour. Cook for 1 to 2 minutes, tossing, until the lamb is glazed and well browned, about 30 seconds. With a slotted spoon, transfer to a large flameproof casserole.

5. Add the wine to the skillet and increase the heat to high. Bring to a boil and cook, scraping up any brown bits from the bottom of the pan, until the wine is reduced to about 3 tablespoons, 3 to 5 minutes.

6. Add the reserved tomatoes, the bouquet garni and the beef stock. Bring to a boil and pour over the lamb. Cover the casserole tightly and bake in the center of the oven for 1½ hours, or until the lamb is tender when pierced with a fork. Remove from the oven. Let cool, cover and refrigerate overnight.

7. Scrape off any congealed fat from the top of the lamb ragout. Remove and discard the bouquet garni. Place the casserole, covered, on top of the stove and warm over moderately low heat.

8. In a medium skillet, heat 1 tablespoon of the olive oil over moderately low heat. Add the red pepper and cook, stirring frequently, until just tender, 6 to 8 minutes.

9. Add the red pepper and the white beans to the ragout. Cook over moderately low heat for 15 minutes. Add the remaining garlic, the parsley and anchovies. Season with additional salt and pepper to taste and serve at once.

—Perla Meyers

MIDDLE EASTERN POTATO AND LAMB GRATIN

8 SERVINGS

3 tablespoons olive oil
2 medium onions, minced
2 large garlic cloves, minced
2 small dried hot peppers, cut in half and seeded
2 pounds lean ground lamb
1½ teaspoons chili powder
½ teaspoon ground cumin
1 teaspoon thyme
1 teaspoon oregano
1 teaspoon marjoram
1 tablespoon tomato paste
1 can (35 ounces) Italian peeled tomatoes, well drained and coarsely chopped
1 teaspoon salt
¼ teaspoon freshly ground black pepper
2 eggs, lightly beaten
4 large baking potatoes (about 2½ pounds)—peeled, thinly sliced and patted dry on paper towels
Cheese Sauce (recipe follows)

1. In a large skillet, heat the oil. Add the onions, garlic and hot peppers and cook over moderate heat until the onions are soft and lightly browned, about 5 minutes. Remove and discard the peppers.

2. Add the lamb and cook, breaking up the meat with a fork, until lightly browned. Add the chili powder, cumin, thyme, oregano and marjoram and cook for 3 minutes.

3. Stir in the tomato paste, chopped tomatoes, salt and black pepper. Bring to a boil, reduce the heat and simmer, uncovered, for about 15 minutes, or until the tomato juices have evaporated. Remove from the heat and let cool.

4. Add the eggs to the cooled meat mixture and blend well. Taste and adjust the seasoning if necessary.

5. Preheat the oven to 350°. To assemble, butter a 13-by-9-by-2-inch (3-quart) baking dish. Layer one-third of the potato slices, overlapping slightly. Season lightly with salt and pepper.

6. Spoon in half of the meat mixture. Top with half the remaining potato slices and season lightly with salt and pepper. Add the remaining meat and top with a final layer of potato slices. Season with salt and pepper and top with the cheese sauce. **(The**

recipe can be prepared ahead to this point and refrigerated or frozen. Let return to room temperature before proceeding.)

7. Put the baking dish on a baking sheet to catch any drips. Bake the gratin for 1½ hours. If the top begins browning too fast, cover loosely with aluminum foil. Remove from the oven and let stand for about 15 minutes before serving.

—*Perla Meyers*

CHEESE SAUCE

MAKES ABOUT 3½ CUPS

3 cups milk
Bouquet garni: ½ teaspoon thyme, 1 bay leaf and 10 parsley stems tied in a double thickness of cheesecloth
5 tablespoons unsalted butter
⅓ cup all-purpose flour
2 egg yolks
Pinch of freshly grated nutmeg
½ cup freshly grated Parmesan cheese
½ teaspoon salt
¼ teaspoon freshly ground pepper

1. In a heavy medium saucepan, bring the milk and bouquet garni to a boil over moderately high heat. Immediately remove from the heat and let stand for 10 minutes. Remove the bouquet garni.

2. In a medium saucepan, melt the butter over moderate heat. Stir in the flour and cook for 2 minutes, stirring constantly, without browning to make a roux.

3. Whisk the hot milk into the roux and bring to a boil. Cook, whisking constantly, until thick and smooth. Remove from the heat and whisk in the egg yolks, nutmeg, cheese, salt and pepper.

—*Perla Meyers*

FRICASSEE OF RABBIT AND WILD MUSHROOMS

Though this dish is somewhat time consuming, it can be made up to two days ahead and reheated.

F&W BEVERAGE SUGGESTION
Fresh young Côtes du Rhône such as Domaine Renjardière

6 TO 8 SERVINGS

2 young rabbits (about 4 pounds each)
6 tablespoons corn oil
4 tablespoons all-purpose flour
3 cups dry red wine, such as Côtes du Rhône
2 cups chicken stock, preferably homemade
12 small white boiling onions, peeled
1 bay leaf
1 garlic clove
1 teaspoon thyme
2¼ teaspoons salt
½ plus ⅛ teaspoon freshly ground pepper
½ pound fresh shiitake mushrooms, cèpes or morels
4 tablespoons unsalted butter

1. Cut each rabbit into 8 pieces: 2 fore legs, 2 hind legs and 2 sections of saddle, each split in half down the spine.

2. In each of 2 large skillets, heat 3 tablespoons of oil. Add the rabbit pieces and sauté, turning, over moderate heat until golden, about 15 to 20 minutes. Transfer the rabbit to a large flameproof casserole.

3. Add 2 tablespoons of flour to one of the skillets and stir the flour into the fat. Cook, stirring constantly, until the mixture becomes golden brown, about 3 minutes. Take care not to let the flour burn. Whisk in 1½ cups of the wine and 1 cup of the stock. Bring to a boil, whisking, until thickened and smooth. Remove from the heat. Repeat with the second skillet and the remaining flour, wine and stock.

4. Strain the sauce from both skillets through a fine-mesh sieve. Pour over the rabbit in the casserole. Add the onions, bay leaf, garlic, thyme, 2 teaspoons of the salt and ½ teaspoon of the pepper. Bring to a boil, reduce the heat and simmer, covered, for 1½ to 2 hours, or until the rabbit is fork tender. (Cooking times for different parts of the rabbit vary greatly, so check the loin and saddle sections after 30 minutes; remove them as soon as they are tender. Cover loosely with aluminum foil and set aside.) Add about ¼ cup water to the pot occasionally if the liquid evaporates. With a slotted spoon, remove the rabbit and onions and set aside.

5. Degrease and clarify the sauce by setting the casserole partly off the burner so that only half of the surface of the liquid gently bubbles. Simmer, skimming the fat and any impurities from the side of the pot frequently, for 30 minutes. Return the rabbit and onions to the sauce and remove from the heat. (**The recipe can be prepared to this point up to 2 days ahead.** Cover and refrigerate.)

6. Rinse the mushrooms and dry with paper towels. Slice or quarter depending on their size.

7. In a large skillet, melt the butter over moderate heat. Add the mushrooms and the remaining ¼ teaspoon salt and ⅛ teaspoon pepper. Cover, reduce the heat to a simmer and cook for 30 minutes, checking occasionally and adding a tablespoon of water if necessary.

8. To serve, reheat the rabbit in the sauce if necessary. With a slotted spoon, transfer the rabbit and onions to a serving platter. Pour the sauce over the rabbit and arrange the mushrooms on top.

—*Lydie Marshall*

NOISETTES OF VENISON WITH ORANGE-ROSEMARY SAUCE

This quick sauté sauced with a combination of crème fraîche, mustard, orange rind and rosemary is a vibrant, intensely flavored dish. Serve with fresh pasta if desired.

F&W BEVERAGE SUGGESTION
Bordeaux, such as Château Cos d'Estournel

4 SERVINGS

4 tablespoons unsalted butter
2 tablespoons olive oil
8 noisettes of venison (4 to 6 ounces each), cut ¾ inch thick from the saddle
2 cups crème fraîche
3 to 4 tablespoons Dijon-style mustard
2 tablespoons freshly grated orange zest
1 tablespoon minced fresh rosemary or 1½ teaspoons dried, crumbled
½ teaspoon salt
¼ teaspoon freshly ground pepper

1. In a large skillet, melt the butter in the oil over moderate heat. Add the venison noisettes and sauté, turning once, for about 3 minutes on each side, until rare. Remove to a warm platter and cover loosely with foil to keep warm.

2. Whisk together the crème fraîche and 3 tablespoons of mustard until blended. Place the skillet with the venison drippings over moderate heat and add the crème fraîche mixture, whisking until incorporated. When the sauce is warmed through, reduce the heat, add the orange zest and rosemary and simmer for 5 minutes. Season with the salt and pepper and up to 1 more tablespoon mustard, to taste.

3. To serve, place two noisettes of venison on each plate and generously coat with the sauce.

—Patricia Wells

HALF-CASTE HOT POT

This variation of a Mongolian hot pot comes with three dipping sauces. Each guest cooks his choice of skewered foods in the seasoned broth—which is eaten as a soup at the end of the meal—then dips it in a sauce and either wraps it in a lettuce leaf or eats it plain. The ingredients are pre-skewered in bite-size portions on many wooden skewers—about 100. Each guest is presented with a plate of skewered tidbits, ready to be cooked in the steaming broth.

F&W BEVERAGE SUGGESTION
Sparkling French wine from the Loire, such as Bouvet Brut

8 TO 10 SERVINGS

¼ pound angel-hair pasta or capellini
4 skinless, boneless chicken breast halves (about 2 pounds), cut cross-wise into ¼-inch-thick slices (see Note) and then into 2-inch lengths
1½ pounds beef tenderloin, cut crosswise into ¼-inch-thick slices (see Note) and then into 2-inch lengths
1 pound medium shrimp, peeled and deveined
1 pound sea scallops, quartered
1 pound large mushrooms, quartered
1 pound shallots, cut in half lengthwise
1 pound pearl onions
4 medium zucchini, cut into ½-inch-thick rounds
2½ quarts chicken stock or canned broth
2 garlic cloves
1 tablespoon minced fresh ginger
4 heads of Bibb lettuce, leaves separated
Horseradish Dipping Sauce (p. 237)
Soy-Sesame Dipping Sauce (p. 237)
Mustard-Caper Dipping Sauce (p. 237)
½ pound fresh spinach, stemmed and shredded
2 medium carrots, very thinly sliced

1. In a large pot of boiling salted water, cook the pasta until tender to the bite. Drain and rinse under cold running water; set aside in a bowl of cold water.

2. Prepare the skewers: thread one group of skewers with a slice of chicken and a slice of beef at the end of each skewer. Thread a second group of skewers with one shrimp and one scallop on each. Thread a third group of skewers with one mushroom, one shallot, one onion and one zucchini piece on each. Divide the skewers among 8 to 10 small platters or large plates. (**The recipe can be prepared ahead to this point.** Cover and refrigerate the noodles and the skewered food.)

3. In a large flameproof casserole or chafing dish, combine the chicken stock, garlic and ginger. Heat until boiling. Place on a heat source, such as Sterno or a hot plate, in the middle of the table and let simmer. Place the lettuce leaves on plates within easy reach of the guests. Place small bowls of the three dipping sauces on the table.

4. To serve, each guest cooks several skewered portions at a time in the stock. Each portion is dipped in a dipping sauce and transferred to a lettuce leaf. The lettuce leaf is rolled up like a mandarin pancake and eaten with the fingers.

5. When all the skewered portions have been eaten, taste the broth for saltiness and dilute with hot water as necessary. Return to a simmer. Add the spinach and carrots to the stock. Drain the pasta and add to the pot. Cook until the ingredients are warmed through, 2 to 3 minutes. Serve in soup bowls.

NOTE: Freeze the meats for 30 minutes until firm enough to slice without tearing.

—W. Peter Prestcott

EGGS & CHEESE

PEPPER AND SPAGHETTI FRITTATA

F&W BEVERAGE SUGGESTION
Beaujolais or California Gamay

6 TO 8 SERVINGS

6 tablespoons extra-virgin olive oil
2 medium onions, chopped
5 medium garlic cloves, minced
10 bell peppers, chopped (about 4 cups)
⅛ teaspoon sugar
½ teaspoon oregano
1 teaspoon salt
¼ teaspoon freshly ground black pepper
6 ounces spaghetti, cooked and drained
8 eggs
½ cup freshly grated Parmesan cheese
¼ cup minced fresh parsley

1. In a large ovenproof skillet, heat the olive oil. Add the onions, garlic and bell peppers, and sauté over moderately high heat, stirring frequently, until the vegetables begin to brown, about 30 minutes. Season with the sugar, oregano, ½ teaspoon of the salt and ⅛ teaspoon of the black pepper.

2. Preheat the oven to 350°. Add the cooked spaghetti to the skillet and toss well. Cook, stirring occasionally, until the pasta is lightly browned, about 10 minutes.

3. In a medium bowl, beat the eggs with ¼ cup of water and the remaining ½ teaspoon salt and ⅛ teaspoon black pepper. Stir in ¼ cup of the Parmesan cheese and 2 tablespoons of the parsley.

4. Pour the egg mixture over the pasta and stir with a fork to distribute evenly. Cook without stirring until the eggs are set around the edges. Place in the oven and bake until the eggs are set, about 10 minutes.

5. Slide the frittata onto a platter and cut into wedges. Toss together the remaining ¼ cup Parmesan cheese and 2 tablespoons parsley and pass separately.

—Anne Disrude

SCRAMBLED HUEVOS RANCHEROS

F&W BEVERAGE SUGGESTION
California dry Chenin Blanc, such as Girard

6 SERVINGS

2 tablespoons unsalted butter
1 small onion, finely diced
12 large eggs, lightly beaten
2 tablespoons minced fresh, green jalapeños
6 ounces hard, aged goat cheese, such as Tomme (about 1½ cups), grated
Crisply fried corn tortillas, preferably blue-corn, as accompaniment

1. In a large skillet, melt the butter over moderate heat. Add the onion and sauté until lightly browned, about 3 minutes.

2. Add the eggs, jalapeños and cheese. Reduce the heat to moderately low and cook, stirring, until lightly scrambled and still soft and moist. Serve with the fried tortillas.

—John Sedlar, St. Estéphe, Manhattan Beach, California

SAVORY CHEESE SOUFFLE

F&W BEVERAGE SUGGESTION
Beaujolais, such as Louis Latour

4 TO 6 SERVINGS

1 stick (¼ pound) unsalted butter
6 tablespoons freshly grated Parmesan cheese
⅓ cup all-purpose flour
1¾ cups milk
1 teaspoon salt
⅛ teaspoon freshly ground black pepper
Pinch of cayenne pepper
½ teaspoon freshly grated nutmeg
1 teaspoon Dijon-style mustard
6 whole eggs, separated
1¼ cups grated Gruyère cheese (about 5 ounces)
1 egg white

1. Preheat the oven to 400°. Use 2 tablespoons of the butter to thoroughly grease a 2-quart soufflé dish. Sprinkle evenly with 2 tablespoons of the grated Parmesan cheese and set aside.

2. In a heavy medium saucepan, melt the remaining 6 tablespoons butter over moderate heat. Add the flour and cook, stirring, for 3 minutes without allowing to color to make a roux.

3. Meanwhile, in another medium saucepan, scald the milk over moderately high heat. Gradually whisk the hot milk into the roux. Bring to a boil, whisking constantly. Cook, stirring, until the béchamel thickens, about 2 minutes. Stir in the salt, black pepper, cayenne, nutmeg and mustard.

4. Remove from the heat and beat the egg yolks into the béchamel base, one at a time.

5. Stir in the grated Gruyère and 2 tablespoons of the remaining Parmesan cheese. (**The soufflé can be prepared ahead to this point.** Simply cover the surface with waxed paper or plastic wrap to prevent a skin from forming. If held for more than 1 hour, refrigerate. Let return to room temperature before continuing.)

6. Beat the 7 egg whites until stiff but not dry or grainy. Stir about one-fourth of the beaten whites into the soufflé base. Working quickly and lightly, blend the lightened base into the remaining egg whites. Turn the mixture into the prepared soufflé dish. Smooth the top with a spatula and run your thumb around the souf-

flé to form a groove around the top about 1 inch in from the rim; this will form the classic "top hat" when the soufflé rises.

7. Bake the soufflé in the lower third of the oven for 35 minutes. Sprinkle the remaining 2 tablespoons Parmesan cheese over the top and bake for about 5 minutes longer, until the cheese is melted. Serve the soufflé immediately.

—John Robert Massie

CARAMELIZED ONION SOUFFLE

F&W BEVERAGE SUGGESTION
Hearty red, such as Côtes-du-Rhône or California Zinfandel

MAKES 8 INDIVIDUAL SOUFFLES OR 1 LARGE SOUFFLE

2 sticks (1/2 pound) unsalted butter
2 pounds Spanish onions, coarsely chopped
2 tablespoons freshly grated Parmesan cheese
1 3/4 cups milk
1/3 cup all-purpose flour
1 teaspoon salt
1/8 teaspoon freshly ground black pepper
Pinch of cayenne pepper
1/4 teaspoon thyme
1 teaspoon Dijon-style mustard
6 whole eggs, separated
1 egg white
Quick Tomato Sauce (p. 234)

1. In a large skillet, melt 1 stick of the butter over moderately low heat. Add the onions and cook, stirring frequently, for about 45 minutes, until deep golden brown.

2. Preheat the oven to 400°. Use 2 tablespoons of the remaining butter to grease one 2-quart or eight 1-cup soufflé dishes. Sprinkle evenly with the grated cheese.

3. In a heavy medium saucepan, melt the remaining 6 tablespoons butter over moderate heat. When the foam subsides, add the flour and cook, stirring, for 3 minutes without allowing to color to make a roux.

4. Meanwhile, in a large saucepan, scald the milk over moderately high heat. Gradually whisk the hot milk into the roux. Bring to a boil, whisking constantly. Cook, stirring, until the béchamel thickens, about 2 minutes. Stir in the salt, black pepper, cayenne, thyme and mustard.

5. Remove from the heat and beat the egg yolks into the béchamel base, one at a time.

6. Scrape the caramelized onions into a food processor and puree until smooth. (Note: If the onion puree is watery, return it to the skillet and cook over moderately high heat, stirring constantly, until the liquid evaporates.) Scrape the puree into the béchamel base and mix well. (**The soufflé may be prepared ahead to this point.** Simply cover the surface with waxed paper or plastic wrap to prevent a skin from forming. If held for more than 1 hour, refrigerate. Let the soufflé base return to room temperature before continuing.)

7. Beat the 7 egg whites until stiff but not dry or grainy. Stir about one-fourth of the beaten whites into the soufflé base to lighten it. Quickly fold the lightened base into the remaining egg whites. Turn the mixture into the prepared soufflé dishes. Smooth the tops with a spatula and run your thumb around each soufflé to form a groove around the top about 1 inch in from the rim; this will form the classic "top hat" shape when the soufflé rises.

8. Bake in the bottom third of the oven until the soufflé is well puffed and browned, about 12 minutes for the 1-cup size, 35 to 40 minutes for the 2-quart size.

9. Using two forks, split open the top of each individual soufflé and ladle in about 1/4 cup of the tomato sauce. For the large soufflé, ladle in about 3/4 cup of sauce. Serve immediately, with the extra sauce on the side.

—John Robert Massie

LEEK AND CABBAGE FLAN

6 TO 8 SERVINGS

6 large leeks (white and 2 inches of the green)
1 small head of cabbage (about 1 1/4 pounds), quartered
4 tablespoons unsalted butter
1 1/4 teaspoons salt
1/2 teaspoon freshly ground pepper
1/4 pound slab bacon, cut into 1/4-inch dice
2 medium onions, minced
1/2 cup coarsely grated Gruyère cheese
8 eggs
1 cup heavy cream
1/3 cup freshly grated Parmesan cheese
2 tablespoons bread crumbs

1. Halve the leeks lengthwise and rinse thoroughly. Thickly slice crosswise and rinse again; drain well.

2. Cook the cabbage in a large saucepan of salted boiling water for 4 minutes; drain, then dry well on a kitchen towel. Cut the tough cores off the cabbage quarters. Thinly slice the cabbage and measure out 3 cups; reserve the remainder for another use.

3. In a large skillet, melt 2 tablespoons of the butter over moderate heat. Add the leeks and season with 1/2 teaspoon of the salt and 1/4 teaspoon of the pepper. Add 1/4 cup of water, cover and simmer until the leeks are tender and all the water has evaporated, about 10 minutes. With a slotted spoon, transfer the leeks to a bowl and set aside.

4. Melt the remaining 2 tablespoons butter in the skillet. Add the

bacon and cook over moderate heat until lightly browned, about 3 minutes. Remove with a slotted spoon and set aside.

5. Preheat the oven to 350°. Discard all but 3 tablespoons of the fat in the skillet. Add the onions and cook until softened but not browned, 2 to 3 minutes. Add the cabbage, cover and cook until soft and translucent, about 5 minutes.

6. In a large bowl, combine the cabbage mixture, leeks, bacon, Gruyère, ¼ teaspoon of the salt and ⅛ teaspoon of the pepper.

7. In another bowl, combine the eggs, cream, half the Parmesan and the remaining ½ teaspoon salt and ⅛ teaspoon pepper. Whisk until well blended. Add this custard mixture to the cabbage and leek mixture and stir well to mix.

8. Butter a 10-inch porcelain quiche pan or deep pie plate. Lightly coat the bottom with some of the Parmesan cheese and bread crumbs. Spoon the cabbage-leek mixture into the pan and top with the remaining Parmesan cheese and bread crumbs.

9. Bake for 1 hour, or until nicely browned on top. Serve hot or warm directly from the dish. (**The flan can be made and baked in advance.** Reheat, covered, in a 250° oven until hot in the center. Any leftover can be refrigerated and reheated the next day.)

—*Perla Meyers*

GOAT CHEESE AND SPINACH TART

F&W BEVERAGE SUGGESTION
California Sauvignon Blanc, such as Cakebread

6 TO 8 SERVINGS

5 tablespoons olive oil, preferably extra-virgin
2 medium garlic cloves, thinly sliced
½ pound fresh spinach, stemmed
Salt and freshly ground black pepper
6 ounces mild goat cheese, such as Montrachet, crumbled
1¼ cups crème fraîche
4 eggs
4 tablespoons freshly grated Parmesan cheese
1 tablespoon finely minced fresh thyme or ½ teaspoon dried
1 teaspoon finely minced fresh rosemary or ¼ teaspoon dried
¼ teaspoon freshly ground white pepper
Basic Tart Shell Dough (p. 202)—in a 10" porcelain quiche dish, blind baked
4 to 6 plum tomatoes, cut crosswise into ¼-inch slices
1 teaspoon fresh thyme leaves (optional)
½ teaspoon fresh rosemary leaves (optional)
12 small oil-cured black olives, preferably Niçoise

1. Preheat the oven to 375°. In a large heavy skillet, heat 3 tablespoons of the oil. Add the garlic and cook over moderate heat, stirring constantly, until golden, about 3 minutes. Remove and discard the garlic.

2. Reduce the heat to low and add the spinach to the oil in the skillet. Toss and sprinkle with a pinch of salt and black pepper. Cover and cook, stirring occasionally, until barely wilted, about 2 minutes. Transfer the spinach to a colander and press lightly to squeeze out excess liquid.

3. In a food processor, combine the goat cheese, crème fraîche, eggs, Parmesan cheese, minced thyme and rosemary. Add ½ teaspoon salt and the white pepper. Process until blended and smooth.

4. Distribute the drained spinach evenly over the bottom of the prebaked tart shell. Pour the cheese mixture over the spinach. Bake in the center of the oven for 30 to 35 minutes, or until the custard is set and golden. Remove the tart from the oven and let cool on a wire rack for about 5 minutes. The cheese custard filling will settle slightly.

5. Preheat the broiler. Arrange the sliced tomatoes, overlapping slightly, in a single layer over the custard. Brush with 1 tablespoon of the olive oil. Sprinkle with ¼ teaspoon black pepper and the whole thyme and rosemary leaves. Cover the pastry edge with foil to prevent burning.

6. Broil the tart about 6 inches from the heat until the edges of the tomatoes are lightly browned, 1 to 2 minutes. Remove from the broiler. Remove the rim of protective foil and brush the tomatoes with the remaining 1 tablespoon oil. Garnish decoratively with the olives. Let the tart cool for about 20 minutes before serving.

—*Perla Meyers*

FRESH GOAT CHEESE

This recipe produces a firm white cheese with a mildness and resiliency reminiscent of mozzarella. It's particularly good drizzled with a fruity olive oil and served with tomatoes, fresh basil and crusty bread. Use a dairy or chocolate thermometer to guarantee the right temperature when heating the milk.

MAKES ABOUT 1½ POUNDS

*4 quarts fresh goat milk**
¼ cup plain active-culture yogurt, such as Dannon, at room temperature
*½ teaspoon vegetable rennet**
**Available at health food stores*

1. Prepare the starter: In a small saucepan, heat 1 cup of the milk to 90°. Remove from the heat and whisk in the yogurt. Pour into a glass bowl or jar, cover with cheesecloth or a kitchen towel and let stand in a warm place overnight. Alternatively, pour into a warmed thermos, cover with the lid and let stand overnight. The

starter will be tart and slightly thickened.

2. In a small bowl, combine the rennet with ½ cup of water at room temperature. Stir to dissolve and set aside.

3. In a large flameproof casserole or noncorrodible saucepan, heat the remaining 3¾ quarts milk to 85°. Remove from the heat and whisk in the starter until blended. Let stand for 20 minutes.

4. Whisk in the dissolved rennet and let stand, without stirring, until curds form, about 40 minutes. The curds will form a smooth soft mass that pulls away from the edges of the casserole, and the whey will collect around the edge. To test the curds, slip a slotted spoon underneath and lift up until the curds break. If the break is clean, the curds are ready; if the curds break in a ragged line or are still soft, let stand for an additional 10 minutes. With a long stainless steel knife, cut the curds into 1-inch chunks.

5. Place the casserole in a larger pot with enough simmering water to reach one-third of the way up the sides. Cook, gently stirring, until the curds have completely separated from the whey and are slightly firm to the touch, about 15 minutes.

6. Line a large sieve or colander with several layers of dampened cheesecloth, leaving enough to hang over the sides by at least 1 inch. Set the sieve over a large bowl. With a slotted spoon, gently transfer the curds to the sieve. Let drain for 5 minutes. Fold the cheesecloth over the curds and turn them over; pour off the whey in the bowl. Refrigerate the sieve and the bowl for at least 2 hours or overnight.

7. Remove the cheesecloth before serving. The cheese can be stored, either wrapped in cheesecloth or waxed paper in the refrigerator for up to 4 days.

NOTE: Be sure all equipment is scrupulously clean throughout the cheese-making process, or the cheese could pick up some unpleasant bacteria. If the finished cheese froths up in a spongelike mass, it has gone bad and should be thrown out.

—*Gail K. LeCompte*

SAVORY WHOLE-MILK CHEESE

This cheese can be served plain, seasoned with herbs, sun-dried tomatoes or olives, or soaked in olive oil. The addition of heavy cream will produce a richer and smoother cheese.

MAKES ¾ TO 1 POUND

2 quarts whole milk
1 cup heavy cream (optional)
4 unpeeled garlic cloves, bruised
2 to 3 tablespoons fresh lemon juice
½ teaspoon coarse (kosher) salt
¼ to ½ teaspoon coarsely cracked pepper

OPTIONAL SEASONINGS:
¼ cup minced sun-dried tomatoes
¼ cup minced black or green olives
2 tablespoons minced fresh herbs, such as tarragon, chives or parsley

OPTIONAL MARINADE:
Olive oil, preferably extra-virgin
Unpeeled garlic cloves

1. In a large, noncorrodible saucepan or flameproof casserole, combine the milk, cream and garlic. Bring to a simmer, reduce the heat to low and steep for 1 hour. Discard the garlic.

2. Stir 2 tablespoons of the lemon juice into the milk. Simmer until the milk curdles, 5 to 10 minutes. (If the milk does not curdle, add the remaining juice and continue cooking for several seconds.)

3. Line a large colander or sieve with several layers of dampened cheesecloth, leaving plenty of overhang. Set the colander in the sink and pour in the curdled milk. Set the colander in a large bowl and let stand until the curds are cooled to room temperature, pouring off the whey as it accumulates in the bowl. Wrap the cheese in the cheesecloth (leaving it in the colander), cover both the colander and bowl with plastic wrap and refrigerate for 8 hours or overnight.

4. Pour off any more whey that has drained from the curds. Turn the cheese into a bowl and stir in the salt and pepper. Season the cheese, if desired, with any of the optional seasonings and pack into a crock or bowl, or shape as follows.

5. To shape into small rounds, line small ramekins or ¼-cup measuring cups with a layer of dampened cheesecloth. Divide the cheese among the molds, pressing to fill evenly.

6. For further flavor, place the rounds, still wrapped in cheesecloth, in a single layer in a shallow dish. Cover with olive oil and add unpeeled garlic cloves to season. Cover the dish with waxed paper and store in the refrigerator for up to 1 week.

—*Anne Disrude*

SWEET WHOLE-MILK CHEESE

This recipe uses the same technique as the Savory Whole-Milk Cheese, but different seasonings. Again, the cream is optional but is particularly nice in a sweet cheese.

MAKES ¾ TO 1 POUND

2 quarts whole milk
1 cup heavy cream (optional)
1 cinnamon stick
6 whole cloves
2 to 3 tablespoons fresh lemon juice

OPTIONAL SEASONINGS:
¼ cup minced dried fruit, such as raisins, pears, sour cherries or peaches, soaked in hot water until softened

1. In a large noncorrodible saucepan or flameproof casserole, combine the milk, cream, cinnamon and cloves. Bring to a simmer, reduce the heat to low and steep for 1 hour to infuse the milk with the spice flavor. Remove and discard the spices.

2. Continue as directed in Steps 2 and 3 of Savory Whole-Milk Cheese. Pour off any more whey that has drained from the curds. Turn the cheese into a bowl and season, if desired, with the optional seasonings. Pack into a crock or bowl, or shape into hearts (see Yogurt Cream Cheese, Step 4) or little rounds (see Savory Whole-Milk Cheese, Step 5).

—*Anne Disrude*

YOGURT CREAM CHEESE

With the addition of different accompaniments, this cheese can be used as a sweet or savory spread.

MAKES 2½ TO 3 CUPS

2 quarts plain, active-culture whole-milk yogurt

SAVORY SEASONINGS:
Freshly ground black pepper
1 cup finely minced scallions
Coarse (kosher) salt

SWEET SEASONINGS:
Sugar
Fresh berries

1. Line a large colander or sieve with several layers of dampened cheesecloth, about 16 inches square, allowing the edges to overhang. Set the colander over a large bowl and pour in the yogurt. Let drain for about 30 minutes.

2. Pour off the liquid in the bowl. Tie the ends of the cheesecloth together with a long piece of string. Tie the string to a faucet so that the cheese is suspended over a sink or suspend the cheese over a large bowl. Let drain for at least 12 hours and up to 24 hours. (The cheese can be eaten after 12 hours but will not have as thick and creamy a texture.)

3. Turn the cheese into a medium bowl, cover with a dish towel and refrigerate. The cheese will keep, refrigerated, for up to 4 days.

4. **To shape and flavor as a savory cheese:** Divide the cheese into three equal amounts. Mound each on a 6-inch square of cheesecloth and, with a blunt knife, smooth into a rough log. Wrap in the cheesecloth and roll into a smooth log about 4 inches long and 1½ inches in diameter. Remove the cheesecloth and roll each log in the pepper, then in the scallions, pressing lightly so that they will adhere. Sprinkle with salt to taste. Serve with toasted French bread or crackers.

To shape and flavor as a sweet cheese: Line 4 heart-shaped noncorrodible molds (see Note) with a layer of dampened cheesecloth. Divide the cheese among the molds, pressing to fill the corners. Turn out onto serving plates and sprinkle with sugar and raspberries. Serve with brioche.

NOTE: Although *coeur à la crème* molds are a natural choice, any heart-shaped mold may be used. It is not necessary to have the drainage holes.

—*Diana Sturgis*

SWISS CHEESE FONDUE

F&W BEVERAGE SUGGESTION
Dry white, such as Alsatian Sylvaner

4 SERVINGS

1 garlic clove cut in half
1⅓ cups dry white wine
1 pound Gruyère or Emmenthaler cheese or a mixture of the two, coarsely grated (about 3½ cups)
1 teaspoon cornstarch
2 tablespoons Cognac or kirsch
Coarsely cracked pepper
1 loaf of French bread, cut into 1-inch slices, then quartered

1. Rub the inside of a fondue pot or a heavy enamel saucepan with the cut garlic clove and discard. Pour in the wine and bring to a simmer. Gradually stir in the cheese and cook, stirring frequently with a wooden spoon, until melted and smooth.

2. In a small bowl, stir the cornstarch into the Cognac until blended. Pour into the melted cheese and stir over high heat until the mixture is blended and slightly thickened, about 2 minutes. Reduce the heat so that the fondue barely bubbles. Serve with the French bread and long-handled fondue forks for dipping.

—*Anne Disrude*

VEGETABLES

VEGETABLES

ARTICHOKE MOUSSE

6 TO 8 SERVINGS

8 large artichokes
3 tablespoons fresh lemon juice
2 tablespoons all-purpose flour
1 tablespoon plus ½ teaspoon salt
2 cups heavy cream
2 tablespoons unsalted butter
¼ cup truffle juice (see Note)
¼ teaspoon freshly ground white pepper

1. Using a stainless steel knife, cut off the stem at the base of the artichoke. Bend back and snap off all the outer leaves. Cut off the inner leaves where they meet at the top of the base. With a paring knife, cut around the base to remove the tough dark green outer skin. Fill a large noncorrodible saucepan with 1 quart of water acidulated with the lemon juice. As you trim the artichokes, drop the hearts into the saucepan to prevent discoloration.

2. Add the flour and 1 tablespoon of the salt to the saucepan and stir well. Bring to a boil over high heat. Reduce the heat to moderate and simmer until the hearts are completely tender, about 30 minutes. Drain and cool.

3. Scoop out and discard the hairy chokes. Cut each heart into quarters.

4. In a food processor or blender, puree the artichoke hearts. Strain the puree through a stainless steel sieve into a medium, noncorrodible saucepan.

5. Over moderately low heat, stir in the cream, butter and truffle juice. Add the remaining ½ teaspoon salt and the pepper and heat through, stirring frequently.

NOTE: Truffle juice is available in 7-ounce cans at specialty food shops.

—Ostaù de Baumanière,
Les Baux-de-Provence, France

TEXAS CAVIAR

4 SERVINGS

1 can (16 ounces) black-eyed peas, drained
1 large red onion, finely chopped
¾ cup vegetable oil
¼ cup red wine vinegar
1 garlic clove
½ teaspoon salt
Cracked black pepper
Cayenne pepper

1. In a bowl, combine the black-eyed peas, onion, oil, vinegar and garlic. Mix thoroughly. Season with the salt and black pepper and cayenne to taste.

2. Cover and refrigerate for at least 2 days and up to 2 weeks. Remove the garlic clove after 1 day. Drain before serving.

—The American Festival Café,
New York City

WHITE BEANS

MAKES ABOUT 3 CUPS

1 cup dried Great Northern white beans
1 medium onion, peeled and stuck with 1 whole clove
1 medium carrot, cut in half
1 medium celery rib with leaves, cut in half
3 peppercorns
Bouquet garni: 1 large sprig of parsley, ¼ teaspoon thyme and 1 small bay leaf tied in a double thickness of cheesecloth
½ teaspoon salt

1. Place the beans in a large flameproof casserole and cover with 2 inches of cold water. Bring to a boil and remove from the heat. Cover and let stand for 1 hour. Preheat the oven to 325°.

2. Drain the beans, return them to the casserole and add cold water to cover by 2 to 3 inches. Add the onion, carrot, celery, peppercorns and bouquet garni. Bring to a boil and immediately remove from the heat.

3. Cover tightly and cook in the oven for 1½ hours, or until tender. Remove the bouquet garni. Season with the salt. If not using the beans immediately, let them cool in their cooking liquid. Drain before using.

NOTE: The cooked beans will keep in their liquid stored in the refrigerator for up to 10 days.

—Perla Meyers

FRIJOLES NEGROS (BLACK BEANS)

Mexican cooks flavor this satisfying side dish with fresh *epazote* leaves, a mild herb. If you can't find it here, use a California bay laurel leaf instead; the flavor won't be the same, but it will be quite delicious.

8 SERVINGS

1 pound dried black beans, rinsed and picked over
8 slices of hickory-smoked bacon, cut into ½-inch squares
1 large onion, chopped
4 garlic cloves, crushed through a press
12 fresh epazote leaves or 1 California bay laurel leaf
1 teaspoon salt, or more to taste

1. Place 6 cups of cold water in a large flameproof casserole. Add the beans and bring to a boil over high heat. Boil for 2 minutes, turn off the

heat and let the beans soak, covered, for 1 hour.

2. Bring to a boil over high heat; reduce the heat to a simmer.

3. Meanwhile, in a medium skillet, cook the bacon over moderate heat, stirring frequently, until the fat is rendered and the bacon is crisp and golden brown. Remove the bacon with a slotted spoon and add it to the beans. Discard all but 2 tablespoons of the bacon drippings.

4. Add the onion to the drippings and sauté over low heat until softened and translucent, about 5 minutes. Add the garlic and cook for 1 minute longer. Scrape the onion, garlic and bacon fat into the beans. Add the *epazote* or bay leaf and simmer, stirring occasionally, for 2 hours, or until the beans are tender. If the beans take longer to cook, add ½ cup water for each additional ½ hour of cooking time. Season with the salt after the beans are tender.

—Jim Fobel

SWEET AND SOUR BEETS

This recipe is easily prepared through Step 2 up to two days before the party. The finishing steps take about 10 minutes on the stovetop.

8 SERVINGS

1½ pounds beets
2 tablespoons unsalted butter
2 tablespoons red wine vinegar
1 tablespoon sugar
½ teaspoon salt

1. Preheat the oven to 425°. Wrap the beets in aluminum foil and bake for 1 hour, or until tender when pricked with a knife. Remove from the oven and let cool.

2. Trim and peel the beets. Cut the beets into ⅛-inch-wide matchsticks. **(The recipe may be prepared to this point up to 2 days ahead.** Cover the beets and refrigerate.)

3. In a large skillet, melt the butter over moderately high heat. Add the beets and cook, tossing frequently, for about 2 minutes. Add the vinegar, sugar and salt and cook the beets until heated through, 3 to 5 minutes.

—W. Peter Prestcott

SHREDDED BRUSSELS SPROUTS WITH PARMESAN CHEESE

The Brussels sprouts may be prepared through Step 3 up to one day ahead and refrigerated. They are quickly reheated on the stovetop.

8 SERVINGS

2 pounds Brussels sprouts
4 tablespoons unsalted butter
¼ cup olive oil
1 cup beef stock or canned broth
1½ cups heavy cream
1 tablespoon fresh lemon juice
1¼ cups freshly grated Parmesan cheese (about 5 ounces)
Salt and freshly ground pepper

1. Shred the Brussels sprouts in a food processor or with a hand grater.

2. In a large heavy skillet over moderately high heat, melt the butter in the oil. When the foam subsides, add the Brussels sprouts and toss until well coated. Reduce the heat to moderate, cover and cook, until the sprouts are heated through, about 5 minutes.

3. Add the beef stock and cook, stirring, until the broth has been absorbed by the sprouts. **(The recipe may be prepared to this point 1 day ahead.** Cover and refrigerate.)

4. Stir in the heavy cream and lemon juice. Cover and cook until the sprouts are cooked through but still somewhat crunchy, 5 to 10 minutes. Stir in 1 cup of the Parmesan cheese and season with salt and pepper to taste.

5. Turn into a warmed serving dish. Sprinkle with the remaining ¼ cup cheese. Serve hot.

—W. Peter Prestcott

COLIFLOR EN CREMA DE QUESO (CAULIFLOWER IN CHEESE SAUCE)

Although complementary to Mexican dishes, this delicious vegetable side dish goes well with many standard main courses. In Mexico, the cream has a flavor and consistency close to *crème fraîche*. I substitute a combination of slightly reduced heavy cream and sour cream. You can prepare this dish a day ahead and serve it chilled or at room temperature. Garnish with the bacon and almonds just before serving.

6 SERVINGS

1 head of cauliflower (about 2 pounds)
1 teaspoon salt
1 tablespoon vegetable oil
1 garlic clove, crushed through a press
1 cup heavy cream
1 cup shredded mild Cheddar cheese (4 ounces)
½ cup sour cream
6 slices hickory-smoked bacon, cut into ¼-inch squares
2 tablespoons sliced blanched almonds

1. Trim away about ½ inch from the bottom of the cauliflower stem; also remove any leaves. Place the whole head in a large saucepan and cover it with cold water. Add ½ teaspoon of the salt, cover the pan and bring the water to a boil over high heat. Reduce the heat slightly and boil until the cauliflower is just tender when pierced with a fork, about 10 minutes after the water comes to a

boil. Let the cauliflower cool to room temperature in the water.

2. In a medium saucepan, heat the vegetable oil. Add the garlic and cook over low heat for 1 minute after the garlic begins to sizzle. Add the cream and bring to a boil over moderate heat. Boil gently for 5 minutes. Stir in the cheese and immediately remove from the heat. Stir in the sour cream and the remaining ½ teaspoon salt. Pour the cheese sauce into a bowl, cover the surface with waxed paper and let cool to room temperature.

3. Place the bacon in a medium skillet over moderate heat. Fry, stirring frequently, until the bacon is crisp and golden brown. Remove with a slotted spoon and drain on paper towels.

4. To serve at room temperature, simply place the cauliflower upright in a serving dish and pour the cheese sauce over it; sprinkle with the reserved bacon and the almonds. To serve chilled, pour the cheese sauce into a bowl just large enough to hold the head of cauliflower. Invert the cauliflower in the sauce, cover and refrigerate until ready to serve. Then transfer, right-side up, to a serving dish and pour the sauce over it. Garnish with the bacon and almonds.

—Jim Fobel

GRATIN OF CAULIFLOWER WITH GOAT CHEESE AND FONTINA

---

4 TO 6 SERVINGS

8 tablespoons unsalted butter
1¼ cups heavy cream
½ teaspoon salt
¼ teaspoon freshly ground white pepper
1 small head of cauliflower (about 1½ pounds), separated into florets
¼ pound lightly smoked ham, cut into ¼-inch dice
¼ pound Italian Fontina cheese, cut into ½-inch dice
¼ cup coarsely crumbled mild goat cheese, such as Montrachet or a fresh American goat cheese (about 2 ounces)

1. In a large heavy saucepan, melt 4 tablespoons of the butter over moderate heat. Add the cream and boil until reduced to ¾ cup, about 10 minutes. Season with ¼ teaspoon salt and ⅛ teaspoon white pepper. Remove from the heat.

2. Preheat the oven to 350°. Meanwhile, steam the cauliflower for 5 to 8 minutes, or until just tender; do not overcook. Remove to a colander and set aside.

3. In a small skillet, melt 2 tablespoons of the butter. Add the ham and sauté over moderate heat until lightly browned, about 2 minutes.

4. Arrange the cauliflower in a well-buttered 6-cup oval gratin dish. Season with the remaining ¼ teaspoon salt and ⅛ teaspoon white pepper. Sprinkle the ham over the cauliflower. Spoon the reduced cream over the cauliflower and sprinkle with the diced Fontina and bits of goat cheese. Dot with the remaining 2 tablespoons butter. **(The recipe can be set aside in a cool place for up to several hours before baking.)**

5. Bake in the center of the oven for 15 minutes. Increase the oven temperature to 450° and bake for 10 minutes, or until the top is nicely browned. Serve hot.

—Perla Meyers

BRAISED CELERY WITH ALMONDS

Those who never think of celery standing on its own as a vegetable will be pleasantly surprised at how appropriate the clean, herbal flavor and crunch of this dish can be in an otherwise rich meal.

8 SERVINGS

3 cups chicken stock or canned broth
1 cup dry white wine
1 medium onion, finely chopped
1 large carrot, finely chopped
6 sprigs of Italian flat-leaf parsley
3 whole cloves
10 peppercorns
1 bay leaf
3 bunches of celery (16 or 18 large outer ribs)
1 large red bell pepper, finely diced
2 tablespoons unsalted butter
2 ounces (about ½ cup) slivered blanched almonds

1. In a medium noncorrodible saucepan, bring the chicken stock, wine, onion, carrot, parsley, cloves, peppercorns and bay leaf to a boil. Reduce the heat to moderately low and boil gently, uncovered, until reduced to 1 cup, 30 to 40 minutes.

2. Strain and reserve the stock. **(The recipe can be prepared to this point 24 hours in advance of serving.** Let cool, cover and refrigerate.)

3. Peel away the celery strings and cut the ribs crosswise on the diagonal into 2-inch pieces. In a large skillet, bring the reserved stock, celery and red pepper to a boil. Reduce the heat to a simmer, cover and cook, stirring often, until the celery is tender but still retains a slight crunch, about 30 minutes.

4. Meanwhile, in a small skillet, melt the butter over moderate heat. Add the slivered almonds and cook,

stirring often, until golden brown, about 5 minutes. Set aside.

5. When the celery is tender, transfer it to a heated vegetable dish with a slotted spoon and cover to keep warm. Return the pan with the stock to high heat and boil rapidly until reduced to a few syrupy spoonfuls, about 5 minutes. Stir the almonds and any butter remaining in the small skillet into the reduced juices. Pour over the celery and serve hot.

—Michael McLaughlin

ROASTED CORN ON THE COB WITH PAPRIKA AND LIME BUTTER

This flavor combination hails from the American Southwest. Any leftover cooked corn can be removed from the cob, wrapped carefully and stored in the freezer. Reheated with butter in a microwave or on the stove, encore corn is a pleasant side dish.

6 SERVINGS

1 stick (1/4 pound) unsalted butter, softened
1/4 cup fresh lime juice
1 teaspoon paprika
6 ears of sweet corn

1. In a blender or food processor, combine the butter, lime juice and paprika. Mix until smooth and well blended. Scrape into a bowl, cover and refrigerate for up to three days.

2. Prepare the corn: Pull down—but do not remove—the husk. Strip off the inner silk. Rub each ear with a heaping tablespoon of the paprika-and-lime butter and replace the husk. Place the corn on a rack over hot barbecue coals or in a preheated 475° oven and roast, turning occasionally, for 20 minutes.

—Molly O'Neill

SAUTEED CUCUMBERS

This elegant dish makes a nice accompaniment to grilled or roasted meats, game, poultry or flavorful fish. Try it with salmon for a striking combination of green and pink.

6 SERVINGS

2 large cucumbers, preferably European seedless
3 tablespoons unsalted butter
1/2 teaspoon salt
1/4 teaspoon freshly ground white pepper

1. Peel the cucumbers and cut in half lengthwise. Using a teaspoon, scoop out and discard any seeds. Slice the cucumbers crosswise into 1/2-inch-wide crescents.

2. In a large saucepan of boiling salted water, blanch the cucumbers for 1 minute after the water returns to the boil; then drain. Rinse under cold running water until cool. Drain well and pat dry. (**The recipe can be prepared to this point up to 1 hour ahead.** Set aside at room temperature.)

3. In a large skillet, melt the butter over moderately high heat until just foaming. Add the cucumbers, season with the salt and pepper and cook, tossing frequently, until heated through, 2 to 3 minutes. Serve hot.

—John Robert Massie

VERONIQUE'S EGGPLANT VINAIGRETTE

This makes a lovely side dish or appetizer. It can be made a day ahead and refrigerated; let return to room temperature before serving, or the oil may congeal. Serve alone or with French bread to sop up the sauce.

4 TO 6 SERVINGS

1 large eggplant, halved lengthwise, then cut lengthwise into 1/2-inch slices
2 tablespoons coarse (kosher) salt
3/4 cup olive oil, preferably extra-virgin
1 small onion, finely chopped
2 tablespoons distilled white vinegar
1 tablespoon red wine vinegar
1 tablespoon fresh lemon juice
1/4 cup ketchup
1/4 cup finely chopped pimiento
1 tablespoon finely chopped dill pickle
4 Calamata olives, pitted and finely chopped
1 garlic clove, minced
1 tablespoon minced fresh parsley
1/4 teaspoon salt
1/8 teaspoon freshly ground pepper
1/8 teaspoon thyume

1. Place the eggplant in a large colander set over a bowl. Sprinkle with the coarse salt, toss to coat both sides and let drain for 1 hour. Rinse well under cold water and pat dry. Place the slices between 2 kitchen towels. Place a cookie sheet on top and weigh down with a large pot of water for 30 to 60 minutes, to press out excess moisture.

2. In a large skillet, warm 3 tablespoons of oil over moderately high heat until shimmering. Working in batches, fry the eggplant in a single layer, turning once, until browned and soft, about 5 minutes on each side. Remove and drain on paper towels. Fry the remaining eggplant, adding more oil as necessary to prevent sticking.

3. In a medium bowl, whisk together the remaining oil (there will be about 4 tablespoons), the onion, white and red wine vinegars, lemon juice, ketchup, pimiento, pickle, olives, garlic, parsley, salt, pepper and thyme. Blend well.

4. Pour half the dressing into a large flat noncorrodible dish. Lay the

eggplant on top in a single layer. Spread the remaining dressing on top of the eggplant. Let stand for 2 hours before serving or refrigerate overnight. Return to room temperature before serving.

—Véronique, Brookline, Massachusetts

MEDITERRANEAN EGGPLANT

Here's my recipe for a great vegetable dish, which is echoed in almost all Mediterranean countries. Long ago people realized that eggplant, tomatoes and pepper makes a delicious dish.

MAKES ABOUT 1½ CUPS

1 large eggplant (about 1¼ pounds)
4 tablespoons olive oil
2 tablespoons thinly sliced scallions
1 small green bell pepper, finely diced
1 large red bell pepper, finely diced
1 tablespoon minced garlic
2 flat anchovy fillets, crushed with a fork
1 medium tomato—peeled, seeded and chopped
2 tablespoons fresh lemon juice
Salt and freshly ground black pepper

1. Preheat the oven to 425°. Prick the eggplant, brush with 1 tablespoon of the olive oil and set in a baking dish. Bake for about 40 minutes, until very soft.

2. Meanwhile, in a heavy medium skillet, heat the remaining 3 tablespoons olive oil. Add the scallions and cook over low heat until soft and translucent, about 2 minutes. Add the green and red bell peppers, the garlic, anchovies and tomato. Cook, stirring, for 15 minutes. Set aside.

3. As soon as it is cool enough to handle, peel the eggplant, reserving about one-fourth of the peel; cut the peel into fine slivers. Cut open the eggplant and scrape away any hard seeds. Squeeze the pulp through your fingers to remove any bitter juices. In a bowl, mash the eggplant with a fork.

4. Add the mashed eggplant and slivered skin to the pepper-tomato mixture in the skillet. Cook over moderate heat, stirring constantly, until all the liquid evaporates and there is only oil and vegetables left, about 15 minutes. (Stir carefully to avoid scorching, but be sure to allow the mixture to become somewhat darker in color.)

5. Season with the lemon juice and salt and black pepper to taste. Set aside to cool; then cover and refrigerate for up to 2 days.

—Paula Wolfert

FIDDLEHEAD FERNS

One basic method of preparation will yield pretty, springy ferns ready to be sauced, sautéed or dressed for salad. The simplest cooking method, boiling, works best; it maintains the best color and texture and eliminates the bitterness that occasionally occurs in these furled sprouts.

Preparation: Trim the base of each fern to leave only a tiny tail beyond the circumference of each circular shape. If there is any of the furry brown covering remaining on the plants, rub it off. Rinse briskly in a colander under running water.

Cooking Method: Drop into a large pot of lightly salted boiling water. Boil until tender throughout—about 5 minutes, testing often. Do not undercook or the full flavor will be lost. Drain well.

Serving Suggestions: 1) Serve the cooked, drained fiddleheads at once with melted butter, or Hollandaise sauce, or a light cream or cheese sauce. 2) Or, after cooking and draining, cool the fiddleheads in a bowl of ice water, then drain and dry. Refrigerate, covered, until serving time. At serving time, heat butter in a large skillet and sauté the fiddleheads until heated through. 3) Or, after cooking and draining, cool the fiddleheads in a bowl of ice water, then drain and dry. Combine with a light mustard vinaigrette, cover and refrigerate until serving time.

—Elizabeth Schneider

GRILLED LEEKS WITH BACON, CAPER AND CREAM SAUCE

4 TO 6 SERVINGS

16 small or 12 medium leeks
¼ pound bacon, minced
1 garlic clove, minced
¾ cup heavy cream
1 tablespoon chopped, drained capers
½ teaspoon freshly ground pepper
1 tablespoon minced Italian flat-leaf parsley
4 tablespoons unsalted butter, melted
¼ teaspoon salt

1. Trim the roots off the end of each leek. Cut off the tough dark green ends to leave the white and tender green. Halve each leek lengthwise, but leave them connected at the root end on the smaller leeks. Split the larger ones completely in half. Rinse carefully under running water to remove all dirt.

2. In a large pot of boiling salted water, cook the leeks until tender when pierced with a knife but still intact, about 5 minutes. Drain and rinse under cold running water; drain well. (**The recipe can be made ahead to this point.** Cover and refrigerate.)

3. In a large skillet, cook the bacon over moderate heat, stirring occasionally, until lightly browned and crisp.

Drain off the excess fat. Add the garlic and cook, stirring, for 2 minutes. Stir in the cream, capers and ¼ teaspoon of the pepper. Simmer until slightly thickened, about 3 minutes. Reduce the heat to low and add the parsley.

4. Light the grill or preheat the broiler. Lightly brush the leeks with the melted butter and season with the salt and remaining ¼ teaspoon pepper. Grill or broil about 4 inches from the heat, basting with the remaining butter and turning occasionally, until the leeks are lightly browned and crisp on the outside and creamy soft inside, about 5 minutes.

5. Meanwhile, reheat the sauce and keep warm over very low heat. Remove the leeks from the heat and cut into 1-inch lengths. Spoon the warm sauce on top.

—*Charlene Rollins, New Boonville Hotel, Boonville, California*

WILD MUSHROOMS EN PAPILLOTE

Wild mushrooms are perfect for this type of cooking because their heady perfume is released in a burst of aroma at the table. The large papillote makes a dramatic presentation. Depending on the season, you can use cèpes, shiitakes or morels. Chanterelles give off too much liquid for this type of enclosed cooking.

F&W BEVERAGE SUGGESTION
St.-Emilion such as Château Pavie

4 TO 8 SERVINGS

1 pound fresh cèpes, shiitakes or morels
¼ cup olive oil
½ cup crème fraîche
¼ cup chopped fresh tarragon or 1 teaspoon dried
2 garlic cloves, minced
1 teaspoon salt
¼ teaspoon freshly ground pepper
1 tablespoon unsalted butter, melted

1. Preheat the oven to 400°. Rinse the mushrooms thoroughly and dry them on paper towels. If they are very large, quarter them; otherwise leave them whole.

2. In a large bowl, combine the oil, crème fraîche, tarragon, garlic, salt and pepper. Add the mushrooms and toss to coat.

3. Cut a 12-inch heart out of parchment paper or heavy-duty aluminum foil. Brush melted butter over the paper. Put the mushrooms on one half of the heart. Fold the other half over the morels and with a series of overlapping crimp folds, seal the papillote. Place on a baking sheet.

4. Bake the papillote in the center of the oven for 20 minutes. Serve at once, cutting the paper open at the table.

—*Lydie Marshall*

CEPES BORDELAISE

8 SERVINGS

1 pound fresh cèpes (see Note)
4 tablespoons unsalted butter
3 garlic cloves, minced
1 teaspoon fresh lemon juice
1 teaspoon salt
½ teaspoon freshly ground pepper

1. Trim the ends off the stems of the cèpes. Separate the stems from the caps. Mince the stems. Set the whole caps aside.

2. In a large skillet, melt the butter over moderate heat. Add the garlic and mushroom stems and sauté, stirring occasionally, until softened, about 5 minutes.

3. Add the whole mushroom caps and 2 tablespoons of water to the pan. Cover, reduce the heat to low and cook gently (adding additional water if the mushrooms begin to stick) until tender, about 40 minutes. (**The mushrooms can be prepared ahead to this point.** Set aside, partially covered, at room temperature.)

4. Before serving, reheat the cèpes. Season with the lemon juice, salt and pepper and serve hot.

NOTE: If fresh cèpes are not available, fresh shiitake (Golden Oak) mushrooms can be substituted.

—*John Robert Massie*

TUSCAN POTATO AND MUSHROOM PIE

F&W BEVERAGE SUGGESTION
Chianti, such as Conte Capponi or Antinori

6 SERVINGS

½ ounce dried porcini mushrooms or cèpes
1 cup chicken stock or canned broth
½ pound slab bacon, cut into ¼-inch dice
6 tablespoons unsalted butter
2 large onions, quartered and thinly sliced
Salt and freshly ground pepper
Pinch of sugar
½ pound fresh mushrooms, cut into ¼-inch slices
2 large garlic cloves, minced
½ cup minced fresh parsley
Basic Tart Shell Dough (p. 202)
3 hard-cooked eggs, finely diced
2 baking potatoes (about 1 pound), peeled and cut crosswise into very thin slices
¾ cup heavy cream
2 whole eggs
1 egg yolk
Coarse (kosher) salt

1. Place the dried porcini in a strainer and rinse under warm run-

ning water to remove any sand or grit. Combine the porcini and stock in a small saucepan. Bring to a boil, reduce the heat, cover and simmer until soft and tender, 25 to 30 minutes; drain. If the porcini still feel gritty, rinse again. Pat dry on paper towels. Cut into ½-inch dice.

2. Meanwhile, in a medium saucepan of boiling water, blanch the bacon for 1 minute. Drain well; pat dry.

3. In a large heavy skillet, melt 2 tablespoons of the butter over moderate heat. Add the bacon and cook, stirring constantly, until lightly browned but not crisp. Transfer with a slotted spoon to paper towels.

4. Discard all but 3 tablespoons fat from the skillet. Increase the heat to moderately high and add the onions. Cook, stirring frequently, until they begin to brown, about 5 minutes. Reduce the heat to low and season with a pinch of salt, pepper and sugar. Cover and cook until very soft and nicely browned, 20 to 30 minutes. Remove with a slotted spoon and set aside.

5. Wipe the skillet clean. Add 1½ tablespoons of the butter and melt over high heat. Add half the sliced fresh mushrooms and sauté until lightly browned, about 3 minutes. Remove to a small mixing bowl with a slotted spoon. Add 1½ more tablespoons of butter to the skillet and sauté the remaining mushrooms.

6. Melt the remaining 1 tablespoon butter in the skillet over moderate heat. Add the diced porcini and garlic and cook, stirring constantly, for 2 minutes. Transfer to the bowl containing the fresh mushrooms. Add the parsley, toss and season lightly with salt and pepper.

7. Preheat the oven to 425°. Lightly oil an 8½-inch tart pan at least 1¾ inches deep with a removable bottom. On a lightly floured surface, roll out half of the dough into a 13-inch circle. Fit the pastry into the prepared tart pan. Do not trim the overhang.

8. Cover the bottom of the tart shell with the sautéed onions. Sprinkle with half of the bacon. Cover with half of the mushroom mixture. Sprinkle with half of the diced hard-cooked eggs. Arrange all the sliced potatoes in an overlapping pattern. Sprinkle with additional salt and pepper. Repeat layering with the remaining mushrooms, bacon and hard-cooked egg.

9. In a small bowl, whisk together the cream, 1 whole egg and the egg yolk until well blended. Season with ¼ teaspoon salt and ⅛ teaspoon pepper and pour over the filling.

10. Roll out the remaining dough into a 13-inch circle. Fit evenly over the filling. Press the edges of the top and bottom dough together. Trim evenly so that the overhang is 1 inch. Roll up the overhang toward the tart pan and crimp to form a decorative edge. Be careful not to tear the pastry. If torn, patch with a piece of excess dough.

11. Make a small hole in the center of the pie to allow steam to escape during baking. Beat together the remaining whole egg with 1 tablespoon of water to make an egg glaze. Brush over the top of the pie and sprinkle the crust lightly with coarse salt.

12. Place on a baking sheet in the center of the oven and bake for 15 minutes. Reduce the heat to 350° and bake for 60 to 75 minutes longer, or until the crust is nicely browned and crisp.

13. Remove the pie from the oven. Let set for 5 minutes. Remove the sides of the tart pan and let the pie cool on a rack for 20 to 25 minutes.

14. To serve, use a wide spatula to carefully slide the pie onto a serving platter. Cut into wedges and serve warm. (**The pie can be made a day ahead.** Reheat, covered with foil, in a 350° oven, until warm.)

—*Perla Meyers*

DEEP-DISH VIDALIA ONION PIE

If you were to cross an Alsatian onion tart and a Sicilian pizza, you might come up with this deliciously plump, chewy pie. Served with a ripe tomato salad and crisp Italian white wine, it makes a lovely lunch or light supper; cut into tiny rectangles and offered with a chilled Riesling or Gewürztraminer, it becomes a luscious hors d'oeuvre.

6 SERVINGS

CRUST:
1 envelope (¼ ounce) active dry yeast
¼ cup warm (105° to 110°) water
¼ teaspoon sugar
⅓ cup milk
2 tablespoons unsalted butter, cut up
1 teaspoon salt
½ teaspoon caraway seeds
About 2¼ cups all-purpose flour

FILLING:
2 tablespoons unsalted butter
4 medium-large Vidalia onions, cut into ½-inch dice (about 3 cups)
1½ tablespoons all-purpose flour
¾ cup milk
¼ teaspoon salt
8 ounces cottage cheese
3 eggs

1. *Make the crust:* In a small bowl, dissolve the yeast in the water with

the sugar. Let proof until fluffy; if the mixture does not bubble up, begin again with fresh ingredients.

2. In a small saucepan, heat the milk, butter, salt and caraway, stirring, until the butter almost melts. Pour the liquid into a large bowl.

3. Stir in ¾ cup of the flour, then the yeast mixture. Stir in 1 cup more flour, then knead in however much more flour is easily absorbed to make a medium-soft dough. Turn the dough out onto a floured surface and knead until it is medium-firm, smooth and no longer sticky, adding flour as needed. Place in a buttered bowl and turn to coat the dough. Cover the bowl with plastic and let the dough rise until at least doubled in bulk, about 1 hour.

4. *Meanwhile, make the filling:* In a large heavy skillet, melt the butter over moderately low heat. Add the onions and cook, stirring frequently, until the onions are golden and soft, about 30 minutes (reduce the heat if the onions begin to brown).

5. Add the flour and cook, stirring, for 2 minutes. Add the milk and salt, increase the heat to moderate and cook, stirring, until the mixture is thick, almost pasty, 2 to 3 minutes.

6. Blend together the cottage cheese and eggs. Stir in the onions. Season to taste with salt.

7. Preheat the oven to 375°. On a lightly floured surface, roll or pat the dough to form a rectangle slightly larger than the baking dish or pan you'll be using, which should be about 12 by 8 by 2 inches. Butter the dish and press in the dough to extend about three-quarters up the sides of the dish. Press the dough well into the dish to cover evenly. Pour in the onion filling.

8. Bake in the center of the oven for 45 minutes, or until the crust is nicely browned and the filling is golden brown. Let cool in the pan for 15 minutes, then gently lift out the pie with large spatulas and let cool slightly on a rack before cutting into serving pieces. (**The pie can be made ahead of time.** Serve at room temperature or reheat in a 350° oven for 15 minutes.)

—*Elizabeth Schneider*

GREEN CHILE STUFFED WITH DUXELLES IN GARLIC CHEVRE SAUCE

F&W BEVERAGE SUGGESTION
California Zinfandel, such as Lytton Springs

8 SERVINGS

6 tablespoons unsalted butter
1½ pounds mushrooms, finely chopped
2¾ cups heavy cream
1 teaspoon salt
¾ teaspoon freshly ground white pepper
8 large fresh green Anaheim chiles
5 garlic cloves, minced
2 shallots, finely chopped
½ cup dry white wine
5 ounces young goat cheese, preferably California chèvre or Montrachet
1 tablespoon peanut oil
¼ cup cayenne pepper

1. In a large heavy saucepan, melt 4 tablespoons of the butter over moderate heat. Add the mushrooms and cook, stirring occasionally, until they have given up their liquid and the liquid has evaporated, 15 to 20 minutes.

2. Add ½ cup of the cream, ½ teaspoon of the salt and ½ teaspoon of the white pepper. Continue to cook over moderate heat until the mixture is very thick, about 5 minutes. Set the mushroom filling aside.

3. Roast the chiles under a broiler or over a gas flame, turning, until completely blackened. Seal in a paper bag for 10 minutes to steam. As soon as the chiles are cool enough to handle, remove the charred skin. Make a lengthwise slit in each pepper and remove the seeds, leaving the stem on.

4. Stuff each pepper with a scant ¼ cup of the mushroom filling. Wrap each individually in plastic wrap. (**The recipe can be prepared up to this point a day ahead.** Refrigerate overnight. Let the peppers return to room temperature.)

5. In a deep medium saucepan, melt the remaining 2 tablespoons butter over moderate heat. Add 4 of the garlic cloves and the shallots and cook until softened and translucent, about 3 minutes. Add the white wine and the remaining ½ teaspoon salt and ¼ teaspoon white pepper. Increase the heat to high and boil until reduced by half, 3 to 5 minutes. Add the remaining 2¼ cups cream, reduce the heat to moderate and boil slowly until the mixture is reduced by about one-third, 10 to 15 minutes.

6. Blend in the goat cheese and cook, stirring, until the cheese is blended and the sauce is moderately thick, about 5 minutes. Strain, pressing on the solids, and keep warm over low heat. (**The sauce can be made several hours ahead.** Rewarm over low heat.)

7. Make "Indian paint" by warming the peanut oil in a small skillet over moderate heat. Add the remaining minced garlic clove and sauté until softened, about 1 minute. Add the cayenne and ⅓ cup of water. Stir until blended, then cook, stirring occasionally, for 3 minutes, until the mixture is

smooth. Strain through a fine sieve. Let cool.

8. To assemble, steam the wrapped chiles for 5 minutes or reheat in a microwave oven until warmed through. Reheat the sauce and divide among 8 warmed plates. Unwrap each chile and place, seam-side down, on the sauce. Using a plastic squeeze bottle or paper cone, drizzle a small, decorative design of "Indian paint" on each plate.

—John Sedlar, Saint Estéphe, Manhattan Beach, California

NEAPOLITAN STUFFED PEPPERS

4 SERVINGS

8 bell peppers
¼ cup plus 2 tablespoons extra-virgin olive oil
½ large onion, chopped
3 garlic cloves, chopped
3 tablespoons chopped fresh parsley
4 plum tomatoes—peeled, seeded and chopped
1 teaspoon tomato paste
3 tablespoons chopped brine-cured black olives
3 tablespoons dry bread crumbs
1½ tablespoons chopped capers
16 flat anchovy fillets

1. Using a small sharp knife, cut around the pepper stems, leaving as small an opening as possible. Pull out the cores. Use a teaspoon to remove the seeds and ribs.

2. Preheat the oven to 350°. In a medium skillet, heat ¼ cup of the oil. Add the onion, garlic and parsley, and sauté over moderate heat until the onion is soft and translucent, 2 to 3 minutes.

3. Add the tomatoes, tomato paste and olives. Cook until the liquid from the tomatoes evaporates, about 5 minutes. Add the bread crumbs and capers. Cook, stirring, for 1 minute.

4. Spoon the filling into the peppers. Place 2 anchovy fillets in each. Spread the remaining 2 tablespoons of oil in a baking dish just large enough to hold the peppers in a single layer. Add the peppers and bake, uncovered, until they collapse, about 1½ hours.

5. Serve hot or cold as a first course, or place peppers on top of pasta and dress with the juices. (**These peppers can be prepared up to 1 week ahead.**)

—Anne Disrude

GRATIN DAUPHINOIS

6 SERVINGS

2 pounds baking potatoes
1 garlic clove, cut in half
3 cups heavy cream
½ teaspoon salt
¼ teaspoon freshly ground pepper
½ cup grated Gruyère cheese

1. Preheat the oven to 350°. Peel the potatoes and slice them ⅛ inch thick. Rinse in cold water and pat dry.

2. Rub the bottom and sides of an 8-cup gratin dish with the cut garlic clove. Discard the garlic.

3. Pour ½ cup of the cream into the dish. Arrange a layer of overlapping potato slices at the bottom. Season with salt and pepper. Continue layering the cream, potatoes and salt and pepper until the dish is filled.

4. Place the dish in a large roasting pan and set the pan on a rack in the lower third of the hot oven. Pour in enough boiling water to reach halfway up the gratin dish. Bake until the potatoes are tender, about 1 hour.

5. Pour out and discard any cream that has not been absorbed. Stir the potatoes gently. Sprinkle with the grated Gruyère and return the dish to the water bath in the oven. Bake until the top is golden, about 30 minutes.

—Ostaù de Baumanière, Les Baux-de-Provence, France

TWICE-BAKED POTATOES WITH CREAM AND WILD MUSHROOMS

4 SERVINGS

2 large russet or other baking potatoes
1 ounce dried mushrooms, such as cèpes or morels
1 teaspoon salt
Pinch of freshly ground pepper
¾ cup heavy cream

1. Preheat the oven to 400°. Pierce the potatoes several times with a fork. Bake for about 50 minutes, or until tender when pierced with a fork.

2. Meanwhile, in a small bowl, soak the mushrooms in 1 cup of hot water until softened, about 30 minutes. Remove from the liquid, squeeze dry and coarsely chop.

3. Reduce the oven temperature to 350°. Scoop out the potatoes and place in a medium bowl (discard the skins or reserve for another use, such as the crisp skin croutons for the Potato Soup with Greens, p. 41). Coarsely break up the potatoes with a fork and mix in the chopped mushrooms, salt and pepper.

4. Spoon the potatoes into a small gratin dish. Pour the cream on top. Bake, uncovered, for 30 minutes, or until bubbling and lightly browned.

—Anne Disrude

POTATOES AND CUCUMBERS WITH MINT DRESSING

8 TO 10 SERVINGS

2½ cups lightly packed fresh mint
1 medium shallot
½ cup safflower or other light vegetable oil
3 tablespoons white wine vinegar
1 tablespoon dry white wine
¼ teaspoon Dijon-style mustard
1 tablespoon plus ½ teaspoon coarse (kosher) salt
¼ teaspoon freshly ground white pepper
4 pounds small red potatoes
2 European seedless cucumbers
2 bunches of watercress, large stems removed

1. In a food processor, finely chop 1½ cups of the mint and the shallot. Transfer to a small bowl and add the oil, 2 tablespoons of the vinegar, the wine, mustard, ½ teaspoon of the salt and the white pepper. Stir to combine and let the dressing sit at room temperature for at least 2 hours.

2. Strain the dressing through a fine sieve, pressing to extract as much liquid as possible. Discard the solids. Set the dressing aside.

3. Trim ¼ inch from each end of the potatoes. Using a sharp paring knife, peel the potatoes by cutting from end to end to produce a faceted oval shape. Cut each in half lengthwise and rinse in cold water.

4. In a large saucepan of boiling salted water, cook the potatoes until tender, about 15 minutes. Drain and place in a bowl. Add half of the dressing and toss gently to coat. Let cool, tossing occasionally. Season with additional salt and pepper to taste.

5. Partially peel the cucumbers, leaving some strips of green skin on for decoration. Cut into 1½-inch lengths, stand on end and cut lengthwise into 4 wedges. Scrape out any seeds. Round each corner to produce a beveled shape similar to the potatoes and place in a bowl. Toss with the remaining 1 tablespoon salt and let sit for 30 minutes. Rinse and pat dry. Add the remaining dressing and 1 tablespoon vinegar, toss to coat and marinate for 30 minutes. Taste and adjust the seasoning.

6. Toss the remaining 1 cup mint with the watercress. Line a large round platter with the greens. Arrange alternating pieces of potato and cucumber, skin-side up, in a circular pattern on top. Combine the dressing that remains in the bowls and drizzle on top. Serve at room temperature.

—Anne Disrude

POTATOES AND SUN-DRIED TOMATOES EN PAPILLOTE

Steaming the potatoes enclosed in paper facilitates the exchange of flavors between the potatoes and seasonings, resulting in a more intensely flavored potato.

4 SERVINGS

1¼ pounds waxy (boiling) potatoes, cut into ⅜-inch dice
¼ cup finely chopped sun-dried tomatoes in oil, drained
1½ tablespoons minced fresh parsley
3 tablespoons olive oil
½ teaspoon salt
¼ teaspoon freshly ground pepper

1. In a large pot of boiling salted water, cook the potatoes until fork-tender, about 10 minutes. Drain well. Place the potatoes in a large bowl.

2. Add the sun-dried tomatoes, parsley, oil, salt and pepper to the potatoes and toss until evenly mixed. **(The recipe may be prepared to this point 1 day in advance.** Cover and refrigerate. Let return to room temperature before proceeding.)

3. Preheat the oven to 400°. Cut a sheet of parchment paper or aluminum foil into an 18-inch square. Mound the potatoes in the center. Fold up two sides over the potatoes and make a tight fold to seal. Fold the ends up and tuck under to form a neat but not tight package. Place the papillote on a baking sheet.

4. Bake in the center of the oven for 20 minutes. Serve the potatoes from the package or turn out into a serving dish.

—Anne Disrude

SPICED POTATO PANCAKES

These pancakes are held together by the starch from the potatoes. When the potatoes are rinsed in cold water, the starch will sink to the bottom of the bowl, where it looks like barely diluted cornstarch. To return the starch to the potatoes, pour off the water, leaving the starch at the bottom, and add the grated potatoes. A choice of flavorings is given. Pick your favorite, or divide the pancake mixture in thirds and sample all three.

4 TO 6 SERVINGS

3 medium all-purpose potatoes
3 eggs, beaten
¾ teaspoon salt
¼ teaspoon freshly ground pepper
1 tablespoon grated fresh ginger or 1 tablespoon minced jalapeño pepper or 1½ teaspoons grated orange zest
Safflower oil, for frying

1. Peel and coarsely grate the potatoes. Place in a large bowl, cover with cold water and stir with your hands to rinse. With a slotted spoon, remove the potatoes and squeeze dry in a

kitchen towel. Let the water stand until the cloudy potato starch settles to the bottom of the bowl, about 5 minutes. Pour off the water, leaving the white starch at the bottom of the bowl.

2. Return the potatoes to the bowl. Add the eggs, salt, pepper and ginger. Stir to combine. Preheat the oven to low. Line a serving platter with paper towels and place in the oven to warm.

3. In a large heavy skillet, warm ¼ inch of safflower oil over moderately high heat until a spoonful of the potato mixture immediately sizzles when dropped in. Drop the potatoes in heaping tablespoons and flatten with the back of the spoon to form pancakes 3 to 4 inches in diameter. Fry until well browned on one side, about 6 minutes. Carefully turn the pancakes and cook until browned on the other side, about 4 minutes.

4. Remove the pancakes to the serving platter and keep warm in the oven. Fry the remaining potatoes in the same manner. Serve as soon as possible.

—Anne Disrude

BASQUE POTATOES

8 TO 10 SERVINGS

3 pounds small new white or red potatoes
6 tablespoons unsalted butter
3 tablespoons olive oil
3 large garlic cloves, crushed through a press
½ cup chopped fresh parsley
1 tablespoon minced fresh thyme or ½ teaspoon dried
1½ teaspoons minced fresh or crushed dried rosemary
1½ teaspoons paprika
Dash of cayenne pepper
½ teaspoon salt
¼ teaspoon freshly ground black pepper

1. Preheat the oven to 375°. Scrub the potatoes well and pat dry.

2. In a large roasting pan, melt the butter in the oil over moderate heat. Add the garlic, parsley, thyme, rosemary, paprika and cayenne. Add the potatoes and roll them in the seasoned butter to coat well.

3. Bake, basting the potatoes occasionally with the butter, for about 40 minutes, or until the potatoes are tender. Season with the salt and black pepper.

—Lila Gault

CURRIED OVEN FRIES

4 SERVINGS

3 russet or other baking potatoes
⅓ cup clarified butter, melted
1½ teaspoons curry powder
½ to 1 teaspoon coarse (kosher) salt, to taste

1. Preheat the oven to 375°. Place a baking sheet in the oven to warm. Without peeling, cut the potatoes into 3-by-1-by-1-inch sticks. Rinse in cold water and pat dry.

2. In a large bowl, combine the butter with the curry powder. Add the potatoes and toss to coat all sides.

3. Remove the baking sheet from the oven. Arrange the potatoes on it in a single layer, return to the oven and bake for 20 minutes. Turn the potatoes and bake for 20 minutes longer. Turn again and bake for 15 minutes, until the potatoes are beginning to brown; then turn once more and bake for 10 minutes, or until browned all over.

4. Remove the potatoes from the oven and place in a large brown paper bag. Sprinkle in the salt, seal the bag and shake gently until the potatoes are evenly coated with salt. Serve the fries piping hot.

—Anne Disrude

OVEN-ROASTED POTATOES

8 SERVINGS

5 pounds baking potatoes, peeled
1 stick (¼ pound) unsalted butter, melted
2 teaspoons salt
1 teaspoon freshly ground pepper

1. Preheat the oven to 425°. Cut the potatoes in half lengthwise. With the cut-side down, cut each half on the diagonal into 4 thick slices. Place in a large bowl and toss with the butter, salt and pepper.

2. Lay the potatoes in a single layer in a large baking pan. Roast for 45 minutes, shaking the pan occasionally to turn the potatoes, until they are lightly browned and slightly crusty all around.

—W. Peter Prestcott

GLAZED SHALLOTS

These flavorful shallots may be prepared through Step 3 up to one day ahead; rewarm in the oven if you're having a roast, or gently reheat over a very low flame on the stovetop.

8 SERVINGS

1 stick (¼ pound) unsalted butter
2 pounds shallots, peeled
2 tablespoons sugar
⅓ cup Calvados or applejack
3 tablespoons sherry vinegar
Salt and freshly ground pepper
2 tablespoons minced fresh parsley

1. In a large deep skillet or flameproof casserole, melt the butter over moderate heat. Add the shallots and sauté, uncovered, shaking the pan occasionally to prevent sticking, until a sharp knife pierces the shallots easily, 20 to 25 minutes.

2. Sprinkle the sugar over the shallots, shaking the pan to coat evenly. Cook until the sugar is caramelized and the shallots are deep golden and glazed, about 10 minutes.

3. Add the Calvados and vinegar and cook, shaking the pan, until the liquid is reduced to a light syrup, 2 to 3 minutes. Season with salt and pepper to taste. (**The recipe may be prepared to this point 1 day ahead.** Cover the shallots and refrigerate.)

4. Just before serving, rewarm the shallots if necessary. With a slotted spoon, remove the shallots to a serving dish. Sprinkle with the parsley.

—*W. Peter Prestcott*

SWEET POTATOES WITH CIDER AND BROWN SUGAR

Here is a deliciously easy treatment for a trusty Thanksgiving standby, inspired by a surviving Jeffersonian menu. As this recipe does not use a lot of sugar, the natural tartness of the cider comes through. (Natural unsweetened cider, by the way, fresh and unfiltered, is preferable to bottled cider or to apple juice.)

8 SERVINGS

4 pounds sweet potatoes, peeled and cut into 1-inch chunks
2½ cups unsweetened apple cider
½ cup dark brown sugar
8 tablespoons (1 stick) unsalted butter
2-inch piece of cinnamon stick

1. In a large noncorrodible saucepan, combine the potatoes, cider, brown sugar, 6 tablespoons of the butter and the cinnamon stick. Bring to a boil over moderate heat. Reduce the heat to a simmer, partially cover and cook, stirring occasionally, until the potatoes are very tender, about 45 minutes.

2. Let cool slightly, remove the cinnamon stick and force the potatoes through the medium disk of a food mill or puree in batches in a food processor. Transfer to an ovenproof serving dish. (**The potatoes can be prepared to this point several days in advance of serving.** Cover tightly and refrigerate. Return to room temperature before proceeding.)

3. Preheat the oven to 325°. Dot the surface of the potatoes with the remaining 2 tablespoons butter, cover tightly with foil and bake, stirring once or twice, until steaming, about 20 minutes. Remove the foil and bake for 5 minutes longer.

—*Michael McLaughlin*

SAVORY TOMATO CHARLOTTES

Served on a bed of Bibb lettuce and watercress, these fragrant tomato charlottes make a delicious accompaniment to an omelet at brunch or to cold meat at lunch or dinner.

4 SERVINGS

1 loaf (1 pound) thinly sliced, firm-textured white bread, slightly stale, crusts removed
¾ cup olive oil
2 medium garlic cloves, bruised
2 large red bell peppers
2 medium shallots, minced
2½ pounds ripe tomatoes—peeled, seeded and coarsely chopped, juices reserved
2 tablespoons chopped fresh basil
1½ teaspoons minced fresh thyme or ½ teaspoon dried
½ teaspoon salt

1. Line the bottom of four 10-ounce custard cups (about 4½ by 1¾ inches each) with a round of bread. Cut out 4 larger rounds of bread to fit the tops. Cut out 16 rectangles of bread, each 3½ by 1¾ inches. Fit 4 rectangles against the sides of each custard cup, trimming with scissors for an even fit.

2. In a large heavy skillet, warm ½ cup of the oil and the garlic over moderately low heat for 3 to 5 minutes to flavor the oil; do not let the garlic brown. Discard the garlic and pour the oil into a small bowl.

3. Remove the bread from the custard cups and lightly brush on both sides with the flavored oil. Working in batches, fry the bread in the same skillet over moderately high heat, turning once, until golden brown on both sides, about 1 minute on each side. Drain well on paper towels. Add more of the flavored oil as necessary, heating well before frying more bread.

4. While the bread is still warm and malleable, line the bottom of the molds with the smaller bread circles and cover the sides with 4 of the rectangles. Reserve the larger rounds to cover the molds.

5. Roast the peppers directly over a gas flame or under a broiler, turning occasionally, until blackened all over, 10 to 15 minutes. Seal in a paper or plastic bag and let steam for about 10 minutes. Rinse and peel. Remove the stems, seeds and ribs. Puree the peppers in a food processor or blender.

6. In a large heavy skillet, heat 1 tablespoon of the oil. Add the shallots and sauté over moderate heat until soft and translucent, about 2 minutes. Add the tomatoes and their juices and sauté over moderately high heat until the juices evaporate, about 10 min-

utes. Reduce the heat to low and stir in the red pepper puree, basil, thyme and salt; remove from the heat and let cool slightly.

7. Divide the filling evenly among the lined molds. Cover with the reserved bread circles. Place a square of plastic wrap or waxed paper on top of each charlotte and weigh down with pie weights or an 8-ounce can. Refrigerate overnight or for up to 2 days.

8. To serve, remove the weights and let the charlottes return to room temperature. Preheat the broiler. Unmold the charlottes onto a cookie sheet. Lightly brush with the remaining 3 tablespoons oil. Broil about 4 inches from the heat until crisp on the top and warmed through, 3 to 4 minutes. Serve the charlottes warm or at room temperature.

—Diana Sturgis

GRATIN OF ZUCCHINI A LA BORDELAISE

This hearty, savory vegetable dish makes a marvelous accompaniment to roasted, grilled or simply sautéed meats or any but the most delicate fish.

6 SERVINGS

4 medium zucchini (about 1¾ pounds)
1 teaspoon salt
3 tablespoons unsalted butter
1 cup light cream or ½ cup heavy cream and ½ cup milk
3 whole eggs
1 egg yolk
½ cup freshly grated Parmesan cheese
¼ teaspoon freshly ground pepper
¼ cup fresh bread crumbs
1 tablespoon olive oil
2 tablespoons minced parsley
2 garlic cloves, minced
1 tablespoon minced shallot

1. Cut the zucchini in half lengthwise and then crosswise into ½-inch slices. Place in a colander. Sprinkle with ½ teaspoon of the salt and let drain for 30 minutes. Dry the zucchini thoroughly on paper towels.

2. Preheat the oven to 350°. In a large skillet, melt 2 tablespoons of the butter over moderately high heat. Add half the zucchini and sauté, tossing, until lightly browned, 3 to 5 minutes. With a slotted spoon, transfer the zucchini to paper towels to drain. Add the remaining zucchini to the skillet and sauté until lightly browned; drain on paper towels.

3. In a large mixing bowl, combine the cream, whole eggs, egg yolk, ¼ cup of the Parmesan, the remaining ½ teaspoon salt and the pepper. Whisk to blend well. Add the sautéed zucchini and stir to mix.

4. Grease a 2-quart oval gratin dish with the remaining 1 tablespoon butter and sprinkle with 2 tablespoons of the bread crumbs. Scrape the zucchini-custard mixture into the prepared dish.

5. Bake for 15 to 18 minutes, or until the custard is almost set.

6. Meanwhile, heat the oil in a small skillet. Add the remaining 2 tablespoons bread crumbs, the parsley, garlic and shallot and sauté over moderately low heat for about 1 minute, until fragrant.

7. Sprinkle the bread crumb-parsley mixture on top of the gratin and return to the oven for 4 minutes.

8. Sprinkle the remaining ¼ cup Parmesan over the top of the gratin and broil 4 to 6 inches from the heat for 30 to 60 seconds, until the top is nicely browned. Let stand for 5 minutes before serving.

—Perla Meyers

MINIATURE VEGETABLES WITH LIME AND BASIL

6 TO 8 SERVINGS

16 miniature zucchini, 2 to 3 inches long
16 miniature carrots, 2 to 3 inches long, with 1 inch of green tops
¼ cup clarified unsalted butter
1 tablespoon olive oil
1 tablespoon walnut oil
16 cherry tomatoes
¼ cup fresh lime juice
1 cup fresh basil leaves, coarsely chopped
Salt and freshly ground pepper
½ cup freshly grated Parmesan cheese

1. Steam the zucchini and carrots until crisp-tender, 5 to 7 minutes. Arrange on a heated serving platter and cover loosely with foil to keep warm.

2. In a large noncorrodible skillet, combine the butter, olive oil and walnut oil over moderately high heat. Add the tomatoes and sauté, shaking the pan, until slightly softened, about 2 minutes. With a slotted spoon, transfer the tomatoes to the platter.

3. Reduce the heat to moderately low. Add the lime juice and basil and cook, stirring, for 1 minute. Season with salt and pepper to taste.

4. To serve, pour the sauce over the vegetables and sprinkle the Parmesan cheese on top.

—W. Peter Prestcott

PASTA, RICE & BREADSTUFFS

FRESH PASTA WITH WILD MUSHROOMS

This is a creation of Jack McClean, a Californian from Orinda, a lucky person who lives near markets where there is a great variety of fresh, wild and cultivated mushrooms. Note that there is no sauce for this dish; hence the great amount of butter to flavor both the mushrooms and the pasta. Remember this, though: the recipe will serve 6 as a main course, 10 as a first course. I generally serve it as a first course; thus the butter is divided among 10 people and is much less extravagant than it appears at first glance.

Though you do not have to make your own fresh pasta, the recipe (which follows) produces an especially light, tender noodle that I think you will enjoy.

F&W BEVERAGE SUGGESTION
Full-flavored white such as Greco di Tufo

6 MAIN-COURSE OR 10 FIRST-COURSE SERVINGS

1 pound fresh shiitake (Golden Oak) mushrooms or 1 pound fresh yellow or black chanterelles or fresh morels
2 sticks (½ pound) unsalted butter
Salt and freshly ground pepper
1 tablespoon coarse (kosher) salt
1 tablespoon olive oil
1 pound Fresh Pasta, preferably homemade (recipe follows)

1. Rinse the mushrooms and dry with paper towels. Cut off the stems and mince them. Slice the mushroom caps into ¼-inch-thick strips.

2. In a large skillet, melt the butter. Add the stems and caps (see Note) and a pinch of salt and pepper; cover and cook the mushrooms over low heat for 20 minutes.

3. In a large pot, bring several quarts of water to a boil; add the coarse salt and oil. Add the pasta and cook for no more than 30 seconds, or until the pasta floats to the surface of the water. Drain well.

4. Pour the mushrooms and butter into a large heated bowl. Add the pasta and toss. Season with salt and pepper to taste.

NOTE: If using chanterelles or morels, add the stems first and cook, covered, for 15 minutes. Then increase the heat to moderate, add the caps and sauté for 3 minutes.

—Lydie Marshall

FRESH PASTA

This fresh pasta is my interpretation of Aunt Chick's, an Oklahoman who was famous for her pies.

MAKES 1 POUND

⅔ cup all-purpose flour
1 ⅓ cups cake flour
½ teaspoon salt
2 small eggs
3 tablespoons heavy cream

1. Process all the ingredients in a food processor for 10 seconds, until the mixture is the texture of coarse meal. Dump out onto a lightly floured work surface and knead until the dough is smooth (add more all-purpose flour if the dough is too sticky; the amount will depend partly on the humidity that day).

2. Roll out the dough according to your pasta machine's instructions, or by hand until paper thin. Cut the dough into ¼-inch strips and let dry.

—Lydie Marshall

SCALLOP AND PINE NUT SAUCE WITH SPAGHETTINI AND BASIL

F&W BEVERAGE SUGGESTION
Italian white, such as Corvo

6 TO 8 SERVINGS

1 pound bay scallops
¼ cup olive oil, preferably extra-virgin
2 medium garlic cloves, minced
⅓ cup pine nuts (pignoli)
2 tablespoons plus ½ teaspoon salt
¼ teaspoon freshly ground pepper
1 pound spaghettini
1 stick (¼ pound) unsalted butter, melted
¾ cup packed fresh basil leaves, coarsely chopped

1. Wash the scallops. Remove the tough tendon on the side and dry well on paper towels.

2. In a large saucepan or flameproof casserole, heat the oil. Add the garlic and cook over moderately low heat until softened but not browned, about 3 minutes. Add the pine nuts, increase the heat to moderate and cook, stirring frequently, until the nuts are lightly browned, about 2 minutes. Remove the sauce from the heat and season with ½ teaspoon of the salt and the pepper.

3. Bring a large pot of water to a boil. Add the remaining 2 tablespoons salt and the spaghettini. Cook until the pasta is just tender to the bite, 8 to 10 minutes.

4. Meanwhile, add the scallops to the garlic and pine nut sauce. Cook over high heat, tossing frequently, until the scallops are just opaque throughout, 2 to 3 minutes. Remove from the heat and season with an additional pinch of salt and pepper.

5. Drain the spaghettini, add to the scallops and toss. Add the butter and basil and toss again. Serve hot.

—Nancy Verde Barr

TOMATO AND OLIVE SAUCE WITH FUSILLI

F&W BEVERAGE SUGGESTION
Italian red, such as Dolcetto

4 TO 6 SERVINGS

½ cup olive oil, preferably extra-virgin
1 medium onion, minced
1 medium garlic clove, minced
1 pound tomatoes—peeled, seeded and chopped—or 1 can (32 ounces) Italian peeled tomatoes, drained and chopped
1 cup brine-cured black olives (or ½ cup each black and green), halved and pitted
2 tablespoons capers, rinsed and drained
2 teaspoons red wine vinegar
2 tablespoons minced fresh oregano or 1 to 2 teaspoons dried
Pinch of sugar
2 tablespoons plus ¼ teaspoon salt
½ teaspoon coarsely cracked pepper
1 pound short fusilli
1 cup freshly grated Pecorino Romano cheese (about 4 ounces) plus additional cheese for passing

1. In a large skillet or flameproof casserole, heat the oil. Add the onion and garlic and cook over moderately low heat, stirring occasionally, until the onion is softened but not browned, 6 to 8 minutes.

2. Add the tomatoes, olives, capers, vinegar, oregano, sugar, ¼ teaspoon of the salt and the pepper and simmer for 15 minutes over low heat.

3. While the sauce is cooking, bring a large pot of water to a boil. Add the remaining 2 tablespoons salt and the fusilli. Stir until the water returns to a boil and cook until just tender to the bite, about 15 minutes; drain.

4. Add the pasta to the sauce and toss. Mix in the cheese and serve immediately with additional grated cheese on the side.

—Nancy Verde Barr

NEAPOLITAN SPAGHETTI WITH SEAFOOD

4 TO 6 SERVINGS

1 tablespoon salt
1 pound spaghetti
⅔ cup olive oil, preferably extra-virgin
2 large garlic cloves, minced
¾ teaspoon crushed hot red pepper
1 pound whole bay scallops or quartered sea scallops
¼ cup minced fresh parsley
Freshly ground black pepper

1. In a large pot, bring 6 quarts of water to a boil. Add the salt and the spaghetti. Cook, boiling, until tender to the bite, 4 to 5 minutes for fresh pasta, 9 to 10 minutes for dried.

2. Meanwhile, in a large heavy skillet, warm the oil over moderate heat. Add the garlic and red pepper and cook until the garlic is slightly golden, 1 to 2 minutes. Add the scallops and sauté, stirring, until opaque, 1 to 2 minutes. Remove from the heat.

3. Drain the pasta and place in a warmed serving bowl. Scrape in the scallops and the flavored oil. Add the parsley and toss well. Season with black pepper to taste and serve hot.

—Diane Darrow & Tom Maresca

FETTUCCINE WITH GORGONZOLA, BELL PEPPERS AND BASIL

4 SERVINGS

5 tablespoons unsalted butter
1 medium red bell pepper, cut into thin julienne strips
1 medium yellow bell pepper, cut into thin julienne strips
1 medium garlic clove, minced
½ teaspoon salt
¼ teaspoon freshly ground black pepper
1 medium zucchini, cut into thin julienne strips
1½ cups heavy cream
3 to 4 ounces Gorgonzola, Saga or Pipo Crem'
1 teaspoon all-purpose flour
⅓ cup freshly grated Parmesan cheese
¼ cup slivered basil leaves
¾ pound fresh fettuccine, preferably green

1. In a large skillet, melt 2 tablespoons of the butter over moderately low heat. Add the bell peppers and garlic and season with the salt and pepper. Toss to coat with the butter. Cover and cook until the peppers are crisp-tender, about 2 minutes. Add the zucchini and cook for 1 minute longer.

2. In a food processor, combine ¼ cup of the cream and the Gorgonzola. Puree until smooth.

3. In a medium saucepan, melt the remaining 3 tablespoons butter over moderate heat. Add the flour and cook, stirring, for 1 minute without browning. Stir in the remaining 1¼ cups cream, reduce the heat to moderately low and simmer until the mixture reduces slightly and lightly coats a spoon. Whisk in the Gorgonzola-cream mixture. Add half of the Parmesan cheese, the pepper-zucchini mixture and the basil. Season with salt and pepper to taste. Keep warm over very low heat.

4. In a large pot of boiling salted water, cook the fettuccine until tender but still firm, about 2 minutes. Drain well and turn into a large, warmed bowl.

5. Pour the warm sauce over the pasta, add the remaining Parmesan cheese and a generous grinding of pepper and toss lightly. Serve at once.

—Perla Meyers

FETTUCCINE WITH GOAT CHEESE, OLIVES AND BASIL

To really heighten the flavors of this dish, be sure to toss the basil and goat cheese with the pasta while it's still hot.

F&W BEVERAGE SUGGESTION
Zinfandel

4 TO 6 SERVINGS

1 tablespoon plus 1 teaspoon salt
1 pound fettuccine
½ cup olive oil, preferably extra-virgin
4 medium garlic cloves, finely chopped
1⅓ cups (6 ounces) Niçoise or Calamata olives, pitted and slivered
¼ teaspoon freshly ground pepper
1⅓ cups coarsely crumbled mild goat cheese, such as Bucheron or Montrachet (about 6 ounces)
20 fresh basil leaves, cut into slivers

1. Bring a large pot of water with 1 tablespoon of the salt to a boil over high heat. Add the fettuccine and cook until tender but still firm to the bite, 8 to 10 minutes.
2. Meanwhile, in a small skillet, heat the olive oil. Add the garlic and sauté over moderately low heat, stirring occasionally, until softened but not browned, 3 to 5 minutes.
3. Add the olives and cook, stirring, for about 30 seconds to warm through. Season with the remaining 1 teaspoon salt and the pepper.
4. Drain the fettuccine well and place in a large warmed serving bowl. Scrape the olive-garlic mixture over the pasta and toss to coat. Add the goat cheese and basil and toss lightly until the ingredients are evenly distributed. Serve the pasta warm or at room temperature.

—Marlena Spieler

FETTUCCINE AL LIMONE

4 SERVINGS

3 tablespoons unsalted butter
1 cup heavy cream
Grated zest of 2 lemons (about 1 tablespoon)
1 pound wide egg noodles
½ cup grated Parmesan cheese, or more to taste
½ teaspoon salt
¼ teaspoon freshly ground pepper

1. In a saucepan, melt the butter without browning. Add the cream and zest and stir until the cream and butter mixture turns a creamy yellow color.
2. In a large pot of boiling salted water, cook the noodles until just al dente. Drain and toss with the cream mixture. Sprinkle with the Parmesan, salt and pepper and toss.

FETTUCCINE WITH BASIL AND TWO SALMONS

F&W BEVERAGE SUGGESTION
Pinot Noir Blanc, such as Sebastiani

2 SERVINGS

3 tablespoons unsalted butter
4 ounces skinned and boned fresh salmon, cut into ½-inch dice
1 medium shallot, minced
1 small tomato—peeled, seeded and coarsely chopped
¼ cup dry white wine
¼ cup fish stock or bottled clam juice
½ cup heavy cream
3 tablespoons chopped fresh basil
8 ounces fresh fettuccine or linguine, or 6 ounces dried
2 ounces thinly sliced smoked salmon, cut into thin strips
¼ teaspoon coarsely cracked pepper
Salt
1 tablespoon chopped fresh parsley

1. In a medium skillet, melt 2 tablespoons of the butter over moderate heat. Add the fresh salmon and cook, tossing, until opaque on the outside, about 30 seconds. Remove with a slotted spoon and set aside. (The salmon will finish cooking later.)
2. Add the shallot and tomato to the butter remaining in the skillet and sauté over moderate heat until the shallot is softened, about 2 minutes.
3. Add the wine and fish stock. Boil over high heat until the liquid becomes syrupy, about 5 minutes.
4. Add the cream and basil. Boil until the sauce thickens slightly, about 2 minutes. Remove from the heat and set aside.
5. Bring a large pot of salted water to a boil over high heat. Add the fettuccine and cook until tender but still slightly firm to the bite, 1 to 2 minutes for fresh, 10 to 12 minutes for dried; drain. Turn the pasta into a warmed bowl and toss with the remaining 1 tablespoon butter.
6. Quickly bring the sauce to a boil over high heat, add the sautéed salmon and remove from the heat. Stir in the smoked salmon. Season with the pepper and salt to taste. Pour the sauce over the pasta and toss. Divide between two warmed plates, sprinkle with parsley and serve hot.

—Jeanette Ferrary & Louise Fiszer

RIGATONI ALLA NORCINA

4 SERVINGS

½ cup olive oil
1 or 2 garlic cloves, to taste
1 whole dried red chile pepper
1 pound sweet Italian sausage, casings removed
1 pound rigatoni
2 cups heavy cream
½ cup grated pecorino Romano or Parmesan cheese

1. In a large skillet, warm the olive oil, garlic and chile pepper over moderate heat (if you do not like very highly seasoned foods, do not break the chile pepper open). Crumble in the sausage meat and brown.

2. Meanwhile, in a large pot of boiling salted water, cook the rigatoni until al dente. Drain, return to the pot and add the sausage and oil, having first removed the chile and garlic.

3. Add the cream and Romano and toss well. Serve immediately.

MORELS WITH PASTA IN LIGHT HERBAL CREAM

F&W BEVERAGE SUGGESTION
California Chardonnay, such as DeLoach

2 GENEROUS SERVINGS

½ cup light or heavy cream
1 tablespoon minced shallot
⅛ teaspoon tarragon
⅛ teaspoon thyme
⅛ teaspoon salt
¼ pound fresh morels, preferably small
½ pound fresh linguine or tagliatelle
Freshly ground pepper

1. In a heavy 1-quart saucepan, combine the cream, shallot, tarragon, thyme and salt. Simmer, covered, until the shallot is soft, about 5 minutes.

2. Meanwhile, trim the morels. Cut off and chop the stems, then slice the caps into ½-inch rounds. (If the morels are medium or large, halve them lengthwise, then cut into half-rounds.) Rinse vigorously in a colander under running water, then dry on a towel.

3. Add the morels to the cream mixture. Cover and simmer gently until tender, 10 to 15 minutes.

4. In a large pot of boiling salted water, cook the noodles until just tender, 1 to 2 minutes. As the pasta is finishing, uncover the cream-morel mixture and boil for a few minutes, if necessary, to thicken the sauce slightly (it should still be liquid, however, not too thick). Drain the pasta and combine at once with the sauce. Season with salt and pepper to taste and serve hot.

—Elizabeth Schneider

MINTED SUMMER SQUASH WITH ZITI

Although the following recipe calls for yellow squash, zucchini can be substituted in the same amount; or a combination of yellow and green squashes could be used.

F&W BEVERAGE SUGGESTION
Italian white, such as Galestro

6 TO 8 SERVINGS

4 medium yellow squash (about 2 pounds)
½ cup olive oil, preferably extra-virgin
3 large garlic cloves, smashed and peeled
¼ cup thinly sliced scallions (white part only)
2 tablespoons plus ½ teaspoon salt
¼ teaspoon crushed hot red pepper
1 pound ziti or similar short tubular macaroni
½ cup chopped fresh parsley
½ cup chopped fresh mint
Freshly ground black pepper

1. Cut the squash into small dice, no larger than ¼ inch.

2. In a large saucepan or flameproof casserole, heat the oil and garlic. Cook over moderate heat until the garlic is well browned. Lift out and discard the garlic.

3. Add the scallions to the oil and cook until tender but not browned, about 2 minutes. Add the squash, ½ teaspoon of the salt and the hot pepper. Cover and cook over moderately low heat, stirring occasionally, until the squash is completely softened, about 15 minutes. (If the squash becomes dry during cooking, add 1 to 2 tablespoons hot water.)

4. Meanwhile, bring a large pot of water to a boil. Add the remaining 2 tablespoons salt and the ziti and stir well. Cook until the pasta is just tender to the bite, about 10 minutes; drain.

5. Add the parsley and mint to the squash. Season with black pepper to taste. Add the drained pasta and toss to combine. Serve hot.

—Nancy Verde Barr

PROSCIUTTO AND SAGE SAUCE WITH ZITI

F&W BEVERAGE SUGGESTION
Chianti Classico

4 TO 6 SERVINGS

¼ cup olive oil, preferably extra-virgin
3 medium garlic cloves, bruised and peeled
6 ounces thinly sliced prosciutto, cut into fine strips
⅔ cup chopped walnuts (about 3 ounces)
2 tablespoons salt
1 pound ziti or similar short tubular pasta

4 tablespoons unsalted butter, melted
1 cup freshly grated Parmesan cheese (about 4 ounces)
30 fresh sage leaves
½ teaspoon coarsely cracked pepper

1. In a large skillet or flameproof casserole, heat the oil. Add the garlic cloves and cook over low heat until golden, 6 to 8 minutes. Remove and discard the garlic.

2. Add the prosciutto and walnuts and cook, stirring occasionally, until the walnuts are lightly toasted and the prosciutto fat is translucent, 8 to 10 minutes. Remove from the heat and set aside.

3. Bring a large pot of water to a boil. Add the salt and the ziti and stir until the water returns to a boil. Cook until just tender to the bite, 12 to 15 minutes.

4. Drain the pasta and toss with the prosciutto. Add the melted butter and the cheese; toss. Add the sage leaves, pepper and salt to taste.

—Nancy Verde Barr

ARUGULA AND PARMESAN CHEESE WITH CAVATELLI

Cavatelli, made from semolina flour and water, are shaped like small seashells. Dried cavatelli are imported from Italy, but it is also possible to find them fresh in some Italian neighborhoods or frozen in some supermarkets or specialty food shops. Often, the fresh or frozen ones have ricotta cheese added to the dough, and these may also be used.

4 TO 6 SERVINGS

½ pound arugula
2 tablespoons plus ½ teaspoon salt
1 pound fresh, frozen or dried cavatelli
6 tablespoons unsalted butter
¼ teaspoon freshly ground pepper
1 cup freshly grated Parmesan cheese (about 4 ounces)

1. Wash the arugula in several changes of cold water; drain and dry well. Discard any tough stems and tear the leaves into bite-size pieces.

2. Bring a large pot of water to a boil. Add 2 tablespoons of the salt, stir in the cavatelli and cook according to the directions on the package; 2 to 3 minutes for fresh, 10 minutes for dried and up to 15 minutes for frozen.

3. Meanwhile, in a large saucepan or flameproof casserole, melt the butter over moderate heat. Add the arugula, pepper and remaining ½ teaspoon salt. Cook until the arugula is wilted and tender, 1 to 2 minutes.

4. Drain the cavatelli. Add to the arugula. Sprinkle on the grated cheese and toss well. Season with additional salt and pepper to taste.

—Nancy Verde Barr

BUCATINI ALLA SALERNITANA

4 SERVINGS

2 eggplants (about 1½ pounds)
3 tablespoons olive oil
1 can (16 ounces) peeled Italian tomatoes, sieved
¼ teaspoon salt
⅛ teaspoon freshly ground pepper
½ cup coarsely chopped fresh basil
1 pound bucatini
½ cup quartered mild, oil-cured, pitted black olives
1 tablespoon drained capers
4 tablespoons grated Parmesan cheese
½ pound thinly sliced mozzarella cheese

1. Peel and cube the eggplants. In a large heavy saucepan, warm the olive oil until hot. Add the eggplant and sauté over moderately high heat. Add the tomatoes, salt and pepper and cook over moderately high heat for 20 minutes. Add the basil and remove from the heat.

2. Preheat the oven to 350°. In a large pot of boiling salted water, cook the bucatini until al dente. Drain and add to the saucepan along with the olives, capers and Parmesan. Toss.

3. Place half of the mixture in a baking dish and cover with half of the mozzarella slices. Add the rest of the pasta and eggplant mixture and the remaining mozzarella. Bake until the mozzarella has melted. Serve at once.

BROCCOLI RABE AND ANCHOVY SAUCE WITH ORECCHIETTE

Orecchiette, which means "little ears," is a small disk-shaped pasta that is a specialty of the southern Italian region of Apulia. Dried imported orecchiette is available in Italian groceries, but any small, shell-shaped pasta can be substituted. The slightly bitter broccoli rabe can usually be found year-round, but if you can't get a hold of any, turnip greens can be substituted.

F&W BEVERAGE SUGGESTION
Vernaccia di San Gimignano

6 TO 8 SERVINGS

1 pound broccoli rabe
2 tablespoons plus ¼ teaspoon salt
1 pound orecchiette
1 can (2 ounces) flat anchovy fillets, drained
4 large garlic cloves, minced
⅓ cup olive oil, preferably extra-virgin
¼ teaspoon freshly ground pepper
1 cup freshly grated pecorino Romano cheese (about 4 ounces)

1. In a large pot, bring 5 quarts of water to a full boil over high heat.

2. Wash the broccoli rabe and peel the stems. Cut into inch-long pieces.

3. Add 2 tablespoons of the salt and the broccoli rabe to the boiling water and cook until almost tender, about 3 minutes. Lift out the broccoli rabe with a slotted spoon or a strainer with a handle and drain in a large colander. Rinse briefly under cold running water. Let the water in the pot return to a boil.

4. Add the orecchiette to the boiling water and cook until just tender to the bite, about 10 minutes.

5. Meanwhile, mash the anchovies and garlic with a fork. Stir in the olive oil. Scrape the mixture into a large saucepan or flameproof casserole and cook over moderately low heat until hot, 2 to 3 minutes.

6. Pour the pasta and its cooking liquid over the cooked broccoli rabe in the colander to reheat it. Add the pasta and broccoli rabe to the sauce in the pan, season with the remaining ¼ teaspoon salt and the pepper and toss. Serve hot. Pass a bowl of the grated Romano cheese on the side.

—Nancy Verde Barr

KOREAN NOODLES AND VEGETABLES (JAP CHAE)

This is a delicious side dish with Korean barbecued meats. It also works well as part of a Western meal of beef or chicken.

4 TO 6 SERVINGS

*1 tablespoon dried tree ears (Chinese black fungus)**
*2 ounces cellophane (bean thread) noodles**
2 tablespoons Oriental sesame oil
2 tablespoons plus 1 teaspoon soy sauce
1 tablespoon sugar
⅛ teaspoon salt
1 teaspoon sesame seeds plus ¼ cup toasted sesame seeds, for garnish
2 tablespoons vegetable oil
2 medium carrots, cut into thin julienne strips
1 large onion, sliced
¼ pound Chinese cabbage, cut into thin julienne strips
1 medium zucchini, cut into thin julienne strips
2 medium scallions, cut into thin julienne strips
**Available at Oriental markets*

1. Place the tree ears in a small bowl, cover with boiling water and soak until soft, about 30 minutes.

2. Place the noodles in a large bowl, cover with boiling water and soak until translucent but still firm, about 8 minutes. Drain and rinse the noodles under cold running water; drain well.

3. Drain the tree ears and squeeze dry. Trim off any hard bits.

4. In a small bowl, combine the sesame oil, soy sauce, sugar, salt and the 1 teaspoon of sesame seeds.

5. In a wok or large heavy skillet, heat the oil. Add the carrots and stir-fry over moderately high heat for 30 seconds. Add the onion and stir-fry for 1 minute. Add the Chinese cabbage and stir-fry for about 2 minutes, or until the cabbage is wilted. Add the zucchini and stir-fry for 15 seconds; then add the scallions and tree ears.

6. Pour in the sauce and stir-fry for 30 seconds longer. Add the noodles and toss until well coated with sauce. Serve immediately, garnished with the toasted sesame seeds.

—Susan Grodnick

CHINESE NOODLES WITH PORK AND BEAN SAUCE

This is a fast and flavorful dish, perfect for a midweek supper.

F&W BEVERAGE SUGGESTION
Alsace Gewürztraminer, such as Trimbach

4 TO 6 SERVINGS

½ cup chicken stock or canned broth
*¼ cup dark miso (soybean paste)**
*1 tablespoon hoisin sauce**
1 teaspoon sugar
*1½ tablespoons Chinese black vinegar or rice wine vinegar**
1 tablespoon vegetable oil
2 garlic cloves, minced
¾ pound lean ground pork
2 scallions, chopped
*½ pound fresh thin Chinese egg noodles**
1 teaspoon plain or hot Oriental sesame oil, or more to taste
**Available at Oriental markets*

1. Bring a large pot of water to a boil over high heat. Meanwhile, in a small bowl combine the chicken stock, *miso*, hoisin sauce, sugar and vinegar; stir until smooth.

2. In a wok or large skillet, heat the vegetable oil. Add the garlic and stir-fry over moderate heat for a few seconds. Add the pork, increase the heat to moderately high and stir-fry, breaking up any chunks of meat, until the pork is no longer pink, about 1½ minutes. Spoon off any accumulated fat and stir in the scallions and the sauce mixture. Bring to a boil, reduce the heat to moderately low and simmer for 5 minutes.

3. Add the noodles to the boiling water and cook until tender but still firm, about 4 minutes. Drain well.

4. Add the sesame oil to the pork mixture. Add the noodles and toss until well coated. Transfer to a serving platter and serve hot.

—Susan Grodnick

CHINESE SHALLOW-FRIED NOODLES WITH SHRIMP SAUCE AND BROCCOLI

F&W BEVERAGE SUGGESTION
Medium-dry Muscat wine, such as Dynasty

4 TO 6 SERVINGS

*½ pound fresh thin Chinese egg noodles**
1 large bunch of broccoli
¾ pound medium shrimp, shelled and deveined
1 tablespoon soy sauce
1 tablespoon Chinese rice wine or dry sherry
3½ teaspoons cornstarch
¾ cup chicken stock or canned broth
1 teaspoon sugar
¼ teaspoon salt
½ cup vegetable oil
1 tablespoon chopped fresh ginger
1 garlic clove, chopped
2 tablespoons fermented black beans, rinsed and coarsely chopped*
**Available at Oriental markets*

1. In a large pot of boiling salted water, cook the noodles until tender but still resilient, about 4 minutes. Drain and rinse under cold running water; drain well.

2. Separate the broccoli into 1- to 1½-inch florets. Trim and peel the stems and cut on the diagonal into thin slices. In a medium saucepan of boiling water, blanch the stems for 30 seconds. Add the florets and blanch for 15 seconds. Drain and rinse under cold running water to refresh.

3. Slice through the shrimp to within ⅛ inch of the back, spreading the sides flat to butterfly the shrimp.

4. In a medium bowl, combine the soy sauce, rice wine and 2 teaspoons of the cornstarch. Add the shrimp and toss to coat well.

5. In a small bowl, combine the remaining 1½ teaspoons cornstarch, the chicken stock, sugar and salt. Set aside.

6. Place a wok or a large skillet over moderately high heat for about 1½ minutes. Add ¼ cup of the oil and heat to just below the smoking point. Add the ginger and garlic; stir-fry for 15 seconds. Add the shrimp and stir-fry until slightly opaque, about 20 seconds. Add the broccoli and black beans and stir-fry for 30 seconds. Pour in the chicken stock mixture, reduce the heat to moderately low and simmer until the broccoli is tender but still firm and the sauce thickens slightly, about 2 minutes. Remove from the heat.

7. In a large skillet, preferably nonstick, heat 3 tablespoons of the oil over moderately high heat. Add the noodles in an even layer and cook, without stirring, until golden and crisp on the bottom, about 4 minutes. Place a plate over the skillet and invert the noodle cake onto the plate; add the remaining 1 tablespoon oil to the skillet. When hot, slide the noodle cake back into the skillet and cook until crisp and golden on the other side, about 4 minutes. Slide onto a large round serving platter.

8. To serve, gently reheat the shrimp sauce and broccoli and pour over the noodle cake. Serve hot.

—Susan Grodnick

DA CELESTINO'S POTATO GNOCCHI WITH TOMATO SAUCE

8 SERVINGS

3 pounds baking potatoes
2 cups all-purpose flour
4 eggs, lightly beaten
1 teaspoon salt
¼ teaspoon freshly ground white pepper
⅛ teaspoon freshly grated nutmeg
1 cup (4 ounces) freshly grated Parmesan cheese
Tomato Sauce with Garlic (p. 234)

1. In a large heavy saucepan of lightly salted boiling water, cook the potatoes until tender when pierced with a fork, about 20 minutes. Drain and set aside to cool, then peel and mash with either a ricer or a food mill.

2. Stir in the flour, eggs, salt, white pepper, nutmeg and Parmesan until just mixed.

3. Lightly flour a work surface. To form the gnocchi, divide the dough into 8 sections. Using your hands, roll each into a cylinder ½ inch in circumference. Cut into 1-inch lengths. (**The recipe can be made several hours ahead of time to this point.** Arrange the gnocchi on baking sheets in a single layer. Refrigerate, covered.)

4. Bring a large pot of lightly salted water to a simmer over moderately high heat. Add one-quarter of the gnocchi and cook until they all rise to the surface, 3 to 5 minutes. Remove with a slotted spoon and drain into a colander. Transfer to a large, warmed serving bowl and cover to keep warm. Cook the remaining gnocchi in 3 more batches; transfer to the bowl.

5. To serve, ladle the hot Tomato Sauce over the gnocchi and toss until well coated. Serve hot.

—Da Celestino, Florence, Italy

Top to bottom: Broccoli Rabe and Anchovy Sauce with Orecchiette (p. 142) and Scallop and Pine Nut Sauce with Spaghettini and Basil (p. 138).

Left to right: Gratin of Sausage and Polenta (p. 151), Gratin of Zucchini à la Bordelaise (p. 136) and Leek and Cabbage Flan (p. 119).

RICE WITH SOUR CREAM AND CHILES

6 TO 8 SERVINGS

2¼ teaspoons salt
1 tablespoon unsalted butter
2 cups converted rice
2 fresh poblano or long green chiles
1 cup sour cream
1 large onion, finely chopped
¼ cup minced fresh coriander
2 tablespoons lard or vegetable oil
1 garlic clove, minced
1 can (16-ounces) corn kernels, drained or 2 cups frozen corn, defrosted
½ pound grated white Cheddar cheese (about 2 cups)

1. In a large saucepan, combine 2 teaspoons of the salt, the butter and 4 cups of water. Bring to a boil. Add the rice and return to a boil, then reduce the heat to very low, cover tightly and cook until all the water is absorbed, 25 to 30 minutes. Fluff the rice up with a fork; set aside.

2. Meanwhile, roast the chiles over an open flame or broil 4 inches from the heat, turning with tongs, until charred all over, about 10 minutes. Seal them in a bag and let steam to loosen the skin, about 10 minutes. Peel under cold running water; pat dry. Remove the stems and seeds. Cut into ¼-inch dice.

3. Preheat the oven to 350°. In a medium bowl, combine the sour cream, ¼ cup of the onion, the coriander and remaining ¼ teaspoon salt.

4. In a large skillet, melt the lard over moderate heat. Add the remaining onion and the garlic. Cook until softened and translucent, about 2 minutes. Add the chiles and cook, stirring, for 1 minute. Remove from the heat. (**The recipe can be made up to this point 3 hours in advance.** Warm gently over low heat before continuing.)

5. Combine the rice with the cooked onion-pepper mixture. Add the corn, cheese and seasoned sour cream and stir until mixed.

6. Turn the rice mixture into a buttered large shallow baking dish. Bake uncovered until it is heated through and slightly crusty on top, about 30 minutes.

—Zarela Martinez, Café Marimba, New York City

BAKED RISOTTO

8 SERVINGS

4 tablespoons unsalted butter
1 tablespoon olive oil
2 medium onions, coarsely chopped
2 generous pinches of saffron threads
2 tablespoons white wine or dry vermouth
3 cups chicken stock or canned broth
2 cups long-grain rice
1 package (10 ounces) frozen green peas, defrosted
2 cups freshly grated Parmesan cheese (about ½ pound)

1. In a heavy medium saucepan, melt the butter in the oil over moderate heat. Add the onions, cover and cook until softened and translucent, about 10 minutes.

2. Meanwhile, sprinkle the saffron over the white wine in a small bowl and set aside. In a saucepan, heat the broth and 1 cup of water until barely simmering.

3. Stir the rice into the onions and cook, stirring, until the rice becomes translucent, about 5 minutes. Increase the heat to moderately high and add the broth all at once. Add the saffron and wine and stir well. Reduce the heat to low, cover and cook until the rice has absorbed all the liquid, 20 to 30 minutes. (**The recipe may be prepared to this point a day ahead.** Tightly cover the rice and refrigerate. Return to room temperature before continuing.)

4. Preheat the oven to 425°. Stir the peas and 1½ cups of the Parmesan into the rice. Turn into a large, shallow ovenproof casserole. Sprinkle the remaining ½ cup cheese on top and bake for 20 minutes, or until the cheese is melted and the rice is heated through.

—W. Peter Prestcott

RISOTTO WITH SHRIMP AND CELERY

6 SERVINGS

¼ cup olive oil, preferably extra-virgin
4⅓ cups finely chopped celery (9 to 10 ribs)
2 medium carrots, coarsely chopped
2 medium leeks (white and tender green), finely chopped
12 to 16 parsley stems
3 pounds fish heads and bones
8 cups beef stock or 4 cups canned broth plus 4 cups water
1 small onion, finely chopped
1 garlic clove, minced
*1½ cups arborio rice**
¾ pound small shrimp, shelled
⅛ teaspoon freshly ground pepper
Salt
1 tablespoon unsalted butter (optional)
**Available in specialty food shops and Italian markets*

1. In a large saucepan or stockpot, heat 2 tablespoons of the oil. Add 4 cups of the celery, the carrots, leeks and parsley stems. Cover and cook over moderate heat until softened, about 15 minutes.

Savory Cheese Soufflé (p. 118).

2. Meanwhile, remove the gills and all traces of blood from the heads and bones. Cut into large pieces and rinse thoroughly under cold running water. Add to the vegetables, cover and cook, stirring occasionally, for 15 minutes.

3. Add the broth and simmer over moderately low heat for 45 minutes. Line a sieve with a double thickness of dampened cheesecloth and strain the stock into a large saucepan; discard the solids. If the stock measures less than 6 cups, add water to make up the difference; if there is more than 6 cups, boil to reduce. Adjust the heat so that the stock continues to simmer.

4. In a large noncorrodible saucepan or flameproof casserole, heat the remaining 2 tablespoons oil. Add the onion and the remaining ⅓ cup celery and cook over moderate heat until the onion is softened and translucent, about 2 minutes. Add the garlic and cook for 30 seconds. Add the rice and stir until coated with oil and slightly translucent, 1 to 2 minutes.

5. Add ½ cup of the simmering stock to the rice and cook, adjusting the heat to maintain a simmer and stirring constantly, until the rice has absorbed most of the liquid. Continue to cook, adding ½ cup of stock at a time and stirring, until the rice is almost tender but still slightly crunchy in the center, 20 to 25 minutes.

6. Add the shrimp; season with the pepper and salt to taste. Continue to cook, stirring and adding ¼ cup of stock at a time, until the rice is tender but firm and the shrimp are pink and just barely translucent in the center, 3 to 4 minutes; reserve any extra stock for another use. Stir in the butter, if desired, and serve immediately.

RISOTTO AL BAROLO

F&W BEVERAGE SUGGESTION
Dolcetto, such as Renato Ratti or Pio Cesare

6 SERVINGS

3½ cups beef stock or canned chicken broth
1¼ cups Barolo wine
3 tablespoons unsalted butter
1 small onion, finely chopped
*1½ cups arborio rice**
½ cup freshly grated Parmesan cheese
¾ teaspoon salt
¼ teaspoon coarsely cracked pepper
2 tablespoons chopped parsley
**Available in specialty food shops and Italian markets*

1. In a medium noncorrodible saucepan, bring the broth and 1 cup of wine to a simmer.

2. Meanwhile, in a large noncorrodible saucepan or flameproof casserole, melt 2 tablespoons of the butter over moderate heat. Add the onion and sauté, stirring occasionally, until softened but not browned, about 2 minutes. Stir in the rice and cook, stirring, until the grains are well coated with butter and slightly translucent, 1 to 2 minutes.

3. Stir in ½ cup of the simmering broth and cook, stirring constantly, until the rice has absorbed most of the liquid. Gradually adding broth, ½ cup at a time, cook, stirring constantly, until the rice is almost tender but still a bit crunchy in the center, 20 to 25 minutes.

4. Stir in the cheese, salt and pepper. Continue to cook, stirring and adding the remaining broth as necessary, ¼ cup at a time, until the rice is tender but still firm and is bound with a creamy sauce, 3 to 6 minutes longer. Stir in the remaining ¼ cup of wine, the parsley and the remaining 1 tablespoon butter. Serve immediately.

—Anne Disrude

WILD RICE AND APPLE CIDER PILAF

6 SERVINGS

2 cups unsweetened apple cider
1 cup wild rice
6 tablespoons unsalted butter
½ cup sliced almonds
½ cup raisins
¾ teaspoon salt
½ teaspoon freshly ground pepper
½ teaspoon cinnamon
¼ teaspoon freshly grated nutmeg

1. In a large noncorrodible saucepan, bring the cider and 1½ cups of water to a boil over high heat. Reduce the heat to moderately low and stir in the wild rice. Simmer, covered, until the rice is tender but still firm, 30 to 40 minutes. Strain, discarding the cooking liquid.

2. In a large skillet, melt the butter over moderate heat. Add the almonds and raisins and cook, stirring, until the almonds are light brown, about 5 minutes.

3. Add the salt, pepper, cinnamon and nutmeg. Stir in the wild rice and cook until warmed through, about 1 minute.

WILD MUSHROOM AND SCALLION PILAF

6 TO 8 SERVINGS

2 ounces dried porcini mushrooms
1 cup boiling water
2 tablespoons unsalted butter
2 tablespoons peanut oil
2 cups converted rice
3 cups hot chicken stock or canned broth
1 cup thinly sliced scallions (white part only)
½ cup freshly grated Parmesan cheese

½ cup coarsely chopped pecans
Salt and freshly ground pepper

1. Place the dried mushrooms in a medium bowl. Cover with the boiling water and soak until softened, about 30 minutes.

2. In a medium skillet, melt the butter in the oil over moderately high heat. Add the rice and sauté, stirring until translucent, about 5 minutes.

3. Add the chicken stock, stir well and bring to a boil. Reduce the heat to low, cover tightly and simmer until almost all of the liquid has been absorbed, about 20 minutes.

4. Preheat the oven to 375°. Drain the mushrooms in a cheesecloth-lined sieve set over a bowl. Add the strained liquid to the rice. Cover and simmer for 5 minutes.

5. Rinse the mushrooms under warm water. Drain on paper towels and chop coarsely. Add the mushrooms, scallions, Parmesan cheese and pecans to the rice. Toss gently to combine. Season with salt and pepper to taste. **(The recipe can be prepared several hours ahead to this point.** Let the rice return to room temperature before proceeding.)

6. Spoon the pilaf into an 8-cup ovenproof serving dish and bake for 20 minutes, until the top is golden.

—W. Peter Prestcott

GRATIN OF SAUSAGE AND POLENTA

6 TO 8 SERVINGS

5 tablespoons olive oil, preferably extra-virgin
2 tablespoons minced shallots
1 tablespoon minced garlic
1 can (35 ounces) Italian peeled tomatoes, drained and coarsely chopped
½ teaspoon oregano
½ teaspoon thyme
2 teaspoons salt
¾ teaspoon freshly ground pepper
1 pound hot Italian sausage, casing removed
3 ounces thickly sliced prosciutto, finely diced
¾ cup yellow cornmeal
8 tablespoons (1 stick) unsalted butter
½ cup freshly grated Parmesan cheese
4 ounces Italian Fontina cheese, thinly sliced

1. In a heavy medium saucepan, warm 3 tablespoons of the oil over moderate heat. Add the shallots and garlic and cook until they are softened but not browned, 1 to 2 minutes.

2. Add the tomatoes, oregano, thyme, ¼ teaspoon of the salt and ¼ teaspoon of the pepper. Reduce the heat to low, partially cover and cook, stirring frequently, until the tomato juices evaporate and a thick puree forms, 45 to 50 minutes. Remove from the heat and set aside.

3. In a medium skillet, heat the remaining 2 tablespoons oil. Add the sausage and cook over moderate heat, breaking up the meat with a fork, until nicely browned, 5 to 10 minutes.

4. With a slotted spoon, transfer the sausage meat to the tomato puree. Add the prosciutto.

5. In a heavy medium saucepan, bring 3 cups of water and 1¼ teaspoons of the salt to a boil over high heat. Stir in the cornmeal in a very slow stream, stirring constantly to avoid any lumps. Reduce the heat to low and cook, stirring, until the polenta pulls away from the sides of the pan, about 15 minutes. Remove from the heat and stir in 6 tablespoons of the butter, ¼ cup of the Parmesan cheese and the remaining ½ teaspoon salt and ½ teaspoon pepper.

6. Butter a large (2-quart) rectangular or oval baking dish, about 2 inches deep. Spread half the polenta in the dish. Top with the Fontina and 1 tablespoon of the Parmesan. Cover the cheeses with the tomato-sausage mixture. Sprinkle with another 1 tablespoon Parmesan. Top with the remaining polenta, smoothing it level with a spatula. **(The recipe can be prepared ahead to this point.** Cover and refrigerate. Let return to room temperature before proceeding.)

7. Preheat the oven to 350°. Dot the top of the gratin with the remaining 2 tablespoons of butter. Sprinkle with the remaining 2 tablespoons of Parmesan cheese.

8. Bake for 35 to 40 minutes, or until golden brown on top. Remove from the oven and let stand for about 15 minutes before serving.

—Perla Meyers

ENZO'S SUGO FOR POLENTA

Use your favorite recipe for polenta, and make this rich meaty sauce to go with it.

8 SERVINGS

3 tablespoons olive oil
2 carrots, chopped (about 1 cup)
3 medium garlic cloves, chopped
1 medium onion, chopped (about ½ cup)
¼ cup chopped fresh parsley
1 rib celery, chopped (about ½ cup)
2 cans (35 ounces each) peeled Italian tomatoes, drained
½ teaspoon salt
¼ teaspoon freshly ground pepper
1 bay leaf
¼ teaspoon rosemary
2 cups medium-dry white wine
16 links of Italian sweet sausage
3 pounds of spareribs, cut into small pieces

1. In a large noncorrodible skillet, warm the olive oil until hot. Add the carrots, garlic, onion, parsley and celery and sauté lightly.

2. Add the tomatoes, salt, pepper, bay leaf, rosemary and wine. Cook the sauce until it is simmering steadily and has thickened somewhat. Add the sausages and spareribs, reduce the heat to low and cook for about 1½ hours, or until the spareribs are fork tender.

3. Remove the sausages and ribs to a platter. Cover with foil and keep in a warm oven. Reduce the sauce by three-fourths, about 20 minutes.

4. Arrange the meat over freshly cooked polenta. Strain the sauce and pour it over the meat and polenta and serve.

KASHA VARNISHKES (BUCKWHEAT GROATS WITH NOODLES)

This dish is an ideal accompaniment to a brisket of beef; the kasha soaks up the rich gravy, which gives the kasha more zip.

8 SERVINGS

1 cup medium buckwheat groats
1 egg, beaten
½ teaspoon salt
2 cups boiling water
1 package (12 ounces) bow tie egg noodles
2 large onions, minced
2 tablespoons vegetable oil
Freshly ground pepper

1. In a medium skillet or saucepan, stir together the buckwheat and the egg over low heat until all the grains are coated. Add the salt and 2 cups boiling water. Cook, covered, until the kasha absorbs all the water, 5 to 10 minutes.

2. In a large pot of boiling salted water, cook the noodles until tender to the bite, 8 to 10 minutes; drain well.

3. Meanwhile, in a medium skillet, sauté the minced onions in the vegetable oil over moderate heat until lightly browned, about 5 minutes.

4. In a large serving bowl, combine the noodles and kasha. Scrape the onions and their oil over the noodles. Toss to coat. Season with salt and pepper to taste.

—Second Avenue Kosher Delicatessen, New York City

BLACK AND RED PEPPER ROLLS

Steven Froman, the pastry chef and chief bread baker at San Francisco's Campton Place restaurant, is the author of these delicious soft rolls.

MAKES 2 DOZEN DINNER ROLLS

1 large red bell pepper
3 tablespoons olive oil
1 teaspoon minced fresh rosemary or ½ teaspoon dried
2 envelopes (¼ ounce each) active dry yeast
1 cup warm milk (105° to 110°)
3 tablespoons sugar
2 eggs
1 tablespoon coarsely ground black pepper
1½ teaspoons salt
4 cups bread flour or all-purpose flour

1. Roast the red pepper over a gas flame or under a preheated broiler, turning occasionally, until blackened all over. Seal in a plastic bag for 10 to 15 minutes. Remove and discard the skin, seeds and stem. Cut the pepper into ¼-inch dice. Cover with the olive oil, stir in the rosemary and set aside. **(This can be done a day ahead** and left at room temperature to infuse.)

2. Combine the yeast, milk and sugar in a large warmed bowl, stirring to dissolve the yeast. Set aside in a warm place until foamy, about 10 minutes.

3. Beat in the eggs, red pepper and seasoned oil, black pepper and salt. Stir in the flour 1 cup at a time until mixed.

4. Turn out onto a lightly floured surface and knead until the dough is smooth and elastic. Dust with additional flour if needed to prevent sticking. Place the dough in a lightly oiled bowl, turn over so that the top will be coated with oil, cover with a dry towel and let rise in a warm draft-free place until doubled in bulk, about 1 hour.

5. Divide the dough into 24 pieces. Roll into balls and place about 1½ inches apart on 2 oiled baking sheets. Let rise again, lightly covered with plastic wrap, until doubled, 40 to 60 minutes. Preheat the oven to 375°.

6. Bake the rolls in the center of the oven until the tops are brown and the bottoms sound hollow when tapped, about 20 minutes. Let cool.

—Barbara Tropp

CARAWAY RYE BREAD

Some rye loaves take many hours or even days to make because of the time it takes for the dough to ferment, but this rye bread develops a tasty rye/caraway flavor in a matter of minutes. The dough can be fashioned into long slender loaves ideal for buffet servings or into large round loaves good for sandwiches. If caraway isn't your seed, make the loaf with sesame or poppy.

MAKES 2 LOAVES

¼ cup dark molasses, preferably unsulphured

3 tablespoons vegetable shortening or lard
3 cups rye flour
2 envelopes (1/4 ounce each) quick-rising yeast
3 tablespoons caraway seeds
2 teaspoons salt
1 egg, at room temperature, beaten
About 3 1/2 cups bread or unbleached all-purpose flour
Egg wash: 1 egg and 1 tablespoon milk beaten together until blended

1. Turn the oven to 300° for 1 minute and then turn off to preheat to 100°. In a small saucepan, combine the molasses, shortening and 2 cups of water. Warm over low heat, stirring to melt the shortening, until the liquid reaches 120° to 130°, or is hot to the touch.

2. Place the rye flour in a large mixer bowl and stir in the yeast, 2 tablespoons of the caraway seeds and the salt. Stir in the molasses mixture. Add the egg and stir until well mixed.

3. Add the white flour, 1/2 cup at a time, stirring with a wooden spoon or using a mixer fitted with a dough hook, until the dough forms a shaggy mass. Turn out onto a lightly floured surface and knead 5 to 6 minutes, or continue to knead in the mixer for about 4 minutes, until the dough sticks together in a smooth ball.

4. Fill a large bowl with hot water until it is warm; pour out the water, wipe dry and lightly coat with oil or butter. Place the dough in the bowl and turn to coat with oil. Cover tightly with plastic wrap. Place in the warm oven for 30 minutes, or until doubled in size.

5. Lightly oil a large baking sheet. Remove the dough from the oven and turn out onto a lightly floured surface. Divide in half. Shape each half into either a slender 14- to 16-inch baguette or a round ball, flattened slightly on top. Place on the baking sheet, cover loosely with waxed paper and return to the oven for 30 minutes, or until almost doubled in size.

6. Remove the dough from the oven and set aside, covered, in a warm place. Preheat the oven to 375°. With a sharp knife or razor, make 1/2-inch-deep diagonal cuts in the top of the long loaves or a tic-tac-toe design on round loaves. Brush with the egg wash and sprinkle with the remaining 1 tablespoon caraway seeds.

7. Bake in the center of the oven for 35 to 40 minutes, or until the bottom is hard and sounds hollow when tapped. Cool on a rack before cutting.

—Bernard Clayton, Jr.

PANETTONE

Although most think of the traditional panettone as a tall, cylindrical loaf, the panettone baked in the *panetterie* near the French border on the Mediterranean is a round loaf into which a deep X has been cut to allow the ball of dough to blossom like a flower.

MAKES 2 LOAVES

About 4 cups bread or unbleached all-purpose flour
1 envelope (1/4 ounce) quick-rising yeast
1/3 cup sugar
1 teaspoon salt
1 1/4 cups milk
6 tablespoons unsalted butter
1 whole egg, at room temperature
2 egg yolks, at room temperature
1 1/2 teaspoons aniseed, crushed or ground
1/3 cup (packed) raisins, chopped
1/4 cup chopped mixed candied fruit or citron
2 tablespoons coarsely chopped pine nuts or almonds

1. Turn the oven to 300° for 1 minute and then turn off to preheat to 100°. In a large bowl, combine 1 cup of the flour, the yeast, sugar and salt.

2. In a small saucepan, warm the milk and 4 tablespoons of the butter over low heat, stirring to melt the butter, until the liquid reaches 120° to 130°, or is hot to the touch. Stir the milk mixture into the flour. Stir in the whole egg, egg yolks and aniseed. Beat with a wooden spoon for 4 minutes or in a mixer for 2 minutes until the batter is completely blended.

3. Add the remaining 3 cups flour, 1/2 cup at a time, stirring with the wooden spoon or in a mixer with a dough hook, until the dough forms a smooth elastic ball. Turn out onto a lightly floured surface and knead, sprinkling with flour if the dough becomes sticky, until smooth and satiny, about 6 minutes. (Alternatively, if using a mixer, knead with the dough hook for an additional 5 minutes.)

4. Fill a large bowl with hot water until it is warm; pour out the water, wipe dry and lightly coat with oil or butter. Place the dough in the bowl and turn to coat with oil. Cover the bowl with plastic wrap, place in the warm oven and let rise for 30 minutes, or until doubled in size.

5. Lightly oil a large baking sheet or two 1-pound coffee cans. Toss together the raisins, candied fruit and pine nuts.

6. Remove the dough from the oven and turn out onto a lightly floured surface. Press into a large fat oval. Pour the fruit and nuts into the center and fold in the sides to completely encase the mixture. Knead the dough gently to evenly distribute the fruit and nuts, about 3 minutes.

7. Cut the dough in half and shape each half into a ball. Place the rounds, seam-side down, at least 3 inches apart on the baking sheet and flatten the tops slightly; alternatively, drop

half the dough into each coffee can. Cover with waxed paper and return to the oven for 30 minutes, or until the dough has almost doubled in size.

8. Remove the dough from the oven and set aside in a warm place. Preheat the oven to 375°. With a razor blade or sharp knife, cut a large cross, ½ inch deep and extending halfway down the sides, on the top of each loaf. Make a similar cross on top of the loaves in coffee cans.

9. Place the loaves in the center of the oven or stand the coffee cans upright on the bottom shelf. After 5 minutes, place 1 tablespoon of butter in the center of the cross on each loaf. Bake for 30 minutes longer, or until the loaves are a deep brown and sound hollow when the bottom is tapped. Remove from the oven and let cool on a rack before cutting.

—*Bernard Clayton, Jr.*

WHITE BREAD WITH POPPY SEEDS

A truly basic loaf, this white bread has only five ingredients—yeast, flour, water, sugar and salt. It is the same recipe as is used for many traditional French loaves. The new fast-rise procedure does not allow time for the open network in the dough to develop fully, making this a dense, but no less delicious, loaf. Because there is so little sugar in the dough to caramelize, the crust will not be a deep brown; be sure to brush the loaf with the egg wash before putting it in the oven.

MAKES 2 LOAVES

5½ to 6 cups bread or unbleached all-purpose flour
2 envelopes (¼ ounce each) quick-rising yeast
2½ cups hot water (120° to 130°)
1 tablespoon salt
1 tablespoon sugar
Egg wash: 1 egg and 1 tablespoon milk beaten together until well blended
1 tablespoon poppy seeds

1. Turn the oven to 300° for 1 minute, then turn off to preheat to 100°. In a large bowl, stir together 3½ cups of flour and the yeast. Add the hot water and stir into a batter. Beat with a wooden spoon for 10 minutes or in a mixer with a dough hook for 8 minutes at medium speed, until the dough is elastic and stringy. Beat in the salt and sugar.

2. Add the remaining 2 cups of flour, ½ cup at a time, stirring until the dough forms a rough, shaggy mass.

3. Turn out onto a lightly floured surface and knead until the dough is smooth and elastic, about 6 minutes, or continue to knead in the mixer for 4 minutes. If the dough is still sticky, sprinkle with flour; the dough should remain soft.

4. Fill a large bowl with hot water until it is warm; pour out the water, wipe dry and coat with oil or butter. Place the dough in the bowl and turn to coat with oil. Cover the bowl tightly with plastic wrap. Place in the warm oven and let rise for 30 minutes, or until doubled in size.

5. Lightly oil two medium (8½-by-4½-inch) loaf pans or a large baking sheet. Remove the dough from the oven and turn out onto a lightly floured surface. Divide the dough in half. To make loaves, press each piece of dough into a flat oval roughly the length of the loaf pan. Fold in half lengthwise, tuck under the ends and place seam-side down in the pan. For a free-standing round loaf, shape each piece of dough into a ball. Place seam-side down, at least 3 inches apart on the baking sheet and lightly flatten the top.

6. Cover the dough with waxed paper and return to the oven for 30 minutes, or until doubled in size.

7. Remove the dough from the oven and set aside, covered, in a warm place. Preheat the oven to 400°. With a sharp knife or razor blade, make 3 diagonal cuts, ½ inch deep, across the top of the loaves in the pan or a tic-tac-toe design on the round loaves. Brush with the egg wash and sprinkle with the poppy seeds.

8. Bake in the center of the oven for 30 to 40 minutes, or until the loaves are golden brown and the bottom sounds hollow when tapped. Remove the loaves from the pans and let cool on a rack before slicing.

—*Bernard Clayton, Jr.*

FRESH CORN TORTILLAS

Masa harina is a special corn flour used to make tortillas. It is available in Latin American groceries and many supermarkets. The easiest way to make homemade tortillas is with a tortilla press, available in specialty cookware stores and Latin American groceries.

MAKES 8 TORTILLAS, 6 INCHES IN DIAMETER

2 cups (8 ounces) masa harina (see Note)
½ teaspoon salt
About 1¼ cups hot water

1. Combine the *masa harina* and salt in a medium bowl and gradually stir in 1¼ cups hot water. Gather the dough into a ball and press into a thick disk between 2 sheets of plastic wrap. If the dough sticks when you

press it between the plastic, it is too wet: knead in 1 or 2 tablespoons of *masa harina*. If the dough breaks when you pull off the plastic, it is too dry: stir in a few drops of water until it holds together. It takes practice to know exactly how moist the dough should be.

2. Place the dough in a plastic bag, twist the top to seal and let rest for 1 hour.

3. Have ready 16 squares of waxed paper and a tortilla press. Divide the dough into 8 equal portions and roll them into balls. Keep those that you are not working with covered. One at a time, flatten a ball of dough between the palms of your hands. Place one square of waxed paper on the tortilla press. Place the flattened dough in the center and top with another square of waxed paper. Press into a 6-inch circle. Remove the tortilla, still between the 2 sheets of paper. Repeat to make 8 tortillas. Set the covered tortillas aside for up to 1 hour before using.

NOTE: Some packages of *masa harina* are labeled "instant," but they will work just as well.

—Jim Fobel

RHODE ISLAND JOHNNYCAKES

A definitive version of this simple but delicious regional specialty, best enjoyed with butter and maple syrup.

MAKES ABOUT 12 CAKES

1 cup stone-ground white cornmeal
1 teaspoon sugar
¼ teaspoon salt
1 to 1½ cups boiling water
¼ cup milk
1 tablespoon unsalted butter, melted

1. In a medium bowl, combine the cornmeal, sugar and salt.

2. Gradually pour the boiling water (it is important that the water be truly boiling, as this begins the cooking process) into the cornmeal mixture, beginning with 1 cup and adding more as necessary until the batter is somewhat thicker than pancake batter yet thinner than mashed potatoes.

3. Add the milk and melted butter and mix well to combine.

4. Brush a heavy medium griddle or skillet with vegetable oil and place over moderate heat. Drop the batter by well-rounded tablespoons onto the griddle and cook, turning once, until lightly browned, 25 to 30 minutes.

—Dovecrest Indian Restaurant, Exeter, Rhode Island

CHEESE AND CHILE CORN BREAD (TORTA DE ELOTE)

6 TO 8 SERVINGS

½ pound (2 sticks) unsalted butter, softened
2 tablespoons sugar
3 eggs, at room temperature
*1½ cups rice flour**
1 tablespoon baking powder
1 teaspoon salt
1 can (16 ounces) corn kernels or 2 cups frozen corn, defrosted
4 ounces white Cheddar cheese, grated (about 1 cup)
1 fresh poblano chile, seeded and finely diced
**Available at health food stores*

1. Preheat the oven to 350°. In a large bowl, cream the butter. Beat in the sugar, 1 tablespoon at a time, and continue beating until light and fluffy. Add the eggs, 1 at a time, beating well after each addition.

2. In a separate bowl, combine the rice flour, baking powder and salt. Add to the butter and beat until just incorporated into a thick batter.

3. In a food processor or blender, chop the corn until minced but not pureed, about 10 seconds. Stir into the batter. Fold in the cheese and chile.

4. Turn the batter into a buttered 6-cup shallow baking dish. Smooth the top with a spatula. Bake until the corn bread is golden brown and crusty on top, or a cake tester inserted in the center comes out clean, 25 to 30 minutes. Serve warm or hot as a side dish.

—Zarela Martinez, Café Marimba, New York City

CHEESE CORNSTICKS

MAKES 2½ DOZEN

2 cups yellow cornmeal
2 cups all-purpose flour
2 tablespoons baking powder
2 teaspoons salt
⅔ cup corn oil or other flavorless vegetable oil
2 cups milk
2 eggs, lightly beaten
¾ cup freshly grated Parmesan cheese (about 3 ounces)
Dash of hot pepper sauce
4 tablespoons unsalted butter, melted

1. Preheat the oven to 400°. Place a heavy 12-stick cornstick pan in the oven to heat. In a large bowl, combine the cornmeal, flour, baking powder and salt.

2. Form a well in the center of the dry ingredients. Pour in the oil, milk and eggs. Beat the liquids together, then blend with the dry ingredients. Stir in the cheese and hot sauce.

3. Paint the preheated cornstick

pan generously with melted butter. Spoon some of the batter into the pan, using 2 heaping tablespoons of batter for each stick. Bake the cornsticks in the center of the oven for 20 minutes, or until the edges are lightly browned. Turn out onto a rack to cool. Repeat with the remaining batter.

—Lila Gault

BANNOCK WITH WILD MUSHROOMS

The term *bannock* means an unleavened bread. This recipe, which comes from my mother-in-law's Scottish family, is more a soufflé than a bread. Mixed with mushrooms, this dish became a big hit in my cooking classes. It is wonderful served with a pan-fried steak or meat stew. Important: Buy fine-quality stone-ground cornmeal.

4 TO 6 SERVINGS

½ pound fresh shiitake (Golden Oak) mushrooms
10 tablespoons unsalted butter
1 large garlic clove, minced
1 teaspoon salt
¼ teaspoon freshly ground pepper
2 cups milk
⅔ cup coarse stone-ground cornmeal
3 eggs, separated

1. Discard the stems of the shiitake. Cut the caps into ¼-inch-thick strips.
2. In a large skillet, melt 6 tablespoons of the butter. Add the mushrooms, garlic, ½ teaspoon of the salt and the pepper. Cover and cook over low heat for 20 minutes, stirring occasionally. Remove from the heat and set aside.
3. Preheat the oven to 350°. Butter a shallow 2-quart baking dish. In a large heavy saucepan, heat the milk. Gradually whisk in the cornmeal in a thin stream. Add the remaining ½ teaspoon salt and cook, stirring, until the mixture is the consistency of thick cream. Add the remaining 4 tablespoons butter, 1 tablespoon at a time, until the butter is melted and incorporated. Remove from the heat.
4. Whisk in the egg yolks, 1 at a time. Add the cooked mushrooms and their juices and fold until mixed.
5. Beat the egg whites until firm but not dry. Fold the egg whites into the cornmeal and mushroom mixture.
6. Pour the batter into the prepared baking dish and bake for about 30 minutes, or until the bannock is puffy and browned. Serve at once.

NOTE: This recipe easily doubles. If you do, bake it in a 3-quart dish.

—Lydie Marshall

COUNTRY HAM AND WILD MUSHROOM STUFFING

My favorite New York gourmet superdeli offers Smithfield ham ready-to-eat, saving me the soaking, scrubbing and simmering otherwise necessary. Those not so fortunate can order the genuine article by mail (see Sources, below).

Step 6 calls for fat and juices from a roast turkey (see Roast Fresh Turkey, page 84). If you are making this stuffing without roasting a bird, substitute chicken broth.

8 SERVINGS

1½ ounces (about 1½ cups) dried porcini mushrooms
2 cups chicken stock or canned broth
10 cups crumbled day-old white bread
6 tablespoons unsalted butter
½ pound country ham, cut into ½-inch cubes
2 medium onions, chopped
1 teaspoon thyme
1 cup finely chopped Italian flat-leaf parsley
½ teaspoon salt
1 teaspoon freshly ground pepper

1. Rinse the porcini thoroughly under cold running water and place in a small bowl. In a small saucepan, bring the stock to a boil. Pour over the mushrooms and let stand, stirring occasionally, for 1 hour.
2. Put the crumbled bread in a large mixing bowl. In a medium skillet, melt 2 tablespoons of the butter over moderate heat until foaming. Add the ham and cook, stirring, until browned, about 10 minutes. With a slotted spoon, transfer the ham to the bowl with the bread.
3. Return the skillet to moderate heat, add the remaining 4 tablespoons butter and heat until foaming. Add the onions and thyme, cover and reduce the heat to moderate. Cook, stirring occasionally, until the onions are tender and lightly colored, 10 to 15 minutes. Pour the onions and butter over the bread in the bowl.
4. With a slotted spoon, lift the whole mushrooms from their soaking liquid and transfer to the mixing bowl. (If making the Madeira Gravy, p. 84, to go with the turkey, reserve the mushroom soaking liquid. Strain the liquid through a funnel lined with a coffee filter or a strainer lined with several thicknesses of dampened cheesecloth.)
5. Add the parsley to the stuffing, season with the salt and pepper and stir well to mix. Transfer to a medium baking dish, preferably with a tight-fitting lid. (**The stuffing can be prepared to this point several hours in advance of baking.** Refrigeration is not necessary.)
6. Preheat the oven to 325°. After removing all of the fat and juices from the turkey roasting pan, you should

have at least 1½ cups. If not, add canned chicken broth to equal that amount. Spoon the juices evenly over the stuffing, cover tightly and bake for 35 to 45 minutes, until the stuffing is steaming and the sides and bottom are crunchy and brown.

SOURCES: Country hams are available by mail from The Smithfield Ham and Products Co., Inc., P.O. Box 487, Smithfield, VA 23430, (804) 357-2121; Taylor Farms Country Hams, 119 S. Walnut, Cynthiana, KY 41031, (606) 234-5015; and S. Wallace Edwards & Sons, Inc., Surry, VA 23883, (800) 222-4267.

SUBSTITUTIONS: Dried cèpes, morels or shiitake mushrooms can all be used to good effect if *porcini* are unavailable. Any good, firm, smoky ham can be sustituted for *Smithfield ham.*

—Michael McLaughlin

BACON AND SCALLION SKILLET BISCUITS

These biscuits are great for brunch, just split and buttered. Or they can be served at a cocktail buffet, filled with smoked ham, turkey or cheese.

MAKES ABOUT 2 DOZEN

2 cups all-purpose flour
2 teaspoons baking powder
1 teaspoon baking soda
¼ teaspoon salt
¼ cup lard, chilled
2 tablespoons chilled unsalted butter, plus 3 tablespoons melted unsalted butter
½ cup plus 1½ tablespoons buttermilk
4 slices of cooked bacon, minced
½ cup chopped scallions

1. Preheat the oven to 375°. Lightly grease a 10-inch ovenproof skillet or cake pan.

2. Into a large bowl, sift together the flour, baking powder, baking soda and salt. Cut in the lard and 2 tablespoons cold butter until the mixture resembles coarse meal. Pour in the buttermilk and mix until just blended.

3. Sprinkle the bacon and scallions on top. Lightly knead and fold the dough until the ingredients are evenly distributed.

4. On a lightly floured surface, roll the dough out into a round, ⅜ inch thick. Dip a 2¼-inch biscuit cutter or glass in flour and cut out as many biscuits as possible. Arrange in the greased skillet tightly packed in a single layer. Gather the scraps and reroll the dough; cut out several more biscuits and fill the skillet.

5. Bake uncovered for 15 minutes. Brush the biscuit tops with the remaining 3 tablespoons melted butter and return to the oven to bake until golden brown on top and cooked through, about 5 minutes longer.

CHANTERELLE AND CHEVRE PIZZA

This pizza from the spa at the Sonoma Mission Inn is low in calories (261 per serving), cholesterol and sodium. To simplify the preparation, use canned low-sodium tomato sauce and substitute lightly toasted whole wheat pita halves for the dough made in Steps 1, 2 and 5.

F&W BEVERAGE SUGGESTION
Sauvignon Blanc, such as Cakebread

6 SERVINGS

2 teaspoons honey
½ cup lukewarm water (105° to 110°)
1¼ teaspoons active dry yeast
1 cup whole wheat pastry flour
⅓ cup unbleached all-purpose flour
¼ teaspoon salt (optional)
2 tablespoons olive oil
1½ pounds fresh chanterelles or cultivated mushrooms
2 tablespoons dry sherry
2 tablespoons dry white wine
1 large shallot, minced
1 cup low-fat cottage cheese
*6 tablespoons low-sodium fresh goat cheese (such as Kendall Farm)**
1 tablespoon chopped fresh dill
1¾ teaspoons chopped fresh thyme or ¾ teaspoon dried
⅛ teaspooon chopped fresh rosemary or a pinch of dried, crumbled
1 tablespoon cornmeal
Low-Sodium Tomato Sauce (p. 235), cooled to room temperature
¼ cup minced fresh parsley
¼ cup minced fresh chives
**Available at health food stores*

1. In a small bowl, dissolve the honey in the warm water. Sprinkle the yeast over the top and let stand for 5 minutes.

2. In a medium bowl, combine the whole wheat flour, all-purpose flour and salt. Make a well in the center, pour in the yeast mixture and 1 tablespoon plus 1 teaspoon of the olive oil. Stir until blended. Turn out the dough onto a lightly floured surface and knead briefly for about 2 minutes, until it forms a smooth mass. Put in a lightly oiled bowl, turn to coat with the oil, cover with a towel and set in a warm place to rise until doubled in bulk, 1 to 1½ hours.

3. Cut the chanterelles into large pieces or thickly slice the mushrooms. Put in a large skillet. Sprinkle the sherry, wine and shallot over the mushrooms. Cover and cook over moderate heat for 10 minutes. Drain off any liquid in the pan; set the chanterelles aside.

4. In a medium bowl, combine the

cottage cheese, goat cheese, dill, thyme and rosemary. Mix to blend well.

5. Preheat the oven to 450°. When the dough has risen once, punch it down and knead for 30 seconds. Form into a 6-inch log shape and cut into 6 equal pieces. Roll out each piece to a 5½-inch circle about ⅛ inch thick. Turn under about ½ inch of dough and pinch to form a raised border. Sprinkle the cornmeal over a heavy baking sheet. Place the dough rounds on the sheet. Cover the rounds lightly and let rise for 20 minutes.

6. Paint the dough rounds lightly with the remaining 2 teaspoons olive oil. Spread a generous 2 tablespoons of the tomato sauce over each pizza. Spoon about 2 tablespoons of the cheese mixture over the sauce. Divide the mushrooms among the pizzas.

7. Bake the pizzas on the lowest rack of the oven for 15 to 20 minutes, until the crust is well browned and cooked through.

8. Sprinkle with the parsley and chives. Serve hot.

—Christian Chavanne,
Sonoma Mission Inn and Spa,
Boyes Hot Springs, California

HOT CAJUN SAUSAGE CALZONE

MAKES 4 CALZONE

DOUGH:
1 tablespoon active dry yeast
Pinch of sugar
¾ cup warm water (105° to 110°)
1 tablespoon olive oil
2½ cups all-purpose flour
½ teaspoon salt

FILLING:
3 tablespoons olive oil
1 pound hot Louisiana or Italian sausage, sliced
2 medium onions, thinly sliced
1 large red bell pepper, sliced
¾ teaspoon thyme
¾ teaspoon oregano
¾ teaspoon paprika
⅔ cup canned black beans, drained
Salt and freshly ground black pepper
Cornmeal

1. *Make the dough:* In small bowl, mix the yeast and sugar with the water. Let stand for about 10 minutes, until foamy. Add the oil to yeast.

2. Place the flour and salt in a food processor. Process briefly to combine. With the machine on, add the yeast mixture through the feed tube and mix until a ball of dough forms on the blade. Remove the dough and knead lightly for about 3 minutes.

3. Place the dough in an oiled bowl; turn to coat. Cover and let rise in a warm, draft-free place until doubled in bulk.

4. *Meanwhile, make the filling:* In a large skillet, heat the oil. Add the sausage and sauté until cooked through, about 8 minutes. Remove the sausage with a slotted spoon and set aside.

5. Add the onions, bell pepper, thyme, oregano and paprika to the oil in the skillet. Cook over low heat until the onion is very soft, about 15 minutes. Add the reserved sausage and the beans and mix. Season with salt and black pepper to taste. (**The filling can be made a day ahead and refrigerated, covered.** Let return to room temperature before proceeding.)

6. Preheat the oven to 500°. Divide the dough into 4 equal portions. On a lightly floured surface, roll out each piece to a circle about ¼ inch thick.

7. Mound one-quarter of the sausage filling on half of each circle, leaving a ½-inch margin. Fold the dough over the filling to make a semicircle. Pinch and crimp the edges well to seal.

8. Sprinkle cornmeal over a large baking sheet and arrange the calzone on top. Bake for 13 minutes, or until golden brown.

—Jeanette Ferrary & Louise Fiszer

SPA TOSTADAS

This generous colorful dish is a dieter's delight. Even those not counting calories will enjoy it, especially with a generous splash of hot sauce.

6 SERVINGS

½ cup dried pinto beans
2 garlic cloves, minced
1 teaspoon cumin
½ teaspoon chili powder
⅛ teaspoon natural hickory smoke extract (optional)
1 large green bell pepper, cut into ½-inch dice
1 large red bell pepper, cut into ½-inch dice
1 small white onion, cut into ½-inch dice
1½ cups finely shredded iceberg lettuce
1½ cups finely shredded red cabbage
1½ cups finely shredded green cabbage
¾ cups coarsely shredded jicama
1 tablespoon fresh lime juice
¼ medium, ripe avocado
¼ cup low-fat plain yogurt
2 teaspoons fresh lemon juice
*¼ teaspoon Vegit seasoning**
Low-Sodium Fresh Salsa (p. 235)
¼ cup safflower oil
6 (6-inch) corn tortillas
6 ounces low-sodium, low-fat Cheddar cheese, shredded (about 1½ cups)
3 cherry tomatoes, halved
**Available at health food stores*

1. Place the beans in a small saucepan and add enough cold water to cover by an inch. Bring to a boil over high heat. Turn off the heat, cover and let stand for 1 hour. Drain the beans, return to the saucepan and cover with 1½ cups of cold water. Bring to a boil, reduce the heat, cover and simmer until soft, 2 to 2½ hours. Add the garlic and cook for 15 minutes. Add ½ teaspoon of the cumin, the chili powder and hickory smoke extract. Cook for 5 minutes longer.

2. Drain the beans, reserving the cooking liquid. In a food processor, puree the beans until smooth. Add about 1½ tablespoons of the cooking liquid to obtain a creamy texture. Scrape into a bowl and set aside. (**The recipe can be prepared up to 3 days ahead to this point.** Cover the bean puree and refrigerate.)

3. In a medium saucepan, combine the green and red bell peppers, the onion and the remaining ½ teaspoon cumin. Add ½ cup of water, cover and cook until softened but still bright in color, about 5 minutes. Drain the peppers and set aside.

4. In a large bowl, toss together the shredded lettuce and red and green cabbage. In a medium bowl, toss the jicama with the lime juice.

5. In another bowl, mash the avocado with a fork until quite smooth. Add the yogurt, lemon juice and Vegit and whisk until well blended. Stir in 1 tablespoon of the Fresh Salsa.

6. In a small skillet, heat the safflower oil over high heat to 385°. Fry the tortillas one at a time, turning, until crisp, about 20 seconds on each side. Drain on paper towels. Pat off any excess oil.

7. To assemble the tostadas, reheat the pureed beans in a small heavy saucepan, stirring until warmed through. Spread about 3 level tablespoons of the bean puree on each tortilla. Divide the pepper mixture among the tostadas. Then layer on the cabbage and lettuce mixture, shredded jicama and shredded cheese. Top each with about 1 tablespoon of the guacamole. Garnish with a cherry tomato half and serve the remaining salsa on the side.

—Christian Chavanne,
Sonoma Mission Inn and Spa,
Boyes Hot Springs, California

BLUEBERRY-NECTARINE SKILLET PIZZA

This recipe makes enough dough for two fruit pizzas. If you want to make both, double the quantities of fruit and sugar for the topping. If you want to make only one, halve the dough in Step 4 and freeze one half for another time.

6 SERVINGS

6 tablespoons unsalted butter
1 envelope (¼ ounce) active dry yeast
3 to 4 tablespoons sugar
1½ cups lukewarm water (105° to 110°)
4½ cups all-purpose flour
½ teaspoon salt
2 large nectarines, peeled and thinly sliced
½ cup blueberries
1 tablespoon vegetable oil
Unsweetened whipped cream, sour cream or crème fraîche (optional)

1. In a small saucepan, melt 4 tablespoons of the butter. Let cool to room temperature.

2. In a small bowl, blend the yeast and 1 tablespoon of the sugar with ½ cup of the warm water. Let stand for 5 minutes, until it begins to bubble. Stir in the cooled melted butter and the remaining 1 cup water.

3. Place 4 cups of the flour in a food processor and add the salt. Turn the machine on and add the yeast mixture through the feed tube. When the dough forms a ball, remove and knead for 5 minutes, working in the remaining ½ cup flour.

4. Lightly oil a large bowl. Form the dough into a ball and place it in the bowl, turning it once to coat it all over with oil. Cover with plastic wrap and let rise in a warm, draft-free place until doubled in bulk, about 1 hour. (If you're making the dough the night before, cover it with plastic wrap and refrigerate overnight.) Unless you are making two tarts (see headnote), divide the dough in half and freeze half for a future pizza (thaw the dough in the refrigerator before using).

5. Preheat the oven to 450°. Coat a 12-inch cast-iron skillet or griddle with the oil and place it in the oven to heat.

6. Form the dough into an even ball, flatten and then roll into a round 13 to 14 inches in diameter. Sprinkle with 1 tablespoon of the sugar.

7. Remove the hot pan from the oven; pour out any excess oil. (Leave the oven on.) Transfer the round of dough to the hot pan, arranging the dough so that there is a small, even rim extending up the sides of the pan.

8. Arrange the nectarine slices in concentric circles starting at the outside. Fill the center with a single layer of blueberries. Sprinkle with 1 to 2 tablespoons of sugar, depending on the sweetness of the fruit. Dot with the remaining 2 tablespoons butter.

9. Return the pan to the bottom shelf of the oven and reduce the temperature to 400°. Bake for 15 to 20 minutes, until the crust is very pale brown.

10. Remove the pizza from the oven and preheat the broiler. Place

the pizza 3 or 4 inches from the heat for about 5 minutes, until the edges of the nectarines are browned.

11. To serve, cut into slices and serve as is or with unsweetened whipped cream, sour cream or crème fraîche.

—*Anne Disrude*

BREAKFAST TATIN

6 TO 8 SERVINGS

1¾ cups all-pupose flour
2½ teaspoons baking powder
¼ teaspoon salt
½ cup plus 1 tablespoon sugar
10 tablespoons cold unsalted butter, cut into small pieces
6 to 8 cooking apples, such as Golden Delicious—peeled, cored and quartered
1 cup milk
Whipped cream (optional)

1. In a food processor, blend the flour, baking powder, salt, and 1 tablespoon of the sugar. Add 6 tablespoons of the butter and process just until crumbly. Remove to a bowl, cover and refrigerate until ready to bake the tart.

2. Place the remaining ½ cup sugar and 4 tablespoons butter in a 9- to 10-inch heavy ovenproof skillet, preferably cast iron, and melt over moderate heat. Remove from the heat. Arrange the apple quarters in overlapping concentric circles, rounded-side down. (The apples will shrink as they cook, so don't worry that they seem crowded in the pan when you start.)

3. Cook over moderately high heat, rotating the pan occasionally for even browning, until the apples are soft and well browned on the bottom and the liquid that remains is thick and syrupy, about 30 minutes. **(The recipe can be made several hours ahead to this point.** Set aside at room temperature until ready to bake.)

4. Preheat the oven to 450°. Add the milk to the biscuit mixture and blend just to incorporate. Distribute the biscuit mixture evenly over the top of the apples. Bake in the middle of the oven for about 15 minutes, or until browned on top.

5. Let the tart rest for 5 minutes, then invert onto a large round serving plate. (If the apple pieces don't come out evenly or some cling to the pan, just stick them back on where they belong.)

6. Cut into wedges and serve with whipped cream if desired.

—*Anne Disrude*

GRAND MARNIER FRENCH TOAST

The slices of bread must be left out overnight or dried in the oven so that they can absorb the liquid without getting soggy.

4 SERVINGS

1 large loaf of Italian bread, cut on the diagonal into 1-inch-thick slices
4 eggs
2 cups milk
1½ teaspoons vanilla extract
⅓ cup fresh orange juice
1½ teaspoons finely grated orange zest
¼ teaspoon cinnamon
¼ cup Grand Marnier or other orange liqueur
1 pint strawberries, halved
2 teaspoons granulated sugar
3 tablespoons unsalted butter
½ cup plus 1 tablespoon vegetable oil
Confectioners' sugar
Maple syrup

1. Arrange the bread slices on a rack and let stand overnight until completely dried out. (Alternatively, place on a rack in a 200° oven for about 1 hour, until dried out but not toasted.)

2. In a large bowl, whisk together the eggs, milk, vanilla, orange juice and zest, cinnamon and Grand Marnier until well blended. (**The recipe can be prepared one day ahead to this point.** Cover and refrigerate.)

3. Preheat the oven to 200°. Line a heatproof platter with paper towels and place in the oven to warm. In a bowl, toss the berries with the granulated sugar. Let stand at room temperature while you make the French toast.

4. Working in batches, soak one-third of the bread slices in the egg mixture, turning once, until saturated, about 5 minutes.

5. In a large skillet, melt 1 tablespoon of the butter in 3 tablespoons of the oil over moderately high heat until foaming. Using a slotted spoon, drain as many bread slices as will fit in the skillet without crowding and place in the skillet. Fry, turning once, until golden brown, about 4 minutes on each side. Reduce the heat to moderate if the bread is browning too quickly. Remove to the platter in the oven. Pour out excess oil from the skillet and wipe with paper towels. Repeat with the remaining bread, butter and oil.

6. Dust the French toast with confectioners' sugar and serve with the strawberries and maple syrup.

—*Piret's, San Diego, California*

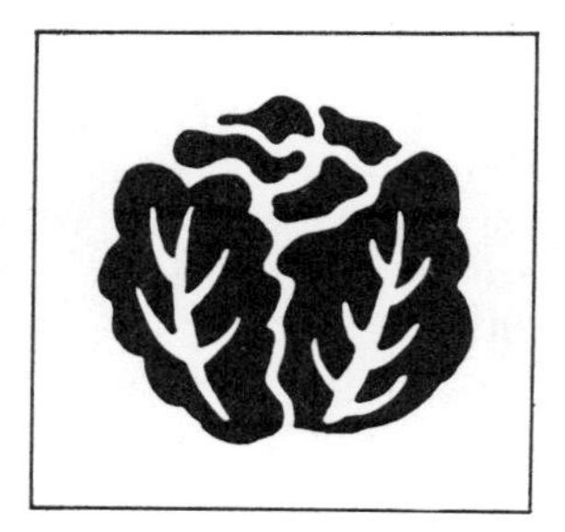

SALADS

MIXED GREENS WITH POLENTA CROUTONS AND GORGONZOLA

6 SERVINGS

1½ teaspoons salt
*1 cup instant polenta**
1 head of radicchio
1 small head of chicory (curly endive)
1 small head of romaine lettuce
1 large Belgian endive
1 tablespoon red wine vinegar
3 tablespoons plus ⅓ cup olive oil, preferably extra-virgin
1 tablespoon walnut oil
½ teaspoon Dijon-style mustard
⅛ teaspoon freshly ground pepper
4 ounces gorgonzola cheese, at room temperature
**Available in Italian markets and specialty food shops*

1. In a heavy medium saucepan, bring 2¼ cups of water to a boil over high heat. Add 1 teaspoon of the salt and stir in the polenta. Cook, stirring constantly with a wooden spoon, until the polenta thickens. Reduce the heat to a simmer and cook, stirring occasionally, until the polenta pulls away from the sides of the pan when stirred, about 15 minutes. (Note: The cooking time, longer than specified on the box, is needed to produce a tight, relatively dry polenta that will hold together when fried.)

2. Scrape the thickened polenta out of the pan onto a noncorrodible baking sheet. Using a lightly oiled wooden or plastic spatula, spread the polenta into an even rectangle about 12 by 6 by ¼ inch. Let cool to room temperature, then cover and refrigerate until well chilled.

3. Meanwhile, prepare the salad greens. Cut the core from the radicchio and separate the head into individual leaves. Separate the chicory and romaine into individual leaves, remove the tough ribs and tear the leaves into bite-size pieces. Separate the Belgian endive into separate leaves. Combine the greens, rinse thoroughly and dry. Wrap the greens in paper towels in a plastic bag and refrigerate if not serving at once. **(The recipe can be made a day ahead to this point.)**

4. In a small bowl, whisk together the vinegar, 3 tablespoons of the olive oil, the walnut oil, mustard, remaining ½ teaspoon salt and the pepper. Set the dressing aside.

5. Preheat the broiler. Remove the polenta from the refrigerator. Cut the polenta into 6 rectangles 6 by 2 inches each. Heat the remaining ⅓ cup olive oil in a large skillet. Add the polenta and sauté over moderately high heat, turning once, until crisp and golden, about 4 minutes. Remove with a slotted spatula and drain on paper towels. **(The recipe can be prepared to this point up to 1 hour ahead).**

6. Spread the gorgonzola over the fried polenta.

7. To assemble the salad, toss the greens with the vinaigrette until coated. Divide among 6 plates.

8. Run the polenta croutons under the broiler, until the cheese melts, about 1 minute. Slice each rectangle crosswise into 6 smaller rectangles or cut into triangles and, while still warm, arrange on top of the salad.

—John Robert Massie

SOUTHERN GREENS SALAD WITH PEPPERED PECANS

Barton Levinson devised this salad for Oakland's Gulf Coast Oyster Bar. She uses collard greens, kale, mustard and red chard, but other hardy greens such as spinach, escarole, beet or turnip greens, or Belgian or curly endive in combination with watercress can be substituted with great success. Toss in the pecans at the end to keep them crisp.

2 SERVINGS

¼ pound (6 slices) bacon
1½ tablespoons olive oil, preferably extra-virgin
¼ cup coarsely chopped red onion
1 small garlic clove, minced
¼ teaspoon coarsely ground black pepper
1 tablespoon balsamic vinegar
½ teaspoon grated lemon zest
½ teaspoon fresh lemon juice
2 teaspoons minced fresh parsley
½ teaspoon minced fresh thyme or ⅛ teaspoon dried
¼ teaspoon coarse (kosher) salt
1½ quarts mixed hearty salad greens (see headnote, above), cleaned and well dried
¼ cup coarsely chopped Peppered Pecans (p. 16)

1. In a medium skillet, cook the bacon over moderate heat, turning, until browned and crisp, 7 to 10 minutes. Transfer to paper towels and pat dry; chop coarsely. Reserve 1½ tablespoons of the rendered bacon fat.

2. Heat a large stainless steel bowl or wok over moderate heat, grasping the rim with a pot mitt. Add the reserved bacon fat and chopped bacon, the olive oil, red onion, garlic and pepper. Sauté until the onion is slightly softened, about 1½ minutes.

3. Add the vinegar, lemon zest, lemon juice, 1 teaspoon of the parsley, the thyme and salt. Cook until the onion is almost translucent, about 30 seconds.

4. Add the greens all at once and toss quickly over heat until the greens are coated with dressing and barely warmed but not wilted, about 30 seconds longer.

5. Remove the bowl from the heat and season with additional salt and pepper to taste. Toss in the chopped Peppered Pecans, then quickly arrange the salad on two heated plates. Sprinkle the reserved 1 teaspoon parsley on top and serve.

—Barbara Tropp

SUMMER GARDEN SALAD

8 TO 10 SERVINGS

1 pound fresh peas, shelled
1 teaspoon sugar
½ cup olive oil
½ cup fresh grapefruit juice
1 tablespoon plus 1 teaspoon white wine vinegar
2 garlic cloves, crushed through a press
½ teaspoon Dijon-style mustard
½ teaspoon salt
¼ teaspoon freshly ground pepper
1 head of romaine lettuce
1 head of Bibb lettuce
1 bunch of spinach, stemmed
¼ pound Chinese snow peas, strings removed
8 scallions, cut into 2-inch sections
1 large grapefruit, peeled and sectioned

1. Bring a large saucepan of water to a boil. Add the peas and sugar and boil until the peas are tender but still firm, about 10 minutes. Drain and rinse under cold running water; drain well.

2. In a small bowl, whisk together the oil, grapefruit juice, vinegar, garlic, mustard, salt and pepper to make a dressing.

3. Wash and dry the romaine and Bibb lettuce and the spinach. Tear the leaves into bite-size pieces and place in large salad bowl. Add the peas, snow peas, scallions and grapefruit.

4. About 30 minutes before serving, pour the dressing over the salad and toss to coat.

—Lila Gault

AUTUMN APPLE, BEET AND WALNUT SALAD

Try this brilliantly colored salad with sandwiches and soup, or with a simple chicken sauté. Use the smallest, tenderest beets you can find.

6 TO 8 SERVINGS

1 head of Boston lettuce, separated into leaves
1½ cups coarsely shredded raw beets
2 medium tart, firm red apples, such as MacIntosh or Empire, diced
¾ cup broken walnut halves
¼ cup buttermilk
¼ cup mayonnaise
½ teaspoon prepared horseradish
1½ tablespoons fresh lemon juice
Freshly ground pepper
1 teaspoon grated lemon zest, for garnish

1. Line a serving platter with the lettuce leaves. Gently squeeze the shredded beets in paper towels to absorb as much juice as possible. In a large bowl, place the apples, beets and walnuts and toss to mix.

2. In a small bowl, combine the buttermilk, mayonnaise, horseradish and lemon juice and whisk until smooth. Season to taste with pepper.

3. Pour over the apple mixture and toss gently until coated. Mound in the center of the platter and sprinkle with the grated lemon zest.

—Jennifer Marshall

SALAD OF WINTER SQUASH, POMEGRANATE AND CHICORY

6 SERVINGS

1 tablespoon freshly grated ginger
½ teaspoon salt
2 tablespoons fresh lemon juice
2 tablespoons cider vinegar
½ cup vegetable oil, preferably corn
1 small butternut squash (about 1¾ pounds) or a 1¾-pound chunk of Hubbard squash or pumpkin
1 large pomegranate
1 medium-small head of chicory (about ¾ pound), cut into small pieces

1. In a jar with a lid, combine the ginger, salt, lemon juice and vinegar; shake to blend. Add the oil and shake again.

2. Halve the squash and remove the seeds. Cut into 2-inch chunks and pare off the rind. Cut the flesh into thin 2-by-⅛-inch julienne strips. Drop into a pot of boiling salted water. Return to a rolling boil and drain immediately; then refresh in a bowl of ice water. Drain and spread on a towel to dry.

3. Combine the squash with three-quarters of the dressing and toss. (**The recipe can be prepared to this point several hours ahead.** Cover and refrigerate.)

4. Seed the pomegranate and set aside; there should be about 1 cup seeds.

5. Just before serving, toss the remaining dressing with the chicory in a serving bowl. Add the squash and pomegranate seeds and toss gently.

—Elizabeth Schneider

WILTED SALAD WITH CHICKEN LIVERS, APPLES AND MUSTARD SEED

In this salad, affordable chicken livers stand in for the more expensive foie gras that might appear on a restaurant menu. The results are almost as luxurious, and the rich flavor of sherry vinegar and the pungent crunch of whole mustard seed make it a robust starter for a hearty but elegant winter meal.

6 SERVINGS

1 bunch of watercress
1 head of red leaf lettuce
1 small head of romaine lettuce
2 teaspoons whole yellow mustard seed
¼ cup sherry wine vinegar
1 pound chicken livers
1 tart apple, preferably Granny Smith
¾ cup olive oil

1. Remove and discard the coarser watercress stems. Trim away the ends and any tough outer leaves from the red leaf and romaine lettuce. Separate into leaves, wash them well and dry. Tear the leaves into bite-size pieces, wrap and refrigerate. **(The greens can be prepared up to a day ahead.)**
2. In a small bowl, stir together the mustard seed and sherry vinegar and let stand for 1 hour.
3. Sort and trim the livers, discarding any that are not whole and firm. Separate the livers into lobes and thoroughly pat dry. Peel and core the apple and cut it into ½-inch chunks.
4. In a large skillet, warm 3 tablespoons of the oil over high heat until very hot. Add the apple and cook, tossing and stirring once or twice, until lightly browned, about 5 minutes. With a slotted spoon, transfer the apple chunks to a bowl.
5. Add 1 tablespoon oil to the skillet and set over moderate heat. Add the chicken livers and cook until stiffened and lightly browned on one side, about 2 minutes. Turn carefully and cook until browned on the other side but still pink and juicy inside, 2 to 3 minutes longer. With a slotted spoon, transfer the livers to the bowl with the apples and cover with foil to keep warm.
6. Put the greens in a large bowl. To the skillet, add the vinegar and mustard seed and the remaining ½ cup oil; bring just to the boil, stirring to scrape up any browned bits from the bottom of the pan. Pour the hot dressing over the greens and toss well.
7. Divide the salad among 6 plates. Spoon the apple chunks and livers over the greens. Pour any dressing remaining in the bowl over the salads and serve at once.

—Michael McLaughlin

WILTED ESCAROLE SALAD WITH PANCETTA AND GARLIC

Escarole is a wide-leafed cousin of the bitter green known as curly endive or chicory as well as of the currently fashionable radicchio. Offer the salad as a first course, if you wish, particularly if the menu is Italian. I like it almost as well, though, served alongside a plainly grilled or roasted meat entrée, rather like an elaborate hot vegetable. In any case, there is a delightful contrast between the coarse ribs, which remain crunchy, and the tender green leaves, which wilt considerably.

6 SERVINGS

2 large heads of escarole
½ pound pancetta or slab bacon, cut into ¼-inch dice
½ cup olive oil
24 large garlic cloves, peeled
24 brine-cured black olives, preferably Calamata
2 tablespoons fresh lemon juice
2 lemons, cut into wedges

1. Trim away the ends and any wilted outer leaves of the escarole. Separate the leaves, wash them well and dry. Tear the leaves into bite-size pieces, wrap and refrigerate. **(The escarole can be prepared up to a day ahead.)**
2. In a medium saucepan of boiling water, blanch the pancetta for 3 minutes. Drain and pat dry.
3. Set a large deep noncorrodible skillet or flameproof casserole over moderately low heat and add the pancetta. Cook uncovered, stirring occasionally, until crisp and golden brown, 20 to 30 minutes. With a slotted spoon, transfer the pancetta to a small bowl. Discard the fat and wipe the skillet clean.
4. Return the skillet to moderately low heat, add the olive oil and garlic cloves and cook, stirring frequently, until the garlic is lightly browned and tender, about 20 minutes. With a slotted spoon, transfer the garlic to the bowl with the pancetta; reserve the oil in the skillet. (**The salad can be prepared to this point up to 3 hours before serving.** Leave the oil in the skillet and rewarm it over moderate heat before proceeding.)
5. Add the olives to the skillet and cook, stirring, for 1 minute. Add the escarole, pancetta and garlic cloves, toss to coat with oil, cover and cook over moderate heat for 1 minute. Sprinkle on the lemon juice, toss again, remove from the heat and let stand, covered, for 1 minute before serving.

6. Divide the salad among 6 plates and garnish with wedges of lemon to squeeze onto the salads to taste.

—Michael McLaughlin

WARM CAESAR SALAD

All the elements of a classic Caesar Salad—anchovy, garlic, Parmesan cheese and Worcestershire sauce—are even zestier when the salad is served warm. Guests are always delighted with this adaptation of an old favorite.

6 SERVINGS

2 medium heads of romaine lettuce
2 tablespoons unsalted butter
¾ cup olive oil
8-ounce loaf of Italian or Viennese bread, cut into ¾-inch cubes
2 hard-cooked eggs
1½ tablespoons anchovy paste
1 tablespoon Worcestershire sauce
1 garlic clove, crushed through a press
3 tablespoons white wine vinegar
¼ cup freshly grated Parmesan cheese
Freshly ground pepper

1. Trim away the ends and any wilted outer leaves from the romaine. Separate the leaves, wash them well and dry. Tear the leaves into bite-size pieces, wrap and refrigerate. **(The romaine can be prepared to this point up to a day ahead.)**

2. In a medium skillet, melt the butter in 2 tablespoons of the oil over moderate heat. When the foam subsides, add the bread cubes and toss to coat. Reduce the heat to moderately low and sauté the bread cubes, stirring often, until crisp and golden brown, 5 to 7 minutes. Set aside.

3. Meanwhile, coarsely chop the eggs; then force them through a sieve into a small bowl. Put the prepared romaine in a large salad bowl.

4. In a small noncorrodible saucepan, combine the anchovy paste, Worcestershire sauce, garlic and vinegar. Whisk to blend well. Whisk in the remaining olive oil. Set the pan over moderate heat and bring just to the boil.

5. Remove from the heat and immediately pour the hot dressing over the lettuce; toss well. Add the Parmesan to the bowl and toss again.

6. Divide the salad among 6 plates. Sprinkle the croutons on top and spoon a small mound of sieved egg into the center of each salad. Season generously with pepper and serve at once.

—Michael McLaughlin

COLD CUCUMBER "FETTUCCINE" SALAD

This dish is a culinary joke; the "fettuccine" is really thin ribbons of cucumber, smoked ham and scallion, tossed together to resemble a pasta salad.

F&W BEVERAGE SUGGESTION
California Chenin Blanc, such as Dry Creek

4 SERVINGS

2 European seedless cucumbers, unpeeled
2 teaspoons coarse (kosher) salt
2 teaspoons Oriental sesame oil
2 eggs, beaten
3 tablespoons light olive oil
1 tablespoon rice wine vinegar
¼ teaspoon Dijon-style mustard
¼ teaspoon coarsely cracked black pepper
1 small bunch of scallions, cut into thin 2-inch strips
¼ pound thinly sliced smoked ham, such as Black Forest, cut into ¼-inch-wide strips as long as possible

1. Using the ¼-inch julienne blade of a mandoline, cut the cucumbers lengthwise into long strands, rotating the cucumbers to avoid cutting the seed core in the center; discard the seed core. (Alternatively, use a swivel-bladed vegetable peeler to remove long, thin ribbons of cucumber, rotating to avoid the seed core. Roll up the ribbons and thinly slice the cylinders crosswise to make long, thin strips.)

2. Place the cucumber in a colander set over a bowl or in the sink. Sprinkle with the salt and toss to mix. Let drain for 30 minutes. Rinse well under cold running water, then drain on paper towels.

3. Brush a heavy medium skillet, preferably nonstick, with sesame oil and heat until shimmering. Pour in 2 to 3 tablespoons of the egg; swirl to cover the bottom of the pan and cook over moderate heat until set but not browned, about 2 minutes. Turn and cook the second side until dry, about 15 seconds. Slide this egg pancake onto a work surface and let cool. Repeat with the remaining egg, brushing the skillet with sesame oil before making each pancake. You will be able to make about 3 pancakes. When cooled, roll up the pancakes and slice crosswise into long strips ¼-inch wide.

4. In a small bowl, whisk together the remaining sesame oil (about 1 teaspoon), the olive oil, vinegar, mustard and pepper until blended.

5. In a serving bowl, toss together the strips of cucumber, egg, scallion and ham. Pour the vinaigrette on top and toss to coat. Serve at once at room temperature.

—Anne Disrude

MOROCCAN TOMATO, RED PEPPER AND PRESERVED LEMON SALAD

This piquant salad is best freshly made.

MAKES ABOUT 2½ CUPS

2 large tomatoes—peeled, seeded and cut into ¾-inch chunks (about 2 cups)
2 or 3 red bell peppers—roasted, peeled, seeded and cut into ¾-inch chunks (about ¾ cup)
3 tablespoons finely chopped red onion or scallion
3 tablespoons olive oil
1 tablespoon fresh lemon juice
½ teaspoon ground cumin
½ teaspoon salt
Pinch of paprika
Pinch of cayenne pepper
4 wedges of Seven-Day Preserved Lemon (p. 238)

1. In a medium glass serving dish, combine the tomatoes and peppers. Add the onion, oil, lemon juice, cumin, salt, paprika and cayenne and toss to mix. Cover and refrigerate for 30 to 60 minutes, until well chilled.

2. Rinse the preserved lemon under running water and cut away and discard the pulp. Cut the peel into tiny 1/16- to ⅛-inch dice.

3. Just before serving, sprinkle the preserved lemon peel over the chilled salad.

—Paula Wolfert

WILD LEEKS VINAIGRETTE

While the potent, earthy aroma of fresh wild leek can be overpowering, the beautiful plants become sweet and gentle when tamed by a few minutes in boiling water.

4 SERVINGS

2 bunches of wild leeks (ramps), about 3 dozen
1 tablespoon fresh lemon juice
1 tablespoon red wine vinegar
1 teaspoon prepared mustard
¼ teaspoon salt, or to taste
3 to 4 tablespoons olive oil, to taste

1. Separate the leek leaves from the bulbs. Clean off and/or remove the first layer of skin from the bulbs. Trim off and discard the roots. Wash the leaves and bulbs thoroughly.

2. In a skillet of boiling, lightly salted water, cook the bulbs until tender, about 2 minutes. Drain, then set on a towel to dry. Gently place the leaves in the water and return the water to a boil; boil 30 seconds, then drain and dry on the towel.

3. Combine the lemon juice, vinegar, mustard and salt in a small jar. Cover tightly and shake to blend. Add the oil and shake until emulsified.

4. Spread the ramps in a serving dish and pour over the dressing. Refrigerate, covered, until serving time.

—Elizabeth Schneider

AVOCADO SALAD WITH CRACKLINGS

8 SERVINGS

1 medium tomato, coarsely chopped
½ cup finely chopped scallion (white and tender green)
⅓ cup minced fresh coriander
3 jalapeño peppers, seeded and finely chopped
½ teaspoon oregano, preferably Mexican
¼ teaspoon salt
2 tablespoons fresh lime juice
¾ cup mayonnaise, preferably homemade
2 ounces (about 1½ cups) pork cracklings, cut into ½-inch pieces
4 ripe avocados—halved, pitted and peeled
1 head of Boston lettuce, leaves separated

1. In a medium bowl, combine the tomato, scallion, coriander, jalapeños, oregano, salt and lime juice. Stir in the mayonnaise and pork cracklings.

2. Heap the salad mixture on top of the avocado halves, dividing evenly. Decoratively arrange the lettuce leaves on 8 salad plates. Place an avocado half on each plate.

—Zarela Martinez, Café Marimba, New York City

WATERCRESS, PEAR AND BLUE CHEESE SALAD

4 SERVINGS

2 tablespoons fresh lemon juice
1 large shallot, minced
2 tablespoons coarsely cracked pepper
1 teaspoon salt
½ cup walnut oil
2 large bunches of watercress, tough stems removed
1 small head of Boston lettuce, leaves separated
2 ripe pears, preferably Bosc or Comice, peeled and sliced
½ cup blue cheese, crumbled
½ cup walnut halves, lightly toasted

1. Whisk together the lemon juice, shallot, pepper, salt and walnut oil.

2. About 15 minutes before serving, place the watercress, lettuce, pears, cheese and walnuts in a salad bowl. Toss with the dressing and let marinate briefly before serving.

—Cindy Black, Sheppard's, San Diego, California

KEY WEST SALAD

Use the ripest, lushest tomatoes you have for this refreshing salad, perfect for a summer picnic or buffet.

8 SERVINGS

3 pounds tomatoes, cut into ½-inch wedges
1 small red onion, thinly sliced
6 ounces Pecorino Romano cheese, coarsely grated (about 1½ cups)
¾ cup olive oil, preferably extra-virgin
¼ cup cider vinegar
2 teaspoons minced fresh basil
2 teaspoons minced fresh parsley
1½ teaspoons minced fresh oregano or ½ teaspoon dried
¼ teaspoon salt

1. In a large bowl, toss together the tomatoes, onion and cheese.
2. In a small bowl, whisk together the olive oil, vinegar, basil, parsley, oregano and salt until well blended. Pour the dressing over the tomatoes and toss to coat. Serve chilled or at room temperature.

—*Creative Seafood Restaurant, Tampa, Florida*

PEPPER AND BLACK BEAN SALAD

8 SERVINGS

1 pound dried black beans
8 medium bell peppers, cut into thin slivers
8 scallions, minced
½ cup chopped fresh parsley
½ cup extra-virgin olive oil
1 teaspoon salt
¼ teaspoon freshly ground black pepper
Boston or romaine lettuce leaves
Jalapeño Mayonnaise (p. 233)

1. Place the beans in a large saucepan, cover with 6 inches of cold water and soak overnight. Alternatively, cover the beans with cold water and bring to a boil over high heat. Boil for 2 minutes, turn off the heat and let the beans soak, covered, for 1 hour; drain.
2. Cover the beans with fresh water. Bring to a boil. Reduce the heat to moderate and simmer until the beans are tender but still maintain their shape, 2 to 2½ hours. Drain and rinse.
3. Place the beans in a large bowl. Add the bell peppers, scallions, parsley, oil, salt and black pepper; toss to mix. Let cool to room temperature.
4. Serve the salad and lettuce leaves separately so that each person can spoon some of the salad into a lettuce leaf, top with Jalapeño Mayonnaise and roll into a package to be eaten out of hand. Or, line a serving platter with the lettuce, mound the salad on top and pass the mayonnaise separately.

—*Anne Disrude*

ZUCCHINI-RADISH SALAD

MAKES ABOUT 2 CUPS

1 medium zucchini (6 ounces), cut into very thin long julienne strips
16 radishes, cut lengthwise into 1/16-inch julienne strips
1 tablespoon safflower or other flavorless vegetable oil
½ teaspoon sherry wine vinegar
¼ teaspoon salt
⅛ teaspoon coarsely cracked pepper

Crisp the zucchini and radish in a bowl of ice water for 15 minutes. Drain and pat dry on paper towels. Just before serving, toss with the oil, vinegar, salt and pepper.

—*Anne Disrude*

SPICY CUCUMBER AND FRUIT SALAD

Here is an intriguing first course, guaranteed to whet the appetite. It has a light, but definite, cucumber taste.

4 SERVINGS

4 Kirby cucumbers, peeled
½ cantaloupe, seeds removed
1½ cups strawberries, hulled and halved or quartered, depending on size
2 tablespoons fresh lime juice
1½ teaspoons finely chopped fresh coriander
1 teaspoon minced seeded jalapeño pepper
⅛ teaspoon salt
1 head of Bibb lettuce—leaves separated, rinsed and patted dry

1. Using a small melon-baller, cut the cucumbers into balls. Place in a large bowl.
2. Using the same melon-baller, scoop out balls from the cantaloupe; reserve the rind. Add the cantaloupe and strawberries to the cucumbers.
3. With your hands, squeeze the cantaloupe rind to collect 1 tablespoon of the juice, then discard the rind. Add the juice to the salad. Sprinkle on the lime juice, coriander, jalapeño pepper and salt; toss to coat well. (**The recipe can be prepared to this point up to 2 hours ahead.** Cover and refrigerate.)
4. To serve, arrange 4 small lettuce leaves in each of 4 salad bowls. Divide the salad evenly among the bowls. Spoon any juices on the bottom of the bowl over the salads.

—*Diana Sturgis*

SMOKED SALMON AND MIXED MELON SALAD

This dish of melon and smoked salmon (inspired by a recipe from Serge Coulon, a chef from the Charente in France) is a first cousin to the classic melon with prosciutto, exploiting the same sort of excellent, yet unexpected, affinity of tastes.

6 SERVINGS

6 ounces smoked salmon, preferably Scotch, sliced
2 cups cranshaw, casaba or Spanish melon cut into ¾-by-¼-inch squares
2 cups honeydew melon cut into ¾-by-¼-inch squares
2 cups cantaloupe cut into ¾-by-¼-inch squares
⅓ cup cubed grapefruit sections
3 tablespoons fresh lemon juice
2 tablespoons fresh orange juice
2 tablespoons olive oil
Salt and freshly ground pepper

1. Cut the smoked salmon slices into ¾-inch squares. Keep chilled. In a large bowl, combine the melon squares and grapefruit. Cover and keep chilled.

2. Just before serving, add the salmon, lemon and orange juices and oil to the fruit. Season lightly with salt and generously with pepper. Toss to mix.

—*Paula Wolfert*

CITRUS SALAD WITH FRESH HORSERADISH DRESSING

12 TO 15 SERVINGS

4 large grapefruit
6 navel oranges
2 tablespoons fresh lemon juice
½ cup peanut or safflower oil
½ cup Lillet or dry vermouth
¼ cup finely shredded fresh horseradish
¼ teaspoon salt
⅛ teaspoon white pepper
2 medium heads of chicory, torn into small pieces
2 medium heads of romaine, shredded

1. With a sharp knife, cut away the peel of the grapefruit and oranges, removing all the white pith. Squeeze the peelings over a small bowl to reserve the juices (about 1 cup total).

2. Cut the fruit crosswise into ¼-inch slices; then cut each round in half. Place the fruit slices in layers in a large baking dish. Strain the reserved juices and pour over the fruit. Cover with plastic wrap and chill. **(The slices can be held overnight in the refrigerator.)**

3. Drain the fruit juices from the sliced fruit, reserving ¼ cup. Make the dressing by whisking together the reserved fruit juices, the lemon juice, oil, Lillet, horseradish, salt and white pepper.

4. To assemble the salad, line a large platter with the greens, tossed together. Arrange concentric circles of overlapping fruit slices on top, then drizzle the dressing over the fruit.

—*Anne Disrude*

SALAD OF PERSIMMONS, KIWIS AND POMEGRANATES

Serve this exquisitely gaudy concoction to take the place of both fruit and salad courses after a rich meal. Or offer it as the opening course for an unusual dinner.

4 TO 6 SERVINGS

1 large pomegranate
1 cup plain yogurt
About 1 tablespoon honey
About 1 tablespoon fresh lemon juice
4 small, ripe persimmons
4 kiwis—peeled, halved lengthwise and cut crosswise into slices

1. Seed the pomegranate; there should be about 1 cup seeds. Set ⅓ cup aside; place the remainder in a bowl and crush lightly to extract some juice. Add the yogurt and 1 tablespoon each of the honey and lemon juice. Taste and add more honey or lemon juice to taste if desired. Refrigerate for 30 minutes or more.

2. Cut out the leaf bases of the persimmons and halve the fruits lengthwise. Carefully slide a sharp paring knife between the skin and the flesh to peel the fruit. (Alternatively, if you have one of the jelly-soft persimmons, you may have to first cut the fruit into lengthwise slices, then delicately pare off the skin from each slice.) Gently cut into slices.

3. Arrange the persimmon and kiwi slices on individual plates. Drizzle some of the yogurt dressing over each and pass the remainder separately. Sprinkle the reserved pomegranate seeds evenly over each salad.

—*Elizabeth Schneider*

PAILLARD OF VEAL WITH BITTER GREENS

This unusual salad, perfect for a luncheon or light supper, was inspired by a dish served at Erminia, an Italian restaurant in Manhattan.

F&W BEVERAGE SUGGESTION
Rosé of Cabernet Sauvignon, such as Simi

4 SERVINGS

1 small head of chicory (curly endive)
1 small head of escarole

1 small head of romaine lettuce
4 veal rib chops (1½ inches thick)—boned, trimmed and pounded to ¼ inch (to save time, ask your butcher to do this)—or 4 large veal scallops, pounded ¼ inch thick
1 teaspoon salt
½ teaspoon freshly ground pepper
3 tablespoons unsalted butter
9 tablespoons olive oil
2 garlic cloves, crushed through a press
½ teaspoon Dijon-style mustard
2 tablespoons red wine vinegar

1. Remove and discard the tough outer leaves from the chicory, escarole and romaine. Separate the heads into individual leaves, remove the tough central ribs and tear the leaves into bite-size pieces. Combine the greens, rinse, dry and set aside in a large bowl.

2. Preheat the oven to 200°. Season the veal on both sides with ½ teaspoon of the salt and ¼ teaspoon of the pepper. In a large skillet, melt the butter in 3 tablespoons of the oil over moderately high heat. Working in batches, sauté the veal paillards, turning once, until well browned and tender, about 5 minutes. As they cook, place them on a heatproof platter, cover loosely with foil and keep warm in the oven.

3. Whisk together the remaining 6 tablespoons oil, the garlic, mustard and remaining ½ teaspoon salt and ¼ teaspoon pepper until blended. Pour over the mixed greens and toss to coat evenly with dressing.

4. When all the paillards are cooked, transfer them to 4 warmed large plates. Pour out the fat in the pan. Return the pan to moderate heat and add the vinegar. Bring to a boil, scraping up any brown bits from the bottom of the pan. Add the mixed greens to the hot pan and toss to mix in the vinegar. Divide evenly among the 4 plates, serving the salad on top of the veal.

—*John Robert Massie*

ITALIAN BEEF SALAD

4 TO 6 SERVINGS

1½ pounds all-purpose potatoes (about 6 medium)—peeled, quartered lengthwise and cut crosswise into ¼-inch slices
⅓ cup minced parsley
1 large red onion, coarsely chopped
¼ cup olive oil, preferably extra-virgin
2½ tablespoons red wine vinegar
2 tablespoons minced fresh basil or 2 teaspoons dried
1 teaspoon salt
½ teaspoon coarsely cracked pepper
1½ pounds cooked beef (such as shin or brisket), cut into ½-inch dice (about 4 cups)
Boston or romaine lettuce leaves, for garnish

1. Bring a medium pot of salted water to a boil over high heat. Add the potatoes and cook until tender, about 15 minutes. Drain and transfer to a serving bowl.

2. Meanwhile, in a small bowl combine the parsley, onion, olive oil, vinegar, basil, salt and pepper. Stir until blended.

3. Add the cooked beef to the bowl with the potatoes. Pour the dressing on top and toss to coat well. Let marinate at room temperature, tossing occasionally, for 30 minutes to 1 hour. Season with additional salt and pepper to taste.

4. To serve, arrange a bed of lettuce on a platter. Mound the beef salad in the center.

MARINATED LAMB SALAD WITH CHERRY TOMATOES

This salad is equally delicious with any leftover cooked meat: beef, veal or even corned beef.

F&W BEVERAGE SUGGESTION
Rosé of Cabernet Sauvignon

6 SERVINGS

½ pound red potatoes (about 2 medium), cut into 2-by-¼-inch julienne strips
½ pound green beans, as thin as possible
1 cup corn kernels (from 2 to 3 ears fresh corn or 5 ounces frozen)
1 pound cooked lamb, cut into 2-by-¼-inch julienne strips
¼ cup cornichons (French gherkin pickles), chopped
1 small red onion, diced
12 cherry tomatoes, halved
2 tablespoons Dijon-style mustard
1½ tablespoons red wine vinegar
⅓ cup olive oil, preferably extra-virgin
½ teaspoon salt
¼ teaspoon freshly ground pepper
3 medium garlic cloves, crushed through a press

1. In a small saucepan, put the potatoes in cold water to cover by 1 inch. Bring to a boil over high heat and cook until tender, about 3 minutes. Drain and let cool.

2. In a medium saucepan of boiling salted water, cook the beans until tender, about 3 minutes. Drain and rinse under cold running water; drain well.

3. In another medium saucepan of boiling water, cook the corn kernels until just tender, about 3 minutes; drain.

4. In a large bowl, combine the potatoes, green beans, corn, lamb, cornichons, onion and tomatoes.

5. In a small bowl, whisk together

the mustard, vinegar, oil, salt, pepper and garlic until well blended. Pour this dressing over the lamb salad and toss to coat. Cover and set aside at room temperature to marinate for 1 hour, tossing once or twice. Serve at room temperature.

—Jeanette Ferrary & Louise Fiszer

THAI-STYLE BEEF AND LETTUCE SALAD WITH CHILE-LIME DRESSING

This dish is inspired by the Steak Yum at Toon's, an admirable Thai restaurant in Greenwich Village. There it is listed as an appetizer; it makes a good one at home, too, preceding an informal meatless main course, such as a cheese omelet. However, there is no reason not to serve the salad as a main course if you wish.

F&W BEVERAGE SUGGESTION
California Gewürztraminer, such as Paul Masson

4 MAIN-COURSE SERVINGS

1 small head of romaine lettuce
1 small head of leaf lettuce
1 small head of curly endive
¾ cup peanut oil
4 tablespoons fresh lime juice
3 tablespoons soy sauce
1 pound fairly lean steak, such as London broil, cut about 1 inch thick
1 tablespoon minced fresh ginger
2 medium garlic cloves, chopped
1 fresh jalapeño or other small hot green pepper, coarsely chopped
¼ cup minced fresh coriander
2 tomatoes (about 1 pound total), cut into 6 wedges each
1 medium red onion, sliced into rings

1. Trim away the ends and any wilted outer leaves of the romaine, leaf lettuce and curly endive. Separate the leaves, wash them well and dry. Tear the leaves into bite-size pieces, wrap and refrigerate. **(The greens can be prepared up to a day ahead.)**
2. In a medium bowl, combine 2 tablespoons of the peanut oil, 2 tablespoons of the lime juice and 1 tablespoon of the soy sauce. Trim any excess fat from the steak, add the steak to the bowl and marinate at room temperature, turning occasionally, for 1 hour.
3. In a food processor, combine ½ cup of the peanut oil, the remaining 2 tablespoons lime juice and soy sauce, the ginger, garlic and jalapeño. Process for 1 minute, or until smooth. Scrape into a bowl and set aside at room temperature.
4. In a medium skillet, warm the remaining 2 tablespoons oil over high heat until it smokes slightly. Remove the steak from the marinade, reserving the marinade. Add the steak to the skillet and sear, turning once, until browned, about 2 minutes on each side. Reduce the heat to moderate and continue to cook, turning once or twice, until the steak is medium-rare, about 5 minutes longer on each side.
5. Meanwhile, stir the reserved marinade into the chile-lime dressing. Put the greens in a large bowl.
6. When the steak is done, transfer it to a cutting board. Remove the skillet from the heat and add the dressing, stirring to scrape up any browned bits from the bottom of the pan. Cover the skillet to keep the dressing warm.
7. With a very sharp knife, cut the steak across the grain into thin slices. Pour the warm dressing over the greens in the bowl and toss well. Add the coriander and toss again.
8. Divide the greens among salad plates. Arrange the steak, with the slices overlapping slightly, on top of the greens. Garnish each plate with 2 tomato wedges and several onion rings. Spoon any dressing remaining in the bowl over the salads and serve at once.

—Michael McLaughlin

POTATO AND CHICKEN SALAD WITH SHREDDED ZUCCHINI

This is a great dish to make with leftovers. You could boil a chicken for chicken stock and use the meat in this salad or use leftover meat from fried or roasted chicken (remove the skin first). Likewise, bake some extra potatoes to have on hand.

10 TO 12 SERVINGS

6 cups diced (½-inch) baked red potatoes (about 2 pounds) or 2 pounds uncooked red potatoes, cut into ½-inch dice
3 cups shredded cooked chicken (from 1 small frying chicken)
4 small zucchini, shredded (about 4 cups)
6 hard-cooked eggs, coarsely chopped
¼ cup minced fresh tarragon or parsley
¾ teaspoon salt
¼ teaspoon freshly ground pepper
¾ cup mayonnaise, preferably homemade
¼ cup chicken stock or canned broth
1 tablespoon white wine vinegar

1. If not using leftover baked potatoes, cook the diced raw potatoes in a large pot of boiling salted water until tender when pierced with a fork, about 15 minutes. Drain and let cool to room temperature.
2. In a large bowl, toss together the potatoes, chicken, zucchini, eggs, tarragon, salt and pepper.
3. In a small bowl, whisk together the mayonnaise, chicken stock and vinegar until blended. Pour over the salad. Toss well and serve the salad at room temperature.

—Anne Disrude

AVOCADO STUFFED WITH CHICKEN AND ARTICHOKE HEARTS

Served on a bed of lettuce, this makes a fine summer supper.

F&W BEVERAGE SUGGESTION
Alsace Gewürztraminer, such as Trimbach or Hugel

2 SERVINGS

1 teaspoon salt
1 tablespoon fresh lemon juice
½ teaspoon freshly ground pepper
3 tablespoons olive oil, preferably extra-virgin
1 tablespoon capers, rinsed and drained
4 artichoke hearts (canned in brine), quartered
2 cooked whole chicken breasts—skinned, boned and cut into bite-size pieces
2 medium avocados, preferably Hass
Lettuce leaves and lemon wedges

1. In a medium bowl, dissolve the salt in the lemon juice. Add the pepper and whisk in the olive oil to make a vinaigrette. Add the capers, artichoke hearts and chicken.

2. Cut each avocado in half lengthwise and remove the pit. Keeping the skin intact, gently run a paring knife between the skin and the fruit to loosen. Without piercing the shell, cut the fruit lengthwise at ½-inch intervals and then horizontally to form bite-size pieces. Using a teaspoon, lift the pieces of avocado from the shell and add to the chicken mixture. Toss gently to mix. Season with additional salt and pepper to taste.

3. Spoon the mixture back into the avocado shells, heaping generously. Serve on a bed of lettuce and garnish with lemon wedges.

—*Molly O'Neill*

CHICKEN AND POTATO SALAD WITH PESTO AND RED PEPPER

6 SERVINGS

6 skinless, boneless chicken breast halves (2 to 2½ pounds)
1 pound red potatoes
1 red bell pepper, cut into thin strips
½ cup fresh basil leaves
2 garlic cloves
½ cup olive oil, preferably extra-virgin
¼ cup white wine vinegar
3 tablespoons freshly grated Parmesan cheese
½ teaspoon oregano
Salt and freshly ground black pepper

1. In a large saucepan of simmering salted water, poach the chicken breasts until white throughout but still juicy, about 15 minutes. Remove the chicken and let cool. (**The chicken can be prepared a day ahead.** Wrap tightly and refrigerate.)

2. Put the potatoes in a large saucepan of cold salted water. Bring to a boil and cook until tender, 10 to 15 minutes. Drain and rinse under cold running water. Remove the skins.

3. Cut the chicken and potatoes into 1-inch cubes. In a large bowl, combine the chicken, potatoes and red pepper.

4. In a blender or food processor, combine the basil, garlic, oil, vinegar, cheese and oregano. Puree until smooth. Season with salt and black pepper to taste.

5. Pour the basil dressing over the salad and toss to coat. Serve slightly chilled or at room temperature.

—*Jeanette Ferrary & Louise Fiszer*

WARM SQUID SALAD WITH CELERY ROOT

F&W BEVERAGE SUGGESTION
Full-flavored Italian white, such as Gavi

8 SERVINGS

1½ pounds squid, cleaned
3 garlic cloves, crushed through a press
½ cup plus 3 tablespoons olive oil, preferably extra-virgin
2 tablespoons fresh lemon juice
6 tablespoons minced fresh parsley
¾ teaspoon salt
½ teaspoon freshly ground pepper
1 medium celery root (about ¾ pound), peeled and cut into 2-inch juilienne strips
2 tablespoons sherry wine vinegar
2 small heads of chicory (curly endive), washed and torn into small pieces
2 cups cooked fresh peas or defrosted frozen

1. Remove the tentacles of the squid and cut crosswise in half. Slit the bodies lengthwise and spread flat. Score with a sharp knife in a crisscross pattern, then cut into 2-inch squares. Place in a bowl.

2. Add the garlic, 3 tablespoons of the olive oil, the lemon juice, 2 tablespoons of the parsley and ¼ teaspoon each of the salt and pepper. Toss to mix. Cover and refrigerate for 4 hours or overnight. Let return to room temperature before proceeding.

3. In a medium bowl, combine the celery root, the remaining ½ cup olive oil, 3 tablespoons of the parsley, ½ teaspoon salt, ¼ teaspoon pepper and the sherry vinegar. Toss to coat well.

4. Divide the chicory among 8 plates. Arrange the celery root in the center. Drizzle any extra dressing from the bottom of the bowl over the chicory.

5. Scrape the squid and marinade into a large skillet. Sauté over moderate heat, stirring frequently, until the squid is opaque, about 3 minutes. Add the peas and toss to warm through. Mound the squid on top of the celery root. Sprinkle with the remaining 1 tablespoon parsley and serve warm.

LOBSTER POTATO SALAD

Coral lobster roe makes a striking garnish for this dish. To obtain lobster roe, simply ask your fishmonger for female lobsters.

F&W BEVERAGE SUGGESTION
Pinot Grigio, such as Santa Margherita

8 TO 10 SERVINGS

2 bottles (8 ounces each) clam juice
2 cups dry white wine
2 imported bay leaves
2 medium onions, quartered
3 female lobsters, 1½ pounds each
1 tablespoon tomato paste
5 pounds waxy (boiling) potatoes, peeled and cut into ⅜-inch dice
¼ cup olive oil
2 tablespoons rice wine vinegar
1 teaspoon salt
½ teaspoon freshly ground pepper
1½ tablespoons fresh lemon juice
1 egg yolk
½ cup plus 2 tablespoons safflower oil
3 tablespoons minced fresh chives
Japanese radish sprouts (2-Mamina) or watercress, for garnish

1. In a large stockpot, combine the clam juice, wine, bay leaves, onions and 4 cups of water. Bring to a boil over high heat. Add the lobsters head first, cover the pot and steam until they turn bright red, about 10 minutes. Remove the lobsters and let cool; reserve the cooking liquid.

2. Disjoint the lobsters, working over a bowl so that no juices will be lost. Remove the meat from the claws, joints and tail and reserve the shells. Place the meat in a small bowl. Remove the green tomalley from the body cavity and the red roe from the tail and place in separate bowls. Cover each bowl with plastic wrap and refrigerate.

3. Crack the lobster shells into pieces and return to the cooking liquid. Add the reserved lobster juices and stir in the tomato paste. Bring to a simmer and cook, uncovered, for 1 hour to infuse the flavors. Strain the broth and return to the pot. Increase the heat to high and boil, uncovered, until the liquid is reduced to 2 cups, about 30 minutes. Set aside. (**The recipe can be prepared to this point up to 6 hours ahead.** Cover and refrigerate.)

4. In a large pot of boiling salted water, cook the potatoes until tender but not falling apart, about 10 minutes. Drain well and place in a large bowl.

5. Pour the lobster broth over the hot potatoes. Add the olive oil, vinegar, salt and pepper. Toss to coat well. Let cool to room temperature, tossing occasionally, about 1½ hours.

6. In a small bowl, whisk together the lemon juice and egg yolk. Whisk in 2 tablespoons of the safflower oil a few drops at a time until the mixture begins to thicken. Continue to whisk in the oil in a slow stream to form a mayonnaise. Whisk in the reserved tomalley until blended.

7. Pour off any excess liquid from the potatoes. Coarsely chop the lobster meat and toss with the potatoes. Add the chives and remaining 2 tablespoons safflower oil and toss. Crumble the red roe on top.

8. Arrange the radish sprouts on a large serving platter. Place the potato salad on top. Pass the mayonnaise separately.

—Anne Disrude

WARM SALAD OF FETA CHEESE AND TOMATOES WITH GARLIC SHRIMP

If you would like to offer this salad as a starter, merely decrease the shrimp accordingly. With *no* shrimp, it makes an unusual warm vegetable to serve alongside roasted or charcoal-grilled lamb.

4 TO 6 SERVINGS

1 bunch of arugula
1 small head of curly endive
1 large head of red leaf lettuce
½ pound feta cheese
¼ cup plus 6 tablespoons olive oil
3 medium garlic cloves, crushed through a press
24 medium shrimp (about 1 pound), shelled but with tails left on
Salt
1 pint (about 20) red, ripe cherry tomatoes
2 tablespoons minced fresh oregano (see Note)
¼ cup red wine vinegar
Freshly ground pepper

1. Trim away the ends and any wilted outer leaves of the arugula, endive and red leaf lettuce. Separate the leaves, wash them well and dry. Tear the leaves into bite-size pieces, wrap and refrigerate. **(The greens can be prepared up to a day ahead.)**

2. Rinse the feta of its salty brine, pat dry and crumble. Reserve at room temperature for up to 2 hours. When you are ready to complete the salad, toss the greens and feta together in a large bowl.

3. In a medium noncorrodible skillet, combine ¼ cup of the olive oil and the garlic. Cook over moderately low

heat, stirring frequently, until the garlic begins to sizzle gently, about 2 minutes. Add the shrimp, season with a pinch of salt and cook, stirring, until they are pink, curled and opaque, about 5 minutes. Do not let the garlic brown. With a slotted spoon, leaving as much garlic behind in the skillet as possible, transfer the shrimp to a bowl and cover with foil to keep warm.

4. Add the remaining 6 tablespoons olive oil, the cherry tomatoes and oregano to the skillet. Cook over moderate heat, tossing and stirring gently, until the tomatoes are heated through and the oregano fragrant, about 5 minutes.

5. Add the vinegar to the pan, increase the heat to high and bring just to a boil. Immediately pour the contents of the skillet over the greens and feta in the bowl and toss well.

6. Divide the salad among 4 or 6 plates. Garnish each salad with 6 or 4 shrimp, season generously with pepper and serve at once.

NOTE: Fresh oregano is preferable here, but if it is unavailable, substitute 1½ teaspoons dry oregano soaked for 1 hour in 2 tablespoons of the olive oil. Add the soaked oregano, along with any oil it has not absorbed, to the skillet with the tomatoes in Step 4.

—Michael McLaughlin

WILD RICE AND MUSSEL SALAD

F&W BEVERAGE SUGGESTION
California Chardonnay, such as Sebastiani Proprietor's Reserve

4 TO 6 SERVINGS

¼ cup pine nuts (pignoli)
1 cup wild rice (about 8 ounces), well rinsed
1½ teaspoons salt
6 tablespoons unsalted butter
2 medium shallots, minced
½ cup dry white wine
1 bouquet garni: 4 parsley stems, 1 bay leaf and ¼ teaspoon thyme tied in a double thickness of cheesecloth
3 pounds mussels—well scrubbed, soaked and beards removed
1 bunch of scallions, thinly sliced (about ¾ cup)
½ teaspoon freshly ground pepper
4 to 6 large leaves of butter lettuce, for garnish

1. Preheat the oven to 375°. Spread the pine nuts in a small baking pan. Bake, shaking the pan occasionally, until the nuts are toasted and lightly browned, 3 to 4 minutes. **(The nuts can be toasted ahead of time.)**

2. In a medium saucepan, combine the rice and 1 teaspoon of the salt with 4 cups of cold water. Bring to a boil over high heat, reduce to a simmer, cover and cook for about 25 minutes, until the rice is barely tender and still slightly chewy. Drain and set aside.

3. Meanwhile, in a large flameproof casserole, melt 3 tablespoons of the butter over moderate heat. Add the shallots and sauté until softened but not browned, about 3 minutes. Add the wine, bouquet garni and mussels. Increase the heat to high, cover and cook, shaking the pan occasionally, for about 3 minutes, or until the mussels open. Remove from the heat. When cool enough to handle, remove the mussels from their shells and place in a small bowl. Strain the cooking liquid through a sieve lined with a double thickness of dampened cheesecloth into a saucepan and boil over high heat until reduced to ½ cup, about 5 minutes.

4. In a large saucepan, melt the remaining 3 tablespoons butter over moderate heat. Add the wild rice, scallions and reduced mussel liquid. Toss gently to combine. Add the pepper, mussels, toasted pine nuts and remaining ½ teaspoon salt. Cook, tossing, until warmed through, about 3 minutes. Arrange each portion on a leaf of lettuce, and serve warm.

—John Robert Massie

WARM SALAD OF SOFT-COOKED EGGS AND SMOKED FISH

This warm salad makes an excellent late-night supper or a perfect first course for an elaborate brunch. Accompany it with bagels—split, toasted and buttered—and pour beer or Champagne. If you're feeling flush, omit the smoked fish and top the eggs, after the salad has been assembled and dressed, with a generous dollop of caviar.

6 SERVINGS

2 medium bunches of spinach (about 1½ pounds)
1 head of Boston lettuce
3 tablespoons white wine vinegar
½ to 1 tablespoon sugar, to taste
2 tablespoons Dijon-style mustard
Pinch of salt
½ cup corn oil or other flavorless vegetable oil
¼ cup heavy cream
¼ cup minced fresh dill
4 tablespoons unsalted butter
8 eggs
¼ pound thinly sliced or flaked smoked salmon, whitefish, sturgeon or trout
1 small red onion, cut into very thin rings

1. Remove and discard the spinach stems. Trim away any wilted outer leaves of lettuce. Wash the spinach and lettuce well and dry. Tear the leaves into bite-size pieces, wrap and

refrigerate. **(The greens can be prepared up to a day ahead.)**

2. In a small noncorrodible saucepan, whisk together the vinegar, sugar, mustard and salt. Gradually whisk in the oil and cream. Set the pan over low heat and bring to just below a simmer. Stir in the dill, remove from the heat and cover to keep warm.

3. Divide the prepared greens among 6 plates. In a medium skillet, melt the butter over low heat. Break the eggs into a bowl, whisk them briefly with a fork (do not overmix and do not add any salt) and pour them into the skillet. Cook, stirring, over low heat until softly set, about 5 minutes.

4. Spoon the hot eggs immediately into the center of each salad. Top the eggs with the smoked fish and spoon the warm vinaigrette over the eggs and greens. Garnish with the onion rings. Serve at once.

—Michael McLaughlin

BAGNA CAUDA SALAD

A classic *bagna cauda* is a traditional Italian hot anchovy dip, usually served with crudités. In this takeoff, the vegetables are cooked briefly to enhance color and texture, then arranged attractively on the plate and served with the tangy anchovy sauce as a dressing.

F&W BEVERAGE SUGGESTION
Italian white, such as Corvo

4 SERVINGS

½ pound red potatoes, cut into 1½-by-¼-inch sticks
1 medium zucchini
¼ pound sugar snap peas
¼ pound green beans
½ small head of cauliflower, broken into ½-inch florets
½ small bunch of broccoli, broken into ½-inch florets
3 large mushrooms, quartered
2 tablespoons fresh lemon juice
¾ cup olive oil, preferably extra-virgin
6 large garlic cloves, thinly sliced
8 flat anchovy fillets, minced
1 tablespoon capers
¼ teaspoon coarsely cracked pepper
½ teaspoon grated lemon zest

1. Cook the potatoes in a medium saucepan of boiling salted water until easily pierced with a fork, 5 to 8 minutes. Drain and set aside.

2. Cut the zucchini crosswise into ¼-inch-thick rounds. Stack the rounds and slice again into ¼-inch sticks. Bring a large saucepan of salted water to a boil. Put the zucchini in a strainer and dip in the boiling water for about 2 seconds to bring out the green color. Rinse under cold running water until cool. Drain on paper towels.

3. Add the sugar snap peas to the strainer and again blanch for about 2 seconds. Rinse under cold running water until cool. Drain on paper towels. Repeat separately with the green beans, cauliflower and broccoli, blanching the beans for 1 minute and the cauliflower and broccoli for 30 seconds each.

4. In a small bowl, toss the mushrooms with the lemon juice.

5. To assemble the salad, arrange the vegetables decoratively on 4 plates.

6. Make the sauce by warming the olive oil in a medium skillet over moderate heat. Add the garlic and slowly cook until light brown, about 10 minutes. Remove and discard the garlic. Add the anchovies to the skillet. Cook, mashing with the back of a spoon, until dissolved. Add the capers, pepper and lemon zest. Pour the hot sauce over the vegetables. Serve warm.

—Anne Disrude

ZUCCHINI AND EGG SALAD WITH DRIED PEPPERS

---

4 SERVINGS

2 medium zucchini, cut into 2-inch-long thin julienne strips
Salt and freshly ground black pepper
4 hard-cooked eggs, halved
1 egg yolk
1 tablespoon white wine vinegar
1 teaspoon dry white wine
¾ cup safflower oil
4 pieces Dried Red Pepper (p. 238)

1. Sprinkle the zucchini lightly with salt and black pepper; toss. Mound the zucchini on 4 chilled plates and place 2 egg halves in the center of each mound.

2. In a medium bowl, whisk together the egg yolk, vinegar, wine and ½ teaspoon salt and ⅛ teaspoon black pepper. Gradually whisk in the oil until the sauce thickens.

3. Spoon 1 tablespoon of the sauce over each egg half. Crumble a piece of the Dried Red Pepper over the top of each serving.

—Anne Disrude

PIES, CAKES & COOKIES

DEEP-DISH BERRY PIE

8 TO 12 SERVINGS

2 cups all-purpose flour
½ teaspoon salt
1 cup plus 3 tablespoons sugar
1½ sticks (12 tablespoons) cold unsalted butter, cut into ¼-inch square slices
3 to 5 tablespoons cold water
1½ pints blueberries
1½ pints raspberries
¼ cup cornstarch
3 tablespoons bourbon
1 tablespoon milk

1. In a large bowl, combine the flour, salt and 2 tablespoons of the sugar. Cut in the butter until the mixture resembles coarse meal. Sprinkle on 3 tablespoons of the water, tossing to moisten the dough. Gather the dough into a ball, sprinkling on more water if necessary. Flatten the ball into a 6-inch disk, wrap and refrigerate for at least 1 hour.
2. Meanwhile, preheat the oven to 350°. In a large bowl, combine the blueberries and raspberries. Add 1 cup of the sugar and the cornstarch; toss to coat the berries evenly. Add the bourbon and toss again. Pour into a shallow 8-cup casserole or baking dish.
3. On a lightly floured surface, roll out the chilled dough about ⅛ inch thick. Place on top of berries and trim to fit the pan. Decorate the top with cut-outs from the pastry scraps if desired. Brush the top with milk and then sprinkle with the remaining 1 tablespoon sugar.
4. Set the pie on a baking sheet to catch any drips and bake in the center of the oven for 1 hour, or until the crust is golden and the filling bubbly. Serve warm or at room temperature.

—*Stephanie Sidell & Bob Sasse*

RHUBARB AND STRAWBERRY PIE

8 SERVINGS

PASTRY:
3 cups all-purpose flour
½ teaspoon salt
1 stick (¼ pound) cold unsalted butter, cut into small pieces
½ cup vegetable shortening, cut into small bits
1 egg
¼ cup ice water

FILLING:
2 pints strawberries, cut into large chunks
1 pound rhubarb, cut into 1-inch pieces (about 4 cups)
⅔ cup plus 1 teaspoon sugar
1 teaspoon finely grated lemon zest (optional)
¼ cup instant tapioca
1 egg beaten with 1 teaspoon water, to make an egg glaze
1 quart vanilla ice cream (optional)

1. *Make the pastry*: Place the flour and salt in a large mixing bowl. Scatter the butter and shortening on top. Cut into the flour, rubbing lightly with fingertips, until it resembles coarse meal with several pea-size bits of fat remaining visible.
2. Lightly beat the egg with the ice water and pour it over the flour mixture. Stir until the mixture just forms a mass. Place the dough on a lightly floured surface, divide in half and press the halves into two 6-inch disks. Wrap separately in waxed paper and chill for 30 minutes or overnight.
3. Preheat the oven to 400°. On a lightly floured surface, roll out one of the pastry disks to a 13-inch circle. Transfer to a 10-inch pie plate and fit the pastry into the dish without stretching; refrigerate.
4. *Make the filling*: In a large bowl, place the strawberries, rhubarb, ⅔ cup of the sugar, the lemon zest and tapioca; toss to combine. Place the fruit filling in the chilled pie shell.
5. Roll the second pastry disk into an 11-inch circle. Dampen the edge of the bottom crust with water. Lay the pastry lid on top and trim away excess pastry. Press the edge to seal and crimp decoratively. Cut out a 1-inch circle from the center as a vent. Brush the crust with the egg glaze.
6. Place the pie in the middle of the oven. Reduce the temperature to 350° and bake for 1 hour, or until the pie is golden. Remove to a rack and sprinkle with the remaining 1 teaspoon sugar. Let cool to room temperature. Serve with a scoop of ice cream if desired.

—*Diana Sturgis*

SAUCE-APPLE PIE

I have never been in agreement with charts claiming to give the best uses for each apple variety. Pie-wise, the results always seem al dente to me, at odds with the quest for a truly tender crust. My first choice for pie is the Cortland, recommended on many apple charts as ideal for sauce, but other varieties—as long as they are listed as not successful for pies or baking whole—will produce a similar effect.

I like to serve the pie à la mode, with a scoop of Maple Ice Cream.

8 SERVINGS

FILLING:
3 pounds Cortland or other "sauce" apples—peeled, cored and cut into ⅛-inch slices
¼ cup unbleached all-purpose flour
½ cup sugar
1½ teaspoons cinnamon
½ teaspoon freshly grated nutmeg
2 teaspoons vanilla extract
¾ cup raisins

PASTRY:
3 cups unbleached all-purpose flour, measured by sifting into a dry-measure cup and sweeping level
½ teaspoon salt
6 tablespoons unsalted butter, chilled
½ cup lard, chilled
4 to 6 tablespoons cold water
About ⅓ cup whole wheat flour (see Note)

GLAZE:
1 egg, beaten
1 tablespoon sugar

1. *Prepare the filling:* In a bowl, combine all the ingredients for the filling and let stand at room temperature, stirring occasionally, while you prepare the crust.

2. *Make the pastry:* In a food processor, combine the all-purpose flour and the salt. Cut the butter and lard into small pieces and add to the processor. With short pulses, cut the butter and lard into the flour until the mixture resembles oatmeal, about 15 seconds. Add the water, 1 tablespoon at a time, pulsing between each addition until a rough dough is formed. (You may not need all the water.)

3. Sprinkle the work surface with 2 tablespoons of the whole wheat flour. Turn the dough out, form it into a ball (it will be crumbly) and divide into two flat 6-inch disks. Wrap each one in plastic wrap and refrigerate for at least 30 minutes.

4. Preheat the oven to 400°. On a work surface lightly sprinkled with whole wheat flour, roll out one pastry disk to form an even circle about 14 inches in diameter. Ease the dough into a 10-inch pie pan. If it tears, patch it by pressing the edges together; it is not necessary to moisten the dough for an effective patch.

5. Spoon the filling and any accumulated juices into the pie shell. Roll out the remaining disk of dough, lightly flouring the work surface with just enough whole wheat flour to prevent sticking. Lay the top crust over the apples. Trim the overhanging dough edges to ½ inch and fold the lower crust over the upper, pinching it gently but firmly to seal. Crimp decoratively if desired and cut 3 or 4 slits into the upper crust.

6. Bake the pie on the lowest rack of the oven for 40 minutes. Brush the crust with the beaten egg, sprinkle evenly with the sugar and bake for another 10 to 15 minutes, until the juices are bubbling up through the slits in the crust and the pie is a rich golden brown. Let the pie cool to room temperature before serving.

NOTE: The whole wheat flour used to roll out the pastry adds extra texture and color to the crust. Unbleached all-purpose flour can be substituted.

—Michael McLaughlin

BERRY CUSTARD TART

A delicate tart with a tender, fragile crust that features ollalieberries, a West Coast native. Raspberries, blueberries or huckleberries can also be used, as long as they are sweet and delicious. *[From Margaret Fox]*

F&W BEVERAGE SUGGESTION
Sauternes, such as Château Suduiraut

MAKES A 9-INCH TART

RICH TART SHELL:
1 cup all-purpose flour
1½ tablespoons sugar
Pinch of salt
1 stick (¼ pound) chilled unsalted butter, cut into ½-inch cubes
½ teaspoon grated lemon zest

FILLING:
3 ounces cream cheese, preferably fresh (with no vegetable gum added), at room temperature*
½ cup crème fraîche
2 egg yolks, at room temperature
3 cups ollalieberries, raspberries, blueberries or huckleberries, or a mixture
3 tablespoons cassis, raspberry syrup or kirsch
1 tablespoon sugar
½ teaspoon fresh lemon juice
**Available at cheese and health-food stores*

1. *Make the tart shell:* In a mixer fitted with a dough paddle or in a food processor fitted with the steel blade, combine the flour, sugar and salt. Scatter the butter and lemon zest on top, then blend until the dough masses around the blade; it will be crumbly. Press into a compact ball. **(The dough can be prepared ahead.** Wrap tightly and freeze or refrigerate. Let return to room temperature before proceeding.)

2. Press the dough into a 9-inch tart pan with a removable bottom to form a ⅛-inch-thick bottom crust and a slightly thicker wall around the sides. Scrape any excess dough cleanly from the rim. Cover and refrigerate the tart shell until cold and firm, 30 to 60 minutes. **(The shell can be refrigerated overnight or frozen.)**

3. Line, weight and bake the tart shell as described in Steps 4 and 5 of Standard Tart Shell on page 180, but after removing the weights, bake until the crust is golden, 12 to 15 minutes.

4. *Make the filling:* Preheat the oven to 375°. In a medium bowl, beat the cream cheese until smooth and light. Add the crème fraîche and egg yolks and beat until smooth. Slide the tart shell onto a baking sheet and scrape the custard into the shell. Bake in the

center of the oven for about 8 minutes, until barely set. The custard will be quivery, not firm. Gently slip the tart from the baking sheet onto a rack. Let stand for at least 30 minutes, until cool, before unmolding.

5. No more than 3 hours before serving, arrange 2 cups of the berries closely together on top of the tart, completely covering the custard with fruit.

6. In a heavy saucepan, combine the remaining 1 cup berries with the cassis and sugar. Cook over moderate heat, stirring to mash the berries and dissolve the sugar, until slightly thickened, 3 to 5 minutes. Strain through a fine-mesh sieve, pressing on the solids to extract as much juice as possible. Stir the lemon juice into the glaze.

7. With a small pastry brush, paint the glaze all over the berries and the uppermost rim of the tart shell.

—Barbara Tropp

CHEESECAKE RAINBOW TART

A dazzling tart that tastes as good as it looks. Strawberries, kiwis and oranges form a particularly jewel-like rainbow, but there are many other possibilities. In season, try a trio of different-colored, halved grapes. *[From Amy Ho]*

F&W BEVERAGE SUGGESTION
Muscat de Beaumes de Venise

MAKES AN 11-INCH TART

1 stick (1/4 pound) unsalted butter, at room temperature
3/4 cup sugar
8 ounces cream cheese, at room temperature
1 teaspoon vanilla extract
2 eggs, at room temperature
1 prebaked Standard Tart Shell (p. 180)
1/4 cup apricot jam
1 pint strawberries, halved
3 large or 4 small kiwis, peeled and sliced
1 large navel orange—peeled, sliced into rounds and then into semicircles

1. Preheat the oven to 375°. In a mixer bowl, cream the butter and sugar on low speed until light and fluffy, 2 to 3 minutes. Add the cream cheese and beat on medium speed until smooth, 2 to 3 minutes. Beat in the vanilla and then the eggs, one by one, blending until smooth and light. (This can also be done in a food processor.)

2. Pour the filling into the prebaked tart shell and slide onto a baking sheet. Bake the tart in the center of the oven until the cheese filling is golden on top, about 30 minutes. Slide the tart gently from the baking sheet onto a rack. Let cool completely before unmolding and arranging the fruit on top. **(The recipe can be prepared to this point several hours ahead of time.)**

3. No more than 1 hour before serving, melt the jam in a small saucepan over low heat, stirring, until smooth. Strain through a sieve.

4. Arrange the strawberries, kiwi and orange slices in alternating rows across the tart, covering the entire surface attractively. With a pastry brush, lightly glaze the fruit with a thin layer of melted jam.

—Barbara Tropp

CRYSTALLIZED LEMON TART

A very pretty, simple tart made from just three ingredients: lemons, sugar and eggs. Prepare the lemons 8 to 24 hours before baking. *[From Amy Ho]*

MAKES AN 11-INCH TART

2 medium-large lemons with thin, unmarked skin (7 ounces total)
1 teaspoon grated lemon zest
1 1/4 cups sugar
2 eggs
1 prebaked Standard Tart Shell (p. 180)

1. Scrub the lemons under warm water until fragrant. Cut off the tip to expose the fruit, then cut crosswise into paper-thin slices. Cut the slices in half. Layer the sliced lemons, grated zest and sugar in a bowl. Toss and set aside for 30 to 60 minutes; toss again. Cover and let stand at room temperature for 8 hours or overnight, stirring once or twice.

2. Preheat the oven to 375°. Stir the lemon mixture gently and remove any seeds. Whisk the eggs until light colored and slightly thickened, 2 to 3 minutes. Add the lemons and fold in with a rubber spatula to mix well.

3. Set the prebaked shell on a baking sheet. Pour in the lemon filling, distributing the lemons evenly and unfolding any curled slices so that they lie flat.

4. Bake in the center of the oven until the filling is bubbling and almost set and the shell is golden, about 25 minutes. Remove the baking sheet from the oven and slide the tart onto a rack to cool before unmolding. The filling will firm as the tart cools.

5. Serve the tart slightly warm or at room temperature, cut into small slices. This tart keeps beautifully overnight. Let cool, wrap well and refrigerate; let return to room temperature before serving.

—Barbara Tropp

GINGER PEAR TART

A lovely looking and exceedingly simple tart that requires little but very firm and fragrant pears. Don't be shy when sniffing them at the grocer's! If there's no smell, there's no taste. Note that the pears must be prepared a day ahead, so plan accordingly. *[From Amy Ho]*

MAKES AN 11-INCH TART

½ cup sugar
2 tablespoons all-purpose flour
1 teaspoon grated lemon zest
1 tablespoon fresh lemon juice
⅓ cup finely chopped ginger in syrup, drained of syrup (see Note)
5 medium, firm pears with a sweet smell
1 prebaked Standard Tart Shell (p. 180)

1. Combine the sugar, flour, lemon zest, lemon juice and ginger in a large shallow bowl; stir to dissolve the sugar. One at a time, peel, core and slice the pears into wedges ⅜ inch thick; drop the slices into the sugar mixture as you work. Stir well to coat the fruit, cover tightly and set aside to stand at room temperature overnight.
2. Preheat the oven to 375°. Arrange the pear slices in the bottom of the prebaked tart shell in concentric circles, overlapping the slices to make a pretty flower pattern; begin at the outside and work in towards the center. Pour the marinating mixture from the pears over the top.
3. Slide the tart onto a baking sheet and bake in the center of the oven for 30 to 40 minutes, until the liquid bubbles and the edge of the crust is lightly browned.
4. Slide the tart onto a rack and let cool for at least 30 minutes before unmolding and slicing.

NOTE: Ginger in syrup is so-called stem ginger, which is young or immature ginger picked several months earlier than usual. It is fiberless and ideal for candying.

—*Barbara Tropp*

HAWAIIAN PINEAPPLE TART

A lush yet light tart invented when pastry chef Jim Dodge of Stanford Court received a perfectly sweet, field-ripened pineapple flown in with a friend from Hawaii. If your own luck isn't as good and you are using a less-sweet store-bought variety, slice the pineapple several hours in advance, toss with ¼ cup sugar, then brush the juices on the sponge filling just before assembling the tart.

MAKES AN 11-INCH TART

TART SHELL:
1 egg yolk
1 teaspoon sugar
¼ teaspoon salt
1 tablespoon flavorless vegetable oil
1½ cups all-purpose flour
1 stick (¼ pound) chilled unsalted butter, cut into ½-inch cubes

FILLING AND ASSEMBLY:
1 stick (¼ pound) unsalted butter, at room temperature
⅓ cup sugar
2 eggs, at room temperature
½ cup cake flour, sifted
1 ripe pineapple
¼ cup apricot preserves

1. *Make the tart shell:* Blend the egg yolk, sugar and salt in a 1-cup liquid measure. Add enough cold water to measure ¼ cup. Blend in the oil.
2. Put the flour in a mixer fitted with the dough paddle. Scatter the butter on top. Blend on low speed until the mixture is the texture of coarse meal. Stir the liquids, beat into the bowl in a thin stream and continue to mix until the dough masses together. (This dough can also be made by hand or in a food processor.) Gather the dough into a ball, press into a 6-inch disk; wrap and refrigerate for 30 to 60 minutes, until cold but still malleable.
3. Roll out the dough, and prebake as directed in Steps 3 through 5 of the Standard Tart Shell on page 180.
4. *Make the filling and assemble the tart:* Preheat the oven to 375°. To make the tart sponge filling, cream the butter and sugar until light. Beat in 1 of the eggs and then half the flour; add the remaining egg and flour, beating until the mixture is smooth and well blended. Scrape the batter into the cooled tart shell and slide it onto a baking sheet.
5. Bake the tart in the center of the oven until the top is golden, about 20 minutes.
6. Slide the tart from the baking sheet onto a rack. Pierce with a fork every ½ inch over the entire surface. Let the tart stand until cool before unmolding.
7. No more than 2 hours before serving, peel, core and slice the pineapple into ¼-inch-thick wedges, working over a bowl to catch the juices. Brush some of the juices over the sponge filling. Arrange the pineapple in a pretty flower pattern, overlapping the slices and working from the outside to the center of the tart.
8. In a small saucepan, melt the apricot preserves with 2 tablespoons of the reserved pineapple juice over low heat, stirring until smooth. Simmer for 1 minute. Strain through a sieve. With a pastry brush, paint a thin glaze over the top and exposed sides of the fruit and along the rim of the shell.

—*Barbara Tropp*

STANDARD TART SHELL

MAKES ONE 11-INCH TART SHELL

1½ cups all-purpose flour
1 tablespoon sugar
Pinch of salt
1 stick (¼ pound) chilled unsalted butter, cut into ½-inch cubes
¼ cup cold water

1. In a large bowl, combine the flour, sugar and salt. Cut in the butter until the mixture resembles coarse meal.

2. Add the water in a thin stream, tossing until the dough begins to mass together. Add a few more drops of water if necessary. Gather the dough into a ball; press into a 6-inch disk. Wrap tightly and refrigerate until cold but still malleable, 30 to 60 minutes.

3. Roll out the dough on a lightly floured surface to a round an even ⅛ inch thick. Fit into an 11-inch tart pan with a removable bottom, pressing the dough against the sides of the pan without stretching it. Trim the excess to leave about 1 inch all around. Fold hem in and press against the pan to reinforce the sides. Neatly trim the crust even with the rim of the pan. Cover with plastic wrap and refrigerate for at least 30 minutes, or freeze, before filling and/or baking. (The unbaked shell can be refrigerated overnight or frozen.)

4. Preheat the oven to 375°. Put the chilled tart shell on a baking sheet. Line with aluminum foil and fill to the rim with pie weights or dried beans.

5. Bake the shell in the center of the oven for 20 to 25 minutes, or until the rim of the shell is dry when the foil is pulled back and the walls have shrunk slightly away from the pan. Remove the foil and weights. Return the shell to the oven and bake for 10 minutes, or until the crust is dry all over. Slide the tart pan off the baking sheet onto a rack and let the shell cool before filling.

—*Barbara Tropp*

FRENCH APPLE TART

8 TO 10 SERVINGS

1⅓ cups all-purpose flour
½ teaspoon salt
1 stick (¼ pound) plus 2 tablespoons unsalted butter, chilled and cut into small pieces
3 to 5 tablespoons ice water
3 tart cooking apples, such as Greening or Granny Smith (about 1¼ pounds)
3 to 4 tablespoons sugar
½ cup apricot preserves
1 tablespoon Barack Palinka (apricot eau-de-vie) or Calvados

1. In a food processor, process the flour, salt and 1 stick of the butter until the mixture resembles small peas, about 8 seconds. Sprinkle 3 tablespoons of ice water over the surface of the mixture and process for 3 seconds. If the dough does not hold together when pinched, sprinkle on 1 more tablespoon of ice water and process for 3 seconds more. (Do not mix until the dough masses together or it will be tough.) If necessary repeat this procedure once more. Turn the dough out onto a work surface and knead lightly, just until it holds together. Form into a smooth ball. Wrap loosely in plastic wrap and flatten into a 6-inch disk. Refrigerate for at least 45 minutes.

2. Roll out the pastry between 2 sheets of lightly floured waxed paper into a 14-inch circle. Slide it, still between both sheets of waxed paper, onto a large heavy cookie sheet; refrigerate the dough until very firm, about 30 minutes.

3. Meanwhile, preheat the oven to 400°. Peel, quarter and core the apples. Cut each quarter lengthwise into ⅛-inch slices.

4. Peel the top sheet of waxed paper from the pastry and invert the pastry onto the cookie sheet. Peel away the remaining paper. Leaving a 1-inch border around the edge of the pastry, arrange the apples in concentric circles overlapping the slices tightly to fit them all in; start with the outer circle and end in the center.

5. Fold the pastry border up and slightly over the edges of the apples; pinch firmly in place. Sprinkle the apples and the rim of the dough with 3 to 4 tablespoons of the sugar, depending on the tartness of the apples. (Brush any sugar off the cookie sheet or it will burn.) Dot the apples with the remaining 2 tablespoons butter.

6. Bake the tart in the lower third of the oven for 40 minutes, or until the apples are lightly colored and the edge of the dough is golden brown. Let cool on the baking sheet for about 10 minutes until warm.

7. Meanwhile, in a small saucepan, warm the apricot preserves over moderate heat, stirring until melted. Press through a sieve into a small bowl and stir in the Barack Palinka. Brush the apples with the warm apricot glaze. Serve warm or at room temperature.

—*Rose Levy Beranbaum*

Clockwise from upper right: Chocolate-Painted Tulip Cups with Raspberries and Whipped Cream (p. 215), "Cigar" Cookies (p. 204), Tuiles (p. 205) and Chocolate-Lace Almond Cookies (p. 205). Following page: Cheesecake Rainbow Tart (p. 178).

Above (left to right), Allspice Bread Pudding (p. 213) and Mace-Scented Carrot Torte (p. 193). Right (clockwise from lower left), Pineapple Poached in Maple Syrup (p. 226), Pineapple Spice Cake (p. 195) and Pineapple Pecan Ice Cream (p. 217).

Above, slices of Anise Butter Cake (p. 194) and a clove- and orange-scented Pomander Cake filled with whipped cream (p. 194). Right, Berry Custard Tart (p. 177) and a glazed Hawaiian Pineapple Tart (p. 179).

APPLE COOKIE-TART

6 SERVINGS

1½ cups all-purpose flour
3 tablespoons sugar
⅛ teaspoon salt
1 stick (¼ pound) unsalted butter, chilled and cut into small pieces
1 tablespoon vanilla extract
4 tablespoons ice water
4 medium, tart baking apples, such as Granny Smith—peeled, cored and cut lengthwise into thin slices
1 tablespoon fresh lemon juice
¼ teaspoon cinnamon
¼ teaspoon allspice
Dash of freshly ground pepper
3 tablespoons seedless raspberry jam

1. In a food processor, whirl the flour, 1 tablespoon of the sugar and the salt until well blended, about 30 seconds. Add the butter and process until the mixture resembles coarse meal, about 10 seconds. Add the vanilla and ice water, 1 tablespoon at a time, and process briefly until the dough begins to mass together. Turn out and flatten into a 4-inch disk; wrap in waxed paper and refrigerate for at least 1 hour.

2. Preheat the oven to 400°. In a bowl, toss the apples with the remaining 2 tablespoons sugar, the lemon juice, cinnamon, allspice and pepper.

3. Roll out the dough into a 10-inch circle, ¼ inch thick. Using the rim of a 9½-inch tart pan as a cookie cutter, cut out a circle of dough. Using a wide spatula, carefully slide the dough onto a cookie sheet.

4. In a small saucepan, melt the jam over low heat. Spread 1 tablespoon of the jam over the surface of the dough. Arrange the apple slices decoratively in a single layer, overlapping slightly. Bake for 20 minutes.

5. Paint the top of the apples with the remaining jam. Reduce the oven temperature to 350° and bake for 30 to 40 minutes longer, or until the apples are tender when pierced with a sharp knife. Serve hot or at room temperature, with whipped cream if desired.

—*W. Peter Prestcott*

Mocha Cream-Filled Profiteroles (p. 214).

WINTER FRUIT TART WITH CHOCOLATE

Glorious to look at, this large fruit mosaic, paved with chocolate and glistening with apricot glaze, could star on any dessert buffet. It is extremely easy to assemble and serves 16 to 20 people. Best of all, you can make it with any seasonal fruit that you think goes well with chocolate.

It can be assembled several hours before serving and is especially appropriate as a showcase dessert on an evening when, for convenience, the other food has been prepared ahead of time or purchased.

16 TO 20 SERVINGS

2¾ cups all-purpose flour
3 tablespoons sugar
¾ teaspoon salt
2 sticks (½ pound) cold unsalted butter, cut into ¼-inch dice
¼ to ⅓ cup cold water
6 ounces extra-bittersweet or bittersweet chocolate
3 large bananas
2 teaspoons fresh lemon juice
3 cans (17 ounces each) peeled apricot halves, drained
About 45 large green seedless grapes
½ cup apricot jam
2 teaspoons Cognac

1. In a large bowl, mix together the flour, sugar and salt. Add the bits of butter and rub quickly between your fingers to flatten and coat with flour. Continue for 1 to 2 minutes, until the mixture resembles coarse oatmeal (do not worry about cutting the butter in well).

2. Sprinkle on about ¼ cup of the water, tossing to moisten the dough; gather loosely into a ball. Add more water to any dry dough at the bottom of the bowl until it can be gathered loosely together.

3. Turn out the dough onto a lightly floured surface and, with quick motions, press bits of the dough away from you with the heel of your hand to blend the flour and butter further. Gather into a ball and flatten into a disk. Wrap in waxed paper and seal in a plastic bag. Refrigerate for 15 to 30 minutes, until the dough firms up. Preheat the oven to 375°.

4. Lay out a couple of sheets of waxed paper, overlapping slightly, and flour lightly. Put the dough on the paper, flour the dough and cover with more waxed paper. Roll out to form a rough rectangle about 16 by 14 inches. Remove the top sheets of paper. Invert a 16-by-14-inch, or larger, baking sheet on top of the dough, and invert to cover the sheet with the dough; peel off the remaining waxed paper.

5. Use your hands to pat the dough into an even rectangle. Fold over about ½ inch of the dough all around and crimp to form a raised edge. Place in the freezer to firm up for about 5 minutes.

6. Cover the dough with foil, fill with pie weights or dried beans and bake for 15 minutes. Remove the weights and foil and bake until the pastry is dry and the edges are beginning to color, 10 to 15 minutes.

7. In a microwave oven or in a

small heavy saucepan over very low heat, melt the chocolate until smooth. Using a rubber spatula, spread a thin layer of chocolate all over the bottom of the pastry. Let stand or refrigerate until set.

8. Peel the bananas and cut crosswise on the diagonal into ⅜-inch-thick slices. Place in a bowl and sprinkle on the lemon juice. Toss gently with your hands to coat the slices with lemon juice to prevent discoloration.

9. Arrange the apricots, grapes and bananas in alternating rows on the tart.

10. In a small heavy saucepan, melt the apricot jam over moderate heat. Let boil, stirring, for 5 minutes. Strain through a wire sieve and stir in the Cognac. Use a pastry brush to dab the glaze lightly over the fruit. The tart can be assembled up to several hours ahead. Serve at room temperature.

—*Susan Wyler*

QUINCE AND ALMOND PASTE TART

8 SERVINGS

1½ pounds quinces (preferably small ones, about 4)
1 cup lightly packed light brown sugar
2-inch piece of vanilla bean
1¼ cups all-purpose flour
Salt
2 tablespoons plus 1 teaspoon sugar
5 tablespoons chilled butter, cut into small bits
2½ tablespoons chilled vegetable shortening, cut into small bits
About 3 tablespoons ice water
1 cup plus 2 tablespoons unblanched whole almonds, toasted
1 egg, lightly beaten
¼ cup milk
⅛ teaspoon almond extract

1. Halve and peel the quinces, reserving the peelings. With a melon ball cutter, remove the seeds and cores and combine with the peelings in a large noncorrodible pot. Add the quince halves and water to cover. Simmer, partially covered, until the quinces are not quite tender, 30 to 45 minutes.

2. Add the brown sugar and vanilla bean and simmer, uncovered, until the fruit is soft. (This can vary from 30 minutes to 1½ hours, so test often, adding water if needed.) With a slotted spoon, remove the quince halves to a dish; cover loosely and refrigerate until chilled. Strain and refrigerate the cooking liquid. **(The recipe can be prepared ahead to this point.)**

3. Meanwhile, make the pastry shell. In a food processor, blend the flour, ¼ teaspoon of salt and 1 teaspoon of the sugar. Add the butter and shortening and process briefly until the mixture resembles oatmeal. Scrape into a bowl. Gradually sprinkle in about 3 tablespoons ice water, tossing the flour with a fork, until the dough masses together. Gather into a ball and press into a ½-inch-thick disk. Cover and refrigerate the dough for 30 minutes.

4. On a lightly floured surface, roll the dough into a circle 12 to 13 inches in diameter. Fit the dough into a fluted 9½-inch tart pan with a removable bottom. Trim the dough, leaving a 1-inch overhang; fold in to form a border. Loosely cover the pastry shell and let rest in the refrigerator for 30 minutes. Preheat the oven to 400°.

5. Line the pastry shell with foil and fill it with pie weights or dried beans. Bake until the edge is set, 7 to 8 minutes. Remove the foil and weights, prick the crust and bake until lightly browned, 10 to 15 minutes. Set on a rack to cool. Reduce the oven temperature to 375°.

6. In a food processor, combine 1 cup of the toasted almonds with the remaining 2 tablespoons sugar and process until finely ground. Add the egg, milk, almond extract and a pinch of salt and whirl to a smooth, light puree. Spread the almond paste on the bottom of the pastry shell.

7. Carefully slice the quinces crosswise on the diagonal into ¼-inch slices. Arrange the slices, closely overlapping, in the pastry shell, with the wide ends next to the tart rim, the smaller ends pointing in toward the center. Fill in all spaces with overlapping quince slices.

8. Bake in the lower third of the oven for 30 minutes.

9. Meanwhile, boil the reserved quince cooking liquid until it is reduced to a very thick, syrupy glaze. After the tart has been in the oven for 30 minutes, brush it with some of the glaze and bake for 15 minutes longer. Remove the tart from the oven and paint it generously with the remaining glaze. Set on a rack to cool.

10. Sliver the remaining 2 tablespoons almonds and scatter them over the tart.

—*Elizabeth Schneider*

CONCORD JAM TARTLETS

These delicate tartlets are best served the same day they're made. Once filled, they don't take kindly to refrigeration. If desired, serve with lightly sweetened whipped cream.

12 SERVINGS

1 package (1¼ pounds, 2 sheets) frozen puff pastry, such as Pepperidge Farm, thawed
1 egg white, lightly beaten
2 teaspoons sugar
1 cup Concord Grape Jam (p. 242)

1. On a lightly floured surface, roll one of the pastry sheets into a 13-by-9-inch rectangle. Preheat the oven to 400°.

2. Flour the blade of a sharp knife and trim the pastry into a 12-by-8-inch rectangle. Reserve the pastry trimmings.

3. Cut the rectangle into six 4-by-4-inch squares. Cutting only halfway through, mark out a square border ¾ inch in from the edge all around each pastry. With a knife, lightly cross-hatch each border.

4. Lightly brush the pastry with the egg white, avoiding the cut lines that mark the border. Sprinkle very lightly with the sugar. Cut leaf shapes from the trimmings, brush with egg white and sprinkle with sugar. Using a spatula, place the pastry shells and leaves separately on a heavy cookie sheet and bake until puffed and golden, about 20 minutes. Remove the leaves after 15 minutes if they are in danger of overbrowning.

5. Meanwhile, repeat the procedure with the second sheet of puff pastry.

6. Transfer the baked pastry squares to a rack to cool. Using the tip of a knife, gently lift out the central square from each tartlet and set aside. If necessary, scoop out and discard any flakes of uncooked pastry. (**The tartlet shells may be prepared several hours ahead to this point.**)

7. To assemble the tarts, spoon about 1½ tablespoons of the jam into each pastry shell; decorate with the lids and leaves.

—*Diana Sturgis*

APPLE TARTLETS

These lovely tartlets may be kept in the refrigerator for a day or two, but they are best eaten the day they are made.

MAKES 8 TARTLETS

¼ cup raisins
1 tablespoon dark rum
Pâte Brisée (recipe follows)
5 small Granny Smith apples
½ cup apple jelly
1 tablespoon sugar
1 teaspoon cinnamon
1 egg, beaten
Chopped toasted nuts or raisins, for garnish

1. In a small bowl, toss the raisins with the rum and set aside.

2. Lightly butter eight 3-inch tartlet tins. On a lightly floured surface, roll out the pastry about ⅛ inch thick. Using a round cookie cutter, 3½ to 3¾ inches in diameter, cut out eight circles of dough and fit into the tins. With a sharp knife, trim off the excess around the rim of each tin and freeze until ready to fill.

3. Core and peel the apples. Halve them lengthwise, place the halves cut-side down and cut crosswise into 12 slices, keeping the slices together. Cut two of the sliced apple halves in half again lengthwise to make a total of 48 small pieces.

4. In a small heavy saucepan, bring the apple jelly to a boil over moderately high heat, stirring until smooth. Remove from the heat and set aside. In a small bowl, combine the sugar and cinnamon.

5. Preheat the oven to 400°. Brush the inside of each pastry shell with some of the hot apple jelly. Set the remaining jelly aside. Dividing the small apple pieces equally, arrange them pinwheel fashion in the bottom of each tin; sprinkle with 1 teaspoon of the cinnamon sugar.

6. Fill the hollowed core of each of the 8 remaining sliced apple halves with one-eighth of the raisins and, holding the slices together, invert quickly onto the center of each tart.

7. Brush the top of each tartlet with the beaten egg and sprinkle all with the remaining 1 tablespoon cinnamon-sugar. Place on a cookie sheet and bake on the lowest rack of the oven until the crust is golden and the apple, when pierced with a knife, is tender but still slightly firm, 20 to 25 minutes. Cool the tartlets in the tins on a rack for 10 minutes; then unmold them.

8. Reheat the apple jelly (adding a drop of water or rum if it has thickened too much) over low heat until melted. Brush lightly over the tartlets. If desired, garnish with chopped toasted nuts or additional raisins.

—*Dorie Greenspan*

PATE BRISEE

ENOUGH FOR ABOUT 20 TARTLETS

1½ cups all-purpose flour
1 tablespoon sugar
¼ teaspoon salt
1 stick (¼ pound) cold unsalted butter, cut into pieces
3 tablespoons ice water

1. In a medium bowl, combine the flour, sugar and salt. Cut in the butter until the mixture resembles coarse meal.

2. Sprinkle the dough with 2 tablespoons of the ice water, tossing with a fork to evenly distribute the moisture. Sprinkle on the remaining 1 tablespoon ice water and, using your fin-

gertips, blend lightly into the dough. Gather the dough into a ball and flatten to a 6-inch disk. Cover with plastic wrap and refrigerate for at least 1 hour.

—Dorie Greenspan

GOLDEN ALMOND BARQUETTES

A plate of these sweets and a cup of lemon tea is a guaranteed cure for sagging holiday spirits. You will need 12 barquette molds or 3-inch tartlet tins.

MAKES 12 BARQUETTES

½ cup finely ground blanched almonds
¼ cup sugar
4 tablespoons unsalted butter, at room temperature
1 egg
½ teaspoon minced lemon zest
1 tablespoon fresh lemon juice
½ cup golden raisins
Pâte Brisée (p. 191)
¼ cup apricot preserves
1 tablespoon dark rum

1. In a small bowl, combine the ground almonds and the sugar. In a medium mixer bowl, beat the butter until light. Beat in half the almond mixture, the egg and then the remaining almond mixture, beating on high speed after each addition until incorporated. Stir in the lemon zest and juice and the raisins. Refrigerate for at least 1 hour. **(The recipe may be prepared ahead to this point and refrigerated for up to 1 week.)**

2. Lightly butter the barquette molds. On a lightly floured surface, roll out the pâte brisée about ⅛ inch thick. Invert a barquette mold on the pastry and cut out a piece ½ inch larger than the mold. Fit the piece of pastry into the mold and cut off the excess around the rim. Repeat with the remaining pastry. Freeze the filled molds for at least 20 minutes before baking.

3. Preheat the oven to 400°. Place the molds on a cookie sheet and bake for 10 minutes, or until slightly firm but not browned. Remove from the oven and let cool; leave the oven turned on.

4. Fill each shell with 1 tablespoon of the almond cream. Bake on the lowest rack of the oven until the tops are well browned, about 15 minutes. Cool the barquettes in the molds on a rack for 10 minutes, then unmold.

5. In a small heavy saucepan, melt the apricot preserves with the rum over low heat. Strain through a fine-mesh sieve and brush lightly over the barquettes.

—Dorie Greenspan

CRANBERRY GEMS

This is a perfect make-ahead sweet for the holidays. The tartlet shells may be baked weeks in advance and frozen. The cranberry filling should be made at least one day in advance; it will keep for several months in the refrigerator. Any leftover filling makes a lovely spread for toast or a relish for turkey, ham or cold meats. You may want to make a second batch of filling just for that purpose. Since there's no need to defrost the shells, these tartlets take just minutes to assemble. The finished product has a sparkling, polished look.

MAKES 16 TO 20 TARTLETS

1 package (12 ounces) cranberries, fresh or frozen
⅓ cup orange or pineapple juice
1 tablespoon grated orange zest
1 tart apple, peeled and chopped
1 medium pear, peeled and chopped
½ cup (3 ounces) raisins
½ cup (3 ounces) dried pears or dried pineapple, finely diced*
1 cup sugar
1½ teaspoons cinnamon
Pinch of nutmeg
⅓ cup coarsely chopped walnuts, pecans or macadamia nuts
3 tablespoons Grand Marnier or dark rum
Pâte Brisée (p. 191)
Whipped cream, for garnish
**Available in natural food stores*

1. Make the cranberry filling: In a medium noncorrodible saucepan, combine the cranberries, orange juice and zest, apple, pear, raisins, dried pears, sugar, cinnamon and nutmeg. Bring to a boil, reduce the heat to moderately low and simmer, stirring occasionally, until thickened, about 20 minutes. Remove from the heat and stir in the nuts and Grand Marnier. Spoon into a 1-quart heatproof jar; cover and refrigerate.

2. Lightly butter 24 tartlet tins 3 inches in diameter and ⅜ inch high. (Any shaped shallow tin of 1½-tablespoon capacity can be used.) On a lightly floured surface, roll out the pastry about ⅛ inch thick. Invert a tin on the pastry and cut out a piece ½ inch larger than the tin. Fit the piece of pastry into the tin and cut off the excess around the rim. Repeat with the remaining pastry. Prick the bottom of each shell with a fork and freeze for at least 20 minutes before baking.

3. Preheat the oven to 400°. Place the tins on a cookie sheet and bake on the lowest rack of the oven for 12 to 15 minutes, until golden. Check the tartlets after 7 minutes and prick them with a fork if the centers start to rise. Cool in the tins on a rack for 10 minutes, then unmold. Freeze in an airtight container until ready to fill.

4. To assemble, place 1 tablespoon of the cranberry filling in each pastry shell. If desired, garnish with whipped cream.

—*Dorie Greenspan*

FRIULIAN ALMOND TORTE

6 TO 8 SERVINGS

3 tablespoons fresh white bread crumbs
1½ cups rye bread crumbs, from 4 to 5 slices seedless rye bread, crusts trimmed
¼ cup light or dark rum
4 eggs
1¼ cups granulated sugar
1¼ cups (about 5 ounces) ground, blanched almonds (see Note)
1 teaspoon grated lemon zest
⅛ teaspoon ground cloves
⅛ teaspoon cinnamon
1½ teaspoons confectioners' sugar

1. Preheat the oven to 350°. Fit a 9-inch circle of waxed paper into the bottom of a 9-inch cake pan. Butter the sides of the pan and the paper and sprinkle with the white bread crumbs.

2. Spread the rye bread crumbs on a plate and sprinkle with the rum. Separate 1 of the eggs.

3. In a medium mixer bowl, beat the 3 whole eggs and 1 yolk. Gradually add the granulated sugar, beating until the mixture turns light yellow and falls in ribbons from the beaters, about 5 minutes. Add the almonds, bread crumbs, lemon zest, cloves and cinnamon. Beat until incorporated.

4. Whip the remaining egg white until it stands in stiff peaks. Gently fold the egg white into the batter. Scrape the batter into the prepared cake pan and smooth the surface.

5. Bake in the center of the oven for 30 minutes or until the center is no longer wet when tested with a toothpick. Slide a knife around the edges of the cake pan and turn the cake onto a rack. Peel off the waxed paper. Let cool then turn right-side up onto a serving dish. Sprinkle with the confectioners' sugar before serving.

NOTE: If you cannot find ground almonds, grate blanched whole almonds with a rotary grater. A food processor will not produce the powdery texture that ensures a light cake.

—*Diane Darrow & Tom Maresca*

CALIFORNIA NUT TORTE

Serve this torte with a simple custard sauce or on its own—an intriguing combination of almonds, hazelnuts, walnuts and coconut, dusted with confectioners' sugar.

10 SERVINGS

1 cup (4 ounces) blanched almonds
2½ tablespoons granulated sugar
3½ tablespoons pastry or cake flour
5 tablespoons cold unsalted butter, cut into small pieces
2 whole eggs
1 egg yolk
1 cup plus 2½ tablespoons (packed) brown sugar
½ cup all-purpose flour
½ teaspoon baking powder
1 cup (4 ounces) hazelnuts (filberts), coarsely chopped
¾ cup (3½ ounces) walnuts, coarsely chopped
*1 cup unsweetened shredded coconut**
Confectioners' sugar, for garnish
**Available at health food stores*

1. Preheat the oven to 350°. In a food processor, grind the almonds with the granulated sugar. Add the pastry flour and process to blend. Add the butter and turn the machine quickly on and off until the mixture resembles coarse meal.

2. Press the almond-butter mixture into the bottom and one-third up the sides of an ungreased 9-inch cake pan.

3. In a mixer bowl, beat the whole eggs, egg yolk and brown sugar until fluffy, 4 to 5 minutes. Combine the flour and the baking powder and blend into the egg-sugar mixture. Fold in the hazelnuts, walnuts and coconut. Pour the filling into the crust.

4. Bake in the center of the oven for about 40 minutes, or until slightly soft in the center and dry 1 inch from the edge when tested with a cake tester. Remove from the oven and let cool in the pan on a rack.

5. Run a sharp knife around the edge of the cake pan. Invert the cake onto a plate. Invert again onto a serving plate and dust with confectioners' sugar.

—*John Ash, John Ash & Co., Santa Rosa, California*

MACE-SCENTED CARROT TORTE

Using a food processor with a steel blade to grind the nuts and mince the carrots makes this torte quick and easy.

8 SERVINGS

1 cup pecans (4 ounces), ground
2 tablespoons all-purpose flour
2 teaspoons baking powder
½ teaspoon ground mace
4 eggs, separated
⅔ cup granulated sugar
2 tablespoons fresh lemon juice
⅔ cup minced carrots (about 2 medium)
Confectioners' sugar, for garnish

1. Preheat the oven to 350°. Butter an 8-inch springform pan. Line the bottom with parchment or waxed paper and butter the paper. Dust the pan with flour; tap out any excess. In a small bowl, combine the pecans, flour, baking powder and mace.

2. In a large bowl, whisk together the egg yolks and granulated sugar until pale. Add the lemon juice, carrots and pecan-flour mixture. Stir until blended.

3. Beat the egg whites until they form stiff peaks. Fold into the carrot mixture; do not overmix. Turn the batter into the prepared pan and smooth the top.

4. Bake in the center of the oven for 60 to 65 minutes, until golden. This type of torte will naturally sink slightly in the center. Let cool on a rack for 10 minutes. Run a blunt knife around the sides of the pan and unmold the cake. Turn right-side up and let cool completely on a rack. Slide onto a platter and garnish with a sprinkling of confectioners' sugar.

—*Dorie Greenspan*

ANISE BUTTER CAKE

This is a moist cake with the aroma and taste of anise—warm and slightly tangy. Although the cake may be frozen, unglazed, it will keep well for several days after finishing and, in fact, improves with a 24-hour rest.

12 SERVINGS

2 cups all-purpose flour
1½ teaspoons baking powder
½ teaspoon baking soda
¼ teaspoon salt
1 tablespoon finely ground aniseed
2 sticks (½ pound) unsalted butter, at room temperature
2 cups sugar
½ teaspoon vanilla extract
2 eggs, at room temperature
1 cup sour cream, at room temperature
½ cup apricot preserves
2 teaspoons Pernod, or other anise liqueur

1. Preheat the oven to 350°. Lightly butter a 10- to 12-cup bundt cake pan. Dust with flour and set aside. In a large bowl, mix together the flour, baking powder, baking soda, salt and aniseed.

2. In a large mixer bowl, beat the butter until light and fluffy. Gradually add the sugar, beating until well blended. Beat in the vanilla and the eggs, one at a time. Continue to beat for 3 minutes after the final addition.

3. Stir in the sour cream; the mixture will appear curdled. Fold in the dry ingredients until just blended. Do not overmix. Spoon the batter into the prepared pan and smooth the top.

4. Bake in the center of the oven for 55 to 65 minutes, or until a cake tester inserted into the center comes out clean and the cake begins to pull away from the sides of the pan. Remove from the oven and cool on a rack for 5 minutes before unmolding. Cool right-side up. (**The cake can be made ahead and frozen for up to 1 month.**)

5. In a small heavy saucepan, combine the apricot preserves and Pernod. Melt over low heat. Strain through a fine-mesh sieve and brush over the cooled cake.

—*Dorie Greenspan*

POMANDER CAKE

Inspired by those pretty, clove-spiked oranges that are made to hang in closets, this cocoa party cake is a variation on the classic genoise. Flavored with ground cloves, moistened with a clove and orange syrup, and dressed with whipped cream and chopped poached oranges, it is rich but still light enough to encourage second helpings.

8 TO 10 SERVINGS

½ cup plus 2 tablespoons all-purpose flour
½ cup unsweetened Dutch-process cocoa powder
¼ cup cornstarch
1 teaspoon baking powder
1½ teaspoons ground cloves
6 whole eggs
1 egg yolk
3 cups granulated sugar
4 tablespoons unsalted butter, melted and cooled to room temperature
8 whole cloves
2 thin-skinned, seedless oranges, thinly sliced
1½ tablespoons orange liqueur, such as Grand Marnier
1½ cups heavy cream
⅓ cup confectioners' sugar

1. Preheat the oven to 350°. Lightly butter two 8-inch round cake pans, 2 inches deep. Line the bottoms of each with parchment or waxed paper and butter the paper. Dust the pans with flour; tap out any excess.

2. Sift together the flour, cocoa, cornstarch, baking powder and ground cloves.

3. In a large metal bowl, combine the whole eggs, egg yolk and 1 cup of the granulated sugar. Whisk together until light in color. Place over a saucepan of simmering water and whisk

until the sugar is dissolved and the mixture is slightly warm to the touch.

4. Remove the bowl from the heat and beat until tripled in volume and thick enough to form a ribbon that holds for 10 seconds when the beater is lifted, about 5 minutes.

5. Sift one-third of the dry ingredients over the eggs and fold in until just blended. Fold in half the melted butter. Repeat with half the remaining dry ingredients and all of the remaining butter. Fold in the last of the dry ingredients.

6. Divide the batter between the 2 prepared pans. Bake in the center of the oven for 25 to 30 minutes, until the tops are springy and a cake tester inserted in the center comes out clean. Remove from the oven and let cool on a rack for 10 minutes. Unmold the cake and remove the parchment. Turn and cool right-side up. (**The cakes can be made ahead to this point.** Cool completely, wrap in plastic and store at room temperature or in the refrigerator for up to 3 days or freeze for one month.)

7. In a medium saucepan, combine the remaining 2 cups granulated sugar and the whole cloves with 2½ cups of cold water. Bring to a boil over high heat and cook until the sugar dissolves and the liquid is clear. Add the orange slices. Return to the boil, reduce the heat to moderately low and simmer until the orange rinds are softened, about 20 minutes. Remove from the heat and let the oranges cool in the syrup for 10 minutes.

8. Remove the oranges and finely chop. Measure out 1 cup of the syrup and stir in the orange liqueur; discard any remaining syrup.

9. Cut each cake layer in half horizontally. Break one of the top layers into pieces, place in a food processor and grind to fine crumbs. Reserve for garnish.

10. Beat the cream until it stands in stiff peaks. Sift the confectioners' sugar over the whipped cream and fold in. Fold the chopped orange into half the whipped cream. Set the remaining whipped cream aside.

11. To assemble, place a bottom layer of the cake, cut-side up, on a platter or cake stand. Brush one-third of the reserved poaching syrup over the layer. Cover evenly with half the whipped cream-chopped orange mixture. Place the other bottom layer, cut-side up, over the filling. Brush with ⅓ cup of the syrup and spread with the remaining orange-cream mixture. Brush the cut side of the top layer with the remaining syrup and place on top, cut-side down.

12. Cover the entire cake with the reserved whipped cream. Press the cake crumbs into the sides of the cake. Refrigerate for 2 to 6 hours before serving. (This cake is best eaten the day it is assembled.)

—Dorie Greenspan

PINEAPPLE SPICE CAKE

Maple syrup is used in a light-textured spice cake, which is filled with pieces of pineapple poached in maple syrup and then iced with a maple buttercream. It is a superb dessert.

8 TO 10 SERVINGS

2½ cups sifted cake flour
1 tablespoon baking powder
½ teaspoon salt
1 teaspoon cinnamon
1 teaspoon allspice
½ teaspoon freshly grated nutmeg
½ teaspoon ground cloves
1 stick (¼ pound) unsalted butter, softened
½ cup sugar
¾ cup pure maple syrup
3 eggs, separated
1 teaspoon vanilla extract
⅓ cup milk
Maple Buttercream (recipe follows)
Pineapple Poached in Maple Syrup (p. 226), prepared through Step 2

1. Preheat the oven to 350°. Grease and lightly flour a 9-by-2-inch round cake pan. Line the bottom with a circle of parchment or waxed paper.

2. In a medium bowl, combine the flour, baking powder, salt, cinnamon, allspice, nutmeg and cloves.

3. In a large mixer bowl, beat the butter on high speed until pale and fluffy, 3 to 4 minutes. Add the sugar and continue beating, stopping occasionally to scrape down the sides of the bowl, until well combined. Add the maple syrup and continue beating until throughly mixed. Scrape down the sides of the bowl again. Add the egg yolks and vanilla and beat on medium speed until incorporated.

4. Alternately add the dry ingredients and the milk in three stages, beating after each addition only until just combined and scraping the sides of the bowl twice.

5. In another bowl, beat the egg whites until stiff but not dry. Stir one-third of the beaten whites into the batter to lighten the mixture. Fold the remaining whites into the batter. Pour the batter into the prepared baking pan.

6. Bake the cake for 50 to 60 minutes, or until the top is a deep golden brown and a cake tester inserted in the center comes out clean. Transfer to a wire rack and let cool for about 15 minutes. As soon as the pan is cool enough to handle, loosen the edges with a small knife and invert to unmold the cake onto the rack. Let the cake cool completely before removing the paper.

7. To assemble, split the cake in half horizontally with a long serrated

knife. Spread ⅓ to ½ cup of the buttercream in a thin layer over the bottom layer of the cake. Arrange the well-drained pineapple wedges on top of the buttercream, covering the entire top surface. Cover the pineapple with another thin layer of buttercream. Put the top of the cake, cut-side down, over the filling. Frost the top and sides of the cake with the remaining buttercream.

—Jim Dodge & Gayle Henderson Wilson

MAPLE BUTTERCREAM

MAKES ABOUT 3 CUPS

2 whole eggs
1⅓ cups maple syrup reserved from Pineapple Poached in Maple Syrup (p. 226), prepared through Step 2
3 sticks unsalted butter, cut into 1-inch chunks, at room temperature

1. In a large bowl, beat the eggs until blended.
2. In a large heavy saucepan, bring the maple syrup poaching liquid to a boil over high heat. Continue to boil until the syrup reaches the soft ball stage, 238° on a candy thermometer.
3. Beating constantly with an electric mixer, pour the boiling liquid into the eggs in a slow steady stream. Continue to beat until the mixture is cooled to room temperature and thick, about 5 minutes.
4. Add the butter in 4 stages, beating until well blended between each stage. Continue to beat until the frosting is fluffy and smooth.

—Jim Dodge & Gayle Henderson Wilson

ARMAGNAC-CINNAMON CAKE WITH PRUNES AND WALNUTS

16 SERVINGS

1 cup cake flour
1 teaspoon cinnamon
⅔ cup (lightly packed) light brown sugar
5 whole eggs
5 egg yolks
6 tablespoons unsalted butter, melted
1½ cups (6 ounces) walnut halves
⅓ cup Armagnac
Prune Puree (recipe follows)
Armagnac-Brown Sugar Buttercream (p. 197)

1. Preheat the oven to 300°. Butter a 10-by-3-inch cake or springform pan. Line the bottom with a circle of parchment or waxed paper; butter the paper. Dust the pan with flour and tap out any excess. Sift together the flour and cinnamon and set aside in a sifter or strainer set over a small bowl.
2. In a large stainless steel bowl, combine the sugar with the whole eggs and egg yolks. Holding the bowl with a mitt, whisk directly over moderate heat until the mixture is hot to the touch (120° on an instant-reading thermometer), about 2 minutes.
3. Remove from the heat and beat with an electric mixer on high speed for 5 minutes, or until the mixture is pale, thick and doubled in volume. Reduce the speed to medium and continue to beat for 5 to 7 minutes, or until a finger run through the batter creates a trough that will not collapse. This may take a few minutes longer if you are using a hand-held mixer.
4. It is important that you work quickly now so the mixture will deflate as little as possible. Remove about 1½ cups of the beaten egg mixture to a medium bowl. Add the melted butter to the 1½ cups beaten egg mixture and fold and stir with a rubber spatula until blended so that there are no streaks of butter visible. Set aside.
5. Sift the dry ingredients over the remaining beaten eggs and fold quickly until blended.
6. Pour the reserved egg and butter mixture over the batter and quickly fold together. Pour the batter into the prepared pan.
7. Bake in the center of the oven for 1 hour, or until the cake begins to pull away from the sides of the pan and a cake tester inserted in the center comes out clean.
8. Remove the cake from the oven and let cool in the pan on a rack for 10 minutes. Loosen the edges, if necessary, with a small sharp knife. Invert to unmold the cake onto the rack, peel off the paper and let the inverted cake cool completely before proceeding to assemble. (**The recipe can be prepared to this point up to 2 days in advance.** Place the cooled cake, flat bottom-side up, on a cardboard round, wrap well in plastic wrap and foil and refrigerate.)
9. Preheat the oven to 325°. Spread the walnuts on a baking sheet and bake, tossing once or twice, for 10 minutes, or until the nuts are lightly toasted. Reserve 10 walnut halves for garnish. Chop the remainder.
10. To assemble, carefully slice the cake horizontally into 3 even layers with a long serrated knife. Sprinkle 1 to 2 tablespoons of the Armagnac on the bottom layer to moisten the cake. Spread half of the prune puree over the bottom layer. Scatter ⅓ cup of the chopped walnuts over the puree. Place the second layer on top; gently press the cake down with the palms of your hands. Sprinkle 1 to 2 table-

spoons of the Armagnac liquid over the cake and repeat with the remaining prune puree and ⅓ cup of walnuts. Place the top layer, flat bottom-side up, on the cake; gently press with the palms of your hands. Sprinkle the remaining Armagnac over the top.

11. Spread the Armagnac-flavored buttercream evenly over the top and sides of the cake, swirling the frosting decoratively if desired. Pat the remaining chopped walnuts into the sides of the cake. Decorate the top with the reserved walnut halves. **(The cake can be assembled up to a day in advance and refrigerated uncovered.** Let stand at room temperature for 2 hours before serving so the flavors fully develop.)

—Jim Dodge & Gayle Henderson Wilson

PRUNE PUREE

MAKES ABOUT 3 CUPS

1¼ pounds pitted prunes (2½ packed cups)
1 cup Armagnac

1. Place the prunes in a large saucepan and cover with water. Bring to a boil over moderately high heat, reduce the heat to moderately low and simmer until the prunes are tender, about 15 minutes; drain.

2. Put the prunes in a shallow dish. Cover with the Armagnac and let the prunes macerate at room temperature for several hours, or overnight. **(The recipe can be prepared to this point and refrigerated, in a tightly covered jar, for 1 to 2 weeks.)**

3. Pass the prunes and liquid through the fine disk of a food mill or puree in a food processor until smooth. Use at once or refrigerate, covered, for up to 2 weeks.

—Jim Dodge & Gayle Henderson Wilson

ARMAGNAC-BROWN SUGAR BUTTERCREAM

MAKES ABOUT 3 CUPS

¾ cup (packed) dark brown sugar
3 sticks (¾ pound) unsalted butter, at room temperature
1 whole egg
4 egg yolks
1 tablespoon Armagnac

1. In a heavy medium saucepan, combine the brown sugar with ⅔ cup of water. Bring to a boil over moderately high heat, stirring to dissolve the sugar. Continue to boil without stirring until the syrup reaches the soft-ball stage, 244° on a candy thermometer, about 10 minutes.

2. Meanwhile, in a mixer bowl, beat the butter until lightly whipped. In another mixer bowl, beat the whole egg and egg yolks on high speed until pale, fluffy and quadrupled in volume, about 5 minutes.

3. Add the boiling syrup to the beaten eggs in a thin, steady stream. Beat until the mixture cools to room temperature, about 5 minutes.

4. Gradually beat in the whipped butter, ¼ cup at a time. Continue to beat until the buttercream is light and fluffy. Beat in the Armagnac.

—Jim Dodge & Gayle Henderson Wilson

CHOCOLATE APRICOT CAKE

16 SERVINGS

⅔ cup cake flour
¼ cup unsweetened Dutch-process cocoa powder
¾ cup sugar
5 whole eggs
5 egg yolks
6 tablespoons unsalted butter, melted
3 tablespoons amaretto liqueur
Apricot Buttercream (recipe follows)
Chocolate Glaze (p. 198)
1 cup (about 5 ounces) coarsely chopped toasted almonds, for garnish

1. Preheat the oven to 300°. Butter a 10-by-3-inch cake or springform pan. Line the bottom of the pan with a circle of parchment or waxed paper; butter the paper. Dust the pan with flour and tap out any excess. Sift together the flour and cocoa. Set aside in a sifter or strainer set over a small bowl.

2. In a large stainless steel bowl, combine the sugar with the whole eggs and egg yolks. Holding the bowl with a mitt, whisk directly over moderate heat until the mixture is hot to the touch (120° on an instant-reading thermometer), about 2 minutes.

3. Remove from the heat and beat with an electric mixer on high speed for 5 minutes, or until the mixture is pale, thick and doubled in volume. Reduce the speed to medium and continue to beat for 3 to 5 minutes, or until a finger run through the batter creates a trough that will not collapse. This may take a few minutes longer if you are using a hand-held mixer.

4. Working quickly, remove about 1½ cups of the beaten egg mixture to a medium bowl. Add the melted butter to the 1½ cups of beaten egg mixture; fold and stir with a rubber spatu-

la until blended so that there are no streaks of butter. Set aside.

5. Sift the dry ingredients over the remaining beaten eggs and fold quickly until blended.

6. Pour the reserved egg and butter mixture over the batter and quickly fold together. Pour the batter into the prepared pan.

7. Bake in the center of the oven for 1 hour, or until the cake begins to pull away from the sides of the pan and a cake tester inserted in the center comes out clean.

8. Remove the cake from the oven and let cool in the pan on a rack for 10 minutes. Loosen the edges, if necessary, with a small sharp knife. Invert to unmold the cake onto the rack, peel off the paper and let the inverted cake cool completely before proceeding to assemble. (**The recipe can be prepared to this point up to 2 days in advance.** Place the cooled cake, flat bottom-side up, on a cardboard round, wrap well in plastic wrap and foil, and refrigerate.)

9. To assemble, carefully slice the cake horizontally into 3 even layers with a long serrated knife. Sprinkle 1 tablespoon of the amaretto liqueur on the bottom layer to moisten the cake. Spread a thin layer of buttercream (about ⅔ cup) over the bottom layer with a metal pastry spatula. Repeat with the second layer. Place the third layer, flat bottom-side up, over the buttercream; gently press the layers together with the palms of your hands. Sprinkle the top of the cake with the remaining 1 tablespoon amaretto. Spread the remaining buttercream over the top and sides. Refrigerate for about 30 minutes to set the frosting.

10. Quickly spread the chocolate glaze over the top and sides of the cake. With a thin spatula, swirl the glaze decoratively or marble with the buttercream underneath. If desired, garnish the sides of the cake with the chopped almonds.

—Jim Dodge and Gayle Henderson Wilson

APRICOT BUTTERCREAM

MAKES ABOUT 2½ CUPS

1 cup (firmly packed) dried apricots (about 8 ounces)
¼ cup sugar
½ cup plus 2 teaspoons amaretto liqueur
3 sticks (¾ pound) unsalted butter, at room temperature

1. In a small saucepan, combine the apricots, sugar, ½ cup of the amaretto and ¾ cup of water. Bring to a boil over high heat. Reduce the heat to moderate and simmer, uncovered, until the apricots are tender and slightly glazed and the liquid has been reduced to about ⅓ cup, 10 to 15 minutes.

2. Remove from the heat and let cool for 5 minutes. Strain the liquid into a small bowl and reserve. Pass the fruit through the fine disk of a food mill or puree in a food processor until smooth.

3. In a large mixer bowl, beat the butter at high speed until very pale and fluffy. Add the apricot puree and beat until well blended. Beat in 2 tablespoons of the reserved apricot syrup and the remaining 2 teaspoons amaretto. (**The frosting can be made up to 2 days ahead.** Refrigerate, tightly covered, or freeze for several weeks. Let return to room temperature and beat to lighten before using.)

—Jim Dodge & Gayle Henderson Wilson

CHOCOLATE GLAZE

This fudgy, spreadable glaze has a rich matte finish. The quantity below will give you enough to mask your 10-inch cake, with an ample quantity left for decoration.

MAKES ABOUT 2⅔ CUPS

¾ cup heavy cream
8 ounces good-quality bittersweet chocolate, broken into pieces
4 tablespoons unsalted butter
1½ cups sifted confectioners' sugar

1. In a saucepan, warm the cream over low heat until hot to the touch but not boiling. Remove from the heat.

2. In a double boiler or stainless steel bowl set over a pan of hot water, warm the chocolate and butter over hot—not simmering—water, stirring occasionally, until melted and smooth.

3. Stir the warmed cream into the chocolate until completely blended. Add the confectioners' sugar and whisk vigorously until it dissolves.

4. Remove from the heat and let the glaze cool at room temperature until thickened to a spreadable consistency, about 30 minutes. Do not refrigerate or cool over ice. (**The recipe can be prepared up to 1 day ahead and refrigerated, covered.** If the glaze becomes too stiff for spreading, reheat over a pan of hot water; then let cool to the desired consistency.)

—Jim Dodge & Gayle Henderson Wilson

SPICE ROLL WITH PERSIMMON AND CREAM FILLING

The taste of this very tender, festive dessert is reminiscent of both pumpkin pie and mango mousse.

8 SERVINGS

¾ cup confectioners' sugar
⅓ cup all-purpose flour
¼ teaspoon salt
1 teaspoon ground ginger
¼ teaspoon freshly ground pepper
1 teaspoon allspice
1 teaspoon cinnamon
1 teaspoon ground coriander
2 teaspoons unsweetened cocoa powder
5 eggs, separated
¼ teaspoon cream of tartar
3 very ripe, medium persimmons
2 tablespoons granulated sugar
2 tablespoons dark rum
1 cup heavy cream
Confectioners' sugar or cocoa powder, for garnish

1. Butter a 10-by-15-inch jelly roll pan and line it with a sheet of waxed paper that extends slightly over the short ends. Butter the waxed paper heavily. Preheat the oven to 350°.

2. Sift together ½ cup of the confectioners' sugar, the flour, salt, ginger, pepper, allspice, cinnamon, coriander and cocoa. Sift again into a bowl.

3. In a large mixer bowl, beat the egg whites until foamy. Add the cream of tartar and beat until soft peaks form. Sift in ¼ cup of the confectioners' sugar and beat until stiff peaks form.

4. Without washing the beaters, beat the yolks in a large bowl until they are pale and thick. On the lowest speed, add the flour mixture, beating just long enough to incorporate. Fold half the beaten whites into this, blending completely. Gently fold in the remainder, half at a time, taking care not to deflate the batter.

5. Spread the batter evenly in the prepared jelly roll pan. Bake on the center rack of the oven for 18 to 20 minutes, or until the cake springs back slightly when pressed in the center; it should no longer sound foamy-wet when pressed.

6. Sprinkle a thin layer of confectioners' sugar on a kitchen towel. Gently invert the cake onto the towel; then carefully peel off the waxed paper. Starting at one short end, roll up the cake and towel to form a neat cylinder. Let cool completely.

7. Halve the persimmons lengthwise and scoop out all the flesh, discarding any area that seems at all unripe (taste to be sure). Chop the fruit coarsely (there will be about 1½ cups) and set aside.

8. Make a rum syrup by combining the granulated sugar and the rum in a small saucepan. Cook over moderate heat until the sugar dissolves and the liquid is clear. Set aside to cool.

9. To assemble, carefully unroll the cake. Paint it with the rum syrup and spread it evenly with the chopped persimmon, leaving a 2-inch margin at one short end.

10. In a mixer bowl, beat the cream until firm peaks form. Spread the whipped cream neatly over the persimmon.

11. Starting at the short end that has filling right up to the edge, gently but firmly roll the cake up. Set the roll seam-side down on a serving dish. Refrigerate, covered, for at least 1 hour and up to 12.

12. To serve, trim away a very thin sliver from each end of the roll to present an attractive swirled appearance. Sieve a thin layer of confectioners' sugar (or cocoa powder if you prefer a dark color) over the roll.

—*Elizabeth Schneider*

ZAUBER TORTE (MAGIC CAKE)

This dramatic cake requires some skill and time to prepare, but the complete glittering presentation is a knockout, to be reserved for very special occasions. To ease the work load, you can make the Caramel Cage and Gold Dust up to several days ahead, and you can soak the dried apricots for the buttercream the night before. If you prefer a simpler dessert, the cake frosted with the apricot buttercream alone is delightful and still dressy.

12 TO 16 SERVINGS

GOLDEN GENOISE:

¾ cup cake flour
⅓ cup cornstarch
12 egg yolks, at room temperature
1 cup superfine sugar
1 teaspoon vanilla extract
6½ tablespoons clarified butter, slightly warm

APRICOT BUTTERCREAM:

1 cup (6 ounces) dried apricots, preferably unsulphured from California
1 tablespoon Barack Palinka (apricot eau-de-vie) or apricot brandy
3 egg yolks
6 tablespoons granulated sugar
¼ cup light corn syrup
2 sticks (½ pound) unsalted butter, at room temperature

ASSEMBLY:

2 tablespoons Barack Palinka (apricot eau-de-vie) or apricot brandy
5 long, thin dripless candles
Caramel Cage and Gold Dust (recipe follows)

1. *Make the genoise:* Preheat the oven to 350°. Grease and flour a 9-cup (9-inch) kugelhopf pan. Sift together the flour and cornstarch.

2. Place the egg yolks and superfine sugar in a large mixing bowl and set over a saucepan with an inch or two of simmering water; do not let the water touch the bowl. Whisk constantly over heat until the mixture is almost hot, about 5 minutes. Remove from the heat.

3. With an electric mixer, beat on high speed until the mixture is very thick and pale and the bowl is cold, about 6 minutes. Lower the speed and quickly beat in the vanilla and ¼ cup of water.

4. Sift one-half of the flour and cornstarch over the batter and gently fold in with a balloon whisk or a perforated skimmer. Repeat with the remaining flour and cornstarch. Gently and quickly, fold in the butter in two stages until just blended.

5. Immediately pour the mixture into the prepared pan and bake for 35 minutes, or until the cake is golden brown and a cake tester inserted in the center comes out clean. Immediately unmold the cake by inverting onto a greased wire rack; let cool. (**The cake can be made a day ahead.** When cool, wrap well in plastic wrap to prevent drying out and store at room temperature.)

6. *Make the buttercream:* Place the apricots in a small saucepan with ¾ cup of water. Let stand at room temperature for at least 2 hours or overnight to soften. Cover and bring to a boil. Reduce the heat to low and simmer for 10 to 20 minutes, until the apricots are completely soft. Puree the apricots with any liquid left in the pan in a food processor or blender; press through a sieve. Stir in the Barack Palinka. Set the apricot puree aside.

7. With an electric mixer, beat the egg yolks on medium-high speed until they are thick and light in color, about 10 minutes. In a small heavy saucepan, combine the granulated sugar and corn syrup. Bring to a rolling boil over moderate heat, stirring constantly.

8. With the mixer still on medium-high speed, beat the syrup into the egg yolks in a thin steady stream. Continue beating until the mixture is cool. On low speed, beat in the butter, 1 tablespoon at a time. Beat in the apricot puree.

9. *Assemble the torte:* Split the cake in half horizontally with a serrated knife. Sprinkle each cut side with 1 tablespoon of the Barack Palinka. Sandwich the pieces together with about ⅓ cup of the apricot buttercream. Spread the remaining buttercream evenly over the outside of the cake; refrigerate for up to several hours until serving time. The cake can be served as is, simply frosted, or finished with the gold dust and cage as follows.

10. Using a small strainer, sift the gold dust over the buttercream, tilting the cake to get an even coating. Place the cake on a large flat platter and cover it with the caramel cage. (If the caramel cage should break when assembling the cake, use the broken pieces as decoration right on the frosting.) Insert the candles through the cage so they radiate from the center.

11. Light the candles at the table. To serve, remove the candles, lift off the cage and break it into pieces. Serve some of the caramel with each slice of cake.

—*Rose Levy Beranbaum*

CARAMEL CAGE AND GOLD DUST

1 cup sugar
⅛ teaspoon cream of tartar
Candied violets (optional)

1. Cover the outside of a 9-inch (9 cup) kugelhopf pan with a sheet of lightweight aluminum foil, fitting it as smoothly as possible to the pan. Trim with a scissors to leave a ½-inch lip for the base of the cage. Lightly oil the foil or spray it with nonstick vegetable spray.

2. In a small heavy saucepan, combine the sugar and cream of tartar with ⅓ cup of water. Cook over moderately low heat, stirring to dissolve the sugar. Wash down any sugar particles from the sides of the pan with a wet brush. Increase the heat to moderately high and boil without stirring until the mixture turns pale amber, about 10 minutes.

3. Quickly place the saucepan in a larger pan of boiling water to stabilize the heat of the caramel. Let stand until the caramel cools to about 240° on a candy thermometer and falls from a fork in fairly thick strands.

4. Working next to the stove, use a wooden spoon to drizzle a thin stream of hot caramel all over the covered cake pan. The strands should be as thick as spaghettini and should be swirled to give an even, lacy covering. Work quickly, reheating the caramel when necessary over moderately low heat to keep it fluid. Strengthen the bottom of the cage with a few extra swirls. If desired, glue crystallized violets decoratively onto the cage with a small dab of caramel. Reserve a thin layer of caramel in the pan for the gold dust.

5. Allow the cage to cool for about 10 minutes, then carefully lift the cage

and foil from the pan. Beginning at the side farthest away from you, gently pull the foil away from the cage, gathering the foil into a ball as you go. **(The cage may be returned to a well-oiled kugelhopf pan and stored in an airtight container for several weeks.)**

6. Reheat the reserved caramel and pour it onto a greased cookie sheet. Let stand until completely hardened. Break up the hard caramel and pulverize it in a food processor. You will need 3 to 4 tablespoons of this gold dust to sprinkle on the cake. **(This may be made ahead and stored in an airtight container for several weeks.)**

—*Rose Levy Beranbaum*

BASIC MADELEINES

MAKES 2 DOZEN 3-INCH CAKES

3 eggs, at room temperature
¾ cup sugar
1 teaspoon vanilla extract
2 teaspoons grated lemon zest
¼ teaspoon fresh lemon juice
1⅓ cups sifted all-purpose flour
¾ cup clarified unsalted butter

1. In a large bowl, whisk the eggs with the sugar until light colored and thick enough to fall in ribbons. Beat in the vanilla, lemon zest and lemon juice.

2. Using a rubber spatula, fold the flour into the eggs. Fold in ½ cup of the butter until just incorporated; do not overfold. Tightly cover the bowl with plastic wrap and refrigerate for at least 1 hour until chilled through. **(The recipe can be prepared to this point up to 24 hours ahead.)**

3. Preheat the oven to 425°. Using a small pastry brush, grease two 12-form madeleine molds of 3-inch-long forms with 2 tablespoons of the butter. Place the mold upside-down over a baking sheet to catch drips so that the butter will evenly coat the molds and won't pool in the bottom; refrigerate until the butter is set, about 10 minutes. Brush again with 2 tablespoons butter and let chill until set.

4. Spoon rounded tablespoons of the batter into the mold. Do not smooth the batter. Bake in the center of the oven for 5 minutes; then reduce the heat to 375° and bake for 7 to 10 minutes, until the madeleines are golden in the center and browned around the edges.

5. Remove from the oven. Sharply rap the mold against a flat surface to loosen the madeleines. Turn out and let cool slightly on a wire rack. Serve warm. **(The madeleines can be loosely wrapped in waxed paper and stored in a loosely covered container for up to 24 hours.)**

—*John Robert Massie*

TEA-SCENTED MADELEINES

F&W BEVERAGE SUGGESTION
Earl Grey tea

MAKES 2 DOZEN 3-INCH CAKES

¾ cup clarified unsalted butter
2 tablespoons Earl Grey tea
3 eggs, at room temperature
¾ cup sugar
1 teaspoon finely grated lemon zest
¼ teaspoon fresh lemon juice
Pinch of salt
1⅓ cups sifted all-purpose flour

1. In a small saucepan, combine ½ cup of the butter with the tea. Gently steep over low heat for 10 minutes to release the aromatic oils; do not boil. Remove from the heat and set aside, uncovered, to infuse for 30 minutes. Strain the butter and discard the tea.

2. Continue from Step 1 of the Basic Madeleines, substituting the tea-flavored butter for the plain clarified butter in Step 2.

—*John Robert Massie*

SPICE MADELEINES

MAKES 2 DOZEN 3-INCH CAKES

¾ cup clarified unsalted butter
3-inch cinnamon stick, broken into pieces
1 tablespoon whole cloves
3 eggs, at room temperature
¾ cup sugar
Pinch of salt
1⅓ cups sifted all-purpose flour

1. In a small saucepan, combine ½ cup of the butter with the cinnamon and cloves. Gently warm over low heat for 10 minutes to release the aromatic oils; do not boil. Remove from the heat and set aside, uncovered, to infuse for 30 minutes. Strain the butter and discard the spices.

2. Continue from Step 1 of the Basic Madeleines, substituting the spice-flavored butter for the plain clarified butter in Step 2.

—*John Robert Massie*

COCOA MADELEINES

MAKES 2 DOZEN 3-INCH CAKES

3 eggs, at room temperature
¾ cup sugar
1 teaspoon rum extract
1 cup sifted all-purpose flour
½ cup Dutch-process unsweetened cocoa
¾ cup clarified unsalted butter

1. In a large bowl, beat or whisk the eggs with the sugar until light col-

ored and thick enough to fall in ribbons. Beat in the rum flavoring.

2. Sift together the flour and the cocoa. Gently fold into the eggs.

3. Fold ½ cup of the butter into the batter until just incorporated; do not overfold. Tightly cover with plastic wrap and refrigerate for at least 1 hour until chilled through.

4. Continue from Step 3 of the Basic Madeleines.

—John Robert Massie

PEPPER MILL SQUARES

These are dense, fudgy cake squares, dotted with golden raisins, spiced with white pepper, black pepper and allspice and finished with a smooth cream cheese frosting.

MAKES 16 SQUARES

½ cup plus 2 tablespoons all-purpose flour
1 teaspoon Pepper Mix (p. 238)
Pinch of salt
10 tablespoons (1 stick plus 2 tablespoons) unsalted butter, at room temperature
½ cup granulated sugar
⅓ cup packed light brown sugar
4 ounces semisweet chocolate, coarsely chopped
2 ounces unsweetened chocolate, coarsely chopped
1½ teaspoons vanilla extract
2 eggs
⅓ cup golden raisins
4 ounces cream cheese, at room temperature
1 cup confectioners' sugar

1. Preheat the oven to 350°. Lightly butter an 8-inch square baking pan. In a small bowl, sift together the flour, pepper mix and salt.

2. In a large heavy saucepan, melt 8 tablespoons of the butter over moderately high heat. Add the granulated and brown sugars and, stirring constantly, bring just to a boil. Stir in the semisweet and unsweetened chocolates and remove from the heat. Continue stirring until the chocolate is melted. Let cool for 5 minutes, until tepid.

3. Stir in 1 teaspoon of the vanilla. Mix in the eggs, one at a time, until blended. Gradually stir in the flour mixture. Add the raisins. Pour the batter into the prepared pan.

4. Bake in the center of the oven for 30 minutes, or until the cake begins to pull away from the sides of the pan.

5. Meanwhile, prepare the frosting. In a medium bowl, beat together the cream cheese and the remaining 2 tablespoons butter. Beat in the confectioners' sugar and the remaining ½ teaspoon vanilla.

6. Remove the cake from the oven and let cool in the pan on a rack for 10 minutes. Loosen the edges with a blunt knife. Unmold and turn right side up; let cool completely on the rack. Spread the frosting over the top. Trim the edges and cut into 2-inch squares.

—Dorie Greenspan

LADYFINGERS

These will keep well stored in an airtight container at room temperature for several days or frozen for several months.

MAKES ABOUT 18

3 eggs, separated
8 tablespoons granulated sugar
1 teaspoon orange-flower water or ½ teaspoon vanilla extract
½ cup all-purpose flour
2 tablespoons confectioners' sugar

1. Preheat the oven to 350°. Beat the egg whites until soft peaks form. Gradually beat in 3 tablespoons of the granulated sugar and continue to beat until stiff peaks form.

2. Beat the egg yolks with the remaining 5 tablespoons granulated sugar until the mixture is thick enough to fall back in a ribbon when the beaters are lifted, about 3 minutes.

3. Stir the orange-flower water into the egg yolk mixture. Fold in the flour until blended. Fold in the beaten egg whites until no streaks of white remain; do not overmix.

4. Using a pastry bag with a plain ¾-inch (#9) tip, pipe narrow 3-inch strips of the batter onto a large parchment-lined or buttered and floured baking sheet. Sift the confectioners' sugar over the ladyfingers. Bake for 15 to 18 minutes, until golden. Let cool.

—Diana Sturgis

SAUTERNES MACAROONS WITH STRAWBERRIES

These macaroons are a delicious accompaniment to a dish of strawberries. Traditionally, the berries are served with an older Saint-Julien poured over them.

6 SERVINGS

2 cups ground, blanched almonds (about 8 ounces)
3 egg whites
¼ cup sugar
4 tablespoons Sauternes
1½ pints strawberries, halved

1. Preheat the oven to 350°. Line a large heavy baking sheet with lightly buttered parchment or waxed paper.

2. In a mixing bowl, combine the ground almonds, egg whites, sugar and 2 tablespoons of the Sauternes.

Beat with a wooden spoon until well blended. The mixture should be firm enough to hold its shape.

3. Spoon tablespoons of the batter at least 1 inch apart onto the prepared baking sheet. Leave the dough rough edged. Brush each cookie lightly with the remaining Sauternes.

4. Bake in the upper third of the oven for 25 to 30 minutes, until lightly browned. Transfer to a rack to cool.

5. Divide the strawberries among 6 dessert dishes and serve accompanied with the macaroons.

—*John Robert Massie*

MINIATURE MACAROONS

Since high humidity softens crisp macaroons, make them on a dry day. They may be stored for several days in an airtight container.

MAKES 5 TO 6 DOZEN

2 eggs whites
½ cup sugar
½ cup ground almonds (about 2 ounces)

1. Preheat the oven to 325°. Beat the egg whites until soft peaks form. Gradually beat in the sugar, then fold in the almonds.

2. Line a large baking sheet with parchment, or butter and flour the sheet. Drop ½ teaspoons of the mixture about 1 inch apart onto the sheet.

3. Place the baking sheet in the oven and immediately reduce the temperature to 200°. Bake for 2 hours. Turn off the heat and let the macaroons dry in the closed oven until they are crisp throughout, preferably overnight.

—*Diana Sturgis*

PALMIERS

MAKES ABOUT 35

1⅓ cups sugar
1-pound sheet of puff pastry, chilled

1. Cut a sheet of parchment paper or aluminum foil into a 16-inch square. Dust with ½ cup of the sugar. Place the pastry on top and sprinkle with ½ cup of the sugar. With a lightly floured rolling pin, roll into a 14½-inch square. Slide the paper and pastry onto a cookie sheet and refrigerate until chilled, at least 15 minutes.

2. Flour the blade of a very sharp knife. Without pulling the pastry, neatly trim ⅛ to ¼ inch from each edge. Fold two opposite sides of the square into the center, leaving a ¼-inch gap in the middle. Fold again to bring the folded edges together, so that the pastry is 4 layers thick. Cover the pastry on the cookie sheet and refrigerate until chilled through, at least 15 minutes.

3. Preheat the oven to 375°. Line a cookie sheet with parchment paper or aluminum foil. Flour the blade of a very sharp knife. Without pulling the pastry, cut the roll crosswise into ⅜-inch slices. Dip the cut sides of each slice into the remaining ⅓ cup sugar. Place 2 inches apart on the cookie sheet and refrigerate until chilled through, about 15 minutes.

4. Remove directly to the oven and bake in the center for 20 minutes, until the palmiers are golden on top. Turn carefully with a wide metal spatula and bake for 5 minutes longer, or until golden brown on both sides. Let cool on a wire rack before serving.

—*Diana Sturgis*

PINWHEELS

MAKES 16

All-purpose flour
1-pound sheet of puff pastry, chilled
1 egg white lightly beaten with 1 teaspoon water, to make an egg glaze
8 teaspoons sugar
2 tablespoons apricot preserves
2 tablespoons black currant jam

1. Cut a sheet of parchment paper or aluminum foil into a 16-inch square. Dust lightly with flour. Place the pastry on top and with a lightly floured rolling pin, roll into a 14½-inch square. Slide the paper and pastry onto a cookie sheet and refrigerate until chilled, at least 15 minutes.

2. Flour the blade of a very sharp knife. Without pulling the pastry, neatly trim about ⅛ inch from each edge. Cut the pastry into 16 squares, 3½ inches each.

3. Make a cut 1½ inches long from each of the square's four corners toward the center, leaving a 2-inch square in the center uncut. Lightly dampen the center of one of the pastry squares with water. Counting each corner as having 2 tips, fold every other tip into the center, pressing lightly to seal, to create a pinwheel shape. Repeat with the remaining pastry squares.

4. Preheat the oven to 375°. Line a cookie sheet with parchment paper or aluminum foil. With a metal spatula, transfer the pinwheels to the cookie sheet. Brush each pastry with the egg glaze. Sprinkle each with about ½ teaspoon sugar. Refrigerate on the cookie sheet for 15 minutes.

5. Remove directly to the oven and bake in the center for 20 to 25 minutes, until golden. Transfer the pastries to a wire rack. While still warm, drop about ½ teaspoon of apricot preserves into the center of 8 of the pinwheels and ½ teaspoon of black currant jam into the center of the remaining 8 pinwheels.

—*Diana Sturgis*

NO-ROLL SUGAR COOKIES

Crisp, light and easy to make, these cookies have a lovely melt-in-the-mouth texture. The recipe can easily be doubled.

MAKES ABOUT 4 DOZEN

2¼ cups all-purpose flour
½ teaspoon baking soda
½ teaspoon cream of tartar
½ teaspoon salt
1 stick (¼ pound) unsalted butter, at room temperature
½ cup granulated sugar
½ cup confectioners' sugar
1 egg
½ cup flavorless vegetable oil
½ teaspoon vanilla extract
Granulated sugar, for dipping

1. Into a large bowl, sift together the flour, baking soda, cream of tartar and salt.
2. In a large mixing bowl, cream the butter, granulated sugar and confectioners' sugar until pale and fluffy. Beat in the egg and oil until well blended. Beat in the vanilla.
3. Add the dry ingredients in three additions, beating until blended after each addition. Cover with plastic wrap and refrigerate until firm, several hours or overnight.
4. Preheat the oven to 375°. Divide the dough into 8 sections. Working with 1 section at a time and keeping the remaining dough in the refrigerator, pinch off about 2 teaspoons of dough at a time and roll between your palms to form 1-inch balls. Place the balls 2 inches apart on ungreased cookie sheets.
5. Moisten the bottom of a 2½-inch glass, then dip it in granulated sugar. Flatten each ball of dough with the sugar-coated glass, dipping the bottom of the glass in sugar before flattening each cookie.
6. Bake the cookies for about 8 minutes, until light golden around the edges. Let cool on a rack. Store in an airtight tin.

—*Leona Foote*

BASIC ALMOND COOKIE BATTER

This Basic Almond Cookie Batter produces cookies that, while still warm, are pliable enough to coax into a number of different shapes. Of course, you can also stop short of the shaping directions to produce delicious and crisp *un*shaped cookies.

MAKES ABOUT 20 4½-INCH OR 60 2-INCH COOKIES

⅔ cup sugar
½ cup all-purpose flour
½ cup finely chopped blanched almonds
1 whole egg, lightly beaten
2 egg whites
½ teaspoon vanilla extract
4 tablespoons unsalted butter, melted
1 to 2 tablespoons water

1. In a medium bowl, mix the sugar, flour and almonds. Add the whole egg, egg whites and vanilla and beat with a wooden spoon until well incorporated. Stir in the butter and 1 tablespoon of water; the batter will be thin and slightly granular. (**The batter may be made 1 day ahead and refrigerated, tightly covered.** Stir before using and add up to 1 tablespoon additional water, if necessary, to restore the consistency.)
2. Follow directions for making Tuiles, "Cigar" Cookies or Chocolate-Lace Almond Cookies (recipes follow) or for the Chocolate-Painted Tulip Cups with Raspberries and Whipped Cream (p. 215).

—*Diana Sturgis*

"CIGAR" COOKIES

Serve these crunchy elegant cookies as an accompaniment to ice cream or espresso.

MAKES ABOUT 30

1 recipe Basic Almond Cookie Batter (at left)

1. Follow the recipe for Tuiles (recipe follows) through Step 2, omitting the almond topping.
2. Bake in the lower third of the oven for 6 to 8 minutes, until the cookies have a golden-brown border 1 inch wide. Have ready 4 long-handled wooden spoons or dowels ½ inch in diameter.
3. Remove the cookies from the oven. Working quickly, slide the back of a wide metal spatula under a cookie, pushing to separate the cookie from the sheet without tearing; the cookie will be soft and pliable. Wrap it around the handle of the spoon and slide down toward the bowl of the spoon. Repeat with the remaining 3 cookies on the other wooden spoons. Leave in place until cooled and set, about 2 minutes; slide off and set aside. If the cookies cool before they can be easily molded, return to the oven for 30 seconds to restore their pliability.

4. Scrape the cookie sheet clean, wipe with a paper towel and lightly butter it. It is not necessary to rewarm the sheet. Repeat Steps 1 through 3 to form the remaining batter into "cigars." (**The recipe may be prepared several days ahead.** The cookies may be frozen, but will also keep well stored in an airtight tin.)

—*Diana Sturgis*

TUILES (TILE COOKIES)

MAKES ABOUT 30

1 recipe Basic Almond Cookie Batter (p. 204)
1 cup (3 ounces) sliced blanched almonds

1. Preheat the oven to 425°. Butter a large heavy cookie sheet. Place in the oven for 1 minute, until the cookie sheet is warm and the butter is melted. Remove from the oven.
2. Using a tablespoon measure, spoon 4 separate half-filled tablespoons of the batter at least 5 inches apart onto the warm cookie sheet. Using the back of a spoon, spread the batter into thin circles 3 inches in diameter, leaving at least 1 inch between circles to allow for spreading during baking. Sprinkle the top of each cookie with 1 rounded teaspoon of the almonds.
3. Bake in the lower third of the oven for 5 to 6 minutes, until the cookies have a golden brown border ½ inch wide. Meanwhile, have ready 1 long or 2 shorter rolling pins or similar curved surfaces about 2 inches in diameter.
4. Remove the cookies from the oven. Working quickly, slide the back of a wide metal spatula under a cookie, pushing to separate the cookie from the sheet without tearing; the cookie will be soft and pliable. Drape the cookie, almond-side up, over the rolling pin and, with your hands, gently mold the cookie to the curve of the pin. Repeat with the remaining 3 cookies. Leave in place to cool and harden, about 2 minutes; set aside. If the cookies cool before they can be easily molded, return to the oven for 30 seconds to restore their pliability.
5. Scrape the cookie sheet clean, wipe with a paper towel and lightly butter it. It is not necessary to rewarm the sheet. Repeat Steps 2 through 4 to form the remaining batter into tuiles. (**Although better fresh, the recipe can be made to this point a few days ahead.** Store the tuiles in an airtight tin or wrap them individually in plastic bags and store in the freezer. Let return to room temperature before serving.)

—*Diana Sturgis*

CHOCOLATE-LACE ALMOND COOKIES

A simple way to pipe the chocolate decoration onto these charming cookies is with a paper cone. To make one, simply roll a sheet of white paper diagonally into a tight cone and fill with the melted chocolate. Snip off the small end of the cone to create any size tip you like.

MAKES ABOUT 60

1 recipe Basic Almond Cookie Batter (p. 204)
4 ounches semisweet chocolate

1. Preheat the oven to 425°. Butter a large heavy cookie sheet. Place in the oven for 1 minute, until the cookie sheet is warm and the butter is melted. Remove from the oven.
2. Using a teaspoon measure, spoon 4 to 6 separate teaspoons of the batter at least 4 inches apart onto the warm cookie sheet. With the back of a spoon, spread the batter into thin circles 2 to 2½ inches in diameter, leaving at least 1 inch between circles to allow for spreading during baking.
3. Bake in the lower third of the oven for 5 minutes, until the cookies have a golden-brown border ½ inch wide.
4. Remove the cookies from the oven. Slide the back of a wide metal spatula under each cookie, pushing to separate the cookie from the sheet without tearing. Transfer to a wire rack and let cool.
5. Scrape the cookie sheet clean, wipe with a paper towel and lightly butter it. It is not necessary to rewarm the sheet. Repeat Steps 2 through 4 with the remaining batter.
6. Melt the chocolate in a double boiler over hot—but not boiling—water. Scrape into a small pastry bag fitted with a plain ⅛-inch tip or into a small paper cone. Pipe decorative swirls onto the cooled cookies and let set. (**Although better fresh, the recipe may be made a few days ahead.** Store the cookies in an airtight tin or stack them with a sheet of waxed paper between each layer, wrap in plastic bags and store in the freezer. Unstack them while still frozen and let come to room temperature before serving.)

—*Diana Sturgis*

HOT GINGER COOKIES

MAKES ABOUT 2½ DOZEN

1 stick (¼ pound) cold unsalted butter, cut into pieces
¾ cup sugar
1½ cups self-rising flour
1 tablespoon powdered ginger
1½ teaspoons freshly ground white pepper
1 egg

2 teaspoons heavy cream
½ cup minced crystallized ginger

1. In a food processor, combine the butter and sugar and process until well mixed, about 40 seconds. Add the flour, powdered ginger and white pepper and process for 30 seconds. Add the egg and cream and process until the dough just masses together.
2. Shape the dough into a cylinder 2 inches thick. Wrap in waxed paper and refrigerate until chilled through and firm, at least 2 hours.
3. Preheat the oven to 350°. Cut the chilled dough into ⅛-inch slices. Place 1½ inches apart on oiled cookie sheets. Sprinkle the crystallized ginger on top and bake until pale golden in color, 8 to 10 minutes.
4. Let the cookies sit for 2 minutes. Then, with a spatula, transfer them to a rack to cool.

—W. Peter Prestcott

GINGER-FUDGE NUGGETS

Rich, fudgy and gently spiced, these cakes are mixed in a saucepan and baked in miniature muffin tins. They may be stored in the refrigerator or freezer, but return them to room temperature before serving.

MAKES 24 LITTLE CAKES

2 teaspoons minced fresh ginger
1 teaspoon granulated sugar
¼ cup plus 2 tablespoons all-purpose flour
⅛ teaspoon powdered ginger
Pinch of salt
4 tablespoons unsalted butter
2½ ounces bittersweet or semisweet chocolate, broken into pieces
⅓ cup brown sugar
¼ teaspoon vanilla extract
1 egg
4 ounces white chocolate, broken into pieces

1. In a small bowl, combine the minced fresh ginger and the granulated sugar; set aside for at least 30 minutes, stirring occasionally. In a medium bowl, combine the flour, powdered ginger and salt.
2. Preheat the oven to 350°. Lightly butter 24 miniature muffin tins, approximately 1½ by ¾ inches.
3. In a heavy medium saucepan, melt the butter, bittersweet chocolate and brown sugar over low heat, stirring constantly, until smooth; remove from the heat.
4. One at a time, add the vanilla, the egg and the ginger-sugar mixture, stirring after each addition until incorporated. Add the flour mixture and mix until combined.
5. Spoon 1 teaspoon of the batter into each muffin cup; the cups should be only half filled. Bake for 9 minutes, or until the tops spring back when touched. Transfer to a rack to cool for about 15 minutes. Unmold and place on the rack until completely cool.
6. Melt the white chocolate in a double boiler over hot water, stirring until smooth. Dip the tops of the cakes into the melted chocolate, or frost the tops with the chocolate, if you wish, using a small spatula. Refrigerate to set the frosting.

—Dorie Greenspan

LINZER SANDWICHES

MAKES 24 TO 30 DOUBLE COOKIES

2 cups hazelnuts (filberts)
1½ cups all-purpose flour
1 tablespoon unsweetened cocoa powder
1¼ teaspoons cinnamon
¼ teaspoon ground cloves
⅛ teaspoon salt
1 stick (¼ pound) unsalted butter, at room temperature
½ cup sugar
½ teaspoon grated orange zest
1 egg
2½ teaspoons orange liqueur, such as Grand Marnier
3 ounces bittersweet or semisweet chocolate
½ cup seedless raspberry jam
Confectioners' sugar, for garnish

1. Preheat the oven to 350°. Spread the hazelnuts on a jelly roll pan and toast in the oven, shaking the pan once or twice, until the nuts are pale brown beneath the skin, about 12 minutes. Rub the hot nuts in a dry kitchen towel to remove as much of the brown skin as possible. Chop the nuts fine, but do not grind them.
2. In a medium bowl, combine the hazelnuts, flour, cocoa, cinnamon, cloves and salt.
3. In a large mixer bowl, beat the butter, sugar and orange zest until light and creamy. Add the egg and 1½ teaspoons of the orange liqueur; beat until smooth.
4. Gradually beat in the flour mixture, occasionally scraping the sides of the bowl with a rubber spatula, until incorporated.
5. Divide the dough in half. Place half on a large sheet of waxed paper and cover with another sheet of waxed paper. Using your hands, flatten the dough into a disk, then roll out ¼ inch thick. Repeat with the other half of the dough. Transfer, still between the waxed paper, to two cookie sheets and freeze until very firm, about 45 minutes.
6. Preheat the oven to 375°. Remove the top sheet of waxed paper from one of the dough rounds. With a 2-inch round cutter, cut into circles and place on a lightly greased or nonstick cookie sheet. (If the dough becomes too soft or sticky, freeze briefly to firm up.) Place in the refrigerator or freezer while cutting the second half of the dough. Gather up the scraps, roll again between waxed paper, chill and cut.

7. Bake the cookies for 11 to 13 minutes, until pale gold. Transfer to a rack and let cool.

8. Meanwhile, melt the chocolate in a double boiler over hot water. With a small spatula, spread a thin layer of chocolate on each cookie.

9. While the chocolate is setting, place the raspberry jam in a small saucepan and cook over moderate heat, stirring until slightly thickened. Stir in the remaining 1 teaspoon orange liqueur; remove from the heat and let cool.

10. Place about ½ teaspoon of the jam on the chocolate side of half the cookies. Gently press the remaining cookies, chocolate-side down, on top of the filling, rotating to spread the jam evenly.

11. Before serving, sift confectioners' sugar over the cookies.

—Dorie Greenspan

CHOCOLATE NUT WAFERS

MAKES 3½ TO 4 DOZEN

1 cup toasted almonds, walnuts or pecans, finely chopped
1¾ cups all-purpose flour
¼ teaspoon ground cloves
Pinch of salt
2 sticks (½ pound) unsalted butter, at room temperature
½ cup sugar
½ teaspoon almond or vanilla extract
12 ounces (2 cups) semisweet chocolate morsels

1. In a medium bowl, combine the chopped nuts, flour, cloves and salt.

2. In another bowl, beat the butter until light and fluffy. Gradually beat in the sugar and almond extract until smooth. Gradually add the nut-flour mixture ½ cup at a time, beating after each addition until incorporated. **(The recipe may be prepared ahead to this point and refrigerated.)**

3. Preheat the oven to 350°. Pinch off heaping teaspoons of the dough and roll into balls about 1 inch in diameter. Place 1½ inches apart on ungreased cookie sheets. Cover with waxed paper and, with the bottom of a glass, gently flatten each ball until ⅜ inch thick. Remove the waxed paper.

4. Bake for 13 to 15 minutes, until slightly colored. Transfer to a rack to cool.

5. Melt the chocolate in a double boiler over hot water until smooth. Partially dip each wafer into the chocolate to coat half the cookie. Let any excess chocolate drip back into the bowl. Gently run the edge of each wafer against the rim of the bowl to remove more excess chocolate. Place the dipped wafers on cookie sheets lined with waxed paper and refrigerate until the chocolate is set.

—Dorie Greenspan

CREAM HORNS

This recipe requires a special metal cornucopia form that is available in specialty cookware stores. Most forms are between 4⅜ and 5½ inches long and range in diameter from 1⅛ to 2½ inches. The main difference between the large and the small ones is the amount of cream needed to fill them. There is no difference in the baking time.

MAKES 16

All-purpose flour
1-pound sheet of puff pastry, chilled
1 egg white lightly beaten with 1 teaspoon water, to make an egg glaze
Sugar
⅓ cup raspberry jam
2 cups heavy cream
½ teaspoon vanilla extract

1. Cut a sheet of parchment paper or aluminum foil into a rectangle at least 17 by 14 inches. Dust lightly with flour. Place the pastry on top. With a lightly floured rolling pin, roll out the pastry into a 16-by-12-inch rectangle. Slide the paper and pastry onto a cookie sheet and refrigerate until chilled through, at least 15 minutes.

2. Flour the blade of a very sharp knife. Without pulling the pastry, trim ⅛ to ¼ inch from the short edges. Cut the pastry crosswise into 16 strips, 1 by 12 inches each.

3. Lightly brush a ⅜-inch border along one long edge of a strip with water. With the dampened side out, wrap the strip around a cornucopia form, starting at the tip and turning the form so that the damp edge is overlapped by pastry as you wrap. Do not stretch the pastry. It is not necessary to completely cover the form. Repeat with the remaining strips.

4. Preheat the oven to 375°. Line a cookie sheet with parchment paper or aluminum foil. Place the horns 2 inches apart on the sheet. Lightly brush the top and sides of the horns with the egg glaze and sprinkle each with a pinch of sugar. Refrigerate until chilled through, at least 15 minutes.

5. Bake the pastries in the center of the oven for 25 to 30 minutes, or until golden. Transfer to a wire rack. While still warm, gently twist the forms to remove them from the pastry.

6. Before serving, brush 1 teaspoon of jam into each horn. In a large bowl, beat the cream, vanilla and 2 teaspoons sugar until stiff peaks form. Spoon the cream into a pastry bag fitted with a ½-inch star tip and pipe into the horns.

NOTE: Tiny horns may be made for hors d'oeuvre by cutting the pastry strips into 5-by-1-inch lengths and wrapping only the bottom part of the form. Fill the baked horns with a savory mixture and rewarm in the oven before serving.

—Diana Sturgis

PAIN AU CHOCOLAT

MAKES 12

All-purpose flour
1-pound sheet of puff pastry, chilled
4 bars (1½ ounces each) bittersweet or semisweet chocolate
1 egg lightly beaten with 1 teaspoon water, to make an egg glaze

1. Cut a sheet of parchment paper or aluminum foil into a 16-inch square. Dust lightly with flour. Place the pastry on top and with a lightly floured rolling pin, roll into a 14-inch square. Slide the paper and pastry onto a cookie sheet and refrigerate until chilled through, at least 15 minutes.
2. Cut each bar of chocolate into 3 even pieces. Flour the blade of a very sharp knife. Without pulling the pastry, neatly trim ⅛ to ¼ inch from each edge. Cut the pastry into 3 even strips, about 4½ by 14 inches each.
3. Working with one strip at a time, place 4 pieces of chocolate ½ inch from the long edge, allowing equal space between each piece and placing the end pieces of chocolate ½ inch from the end of the strip. Lightly dampen the edges of the pastry and the spaces between the chocolate with water. Fold the pastry lengthwise in half to enclose the chocolate. Gently press the dough along the edges and between the chocolate pieces to seal. Repeat with the remaining pastry and chocolate.
4. Preheat the oven to 400°. Line a cookie sheet with parchment paper or aluminum foil. Cut each pastry strip crosswise between the chocolate sections to yield 4 pieces. Using a metal spatula, transfer to the cookie sheet. Lightly brush with the egg wash. Freeze for at least 20 minutes.
5. With a very sharp knife, make 6 slashes crosswise across the top of each pastry almost through to the chocolate. Transfer the pastries directly from the freezer to the oven and bake in the center for 20 minutes, or until puffed and golden. Let cool on a wire rack before serving.

—Diana Sturgis

APPLE ALMOND SQUARES

MAKES 9

All-purpose flour
1-pound sheet of puff pastry, chilled
3 ounces almond paste
⅔ cup unsweetened applesauce, preferably homemade
1 egg white lightly beaten with 1 teaspoon water, to make an egg glaze
About 1 tablespoon sugar
¼ cup sliced blanched almonds

1. Cut a sheet of parchment paper or aluminum foil into a 16-inch square. Dust lightly with flour. Place the pastry on top and with a lightly floured rolling pin, roll into a 14½-inch square. Slide the paper and pastry onto a cookie sheet and refrigerate until chilled, at least 15 minutes.
2. Flour the blade of a very sharp knife. Without pulling the pastry, trim ⅛ to ¼ inch from each side. Cut into 9 squares, 4½ inches each.
3. Roll out the almond paste into a 6-inch square. Cut into 9 squares, each one 2 inches. Place an almond paste square in the center of each pastry square. Spoon about 1 tablespoon of the applesauce on top of each almond paste square.
4. Lightly brush the edges of each pastry square with water. Bring the points of the pastry square together over the filling. Pinch the edges of the pastry together, leaving a small vent in the center.
5. Preheat the oven to 400°. Line a cookie sheet with parchment paper or aluminum foil. With a metal spatula, transfer the pastries to the cookie sheet. Brush each pastry with the egg glaze. Sprinkle each with about ¼ teaspoon of sugar and about 1 teaspoon of the almonds. Set the pastries 2 inches apart from each other on the cookie sheet. Refrigerate until chilled through, at least 15 minutes.
6. Bake in the center of the oven for 20 to 25 minutes, until golden brown. Let cool on a wire rack.

—Diana Sturgis

BASIC TART SHELL DOUGH

MAKES A 10-INCH TART SHELL

1½ cups unbleached all-purpose flour
½ teaspoon salt
9 tablespoons cold unsalted butter, cut into tablespoons
3 to 4 tablespoons ice water

1. In a food processor, combine the flour, salt and butter. Turn quickly on and off until the mixture resembles oatmeal.
2. Add 3 tablespoons of ice water and pulse again. Stop when the mixture just begins to mass together; do not let it form a ball. Turn the mixture out onto a work surface and shape into a ball. If the mixture is too dry and crumbly, add the remaining 1 tablespoon ice water. Flatten the dough into a disk. Wrap in plastic and refrigerate for at least 30 minutes, or until firm.

—Perla Meyers

DESSERTS

MRS. SIMPSON'S LEMON MOUSSE

At Mrs. Simpson's, this light and tart mousse is garnished with a spoonful of strawberry or raspberry puree and a dollop of whipped cream. Candied lemon peel is also a nice touch.

10 TO 12 SERVINGS

1 cup plus 2 tablespoons fresh lemon juice (from about 6 large lemons)
1 tablespoon plus 1/4 teaspoon grated lemon zest
12 eggs, separated
1 1/3 cups sugar
2 cups heavy cream, chilled

1. In a small heavy saucepan, combine the lemon juice, zest, egg yolks and 1 cup of the sugar. Stir to dissolve the sugar. Cook over low heat, stirring frequently, until thick enough so that a spoon drawn through the mixture will leave a trail, about 30 minutes. Do not boil.

2. Remove from the heat. Place the saucepan in a bowl of ice and water and let cool, stirring occasionally to prevent a skin from forming, until chilled through, about 15 minutes.

3. Transfer the lemon mixture to a large bowl. In a large mixer bowl, whip the cream until it forms soft peaks. Stir one-quarter of the cream into the lemon mixture to lighten it, then fold in the remaining whipped cream.

4. In a large mixer bowl, beat the egg whites until foamy. Gradually add the remaining 1/3 cup sugar and beat until the whites are stiff but not dry.

5. Fold the egg whites into the lemon-cream mixture. Transfer the mousse to an 8-cup soufflé dish or glass serving bowl and refrigerate until thoroughly chilled, at least 2 hours. (**The recipe can be made to this point up to 2 days ahead.** Cover and refrigerate.) To serve, spoon onto chilled plates.

—*Mrs. Simpson's, Washington, D.C.*

GRAPE JELLY WITH ORANGE CUSTARD

4 SERVINGS

JELLY:
1 pound Concord grapes, stemmed (about 3 cups)
2 teaspoons unflavored gelatin
3 tablespoons sugar

ORANGE CUSTARD:
1 1/3 cups milk
1 1/2 teaspoons unflavored gelatin
4 egg yolks
1 egg white
2 tablespoons sugar
1 1/4 teaspoons vanilla extract
1 teaspoon grated orange zest

TOPPING:
3/4 cup heavy cream, chilled
1 teaspoon sugar
1/4 teaspoon vanilla extract
1 teaspoon chopped orange zest

1. *Make the jelly*: In a small saucepan, combine the grapes with 1/4 cup water. Cover and cook over moderately low heat until the grapes are completely collapsed and exude their juice, about 15 minutes. Strain through a sieve, pressing on the solids with a wooden spoon; discard the solids in the sieve. Measure the liquid and, if necessary, boil until reduced to 1 1/4 cups.

2. Meanwhile, place 1/4 cup of warm water in a small bowl. Sprinkle on the gelatin and let stand until softened, about 5 minutes.

3. Off the heat, add the liquid gelatin to the hot grape juice and stir until the gelatin dissolves, about 1 minute. Add the sugar and stir until dissolved, about 1 minute.

4. Spoon the jelly into 4 stemmed glasses and refrigerate, covered, until set, about 2 hours.

5. *Prepare the orange custard*: Place the milk in a small heavy saucepan and sprinkle on the gelatin. Let stand until softened, about 5 minutes.

6. In a medium heatproof bowl, beat the egg yolks and egg white with 1 tablespoon of the sugar and the vanilla until pale and thickened, about 2 minutes.

7. Add the remaining 1 tablespoon sugar and the grated zest to the milk mixture and whisk until the gelatin and sugar are well combined. Bring to a simmer over moderate heat.

8. Gradually whisk the hot milk into the egg mixture in a thin stream. Pour the mixture into a clean heavy saucepan. Cook over moderately low heat, stirring constantly with a wooden spoon, until the custard thickens enough to coat the back of the spoon, about 5 minutes. (Do not let boil, or the custard will separate.)

9. Pour at once through a fine sieve into a clean bowl. Let cool to room temperature. When the grape jelly has set, spoon a layer of orange custard into each glass on top of the jelly. Refrigerate, covered, until set, about 2 hours.

10. *Prepare the topping*: In a medium bowl, beat the cream until soft peaks form. Add the sugar and vanilla and beat until stiff. Pipe or spoon the cream into each glass on top of the orange custard layer. Sprinkle with the chopped orange zest. Serve chilled.

—*Diana Sturgis*

ZABAGLIONE

Zabaglione can be served hot or cold. To chill, at the end of Step 1, place the zabaglione pot in a bowl of ice and water and stir until the mixture is cold. Spoon immediately into chilled glasses or over fruit and serve at once.

6 TO 8 SERVINGS

6 egg yolks
½ cup sugar
⅔ cup dry Marsala
1½ to 2 teaspoons finely grated lemon zest (optional)

1. In an 8-inch copper zabaglione pan or a 3- to 3½-quart metal bowl, combine the egg yolks, sugar and Marsala. Place over a pan of simmering water and whisk until light and frothy. Continue beating over the water until quadrupled in volume, very thick and hot to the touch, about 10 minutes.
2. Immediately spoon into warmed glasses. Top with a pinch of finely grated lemon zest if desired and serve at once.

SABAYON:
Follow the instructions for Zabaglione (above), using 6 egg yolks, ⅓ cup sugar and ⅔ cup Sauternes, and garnish with toasted sliced almonds.

—*Diana Sturgis*

GINGERED FLOATING ISLAND WITH RASPBERRY SAUCE

8 SERVINGS

8 eggs, separated
1¼ cups sugar
2 cups milk
1 teaspoon vanilla extract
½ cup crystallized ginger, finely chopped
1 package (10 ounces) frozen raspberries in syrup, thawed
2 tablespoons raspberry liqueur, such as Chambord

1. Beat the egg yolks with ½ cup of the sugar until pale yellow and thick enough to fall in ribbons from the whisk.
2. In a large heavy saucepan, bring the milk to a boil. Remove from the heat and skim off any skin that has formed. Stir in the vanilla. Gradually whisk about 1 cup of the hot milk into the beaten egg yolks to warm them gently. Whisk the yolks back into the remaining milk in the saucepan. Cook over low heat, stirring constantly, until the custard thickens enough to coat the back of a wooden spoon, about 10 minutes.
3. Strain the custard into a bowl set in a larger bowl of ice and water. Stir to quickly cool the custard to room temperature, about 5 minutes. Remove from the ice and set aside, stirring occasionally to prevent a skin from forming. (**The custard sauce may be made ahead to this point 1 day in advance.** Cover the surface of the custard with buttered plastic wrap to prevent a skin from forming and refrigerate. Stir before using.)
4. Preheat the oven to 350°. In a large mixer bowl, beat the egg whites until stiff peaks form. Gradually add the remaining ¾ cup sugar, beating constantly, until the meringue is shiny and thick. Gently fold in the ginger.
5. Butter a 4-cup mold. Lightly dust with sugar to coat all sides. Turn the meringue into the mold and lightly cover with buttered parchment paper.
6. Place the mold in a roasting pan or large casserole and pour in enough hot water to reach three-quarters of the way up the sides of the mold. Bake for 30 minutes, or until the meringue is firm to the touch and begins to shrink away from the sides of the mold.
7. Remove from the water bath and let cool to room temperature. Unmold the meringue onto a large round platter. (**The meringue may be made to this point the morning of the party.** Cover with a large bowl and refrigerate until ready to assemble.)
8. In a blender or food processor, puree the raspberries and their syrup with the raspberry liqueur until smooth. Strain through a fine-meshed sieve to remove the seeds.
9. To assemble, pour about 1½ cups of the custard sauce around the meringue. Pour about ½ cup of the raspberry sauce in a thin circle on top of the custard. Draw a knife at 2-inch intervals through the raspberry sauce from the edge of the meringue outward to create a marbled pattern. Pour about ¾ cup of the raspberry sauce on top of the meringue, so that a pool forms on top and ribbons of puree drip down the sides. Chill the floating island for at least 1 hour. To serve, pass the remaining custard and raspberry sauces separately.

—*W. Peter Prestcott*

ORANGE TRIFLE

10 SERVINGS

CUSTARD:
2½ cups milk
¼ cup sugar
⅓ cup cornstarch
2 egg yolks
1 tablespoon vanilla extract
1 tablespoon orange liqueur (optional)
1 tablespoon grated orange zest

ASSEMBLY:
3 navel oranges
About 18 Ladyfingers (p. 202)
½ cup seedless raspberry jam

6 tablespoons medium-dry sherry
5 to 6 dozen Miniature Macaroons (p. 203)
¾ cup plus 2 tablespoons chopped walnuts
1 cup heavy cream

1. *Make the custard*: In a heavy medium saucepan, combine 2 cups of the milk with the sugar. Heat to boiling, stirring to dissolve the sugar.

2. In a medium bowl, mix the remaining ½ cup milk and the cornstarch until it forms a smooth paste. Stir in the boiling milk, scrape the mixture back into the saucepan and bring to a simmer over low heat. Cook, stirring, until thickened and smooth, about 1 minute. Remove from the heat.

3. In a small bowl, mix the egg yolks and vanilla until blended. Gradually stir in about ¼ cup of the hot milk mixture. Immediately stir back into the remaining milk mixture in the saucepan; the egg yolks will thicken slightly on contact with the hot liquid.

4. Scrape the custard into a bowl and beat or whisk until cooled. This lightens the custard and prevents a skin from forming. Stir in the orange liqueur and orange zest.

5. *Assemble the trifle*: With a zester, remove the zest from one of the oranges or coarsely grate enough to measure 1 tablespoon; set aside for garnish. Using a small sharp knife, peel the oranges and cut on either side of the dividing membranes to remove each section without any skin. Spread the flat sides of the ladyfingers with jam.

6. Arrange about 6 of the ladyfingers, jamside up, in the bottom of a 2-quart deep glass bowl or soufflé dish. Sprinkle with 2 tablespoons of the sherry. Scatter about one-third of the orange sections over the ladyfingers and top evenly with about 1 dozen of the macaroons. Sprinkle with ¼ cup of the nuts and spoon on one-third of the custard to complete the first layer of the trifle. Repeat 2 more times to make 3 layers. Cover and refrigerate for 2 to 4 hours, until chilled.

7. Shortly before serving, whip the cream, then cover the surface of the trifle with it. Decorate with the remaining 2 tablespoons walnuts, the orange zest and about a dozen of the remaining macaroons.

—*Diana Sturgis*

CHOCOLATE SOUFFLE WITH COFFEE ICE CREAM

These hot soufflés are topped with a dollop of intensely flavored coffee ice cream, then garnished with whipped cream. If you choose to make the ice cream (p. 216), save five of the egg whites for these soufflés.

12 SERVINGS

1 cup sugar
1 stick plus 2 tablespoons unsalted butter, cut into small pieces, at room temperature
8 ounces bittersweet chocolate, broken into ½-inch pieces
5 whole eggs, separated, at room temperature
5 egg whites, at room temperature
Pinch of salt
Coffee Ice Cream (p. 216)
Whipped cream, for garnish

1. Preheat the oven to 425°. Lightly coat the inside of twelve 1-cup soufflé dishes with butter. Dust with ½ cup of the sugar; tap out any excess.

2. Melt the 1 stick plus 2 tablespoons butter and the chocolate in a double boiler over hot, but not boiling, water, stirring occasionally. Scrape into a large bowl.

3. Meanwhile, put the egg yolks in a mixer bowl. Add ½ cup lukewarm water and beat at high speed until light and fluffy, about 10 minutes. Fold into the chocolate.

4. Beat the 10 egg whites with the salt until soft peaks start to form. Slowly sprinkle in the remaining ½ cup sugar and continue beating until glossy and stiff. Gently fold into the chocolate mixture, one-third at a time.

5. Ladle into the prepared soufflé dishes, filling up to the rim. Bake in the lower third of the oven until puffed, about 10 minutes. Place a small scoop of coffee ice cream in the middle of each soufflé, which will collapse and enfold the ice cream. Top with a dollop of whipped cream and serve at once.

—*Barry Wine,*
The Quilted Giraffe, New York City

SWEET POTATO PECAN SOUFFLE WITH TAMARIND SAUCE

6 SERVINGS

2 tablespoons plus 1 teaspoon unsalted butter
⅓ cup plus 2 tablespoons granulated sugar
1 medium sweet potato (about 6 ounces), peeled and cut into 1-inch dice
1 teaspoon cinnamon
¼ teaspoon freshly grated nutmeg
2 whole eggs, separated
2 tablespoons dark rum
½ cup toasted pecans (see Note), finely chopped
2 egg whites
Confectioners' sugar, for garnish
Tamarind Sauce (recipe follows)

1. Preheat the oven to 350°. Lightly butter a 6-cup soufflé dish with 1 teaspoon of butter. Dust with 1 tablespoon of the granulated sugar.

2. In a small saucepan, melt the re-

maining 2 tablespoons butter over moderate heat. Add 1 tablespoon of the sugar, the sweet potato, cinnamon and nutmeg. Reduce the heat to moderately low, cover and cook, stirring occasionally, until the potato is tender, about 15 minutes. Scrape into a food processor or blender and puree until smooth. For an even silkier texture, pass the mixture through the fine disk of a food mill or a fine-mesh sieve. Let cool slightly.

3. Stir the egg yolks, rum and pecans into the sweet potato mixture.

4. Beat the 4 egg whites until thick enough to leave a trail. Gradually beat in the remaining ⅓ cup sugar and continue beating until soft peaks form.

5. Fold ⅓ of the egg whites into the sweet potato mixture to lighten it. Fold the potato mixture into the remaining egg whites. Scrape the mixture into the prepared soufflé dish.

6. Bake in the lower third of the oven for about 30 minutes, or until well puffed and lightly browned. Dust lightly with the confectioners' sugar and serve hot with the Tamarind Sauce.

NOTE: To toast pecans, spread in a single layer on a baking sheet. Bake in a 350° oven, shaking the pan occasionally, for about 10 minutes.

—Brennan's of Houston, Houston, Texas

TAMARIND SAUCE

MAKES ABOUT 1½ CUPS

3 egg yolks
¼ cup sugar
1 cup heavy cream
½ teaspoon vanilla extract
Pinch of freshly grated nutmeg
1 teaspoon tamarind concentrate, or 1 tablespoon dissolved tamarind paste (see Note)*
**Available in Oriental and Indian groceries*

1. In a double boiler, combine the egg yolks and sugar. Beat over simmering water until the mixture falls in ribbons when the whisk is lifted.

2. Meanwhile, in a saucepan, bring the cream to a boil. Over simmering water, whisk the hot cream into the thickened egg yolks and cook, stirring constantly, until the sauce is thick enough to coat the back of a spoon.

3. Stir in the vanilla, nutmeg and tamarind concentrate. Serve warm or chilled.

NOTE: To make tamarind paste, soak 1 tablespoon of tamarind pulp in 3 tablespoons of hot water, stirring occasionally, until dissolved, about 30 minutes. Strain through a fine-mesh sieve.

—Brennan's of Houston, Houston, Texas

LECHECILLA DE ALMENDRA (MILK AND ALMOND PUDDING)

The sweet, rich, earthy flavors of this creamy pudding are typical of the desserts served in Oaxaca, Mexico.

6 SERVINGS

¼ cup (packed) raisins
3 tablespoons dark rum or water
½ pound (about 1½ cups) whole blanched almonds, toasted (see Note)
2 cups milk
1 cup sugar
4 egg yolks
3 tablespoons all-purpose flour
2 cups heavy cream
1 tablespoon vanilla extract

1. In a small saucepan, bring the raisins and rum to a boil. Remove from the heat and let stand while you prepare the pudding.

2. Place the almonds, milk, sugar and egg yolks in a blender or food processor. Process until the nuts are finely ground, about 1 minute. With the machine on, gradually add the flour.

3. Pour the almond mixture into a heavy, medium saucepan. Stir in the heavy cream. Cook over moderately low heat, stirring constantly, until the mixture just comes to a boil. Immediately remove from the heat and stir in the vanilla.

4. Pour the pudding into a heatproof serving bowl. Drain the raisins and scatter them over the top. Let cool to room temperature, cover and refrigerate until chilled.

NOTE: To toast the almonds, place them in a small baking pan and roast in a 325° oven, shaking the pan occasionally, for 10 to 15 minutes, until the almonds are lightly browned.

—Jim Fobel

ALLSPICE BREAD PUDDING

These individual cups of cream-drenched pudding are lovely brunch desserts and perfect teatime treats.

8 SERVINGS

1½ cups milk
1 cup heavy cream
¾ cup packed light brown sugar
1½ tablespoons whole allspice berries, bruised
8 thin slices of firm-textured white bread, crusts removed
¾ cup (4 ounces) prunes, cut into ⅜-inch dice
3 whole eggs
2 egg yolks
¾ teaspoon vanilla extract
2 tablespoons granulated sugar

1. In a heavy medium noncorrodible saucepan, combine the milk,

cream, brown sugar and allspice berries. Bring to a boil. Remove from the heat, cover and let steep for 10 minutes; the mixture will look curdled.

2. Preheat the oven to 375°. Butter eight 6-ounce ramekins or custard cups. Cut the bread into ½-inch dice; distribute among the ramekins. Add the prunes and toss them with the bread to mix.

3. In a large bowl, whisk together the whole eggs, egg yolks and vanilla. Strain the allspice milk mixture, discarding the berries. Whisk the liquid into the eggs.

4. Place the ramekins in a large roasting pan. Ladle about ⅓ cup of the custard into each ramekin. Push the bread down into the custard. Add additional custard to fill the cups. Let stand for 10 minutes.

5. Sprinkle the granulated sugar on top of the puddings. Fill the roasting pan with enough cold water to reach almost halfway up the sides of the ramekins. Bake in the center of the oven for 20 to 25 minutes, or until a knife inserted near the center of a pudding comes out clean and the tops are puffed and golden. Remove the ramekins to a rack and let cool. Serve warm, at room temperature or chilled.

—Dorie Greenspan

BAKED INDIAN PUDDING

This spicy pudding is generally served warm, topped with vanilla ice cream.

8 TO 10 SERVINGS

4 cups milk
½ cup sugar
½ cup stone-ground white cornmeal
2 tablespoons unsalted butter
3 eggs, lightly beaten
1 teaspoon grated orange zest
1 teaspoon ground ginger
½ teaspoon cinnamon
1 teaspoon salt
1 cup unsulphured molasses

1. Preheat the oven to 300°. In a heavy medium saucepan, scald the milk with ¼ cup of the sugar over moderately high heat. When the milk begins to foam, remove from the heat and gradually sprinkle in the cornmeal, whisking constantly. Add the butter and stir until smooth and slightly thickened, about 3 minutes.

2. Whisk in the eggs, orange zest, the remaining ¼ cup sugar, the ginger, cinnamon, salt and molasses. Pour the batter into an 8-inch square baking dish. Set the baking dish on a cookie sheet and bake until a skewer inserted in the center comes out clean, about 1 hour. The pudding will be wobbly in the center, but will set as it cools.

—Dovecrest Indian Restaurant,
Exeter, Rhode Island

MOCHA CREAM-FILLED PROFITEROLES

The cream puffs for these profiteroles can be made ahead of time and kept refrigerated, or they can be made up to 3 months ahead and stored, tightly wrapped, in the freezer. Although the mocha filling can be made an hour or so ahead of time (and held in a cheesecloth-lined strainer in the refrigerator), the profiteroles should not be filled until just before serving, or they will become soggy.

4 SERVINGS

4 tablespoons unsalted butter, cut into small bits
¾ cup all-purpose flour
2 teaspoons sugar
Pinch of salt
3 eggs, at room temperature
1 cup heavy cream, chilled
1 tablespoon instant coffee powder
1 tablespoon dark rum
2 ounces semisweet chocolate, cut into small pieces
Strawberries, for garnish

1. Make the cream puffs: Preheat the oven to 400°. Place ¾ cup of water and the butter in a medium saucepan. Bring to a boil and cook until the butter melts, about 1 minute.

2. In a small bowl, combine the flour, sugar and salt. Remove the pan from the heat and add the flour mixture all at once. Stir until well blended. Return to moderate heat and cook, stirring, until the mixture pulls away from the sides of the pan, 1 to 2 minutes. Remove from the heat.

3. Break one egg into the hot dough and beat vigorously with a wooden spoon until the egg is completely incorporated and the paste is no longer slippery. Repeat with the other eggs, one at a time.

4. Spoon the mixture into a pastry bag fitted with a ½-inch plain tip and pipe 1-inch mounds 2 inches apart on a buttered and floured cookie sheet. The pastry can also be dropped from teaspoons.

5. Bake for 10 minutes. Reduce the oven temperature to 350° and bake for 20 minutes longer, or until the pastry puffs are golden and firm to the touch. Remove from the oven and turn off the heat. Pierce each puff with the tip of a small sharp knife and return to the oven. Leave the oven door ajar and let the puffs dry out in the warm oven for 10 minutes. Let cool on a wire rack. (**The cream puffs can be made up to 3 months ahead and frozen.** Reheat frozen puffs in a 325° oven until warmed through, about 10 minutes. Let them cool before filling.)

6. Meanwhile, make the mocha filling: Whip the cream until soft peaks form. Add the instant coffee and rum and beat until stiff.

7. In a small, heavy saucepan, melt the chocolate over very low heat, stirring until smooth. Remove from the heat.

8. Make a slit in the cream puffs about ⅓ from the top, making sure not to cut all the way through. Spoon the mocha cream into a pastry bag fitted with a ½-inch plain round tip. Pipe the cream into the puffs.

9. Place 4 filled puffs on each plate and stack a fifth puff on top. Drizzle each portion with a little melted chocolate. Serve garnished with whole strawberries if desired.

—W. Peter Prestcott

CHOCOLATE-PAINTED TULIP CUPS WITH RASPBERRIES AND WHIPPED CREAM

One of the most adaptable shapes, tulip cups—painted with chocolate or served plain—can be used as containers for sherbet or mousse.

MAKES ABOUT 20

1 recipe Basic Almond Cookie Batter (p. 204)
2 ounces semisweet chocolate
1 cup heavy cream, chilled
2 teaspoons sugar
½ teaspoon vanilla extract
1 cup raspberries
Chocolate shavings, for garnish

1. Preheat the oven to 425°. Butter a large heavy cookie sheet. Place in the oven for 1 minute, until the cookie sheet is warm and the butter is melted. Remove from the oven.

2. Using a tablespoon measure, drop 4 separate tablespoons of the batter at least 5 inches apart onto the warm cookie sheet. Using the back of a spoon, spread the batter into thin circles 4 inches in diameter, leaving at least 1 inch between circles to allow for spreading during baking.

3. Bake in the lower third of the oven for 6 to 8 minutes, until the cookies have a golden-brown border 1 inch wide. Meanwhile, cut 4 pieces of aluminum foil into 4-inch squares and set out 4 narrow glass jars (such as store-bought spice jars or other cylindrical containers 1½ to 2 inches in diameter) bottom-side up on the work surface.

4. Remove the cookies from the oven. Working quickly, slide the back of a wide metal spatula under a cookie, pushing to separate the cookie from the sheet without tearing; the cookie will be soft and pliable. Invert the cookie and drape it over the spice jar. Place a square of foil on top to protect your fingers and with your hands, gently mold the cookie around the jar into a tulip shape. Repeat with the remaining 3 cookies on the other spice jars. Leave in place until cooled and set, about 2 minutes; set aside. If the cookies cool before they are molded, return to the oven for 30 seconds to restore their pliability.

5. Scrape the cookie sheet clean, wipe with a paper towel and lightly butter it. It is not necessary to rewarm the sheet. Repeat Steps 2 to 5 to form the remaining batter into tulip cups. (**Although better fresh, the recipe can be made to this point a few days ahead.** Store tulip cups in an airtight tin or wrap them individually in plastic bags and store in the freezer. Let the tulip cups come to room temperature before using them.)

6. Melt the chocolate in a double boiler over hot—but not boiling—water. With a dry pastry brush, lightly paint the inside of each tulip cup with melted chocolate and let set.

7. In a medium bowl, beat the cream until soft peaks form. Add the sugar and vanilla and continue to beat until stiff peaks form.

8. Up to an hour before serving, spoon or decoratively pipe the whipped cream into the tulip cups. Dot with the raspberries and sprinkle chocolate shavings on top.

—Diana Sturgis

DOLCE OF RICOTTA AND PLUM

4 SERVINGS

1 pound whole-milk ricotta cheese
½ cup Fresh Plum Sauce (p. 225)
4 tablespoons honey
2 tablespoons grated orange zest

Divide the ricotta cheese evenly among 4 individual dessert bowls. Top each with 2 tablespoons Plum Sauce. Drizzle each with 1 tablespoon of honey and sprinkle with ½ tablespoon orange zest.

—W. Peter Prestcott

GOLDEN GLORY CHEESECAKE

BEVERAGE SUGGESTION
Full-bodied dessert wine, such as Tokay from Hungary

8 TO 10 SERVINGS

1 cup (6 ounces) dried apricots, preferably unsulphured from California
3 tablespoons superfine sugar
2 teaspoons plus 2 tablespoons fresh lemon juice
1¼ cups cookie crumbs made from lemon wafers or gingersnaps (about 17 cookies)
2 packages (8 ounces each) cream cheese, at room temperature
1 cup granulated sugar

1 tablespoon cornstarch
3 eggs, at room temperature
1½ teaspoons vanilla extract
¼ teaspoon salt
3 cups sour cream
½ cup apricot preserves
1 tablespoon Barack Palinka (apricot eau-de-vie) or apricot brandy

1. Place the apricots in a small saucepan with ¾ cup of water. Let stand at room temperature for at least 2 hours or overnight to soften. Cover and bring to a boil. Reduce the heat to low and simmer until the apricots are completely soft, 10 to 20 minutes. Puree the apricots with any liquid left in the pan in a food processor or blender; press through a sieve. Add the superfine sugar and 2 teaspoons of the lemon juice. Stir to dissolve the sugar. Set the apricot puree aside.
2. Preheat the oven to 350°. Butter an 8-by-3-inch round cake pan or an 8-inch springform pan at least 2½ inches deep (an 8-by-2-inch pan will not be deep enough) wrapped in a double layer of aluminum foil to prevent water seepage. Line the bottom of the pan with an 8-inch circle of waxed paper or parchment; butter the paper.
3. Sprinkle ¾ cup of the cookie crumbs over the bottom of the pan, distributing them evenly. Pat gently into place. Reserve the remaining cookie crumbs.
4. Beat the cream cheese until smooth. Gradually add the granulated sugar and beat until light and fluffy, 7 to 10 minutes. Beat in the cornstarch. Add the eggs, one at a time, beating until smooth after each addition. Add the remaining 2 tablespoons lemon juice, the vanilla and salt. Beat only until well blended; do not overbeat. Gently stir in the sour cream until just blended.
5. Pour one-third of the cheese filling into the prepared pan. Dot half of the apricot puree over the cheese mixture in rounded teaspoonfuls. Add another one-third of the cheese filling and dot with the remaining apricot puree. Top with the remaining filling. Using a small spatula and carefully avoiding the crumb crust, swirl the apricot puree through the filling as if to marble a cake.
6. Set the pan into a larger pan and surround it with about 1 inch of boiling water. Bake for 45 minutes. Turn off the oven, but *do not* open the door; let the cheesecake cool in the oven for 1 hour. Remove to a rack and let cool to room temperature, about 3 hours. Cover with plastic wrap and refrigerate overnight.
7. To unmold the cake, run a thin metal spatula around the sides of the pan. Warm the base of the pan over low heat for 10 seconds. Place a flat plate lined with plastic wrap on top of the pan and invert to unmold. Peel off the waxed paper and invert the cake onto a serving platter.
8. Pat the reserved ½ cup cookie crumbs onto the sides of the cake.
9. In a small saucepan, warm the apricot preserves over moderately low heat until melted. Press through a sieve into a small bowl and stir in the Barack Palinka. Spoon this glaze over the top of the cake, spreading it from the center to the sides. Serve the cheesecake chilled.

—Rose Levy Beranbaum

AVOCADO-PISTACHIO ICE CREAM

Florida avocados are perfect for this frozen dessert.

4 SERVINGS

2 large avocados, peeled and pitted
1 cup heavy cream
1 cup milk
½ cup sugar
⅛ teaspoon salt
¼ cup shelled natural-colored unsalted pistachio nuts, coarsely chopped
3 tablespoons dark rum

1. In a blender or food processor, combine the avocados, cream, milk, sugar and salt. Puree until smooth, about 3 minutes.
2. Pour into an ice cream maker and freeze according to the manufacturer's instructions.
3. Scrape the ice cream into a bowl. Fold in the pistachios and rum. Cover and freeze until firm, about 3 hours.

—Molly O'Neill

QUILTED GIRAFFE'S COFFEE ICE CREAM

MAKES ABOUT 1 QUART

2 cups heavy cream
1 cup milk
½ cup ground coffee (not instant)
6 egg yolks
⅔ cup of sugar
¼ teaspoon salt

1. In a large heavy saucepan, combine the cream and milk. Bring to a simmer over moderately high heat. Remove from the heat and stir in the coffee. Let stand for 20 minutes, stirring occasionally.
2. Meanwhile, beat the egg yolks with the sugar until light in color and thick enough to fall in ribbons from the whisk.
3. Strain the coffee grounds from the cream through a fine sieve lined with several layers of dampened cheesecloth. Return the cream to the saucepan. Gently heat the cream but do not boil.
4. Gradually whisk 1 cup of the hot cream into the egg yolks. Whisk the

mixture back into the saucepan. Cook over moderate heat, stirring constantly, until the custard thickens enough to coat the back of a spoon. Do not let boil or the custard will curdle.

5. Strain the custard into a metal bowl. Cool quickly by setting in a larger bowl of ice and water and stirring. Add the salt and pour into the canister of an ice cream machine and process according to the manufacturer's instructions.

—Barry Wine, The Quilted Giraffe, New York City

CREMET D'ANJOU WITH RASPBERRY COULIS

If *fromage blanc* is not available, use whole-milk ricotta.

4 SERVINGS

¾ cup fromage blanc
¾ cup crème fraîche
2 egg whites
3 tablespoons sugar
3 cups (1½ pints) raspberries
4 sprigs of mint, for garnish

1. In a food processor, process the *fromage blanc* until smooth, about 1 minute, stopping once to scrape down the sides of the bowl. Set aside.

2. In a large bowl, beat the crème fraîche until thick and fluffy. Set aside.

3. In another large bowl, beat the egg whites until soft peaks form. Sprinkle in 2 tablespoons of the sugar and continue beating until stiff peaks form.

4. Gently fold the crème fraîche into the *fromage blanc*. Then fold in the egg whites, combining thoroughly.

5. Line 4 coeur à la crème molds with a double layer of dampened cheesecloth. Divide the cheese mixture evenly among the molds. Tap the molds gently on the work surface to settle the cheese. Wrap the cheesecloth over the tops. Place the molds in a shallow pan and allow to drain in the refrigerator for at least 12 hours.

6. In a food processor, puree 1 pint of the raspberries with the remaining 1 tablespoon sugar. Pass through a fine mesh sieve. Taste and add more sugar if necessary.

7. Gently unmold the Cremets d'Anjou on individual dessert plates. Surround each with the raspberry *coulis* and garnish with the remaining whole raspberries and the mint sprigs.

—Chef Hubert, Le Bistro d'Hubert, Paris, France

FRENCH VANILLA ICE CREAM

This ice cream is exceedingly rich, and a little goes a long way. A quart should be enough to serve 8 to 12 people, especially if it is presented à la mode on top of a berry pie.

MAKES ABOUT 1 QUART

2 cups heavy cream
1¼ cups milk
2 vanilla beans, split
10 egg yolks
½ cup plus 2½ tablespoons sugar

1. In a large saucepan, combine 1¼ cups of the cream, the milk and the vanilla beans. Bring just to a boil over high heat. Reduce the heat to low.

2. In a large bowl, whisk the egg yolks until light in color. Gradually whisk in the sugar until well blended.

3. Gradually whisk the hot cream mixture into the eggs. Return the custard to the saucepan and cook over moderate heat, stirring constantly, until the mixture thickens enough to coat the back of a spoon, about 3 minutes. (Do not overcook, or the eggs may curdle.) Pour the custard into a bowl, cover and let it cool to room temperature.

4. Remove the vanilla beans and scrape the seeds inside into the custard. Stir in the remaining ¾ cup cream; strain through a sieve. Pour the custard into an ice cream maker and freeze according to the manufacturers' instructions.

—Stephanie Sidell & Bob Sasse

PINEAPPLE PECAN ICE CREAM

MAKES ABOUT 2 QUARTS

½ cup coarsely chopped pecans
2 cups heavy cream
1 cup milk
1¼ cups poaching liquid from the poached pineapple (see below), chilled
2 cups Pineapple Poached in Maple Syrup (p. 226), prepared through Step 2

1. Preheat the oven to 325°. Scatter the pecans in a small baking pan and bake for 10 to 15 minutes, shaking the pan once or twice, until the nuts are toasted. Transfer to a plate and let cool.

2. In a large bowl, combine the cream, milk and maple syrup poaching liquid. Blend well. Cover and refrigerate until chilled.

3. Working in two batches if necessary, pour the maple cream into the canister of an ice cream maker and freeze according to the manufacturer's instructions until the mixture is almost firm. Add the pineapple and toasted pecans and process briefly in the ice cream maker to blend thoroughly. Transfer the ice cream to a container with a tight-fitting lid and place in the freezer for about 3 hours, or until firm.

—Jim Dodge & Gayle Henderson Wilson

MAPLE ICE CREAM

Although maple as an all-purpose seasoning is not used with the frequency it was two or three hundred years ago, a hardy cottage industry still exists. Seek out a good-quality maple syrup for this recipe, since the cooking process used will intensify the flavor.

MAKES ABOUT 1½ QUARTS
2 cups genuine maple syrup
2 cups milk
2 cups heavy cream
4 egg yolks

1. In a medium saucepan, bring the maple syrup to a boil over moderate heat. Reduce the heat to very low and simmer until reduced by half, about 45 minutes. (Counteract the tendency of the syrup to boil over by stirring often with a metal spoon.) At the end of the reduction process you will have what appears to be a combination of maple syrup and maple sugar.
2. Let the reduced syrup cool slightly; then slowly whisk in the milk and cream. Return to moderate heat and bring to a boil, stirring to dissolve the solids.
3. In a medium bowl, whisk the egg yolks thoroughly. Slowly whisk the hot maple syrup mixture into the egg yolks in a thin stream. Return this mixture to the pan and stir constantly over low heat until the mixture is steaming and has thickened enough to coat the back of a spoon heavily, 3 to 5 minutes. Do not let the mixture come close to a boil or it will curdle.
4. Remove from the heat, let cool to room temperature and refrigerate, covered, until very cold, at least 4 hours or preferably overnight.
5. Churn the chilled maple mixture in an ice cream maker, according to the manufacturer's instructions. Transfer to a storage container, cover and freeze. (**This ice cream can be prepared several days in advance of serving.** Allow it to soften in the refrigerator for 10 minutes or so, if necessary, before serving.)

—Michael McLaughlin

CARDAMOM ICE CREAM

Although the flavor sounds exotic, this cardamom-scented ice cream will appeal to less adventurous palates as well.

MAKES ABOUT 1 QUART
3 cups milk
1 cup heavy cream
16 cardamom pods
6 egg yolks
1 cup sugar
¾ teaspoon vanilla extract

1. In a large heavy saucepan, combine the milk, cream and cardamom pods. Bring to a boil over high heat. Remove from the heat, cover and steep for 10 minutes.
2. Meanwhile, in a medium bowl, combine the egg yolks and sugar. Beat together until the mixture is pale and falls in thick ribbons when the beater is lifted.
3. Gradually beat the hot milk (with the cardamom) into the egg-sugar mixture. Return the custard to the saucepan and cook over moderate heat, stirring constantly, until thick enough to coat the back of a spoon; do not let boil. Remove from the heat. Stir in the vanilla extract.
4. Strain the custard into a bowl; discard the cardamom pods. Place over a larger bowl of ice and water and stir until cool. (**The mixture can be made ahead to this point.** Cover and refrigerate for up to 3 days.) Freeze in an ice cream maker according to the manufacturer's instructions.

—Dorie Greenspan

CAFE RENNI'S HONEYDEW GRANITE

Serve this refreshing ice as a palate cleanser.

4 SERVINGS
1 medium honeydew melon
2 tablespoons light corn syrup
1 teaspoon fresh lemon juice
Fresh mint sprigs, for garnish

1. Halve and seed the melon. Working over a sieve to catch the juice, scoop out the flesh. Reserve the juice.
2. Puree the flesh in a food processor or blender. Strain through a fine-mesh sieve, pressing lightly so that no pulp is forced through. Combine with the reserved melon juice.
3. Stir the corn syrup and lemon juice into the melon juice. Place in an ice cream machine and freeze according to the manufacturer's instructions.
4. Serve in chilled glasses, garnished with a sprig of mint.

—Mark Carrozza, Café Renni, Frenchtown, New Jersey

GRANITA DI ESPRESSO

MAKES ABOUT 1½ QUARTS
1½ cups finely ground espresso
4½ cups boiling water
¾ cup plus 2 teaspoons superfine sugar
¼ cup coffee liqueur, such as Tia Maria or Kahlúa
¾ cup heavy cream
1 tablespoon Cognac or brandy
Strips of lemon zest, for garnish

1. Brew the coffee using 1½ cups of the espresso and all the boiling water.
2. Combine the hot coffee with ¾ cup of the sugar and the coffee liqueur. Stir until the sugar is dissolved. Let cool.
3. Pour into a shallow noncorrodible pan and freeze for about 5 hours, stirring every hour to break up any large ice crystals that have formed. Pack into a decorative 6-cup mold and freeze again.
4. Before serving, whip the cream until it forms soft peaks. Add the remaining 2 teaspoons sugar and the Cognac; whip for 30 seconds more. Unmold the granita onto a large platter. Mound or pipe the whipped cream around it and garnish with strips of lemon zest.

—W. Peter Prestcott

APPLE SORBET "A LA MODE"

This low-calorie (116 per serving) sorbet is delicious with real sugar as well.

6 SERVINGS

*1 quart unfiltered natural apple juice**
2 tablespoons fresh lemon juice
2 teaspoons cinnamon
Pinch of ground cloves
⅓ cup evaporated skim milk
5 drops maple extract
3 packages low-calorie, artificial sweetener, preferably Equal
¼ cup granola or chopped toasted almonds

**Available at health food stores*

1. Put the apple juice, lemon juice, cinnamon and cloves in a blender or food processor. Mix for 15 seconds, until well blended.
2. Pour into an ice cream maker and freeze according to the manufacturer's instructions. Place in the freezer for up to 30 minutes while you make the topping. (The sorbet will crystallize if you hold it much longer.)
3. Pour the milk into a glass measuring cup and freeze until almost solid, about 15 minutes. Add the maple extract and sweetener. With an electric hand mixer, beat on high speed until thick, about 15 minutes.
4. To serve, scoop the sorbet into chilled dessert dishes. Spoon on a dollop of the whipped topping and sprinkle with granola.

—Christian Chavanne,
Sonoma Mission Inn and Spa,
Boyes Hot Springs, California

CANTALOUPE SORBET WITH PEPPER AND PORT

In Italy this type of dish is called an *intermezzo.* We call it a palate-refresher and serve it between courses, but it works just as well as a light dessert.

MAKES ABOUT 3½ CUPS

2 small cantaloupes
¼ cup sugar
1 tablespoon fresh lemon juice
½ teaspoon freshly ground pepper
Pinch of salt
Ruby port, chilled

1. Working on a large platter to catch the juices, split and seed the cantaloupes, cut into chunks and remove the rind. Strain the reserved juices to remove the seeds.
2. Combine the cantaloupe juice with enough water to equal ¼ cup. Pour into a small heavy saucepan and add the sugar. Bring slowly to a boil, stirring to dissolve the sugar. Boil for 1 minute, remove from the heat and let cool.
3. Place the sugar syrup, melon, lemon juice, pepper and salt in a food processor. Puree until smooth. Strain through a sieve; to avoid any graininess, do not press on the solids.
4. Pour the puree into an ice cream maker and freeze according to the manufacturer's instructions. To serve, scoop into individual glasses and pour about 1 tablespoon of port on top of the sorbet.

—Enoteca Pinchiorri, Florence, Italy

GREEN GRAPE SORBET

8 SERVINGS

6 cups seedless green grapes (2 pounds)
1 cup brandy
3 tablespoons honey
3 tablespoons golden raisins, coarsely chopped

1. In a blender or food processor, puree the grapes until very liquid and as smooth as possible, about 2 minutes. Strain into a medium bowl, pressing on the skins with the back of a spoon to extract as much juice as possible.
2. In a small heavy saucepan, combine the brandy and honey. Bring to a simmer over low heat, stirring occasionally, and cook for 2 minutes, being careful not to ignite the brandy. Remove from the heat and let cool to room temperature.
3. Combine the honey mixture with the grape juice. Stir in the chopped raisins. Scrape the mixture into an ice cream maker and freeze according to the manufacturer's instructions. Place in the freezer for 1 to 2 hours for extra firmness if desired.

—W. Peter Prestcott

SPUN SUGAR NESTS

These crunchy, sparkling little jewels make a perfect nest for three small ovals of different-colored sherbet or ice cream for an unforgettable presentation. Spun sugar is easy to make, but a bit of a production. To produce in sufficient quantity for six nests, you'll need a special tool: either a wire whisk whose loops have been snipped or an inexpensive forked cake breaker (see Sources, below) with each tine bent slightly in opposite directions.

MAKES 6 SMALL NESTS

¾ cup sugar
½ cup light corn syrup

1. Cover a large section of floor near your counter with newspaper. Grease two yardsticks or the handles of two long wooden spoons. Weigh them down or tape them to the counter top 1 foot apart with the handles extending well beyond the edge to catch the spun sugar. Spray 6 small (6-ounce) heatproof custard cups lightly with nonstick vegetable spray.

2. In a heavy medium saucepan, stir together the sugar and corn syrup. Bring to a boil over moderate heat, stirring constantly. When the syrup boils, increase the heat to moderately high and boil without stirring until the liquid turns deep amber, 350° on a candy thermometer. Immediately remove from the heat and dip the bottom of the pan in cold water for several moments to stop the cooking. If the temperature exceeds 360°, the spun sugar will look brassy not golden.

3. Let the syrup cool for a few minutes, until a small amount lifted with a fork forms threads instead of falling back into the pot in separate droplets.

4. To spin the sugar, dip the cut whisk or bent cake breaker into the syrup and wave back and forth above the wooden handles, letting the sugar fall in long, thin threads. If the liquid thickens too much, reheat briefly. Continue until most of the syrup has been used.

5. With dry hands, gather up the strands of spun sugar and place on the counter. Working quickly, divide the spun sugar into 6 bunches and press each bunch into one of the prepared custard cups, holding until the strands mold to the inside of the cup.

6. Unmold the spun sugar nests and serve. (If made ahead, return the nests to their molds and store airtight at room temperature for several weeks.)

SOURCES: Available by mail order from H. Roth & Son, 1577 First Ave., New York, NY 10028.

—*Rose Levy Beranbaum*

BELLE EPOQUE CHERRIES JUBILEE

For flambéeing, it is best not to use little book matches. Wooden matches or, best of all, fireplace matches are recommended. Also remember to stand well back when igniting any spirits.

4 SERVINGS

1 can (1 pound) pitted Bing cherries
½ cup sugar
2 tablespoons grated orange zest
1 tablespoon arrowroot
⅓ cup kirsch
1 pint vanilla ice cream, frozen hard
Chocolate curls, for garnish
Strips of orange zest, for garnish

1. Drain the cherries, reserving the juice. Measure the juice and add enough water to equal 1½ cups; pour into a small saucepan. Add the sugar and orange zest and simmer uncovered over low heat for 10 minutes.

2. Add 2 tablespoons of water to the arrowroot, stirring to dissolve. Gradually stir the arrowroot mixture into the cherry liquid in the pan. Simmer, stirring frequently, until thick, about 10 minutes. Add the cherries.

3. In a small saucepan, warm the kirsch over moderate heat, about 1 minute. Meanwhile, scoop the ice cream into a serving bowl or individual dessert dishes. At table, pour the warm kirsch into the cherry sauce and ignite. Carefully pour the flaming sauce over the ice cream at once and garnish with the chocolate curls and strips of orange zest if desired.

—*W. Peter Prestcott*

FRESH PLUM FOOL

6 SERVINGS

3 cups Fresh Plum Sauce (p. 225)
1 cup sour cream
2 tablespoons blackberry brandy
1½ cups heavy cream, chilled
½ cup granulated sugar
½ cup brown sugar

1. In a medium bowl, stir together the plum sauce, sour cream and blackberry brandy. Set aside.

2. Whip the cream until soft peaks form. Beat in the granulated sugar. Fold in the plum mixture until partly blended, leaving streaks of color.

3. Turn the fool into a decorative bowl. Sprinkle the brown sugar on top. Chill for several hours before serving.

—*W. Peter Prestcott*

Apples Baked on Cabbage Leaves (p. 227).

Left, Belle Epoque Cherries Jubilee (p. 220). Above, Spun Sugar Nests (p. 220) and Golden Glory Cheesecake (p. 215).

FRESH PLUM SAUCE

MAKES ABOUT 3 CUPS

2 pounds sweet, ripe red plums, quartered and pitted
1 cup large pitted prunes (about 6 ounces), coarsely chopped
½ cup sugar
1 cup ruby port
2 tablespoons fresh lime juice
2 teaspoons Angostura bitters

1. In a medium noncorrodible saucepan, combine the plums, prunes, sugar, port, lime juice and bitters. Cook over very low heat, stirring occasionally, until the sauce is thick, about 1 hour.

2. Remove from the heat, pour into a bowl and let cool. Store, tightly covered, in the refrigerator. **(This recipe can be made at least 3 days ahead.)**

—W. Peter Prestcott

SOUFFLE OMELET WITH FRESH PLUM SAUCE

4 SERVINGS

3 eggs, separated
1 teaspoon almond extract
1½ tablespoons all-purpose flour
1 egg white
Pinch of salt
⅛ teaspoon cream of tartar
2 tablespoons granulated sugar
1 tablespoon minced toasted almonds,
1 tablespoon confectioners' sugar
1 cup Fresh Plum Sauce (above), heated

1. Preheat the oven to 400°. In a medium bowl, whisk together the egg yolks and almond extract. Gradually whisk in the flour.

2. Beat the egg whites, salt and cream of tartar until soft peaks form. Sprinkle on the granulated sugar and beat until stiff but not dry.

3. Fold about ½ cup of the beaten egg whites into the egg yolk mixture to lighten it. Fold in the remaining egg whites just until blended.

4. Generously butter a shallow oval baking or gratin dish. Spoon the soufflé mixture into three mounds in the dish. Bake for 10 minutes, or until golden.

5. Sprinkle with the toasted almonds and confectioners' sugar. Serve the warm Plum Sauce on the side.

—W. Peter Prestcott

Zabaglione (p. 211) over fresh berries.

PEACH, STRAWBERRY AND ORANGE GRATIN

6 SERVINGS

½ recipe (about 2½ cups) Zabaglione or Sabayon (p. 210)
2 cups fresh peach slices or 1 package (16 ounces) frozen peach slices, thawed
1 pint (2 cups) strawberries, halved if large
2 navel oranges, peeled and sectioned

1. Preheat the broiler. Prepare the zabaglione and cool it quickly by setting the pan in a bowl of ice and water and stirring gently until the mixture is cool.

2. Combine the peaches, strawberries and orange sections and arrange in a layer in a large shallow ovenproof gratin dish or in 6 individual dishes. Top with the zabaglione, allowing some fruit to show at the edges.

3. Broil at once, about 4 inches from the heat, for 15 to 20 seconds, or until the zabaglione is glazed and lightly browned. Serve at once.

—Diana Sturgis

SUMMER BERRY CHARLOTTE

Different varieties of berries may be substituted for each other. Some, however, are naturally tarter or sweeter than others; add sugar with a cautious hand, as the amount may vary by as much as a quarter of a cup. Do not substitute strawberries, since they do not have the same texture.

F&W BEVERAGE SUGGESTION
California Moscato, such as Robert Pecota

12 SERVINGS

1 loaf (1 pound) thinly sliced, slightly stale firm-textured white bread, crusts removed
½ pound fresh blueberries
1¼ cups plus 1 tablespoon sugar
1¼ pounds (2 pints) fresh or individually quick-frozen raspberries
¾ pound fresh red currants
1 to 3 teaspoons fresh lemon juice
2 cups heavy cream, chilled
Fresh berries, for garnish

1. Cut out 2 paper circles, one the size of the bottom and one the size of the top of the mold. Fold each circle in half and then into thirds to produce 6 equal triangles. Cut 6 triangles of bread to fit the bottom template; repeat so that you have 12 triangles the same size. Cut out 6 larger triangles of bread to fit the top template. Cut out 6 squares of bread, 3½ inches on each side.

2. Line a 7-cup charlotte mold (about 6½ by 3½ inches) with a sheet of plastic wrap large enough to hang over the edges of the mold by a few inches. Smooth out any wrinkles in the plastic.

3. Line the bottom of the mold with 6 of the smaller bread triangles. Fit the bread squares against the sides of the mold, trimming the bottoms with a scissors for an even fit or, alternatively, overlapping the sides slightly.

4. Place the blueberries in a heavy medium noncorrodible saucepan and sprinkle with ¼ cup of the sugar. Place the raspberries on top and sprinkle with ½ cup of sugar. Top with the currants and sprinkle with ½ cup of sugar.

5. Cover and cook over moderately low heat until the juices are drawn out and the fruit is soft but not mushy, 5 to 10 minutes, depending on the ripeness of the fruit.

6. Using a slotted spoon, transfer enough fruit to the mold to fill it halfway; reserve the juices in the pan. Fit the 6 remaining smaller bread triangles on top of the fruit. Fill the mold with the remaining fruit and cover with the 6 large triangles of bread, trimming if necessary; do not let the bread overlap the square pieces at the sides of the mold.

7. Stir the fruit juices in the saucepan to dissolve all the sugar. Strain to remove any seeds if necessary. Add lemon juice to the desired degree of tartness. Spoon the juices over the mold to saturate it evenly.

8. Place the mold on a large plate to catch any overflowing juice. Place a plate just large enough to fit inside the mold on top and weigh down with 4 to 5 pounds. Refrigerate the charlotte overnight.

9. Just before serving, beat the cream and remaining 1 tablespoon sugar until the cream stands in stiff peaks.

10. To serve, pour off and reserve any juices that have collected from the mold. Remove the weights and the plate. Invert to unmold onto a large serving platter. Peel off and discard the plastic wrap. Cut the charlotte into wedges with a sharp knife. Spoon the reserved juice around the charlotte and garnish with fresh berries. Serve with the whipped cream on the side.

—Diana Sturgis

PINEAPPLE POACHED IN MAPLE SYRUP

4 TO 6 SERVINGS

1 ripe pineapple
2 cups pure maple syrup
1 cup plain yogurt, at room temperature
3 tablespoons heavy cream

1. Cut off the top and bottom of the pineapple. Stand the pineapple upright and slice off about a ¼-inch layer all around to remove the skin and "eyes." Cut the pineapple into lengthwise quarters. Cut out the tough woody core of each quarter and discard. Cut each quarter crosswise into ½-inch slices; then cut each slice into 2 wedges.

2. In a heavy medium saucepan, bring the maple syrup to a boil over high heat, being careful to keep the syrup from boiling over. Immediately turn off the heat and add the pineapple chunks. With a large spoon, push the chunks down into the hot liquid. Let the fruit steep off heat, pressing down occasionally, until it is tender when pierced with a fork and the syrup is slightly warm to the touch, about 25 minutes. Drain the pineapple through a sieve, reserving the maple syrup. (**The recipe can be prepared ahead to this point.** Refrigerate the poached pineapple and maple syrup separately.)

3. If there is liquid on top of the yogurt, pour it off. Put the yogurt in a small bowl and whisk in the cream 1 tablespoon at a time, until the mixture is the consistency of crème fraîche or slightly beaten whipped cream.

4. To serve, place the pineapple in shallow dessert bowls. Add 2 tablespoons of the maple syrup and top each with about 2 tablespoons of the yogurt-cream sauce.

—Jim Dodge & Gayle Henderson Wilson

MINTED GINGER CANTALOUPE

4 SERVINGS

1 medium cantaloupe, cut into 1-inch dice
4 teaspoons ginger juice
1 tablespoon fresh lemon juice
1 teaspoon sugar
1 tablespoon minced fresh mint
Sprigs of mint, for garnish

1. Place the melon in a bowl and sprinkle with the ginger juice, lemon juice, sugar and mint; toss gently. Cover and refrigerate for 30 minutes.

2. With a slotted spoon, transfer the melon to individual serving bowls. Garnish with mint. Serve chilled.

—Diana Sturgis

CONCORD PEARS

Serve these luscious pears plain with their syrup or in a decorative "flower" presentation: cut each pear into eight sections and arrange in a petal formation on a large plate. Decorate with lightly sweetened whipped cream and strips of lemon zest.

6 SERVINGS

1 pound Concord grapes, washed and stemmed (about 3 cups)
2 cups dry white wine
¾ cup sugar
3 strips of lemon zest, each about 3 inches long
6 medium slightly underripe pears, such as Bartlett or Bosc
½ teaspoon vanilla extract

1. In a large noncorrodible saucepan, combine the grapes, wine, sugar and lemon zest.

2. Bring to a boil over moderately low heat, stirring occasionally to dissolve the sugar. Cover, reduce the

heat to very low and simmer for 10 minutes. Crush the grapes with a potato masher or a slotted spoon. Simmer for 10 minutes longer.

3. Strain the mixture through a sieve into a large bowl, pressing on the solids with a wooden spoon to extract as much juice as possible; discard the solids. Pour the syrup into a clean noncorrodible saucepan.

4. Peel and core the pears and place in the saucepan with the grape syrup. Add the vanilla. Cover and simmer over low heat, turning the pears occasionally, for 20 to 30 minutes, until the pears are tender when pierced with a fork. Let cool in the syrup. Serve warm, at room temperature or chilled. (**The whole pears may be refrigerated, covered in syrup, for up to 3 days before serving.** They will take on a deeper, more dramatic color.)

—Diana Sturgis

APPLES BAKED ON CABBAGE LEAVES

You probably never thought of eating cabbage leaves for dessert. Neither did I. But when I first read about this dish, called *grimolles*, in a book about the food of the Poitou, I remembered a line from Samuel Foote: "So she went into the garden to cut a cabbage-leaf, to make an apple pie . . ."

In this recipe the cabbage leaves are used in place of a pie crust. A skillet is lined with them and then apples—mixed with a thick crêpe batter flavored with Cognac and orange flower water—are baked on top. The result is earthy and sophisticated. The slightly burnt cabbage, which can be eaten or not, imparts a marvelous smoky flavor to the fruit. This, I guarantee you, will be a memorable dessert.

F&W BEVERAGE SUGGESTION
Alsace Gewürztraminer, such as Hugel

6 SERVINGS

3 tablespoons granulated sugar
2 eggs
1 tablespoon unsalted butter, melted, plus 2 tablespoons cold butter
1/8 teaspoon salt
1 cup all-purpose flour
1/2 cup milk
1/4 cup heavy cream
2 tablespoons Cognac
1 1/2 tablespoons orange flower water (optional)
1 pound tart apples, such as Granny Smith
About 6 large outer green cabbage leaves
2 to 3 tablespoons light brown sugar

1. About 2 1/2 hours before serving (so the batter has time to sit), combine the granulated sugar, eggs, melted butter and salt in a medium bowl. Sift the flour over the mixture and stir to combine. Gradually stir in the milk, cream, Cognac and orange flower water. If the batter is not smooth, strain; it will be thick.

2. Peel and quarter the apples. Cut into 1/8-inch slices and fold into the batter. Cover and let stand at room temperature.

3. One hour before serving, preheat the oven to 475°.

4. Spread the cabbage leaves out in a 12- to 14-inch cast-iron skillet or black pizza pan or round griddle. Set over moderate heat. When the leaves begin to wilt and soften, flatten them out to cover the pan without overlapping more than is necessary.

5. Spread the apple batter over the cabbage in a thin, even layer. Sprinkle the brown sugar on top and bake in the top third of the oven until set and golden, about 25 minutes. (The center should still be slightly supple.) Remove the skillet from the oven; increase the heat to broil.

6. Let the dessert rest for 10 minutes. Dot with the remaining 2 tablespoons butter. Broil for 1 to 2 minutes, until glazed. Serve this apple dessert in the pan while still warm.

—Paula Wolfert

BAKED STUFFED APPLES

6 SERVINGS

6 large baking apples, such as Rome Beauties or Golden Delicious
2 tablespoons fresh lemon juice
1/2 cup ground blanched almonds
1/4 cup sugar
1/4 cup raisins
1/2 teaspoon cinnamon
1 cup apple juice

1. Preheat the oven to 350°. Core the apples to within 1/2 inch of the bottom. Peel off a 1-inch strip of the skin around the top of the apples. Brush the inside and peeled sections of the apples with the lemon juice to prevent discoloration. Arrange the apples in a baking dish.

2. In a small bowl, combine the almonds, sugar, raisins and cinnamon. Spoon into the cored apples. Pour the apple juice and 1/4 cup of water into the baking dish around the apples.

3. Bake in the center of the oven, basting occasionally with the pan juices, until tender when tested with a knife, 45 to 60 minutes. Remove the apples from the pan and transfer to serving plates. Pour the pan juices into a small saucepan and boil over moderate heat until reduced by half. Pour over the apples. Serve warm or at room temperature.

—Diana Sturgis

CARAMEL APPLES WITH RUM AND ICE CREAM

This is best served immediately as the apples become watery upon standing.

6 SERVINGS

12 tablespoons (1½ sticks) unsalted butter
⅔ cup sugar
1 teaspoon fresh lemon juice
1½ tablespoons dark rum
6 small or 4 large apples—peeled, cored and cut into thin slices
1½ pints coffee ice cream

1. In a large skillet, combine the butter, sugar, lemon juice and ¼ cup of water. Stir together over moderate heat until the sugar dissolves. Simmer until thickened and caramel colored, about 10 minutes. Stir in the rum.
2. Add the apples. Toss to coat with the sauce. Cook, turning, until slightly softened, about 2 minutes.
3. Scoop the ice cream into 6 dessert dishes. Top with the apples and sauce.

—*Jimmy's Place, Chicago, Illinois*

NUTTED PERSIMMON HALVES

1 SERVING

1 ripe persimmon
2 to 3 teaspoons hazelnut or almond liqueur to taste
1 tablespoon whole unblanched almonds, toasted and chopped
Tiny bunch of grapes or sliced fresh fig, for garnish

1. Cut out the leaf base of the persimmon and halve the fruit lengthwise. Set skin-side down on a serving dish and, with a sharp paring knife, deeply score a diamond pattern into the flesh, reaching almost to the skin.
2. Drizzle the liqueur slowly over each persimmon half, squeezing the fruit gently to let the liqueur run into the cracks. Sprinkle with the toasted almonds. Garnish with grapes or figs and serve.

—*Elizabeth Schneider*

TROPICAL FRUIT COMPOTE

This compote must macerate overnight, so plan accordingly.

6 TO 8 SERVINGS

1 bottle sweet white wine, such as Sauternes or Muscat
1 cup sugar
1 vanilla bean
6 strips of orange zest, about 2 inches long
4 ripe kiwi fruits, peeled and cut crosswise into ¼-inch slices
2 ripe papayas—peeled, seeded and cut into thin wedges
2 ripe pears—peeled, cored and cut crosswise into ⅛-inch slices
24 strawberries, halved lengthwise
1 orange, peeled and cut into sections
1 cup lightly packed fresh mint leaves, for garnish

1. In a large heavy skillet, combine the wine, sugar and vanilla bean. Bring to a boil over moderately high heat and cook, stirring occasionally, until reduced by one-fourth, about 10 minutes.
2. Meanwhile, arrange the fruit decoratively in a shallow heatproof dish.
3. Carefully strain the hot syrup over the fruit. Let stand until cool, then cover with plastic wrap and refrigerate overnight.
4. Garnish with mint leaves before serving.

—*W. Peter Prestcott*

PRUNE TRUFFLES WITH ARMAGNAC

MAKES 30 TRUFFLES

¾ cup (4 ounces) pitted prunes, cut into eighths
¼ cup Armagnac
⅓ cup heavy cream
6 ounces bittersweet chocolate, such as Lindt or Tobler, broken into small pieces
1 tablespoon unsalted butter, at room temperature
½ cup (2 ounces) toasted pecans, finely chopped
Unsweetened cocoa powder, for coating

1. In a small bowl, combine the prunes and the Armagnac. Cover tightly and let macerate at room temperature for at least 1 hour.
2. In a small saucepan, bring the cream to a boil over moderately high heat. Add the chocolate and remove from the heat. Whisk until the chocolate is melted and the mixture smooth. Beat in the butter.
3. Drain the prunes, reserving 1 tablespoon of the Armagnac. Add the prunes, the reserved Armagnac and the pecans to the chocolate mixture, mixing until well combined. Transfer the mixture to a shallow bowl and refrigerate, uncovered, until firm, at least 3 hours.
4. Coat your palms with the cocoa. For each truffle, form about a teaspoonful of the cold truffle mixture into a ball, rolling it between your palms. Place the truffles on sheets of waxed paper.
5. When the truffles are shaped, dredge them lightly in the cocoa, then toss gently from palm to palm to remove any excess. Place each truffle in a paper petit four cup and refrigerate for at least 1 day to let the flavors mellow.

—*Dorie Greenspan*

SAUCES & CONDIMENTS

BROWN STOCK

Deep, amber, flavorful brown stock forms the basis for many sauces.

MAKES 4 TO 5 QUARTS

6 pounds beef shin with bones
6 pounds veal bones
6 carrots, cut into 2-inch lengths
3 onions—unpeeled, halved and each half stuck with 1 whole clove
3 leeks (white part only), split lengthwise, plus 1 leek (including green top), quartered
2 celery ribs with leaves, cut into 2-inch lengths
1 small white turnip
2 cups coarsely chopped tomatoes, canned or fresh
Bouquet garni: 6 sprigs of parsley, 1 teaspoon thyme, 1 large bay leaf, 7 peppercorns and 2 unpeeled garlic cloves tied in a double thickness of cheesecloth

1. Preheat the oven to 450°. Place the meat and bones in a large roasting pan in 1 or 2 layers, or in 2 roasting pans if necessary. Bake, uncovered, for 30 minutes. Add the carrots and onions and bake, turning occasionally, until the bones are deep brown but not charred, 30 to 60 minutes longer.

2. Transfer the bones and vegetables to a large stockpot. Pour off and discard any fat from the roasting pan. Add 2 to 3 cups of cold water to the pan and deglaze over medium heat, scraping up any browned particles that cling to the bottom. Pour the liquid into the stockpot, add enough additional cold water to cover the bones—about 4 quarts—and bring the water slowly to a simmer over low heat; to insure a clear stock, this slow heating should take about 1 hour. Skim off all the scum that rises to the surface.

3. Add the leeks, celery, turnip, tomatoes, bouquet garni and enough additional water to cover. Simmer, partially covered, over low heat for 5 to 8 hours, skimming the surface occasionally. Add additional water to cover as necessary.

4. Carefully ladle the stock into a large bowl through a colander lined with several thicknesses of dampened cheesecloth. Do not press on the bones and vegetables, or the resulting stock will be cloudy. Refrigerate, uncovered, overnight; then remove any fat from the surface. The stock may be refrigerated for 3 to 4 days, then reboiled, or frozen for several months.

WHITE VEAL STOCK

Use this clear, delicate stock to create sauces for veal, chicken or fish dishes.

MAKES 2 TO 3 QUARTS

4½ pounds veal bones
3 pounds veal stew meat, such as shank, breast, neck
2 leeks (white part only), cut into 2-inch lengths
2 medium onions, quartered
2 celery ribs with leaves, cut into 2-inch lengths
2 carrots, cut into 2-inch lengths
Bouquet garni: 6 sprigs of parsley, ½ teaspoon thyme, 1 bay leaf, 2 unpeeled garlic cloves, 3 whole cloves and 4 peppercorns tied in a double thickness of cheesecloth

1. Place the veal bones and meat in a large stockpot. Add enough cold water to cover, about 3 quarts. Cover the pot and bring to a boil over high heat. Lower the heat to moderate and boil gently for 5 minutes. Drain, discarding the water, and rinse the bones under cold running water. Rinse out the pot. Return the bones and meat to the stockpot and add enough cold water to cover. Bring to a simmer over low heat and skim off any scum that rises to the surface. Add 1 cup cold water and when the liquid has returned to a simmer, skim again. Repeat the cold water-skimming process until the liquid is clear.

2. Add the leeks, onions, celery, carrots and bouquet garni. Simmer, partially covered, for 4 to 5 hours, adding water to cover as necessary.

3. When the stock is ready, carefully ladle it through a colander lined with several thicknesses of dampened cheesecloth into a large bowl. Allow to cool. Cover and refrigerate. After the stock has jelled, remove any fat that has accumulated on the surface.

RICH CHICKEN STOCK

Although this deliciously rich stock calls for two whole chickens in addition to chicken parts, the whole birds are removed as soon as they are cooked, so you can eat them as is or use the meat for other dishes, salads or sandwiches. You may substitute additional chicken parts for the whole chickens. Use this stock as a base for soups or sauces.

MAKES ABOUT 3 QUARTS

4 pounds chicken backs, necks and/or wings
2 whole chickens (about 3 pounds each), including neck and gizzards
3 large carrots, sliced
2 large onions, sliced
4 medium leeks—split lengthwise, rinsed and sliced crosswise (or, substitute 1 extra onion)
2 celery ribs with leaves, sliced

Bouquet garni: 8 sprigs of parsley, 1 teaspoon thyme, 1 bay leaf, ½ teaspoon peppercorns and 3 whole cloves tied in a double thickness of cheesecloth

1. Place the chicken parts in a large, heavy stockpot; place the whole chickens on top. Add 6 quarts of cold water and place over low heat. Heat to simmering without stirring; for a clear stock, this should take about an hour. While the water is heating, skim off any scum that rises to the surface.

2. Add the carrots, onions, leeks, celery and bouquet garni. Simmer, partially covered, without stirring, for about 45 minutes. Remove both chickens. Continue simmering the stock, without stirring, for about 4 hours, skimming occasionally. (The meat can be removed from the two chickens as soon as they are cool enough to handle and the bones returned to the pot.)

3. Ladle the stock carefully through a colander lined with several layers of dampened cheesecloth. Strain a second time, if desired, for an even clearer stock. Let cool to room temperature; then cover and refrigerate. Remove the congealed fat from the top. If using the hot stock immediately, remove the fat by first skimming and then blotting the surface with paper towels, or use a degreasing utensil designed for that purpose.

CHICKEN STOCK

MAKES ABOUT 4 QUARTS

5 pounds chicken necks, backs and bones
1 calf's foot, split (optional)
2 medium onions, quartered
2 carrots, coarsely chopped
2 celery ribs, coarsely chopped
3 garlic cloves, crushed
3 leeks, green tops only, coarsely chopped
Bouquet garni: 10 parsley stems, ½ teaspoon dried thyme, 10 peppercorns and 1 bay leaf tied in cheesecloth

1. In a large stockpot, combine all the ingredients. Add 4½ quarts of water. Bring to a boil over moderate heat, skimming off the foamy scum as it rises to the surface. Lower the heat to maintain a slow simmer. Cook, skimming occasionally, for 4 hours.

2. Strain the stock through a fine-mesh sieve lined with a double layer of dampened cheesecloth.

—*John Robert Massie*

FISH STOCK

When cleaning whole fish, save the heads and frames for stock; or, inquire at your local fish market. Use this stock for a variety of sauces.

MAKES ABOUT 2 QUARTS

4 pounds fish bones and trimmings (heads, tails, skin)
3 tablespoons vegetable oil
1 medium onion, cut into eighths
1 large celery rib, cut into 1-inch lengths
1 large carrot, cut into 1-inch lengths
Bouquet garni: 3 sprigs of parsley, ½ teaspoon thyme, 1 bay leaf and 8 to 10 peppercorns tied in a double thickness of cheesecloth

1. Rinse the fish bones and trimmings under cold running water to remove any blood; drain.

2. Heat the oil in a large, heavy stockpot. Add the fish bones and trimmings and sauté over moderate heat for 5 minutes, breaking them up occasionally with a wooden spoon. Cook, partially covered, for 5 minutes longer.

3. Add the onion, celery, carrot and bouquet garni. Pour in 3 quarts of cold water. Bring the mixture to a boil over high heat, skimming off any foam from the surface. Reduce the heat to low and simmer, uncovered, for 30 minutes. Strain through a fine sieve lined with several layers of dampened cheesecloth.

RICH FISH STOCK

The fish bones and heads for this stock should be as fresh as possible.

MAKES 3 CUPS

3 pounds fish bones and heads
¼ pound fresh mushrooms
2 tablespoons unsalted butter
1 medium onion, sliced
10 sprigs of parsley
¾ cup dry white wine
5 peppercorns

1. Rinse the fish bones and heads under cold running water to remove any blood; drain. Separate the caps and stems of the mushrooms. Slice off the bottom of the caps to remove the dark gills.

2. In a large noncorrodible saucepan, melt the butter over moderate heat. Add the onion, parsley and mushroom caps and stems. Sauté gently for about 3 minutes, without browning.

3. Add the fish heads and bones. Cover and cook for 15 minutes.

4. Add the wine and the peppercorns. Bring to a boil over high heat, skimming off any foam from the surface. Boil until reduced by half, about 3 minutes.

5. Add 3 cups of cold water and return to a boil. Reduce the heat to moderate and simmer for 15 minutes. Strain through a fine-mesh sieve. There should be 3 cups. If there is more, boil until reduced to 3 cups; if there is less, add water.

—*Richard Grausman*

VEGETABLE STOCK

MAKES ABOUT 1½ QUARTS

3 celery ribs, cut into 2-inch lengths
2 large carrots, cut into 2-inch lengths
2 small onions, unpeeled and quartered
1 large boiling potato, cut into 1-inch slices
½ pound mushrooms, roughly chopped
4 small leeks (white part only), split lengthwise
2 small white turnips, peeled and quartered
6 garlic cloves, unpeeled
1½ teaspoons salt
1½ teaspoons Hungarian sweet paprika
Bouquet garni: 10 sprigs of parsley, 1½ teaspoons marjoram, 2 bay leaves and 8 peppercorns tied in a double thickness of cheesecloth

1. Place all the vegetables in a stockpot. Add the garlic, salt, paprika, bouquet garni and 3 quarts of water and bring to a boil over moderate heat.
2. Reduce the heat to low and simmer the stock, partially covered, until reduced by half, about 1½ hours.
3. Strain through a double thickness of dampened cheesecloth, pressing lightly on the vegetables with the back of a spoon.

PORK STOCK

If you're making this pork stock for Holiday Choucroute (p. 104) and are including the Confit of Quail and Spareribs (p. 88), add the quail necks and gizzards and the trimmings from the pork ribs to make an extra rich stock.

MAKES ABOUT 6 CUPS

5 pounds pork neck bones, cut into 2-inch sections

1. Place a large roasting pan in the oven and preheat the oven and pan to 425°. Place the pork bones (and rib trimmings, quail necks and gizzards, if using) in the pan and bake, turning occasionally, until deep brown, 1 to 1½ hours.
2. Transfer the meat and bones to a large stock pot. Pour off and discard all fat from the roasting pan; blot up any remaining film of grease with paper towels. Add enough cold water to cover the bottom of the roasting pan and bring to a boil over high heat, scraping up any browned bits that cling to the bottom. Pour this liquid into the stock pot. Add enough cold water to cover the meat and bones by 1 inch.
3. Bring the water slowly to a simmer over moderate heat, skimming occasionally. Reduce the heat to low and simmer, skimming the surface occasionally, for 4 hours.
4. Drain the stock. Let cool to room temperature, then refrigerate.
5. Strain the chilled stock through a fine sieve lined with several layers of dampened cheesecloth into a large saucepan. Boil the stock, skimming occasionally, until reduced by half, about 1 hour. Let cool to room temperature, then refrigerate for up to 3 days before using.

—Anne Disrude

BASIC MAYONNAISE

Mayonnaise works best if all the ingredients are at room temperature before you begin. The emulsion (the suspension of the particles of oil within the yolk) will not form if the oil or the yolks are too cold. On a chilly day, warm the bowl and whisk in hot water, then dry well before starting.

MAKES ABOUT 1½ CUPS

3 egg yolks, at room temperature
1 teaspoon Dijon-style mustard
½ teaspoon salt
Pinch of white pepper
1 tablespoon fresh lemon juice
½ cup olive oil mixed with ½ cup light vegetable oil (see Note)
1 tablespoon white wine vinegar
1 tablespoon boiling water

1. In a medium bowl, whisk the egg yolks until they lighten in color and begin to thicken. Beat in the mustard, salt, pepper and lemon juice and continue whisking until the mixture thickens enough to leave a trail when the whisk is drawn across the bottom of the bowl.
2. Very gradually, begin whisking in the oil by droplets. The emulsion will not form if the oil at this stage is added too quickly.
3. Once the emulsion forms and the mayonnaise begins to thicken, you can add the oil more rapidly, but never faster than in a thin stream.
4. After all the oil has been incorporated, whisk in the vinegar and the boiling water. (The vinegar will lighten and flavor the sauce, the boiling water will help stabilize it.) Taste the mayonnaise and adjust the seasonings according to your taste and the planned use. Cover and refrigerate for up to 5 days.

NOTE: We find this combination of oils produces the perfect balance of flavor and lightness for an all-purpose mayonnaise. You can adjust the proportions according to your taste and particular use.

JALAPENO MAYONNAISE

MAKES ABOUT 1½ CUPS

1 egg yolk
¼ teaspoon Dijon-style mustard
1 tablespoon dry white wine
1 tablespoon white wine vinegar
½ teaspoon salt
Pinch of sugar
Pinch of freshly ground pepper
1 garlic clove, crushed through a press
3 jalapeño peppers—seeded, deribbed and minced
¾ cup safflower or corn oil
½ cup extra-virgin olive oil

In a medium bowl, whisk together the egg yolk, mustard, wine, vinegar, salt, sugar, pepper, garlic and jalapeños. Drizzle in the oils very slowly, whisking constantly, until all the oil is incorporated.

—*Anne Disrude*

GREEN MAYONNAISE

This hand method produces an especially rich, velvety sauce.

MAKES ABOUT 2 CUPS

2 egg yolks
2 tablespoons fresh lemon juice
1 teaspoon Dijon-style mustard
½ teaspoon salt
Dash of cayenne pepper
1 cup olive oil
½ cup plus 2 tablespoons safflower oil
2 tablespoons hot water
1 tablespoon white wine vinegar
½ cup coarsely chopped watercress
¼ cup coarsely chopped chives
¼ cup coarsely chopped fresh dill

1. In a medium bowl, whisk together the egg yolks, 2 teaspoons of the lemon juice, the mustard, salt and cayenne until blended. Gradually whisk in the olive oil by drops until the mixture thickens. Then beat in the remaining olive oil and ½ cup of the safflower oil in a thin stream to make a mayonnaise. Beat in the remaining 4 teaspoons lemon juice. (**The recipe can be made to this point a day ahead.** Cover and refrigerate.)

2. Up to several hours before serving, combine the remaining 2 tablespoons safflower oil, the hot water, vinegar, watercress, chives and dill in a food processor. Puree until smooth. Whisk into the mayonnaise.

—*Susan Wyler*

CREME FRAICHE

MAKES ABOUT 2¼ CUPS

2 cups heavy cream
⅓ cup active-culture buttermilk

1. In a small saucepan, gently heat the cream and buttermilk to just under 100° (higher will kill the culture).

2. Pour into a clean glass jar, cover and place in a saucepan filled with warm (100°) water; or put in a thermos bottle. Allow to stand for 8 to 36 hours, or until thickened, replenishing the warm water occasionally. The longer you culture the cream, the tangier it will become.

3. Refrigerate until chilled. Crème fraîche will keep in the refrigerator for a week to 10 days.

SHERRY VINEGAR BEURRE BLANC

MAKES ABOUT 1½ CUPS

¾ cup sherry wine vinegar
¾ cup dry vermouth
¾ cup minced shallots (4 ounces)
¼ teaspoon salt
¼ teaspoon freshly ground white pepper
3 sticks (¾ pound) cold, lightly salted butter, cut into tablespoons

1. In a medium noncorrodible saucepan, combine the vinegar, vermouth, shallots, salt and white pepper. Bring to a boil over moderately high heat. Cook until the shallots are soft and the liquid has reduced to a syrupy consistency, 10 to 12 minutes.

2. Force the shallot mixture through a fine-mesh sieve.

3. Return the puree to a clean saucepan and rewarm over low heat. Whisk in the cold butter, 3 tablespoons at a time, adding more butter only when the previous amount has been incorporated. The butter should soften to create a thick, creamy sauce; it should not become oily. Season with additional salt and pepper to taste.

4. The sauce can be prepared up to 1 hour before serving and held over warm water. If the sauce gets too hot, it will separate.

—*W. Peter Prestcott*

BEURRE BLANC

Although our recipes usually call for unsalted butter, Grausman believes that lightly salted butter produces a fuller, rounder-tasting sauce.

MAKES ABOUT 1½ CUPS

4 medium shallots, minced
¾ cup distilled white vinegar
⅛ teaspoon finely ground black pepper
3 sticks (¾ pound) lightly salted butter, cut into tablespoons, at room temperature
Salt

1. In a heavy noncorrodible saucepan, combine the shallots, vinegar and pepper. Bring to a boil over mod-

erately high heat and continue to boil until the liquid is reduced to a syrup, about 5 minutes.

2. Reduce the heat to very low. Whisk in the butter, 1 tablespoon at a time. Season with salt to taste. (This sauce can be kept warm in its pan set in a larger pan of warm water for up to 30 minutes.)

—Richard Grausman

WATERCRESS BEURRE BLANC

The addition of pureed watercress gives this beurre blanc a vivid green color and an intriguing taste.

MAKES ABOUT 1 CUP

½ recipe Beurre Blanc (above)
1 bunch of watercress, tough stems removed

1. Make the Beurre Blanc as directed above.

2. In a large saucepan of boiling water, blanch the watercress for 1 minute. Rinse under cold running water to refresh; drain well.

3. In a blender or food processor, puree the watercress. Drain the puree in a fine sieve; press to extract as much liquid as possible. Turn out the solids onto paper towels and squeeze dry.

4. Stir the pureed watercress into the finished beurre blanc. Taste and adjust the seasonings if necessary. (This sauce can be kept warm in its pan set in a large saucepan of warm water for up to 30 minutes.)

—Richard Grausman

CREOLE SAUCE

This sauce will keep in the refrigerator, tightly covered, for up to four days. It can also be frozen.

MAKES ABOUT 3 CUPS

2 tablespoons unsalted butter
1 medium onion, choppped
1 green bell pepper, chopped
2 celery ribs, chopped
5 garlic cloves, finely chopped
2 teaspoons Creole Seafood Seasoning (p. 238), or more to taste
1 teaspoon paprika, preferably hot
⅛ teaspoon cayenne pepper
4 imported bay leaves
1¼ cups chicken stock or canned broth
4 medium tomatoes—peeled, seeded and diced—or 1 can (35 ounces) Italian peeled tomatoes, drained and coarsely chopped
1 tablespoon Worcestershire sauce
1 teaspoon Louisiana Red Hot Sauce or other hot pepper sauce
½ teaspoon salt
3 scallions, chopped

1. In a large skillet, melt the butter over moderately high heat. Add the onion, bell pepper, celery and garlic. Cook, stirring occasionally, for about 5 minutes or until the vegetables are softened, but not browned.

2. Add the Creole Seafood Seasoning, paprika, cayenne pepper, bay leaves and chicken stock. Bring to a boil and cook until slightly reduced and thickened, about 5 minutes.

3. Stir in the tomatoes and cook, stirring occasionally, for 10 minutes longer, until thick.

4. Stir in the Worcestershire sauce, hot sauce, salt and scallions, reduce the heat to low and simmer for 10 minutes.

—Emeril Lagasse, Commander's Palace, New Orleans, Louisiana

QUICK TOMATO SAUCE

MAKES ABOUT 2 CUPS

1 can (35 ounces) Italian peeled tomatoes—drained, seeded and chopped
2 tablespoons tomato paste
1 teaspoon fresh lemon juice
¼ teaspoon salt
⅛ teaspoon freshly ground pepper
1 small tomato—peeled, seeded and diced

In a medium noncorrodible saucepan, bring the canned tomatoes, tomato paste, lemon juice, salt and pepper to a boil over moderate heat. Reduce the heat and simmer for 10 minutes, stirring occasionally to break up the tomatoes. Stir in the fresh tomato and heat through.

—John Robert Massie

TOMATO SAUCE WITH GARLIC

This long-simmered sauce can be made up to 3 days ahead and stored, covered with plastic wrap, in the refrigerator or frozen for several months.

MAKES ABOUT 3 CUPS

1 can (28 ounces) Italian peeled tomatoes, with their juice
3 tablespoons olive oil
5 medium garlic cloves, crushed through a press
½ teaspoon salt
¼ teaspoon freshly ground pepper
¼ teaspoon sugar

1. Puree the tomatoes with their juice in a food processor or blender.

2. In a heavy medium noncorrodible saucepan, heat the oil. Add the crushed garlic and sauté over moderate heat, stirring occasionally, until golden, 6 to 8 minutes.

3. Add the pureed tomatoes, salt, pepper and sugar; stir until blended. Reduce the heat to low, partially cover and simmer, stirring occasionally, until the sauce is thickened, 1 to 1½ hours.

—Da Celestino, Florence, Italy

TOMATO-BASIL COULIS

MAKES ABOUT 2 CUPS

3 pounds ripe tomatoes (about 8 medium)—peeled, seeded and diced—or 2 cans (28 ounces each) Italian peeled tomatoes—drained, seeded and chopped
2 tablespoons tomato paste
½ teaspoon salt
¼ teaspoon freshly ground pepper
½ cup chopped fresh basil

1. In a large noncorrodible skillet, combine the tomatoes, tomato paste, salt and pepper. Cook over moderately high heat, stirring occasionally, until the tomatoes are reduced to a thick sauce, 5 to 10 minutes. (**The recipe can be prepared ahead to this point.** Cover and refrigerate.)

2. Reheat if necessary and stir in the basil shortly before serving.

—Richard Grausman

SALSA FRESCA

Spoon this lively sauce liberally over Quesadillas (p. 20) or use as a dip.

MAKES ABOUT 2 CUPS

2 medium tomatoes, finely diced
½ teaspoon salt
1 small onion, minced
¼ cup minced fresh coriander (cilantro)
2 fresh hot chiles, preferably serrano —seeded, deribbed and minced

Place the tomatoes in a small noncorrodible bowl and sprinkle with the salt; let stand for 10 minutes. Mix in the onion, coriander, chiles and 2 tablespoons of cold water. Serve at room temperature.

—Jim Fobel

LOW-SODIUM FRESH SALSA

MAKES ABOUT 2 CUPS

1 pound ripe tomatoes, seeded and coarsely chopped
*½ cup low-sodium tomato juice**
1 tablespoon fresh lime juice
1 tablespoon fresh lemon juice
¼ teaspoon oregano
1 scallion, chopped
1 small red onion, chopped
2 teaspoons chopped fresh coriander or flat Italian parsley
1½ teaspoons Vegit seasoning*
½ small fresh serrano or jalapeño pepper, finely chopped
**Available at health food stores*

In a medium bowl, combine the tomatoes, tomato juice, lime juice, lemon juice, oregano, scallion, red onion, coriander, Vegit and serrano pepper. Stir to combine. Cover and refrigerate for 2 to 3 hours.

—Christian Chavanne,
Sonoma Mission Inn and Spa,
Boyes Hot Springs, California

LOW-SODIUM TOMATO SAUCE

MAKES ABOUT 1½ CUPS

1 teaspoon olive oil
1 small onion, finely chopped
3 garlic cloves, minced
1½ pounds plum tomatoes—peeled, seeded and coarsely chopped
*¼ cup low-sodium tomato juice**
¼ cup minced fresh parsley
½ teaspoon chopped fresh or dried thyme
Pinch of chopped fresh or dried crumbled rosemary
**Available at health food stores*

In a medium noncorrodible saucepan, heat the oil. Add the onion and sauté over moderate heat, stirring frequently, until softened but not browned, about 3 minutes. Add the garlic and cook for 1 minute longer. Add the tomatoes, tomato juice, parsley, thyme and rosemary. Cover and cook the sauce, stirring occasionally, for 40 minutes.

—Christian Chavanne,
Sonoma Mission Inn and Spa,
Boyes Hot Springs, California

LOW-CALORIE LEMON PESTO

MAKES ABOUT ⅔ CUP

2 cups packed basil leaves (¼ pound basil)
2 ounces peeled garlic cloves (about 12 cloves), chopped
1½ teaspoons olive oil
½ teaspoon pine nuts
¼ teaspoon grated lemon zest
1½ tablespoons fresh lemon juice

In a food processor or blender, combine the basil, garlic, olive oil, pine nuts, lemon zest and lemon juice. Process for about 5 minutes, scraping down the sides of the bowl 2 or 3 times, until the pesto is creamy.

—Christian Chavanne,
Sonoma Mission Inn and Spa,
Boyes Hot Springs, California

SAFFRON SAUCE

The clarification process employed here is similar to that used for stocks. It produces a rich, velvety sauce.

MAKES 2 TO 2½ CUPS

6 tablespoons unsalted butter
¼ cup all-purpose flour
1 recipe Rich Fish Stock (p. 231)
2 pinches of thread saffron, crushed
¼ teaspoon salt
Pinch of white pepper

1. In a heavy medium saucepan, melt 3 tablespoons of the butter over moderately high heat. Whisk in the flour and cook for 5 to 10 seconds; whisk again.

2. Whisk in the fish stock and the saffron and bring to a boil over high heat. Reduce the heat to moderately low and with the pan off to the side of the burner, simmer for 1 hour. The sauce should bubble gently up one side of the pan. Skim frequently to remove the butter and impurities as they rise to the surface. Season with the salt and pepper. (**The recipe can be prepared up to a day ahead to this point.** Cover and refrigerate.)

3. Just before serving, reheat the sauce if necessary. Remove from the heat and swirl in the remaining 3 tablespoons butter. Do not allow the sauce to boil after this point.

—*Richard Grausman*

SPRING HERB SAUCE

If you can't find all of the fresh herbs, rather than substitute dried herbs, increase the quantity of the fresh herbs you do have.

MAKES ABOUT 2½ CUPS

2 quarts chicken stock (see Note)
3 tablespoons minced shallots
2 tablespoons minced fresh chives
2 tablespoons minced fresh tarragon
2 tablespoons minced fresh parsley
2 tablespoons minced fresh thyme
½ teaspoon minced fresh marjoram
½ teaspoon salt
¼ teaspoon freshly ground pepper
1 stick (¼ pound) unsalted butter, at room temperature
2 tablespoons all-purpose flour

1. In a large saucepan, combine the stock with 2 tablespoons of the shallots, 1 tablespoon of the chives, 1 tablespoon of the tarragon, 1 tablespoon of the parsley and 1 tablespoon of the thyme. Bring to a boil over high heat and cook until reduced to about 2 cups, 15 to 20 minutes. Strain through a fine-mesh sieve into another, smaller saucepan.

2. Meanwhile, in a food processor, combine the remaining 1 tablespoon each of shallots, chives, tarragon, parsley and thyme, the marjoram, salt and pepper with 6 tablespoons of the butter. Process to a smooth paste. Set the herb butter aside.

3. Cut the remaining 2 tablespoons butter into small pieces and place in a small bowl. Blend with the flour until smooth, to form a beurre manié. Bring the reduced stock to a boil over moderately high heat. Whisk in the beurre manié, 1 tablespoon at a time, and boil until the sauce thickens, 1 to 2 minutes. Remove from the heat and whisk in the herb butter, 1 tablespoon at a time.

NOTE: If you're making this sauce to go with Poached Capon with Spring Herb Sauce (p. 236), use the poaching liquid instead of chicken stock.

—*John Robert Massie*

LOW-CALORIE FRESH HERB DRESSING

Thick, creamy and truly low in calories, this fresh herbal dressing can be used over any tossed salad.

MAKES ABOUT 1¼ CUPS

*2 teaspoons Irish moss powder**
2 small garlic cloves, chopped
2 tablespoons fresh lime juice
1 tablespoon fresh lemon juice
¼ teaspoon white pepper
2 tablespoons plus 2 teaspoons olive oil, preferably extra-virgin
2 tablespoons plus 2 teaspoons white wine vinegar
1½ tablespoons chopped fresh basil
1½ teaspoons each of minced fresh dill, coriander, tarragon and chives
1 small shallot, chopped
1 teaspoon Vegit seasoning*
1 tablespoon chopped fresh parsley
**Available at health food stores*

1. Put 1½ cups water into a blender or food processor. Add the Irish moss powder and blend for 1 minute.

2. Pour into a medium saucepan and bring to a boil over high heat, stirring constantly. Boil, stirring, for 2 minutes. Pour into a small bowl and let cool until set to a firm gel.

3. Put the Irish moss gelatin into the blender or food processor. Add all the remaining ingredients and process until smooth and creamy, about 5 minutes.

—*Christian Chavanne, Sonoma Mission Inn and Spa, Boyes Hot Springs, California*

SPICY TOMATO VINAIGRETTE

MAKES ABOUT 2 CUPS

1 can (8 ounces) Italian peeled tomatoes, juices reserved
1 garlic clove
½ teaspoon salt
¼ teaspoon hot pepper sauce
Dash of freshly ground black pepper
2 tablespoons olive oil
¼ cup minced fresh coriander

1. In a blender or food processor, combine the tomatoes and their juice, the garlic, salt, hot sauce and black pepper. Purée until smooth. With the machine on, slowly add the olive oil. Pour into a serving bowl. Cover and refrigerate for up to 2 days.

2. Just before serving, stir in the minced coriander.

—*Molly O'Neill*

SEAFOOD COCKTAIL SAUCE

MAKES ABOUT 2 CUPS

4 ounces prepared white horseradish
1 bottle (12 ounces) ketchup
⅓ cup bottled chili sauce
2 tablespoons fresh lemon juice
⅛ teaspoon hot pepper sauce
1 tablespoon Worcestershire sauce

1. Put the horseradish in a sieve and rinse under cold running water. Drain and press out the moisture.

2. In a medium bowl, combine the horseradish, ketchup, chili sauce, lemon juice, hot sauce and Worcestershire sauce. Cover and refrigerate until serving time.

—*Stephanie Sidell & Bob Sasse*

MUSTARD-CAPER DIPPING SAUCE

MAKES ABOUT 2 CUPS

2 egg yolks
¼ cup capers, drained
2 tablespoons Dijon-style mustard
2 tablespoons fresh lemon juice
1 teaspoon tarragon vinegar
¾ cup olive oil
¾ cup flavorless vegetable oil
Salt and freshly ground pepper

1. In a food processor or blender, combine the egg yolks, capers, mustard, lemon juice and vinegar. Process until the capers are coarsely chopped, about 1 minute.

2. With the machine on, slowly add the olive oil and vegetable oil in a thin stream. Season with salt and pepper to taste.

—*W. Peter Prestcott*

HORSERADISH DIPPING SAUCE

MAKES ABOUT 2¼ CUPS

1 cup plain yogurt
1 cup sour cream
¼ cup prepared white horseradish
2 teaspoons salt
1 teaspoon dried dillweed

In a medium bowl, combine all of the ingredients and stir to blend.

—*W. Peter Prestcott*

SOY-SESAME DIPPING SAUCE

MAKES ABOUT 1¼ CUPS

½ cup soy sauce
½ cup dry sherry
¼ cup Oriental sesame oil
¼ cup minced scallions
1 medium garlic clove, minced

In a small bowl, combine all of the ingredients and stir to blend.

—*W. Peter Prestcott*

CHARRED ONION POWDER

Charred Onion Powder adds a dark, sweet taste to meats and fish. Use it as you would any seasoning before sautéing a piece of meat, poultry or fish, or try it in one of the two recipes it was designed for: Onion-Charred Chicken (p. 79) or Onion-Charred Ribs (p. 102).

MAKES ABOUT ½ CUP

2 pounds white onions, peeled and thinly sliced

1. Cook the onions in a large cast-iron skillet over high heat for about 30 minutes, until deep black-brown (but not carbonized). Stir frequently for even charring.

2. If the onions are not completely dry at the end of 30 minutes, spread them on paper towels and let dry overnight at room temperature or for 1 or 2 hours in a 200° oven.

3. Grind to a fine powder in a spice grinder.

—*Anne Disrude*

SHRIMP POWDER

Much the way shrimp shells add to the flavor of fish stocks, shrimp powder enhances soups and sauces, such as the cream sauce for Sole and Shrimp with Shrimp Sauce (p. 57).

MAKES ABOUT ½ CUP

Shells from 2 pounds of shrimp

1. Spread the shells in one layer on baking sheets and roast them in a preheated 350° oven for about 15 minutes. Toss them occasionally for even drying.

2. Roughly grind the shells in a food processor, then grind to a fine powder in a spice or coffee mill.

—*Anne Disrude*

CREOLE MEAT SEASONING

MAKES ABOUT 2¾ CUPS

1 cup salt
¾ cup garlic powder
¾ cup black peppercorns
½ teaspoon cayenne pepper
¼ cup paprika, preferably hot

In a large spice mill or a food processor, combine all the ingredients. Process for about 1 minute, or until evenly pulverized and blended. Store in an airtight container. Will keep well for up to 1 year.

—*Emeril Lagasse, Commander's Palace, New Orleans, Louisiana*

CREOLE SEAFOOD SEASONING

MAKES ABOUT 1¾ CUPS

⅓ cup salt
¼ cup garlic powder or flakes
¼ cup black peppercorns
2 tablespoons cayenne pepper
2 tablespoons thyme
2 tablespoons oregano
⅓ cup paprika, preferably hot
3 tablespoons onion powder or flakes

Combine all the ingredients in a large spice mill or food processor. Process for about 1 minute or until evenly pulverized and blended. Store in an airtight container. Will keep for up to 9 months.

—*Emeril Lagasse, Commander's Palace, New Orleans, Louisiana*

PEPPER MIX

This fragrant pepper-allspice combination was made famous by the French food purveyor Hédiard; the proportions for this mixture were inspired by Madeleine Kamman. Use it in the Pepper Mill Squares (p. 202) or as a seasoning in place of your usual pepper.

MAKES ABOUT 2½ TABLESPOONS

1 tablespoon black peppercorns
1 tablespoon white peppercorns
1½ teaspoons whole allspice berries

Mix the black and white peppercorns and the allspice berries together. Grind to a powder in a pepper or spice mill.

—*Dorie Greenspan*

DRIED RED PEPPERS

Dried Red Peppers make a great snack, and with their sweet nutty flavor and crunch, they liven up dishes such as Zucchini and Egg Salad with Dried Peppers (p. 174).

Unblemished red bell peppers—quartered, cored and deribbed

1. Preheat the oven to 140°. In a large steambasket, steam the peppers for 10 minutes. Dry on paper towels.

2. Place the peppers, cut-side down, on cheesecloth-covered racks. Set the racks on baking sheets

3. Dry the peppers in the oven for 8 to 10 hours, or until crisp. Keep the oven door propped open to allow moisture to escape.

4. Let the peppers cool completely before packing in airtight containers.

—*Anne Disrude*

SEVEN-DAY PRESERVED LEMON

Preserved lemons are a Moroccan specialty, with a very special flavor that cannot be duplicated with fresh lemon juice or rind. Here is a new seven-day method to replace the traditional month-long preparation.

MAKES ½ PINT

2 ripe lemons
⅓ cup coarse (kosher) salt
⅓ cup fresh lemon juice
Olive oil

Scrub the lemons and dry well. Cut each into 8 wedges. Toss with the salt and place in a ½-pint glass jar with a plastic-coated lid. Pour in the lemon juice. Close tightly and let ripen in a warm place for 7 days, shaking the jar each day to distribute the salt and juice. To store, add olive oil to cover and keep in the refrigerator for up to 6 months.

—*Paula Wolfert*

SWEET AND SOUR PRUNES

These tart-sweet preserved prunes are a delicious accompaniment to the Rum-Marinated Rabbit Terrine (p. 37) or to roast game or pork. They keep well for months when stored in the refrigerator.

MAKES ABOUT 1 PINT

2 cups pitted prunes (about 12 ounces)
1 cup red wine vinegar
⅔ cup sugar
Zest of 1 orange, cut into 1-inch-long julienne strips
12 allspice berries

1. Place the prunes in a bowl and

pour in 2 cups of boiling water. Set aside for 15 minutes; then drain.

2. Meanwhile, in a small noncorrodible saucepan, combine the vinegar and the sugar. Bring to a boil over moderately high heat, stirring to dissolve the sugar. Reduce the heat to moderate and simmer for about 4 minutes.

3. Scald a 1-pint canning jar with boiling water and drain well. Fill the jar with the prunes, interspersing the orange zest and allspice berries. Pour in the hot vinegar mixture; the liquid should overflow the jar. Wipe the rim, seal the jar and let stand until cool. Store in a cool dark place for at least 3 weeks before opening. Refrigerate after opening.

—Patricia Wells

PEARL ONIONS IN WINE

These sweet preserved onions keep for months in the refrigerator.

MAKES ABOUT 1 PINT

2 pints (1¼ pounds) tiny white boiling (pearl) onions
1 bottle Gewürztraminer or other spicy white wine
½ cup sugar
5 imported bay leaves

1. In a large saucepan, bring 2 quarts of water to a boil. Add the onions. When the water returns to a boil, drain the onions. Slip off the skins and trim the root ends.

2. In a medium noncorrodible saucepan, bring the wine, sugar and bay leaves to a boil over high heat. Boil until the liquid is reduced to 2 cups, about 15 minutes.

3. Add the onions and reduce the heat to moderate. Simmer for about 10 minutes, until an onion can be easily pierced with the tip of a knife.

4. With a slotted spoon, remove the onions to a 1-pint jar. Boil the liquid until it is syrupy and reduced to about ¾ cup. Pour the syrup over the onions and add the bay leaves. Let stand uncovered until cool. Wipe the rim of the jar, cover and refrigerate.

—Anne Disrude

ROASTED PEPPERS IN OLIVE OIL

The great bonus of preserving peppers this way is the flavorful oil that results. For flavorful variations, see the two suggestions that follow.

MAKES ABOUT 1 QUART

6 pounds red or yellow bell peppers
1 tablespoon red or white wine vinegar
¾ cup extra-virgin olive oil, or to cover

1. Roast the peppers directly over a gas flame or under the broiler, as close to the heat as possible, turning frequently, until blackened all over. Place the peppers in a paper or plastic bag and let steam for 10 minutes. When cool enough to handle, peel off the skins under running water. Place the peeled peppers in a large bowl.

2. Halve the peppers and remove the cores, seeds and ribs over the bowl to catch the juices. Place the peppers in a wide-mouth quart jar. Strain the juices over the peppers.

3. Add the vinegar and enough oil to cover the peppers. Stir to release any air bubbles. These peppers will keep for 2 to 3 months refrigerated.

—Anne Disrude

ROASTED PEPPER VARIATIONS

Roasted Peppers with Anchovies and Capers: Prepare Roasted Peppers in Olive Oil through Step 2. Drain, rinse and pat dry 1 can of flat anchovy fillets. Add the anchovies, 1½ tablespoons drained capers, 2 imported bay leaves and 4 garlic cloves to the peppers. Proceed with Step 3.

Roasted Peppers with Olives and Thyme: Prepare Roasted Peppers in olive oil through Step 2. Add 6 brine-cured black olives, 2 sprigs of fresh thyme and 2 peeled garlic cloves. Proceed with Step 3.

—Anne Disrude

JICAMA RELISH

The relish should sit for four hours or overnight, so plan accordingly.

6 TO 8 SERVINGS

2 small carrots, peeled and cut into ¼-inch dice
1 medium jicama (about 1¼ pounds), peeled and cut into ¼-inch dice
1 medium onion, finely chopped
2 small zucchini, cut into ¼-inch dice
3 tablespoons minced fresh coriander
4 garlic cloves, minced
1 canned chipotle chile, seeded and minced (about 2 teaspoons)
1 bay leaf
8 black peppercorns, crushed
1 teaspoon oregano, preferably Mexican
¼ teaspoon salt
½ cup distilled white vinegar
⅓ cup olive oil

1. In a large saucepan of boiling water, blanch the carrots until crisp-tender, 1 to 2 minutes. Drain and rinse under cold water; drain well.

2. In a large bowl, combine the blanched carrots and the rest of the ingredients. Add ½ cup of cold water

and toss to mix well. Cover and refrigerate for at least 4 hours or overnight. Let return to room temperature and remove the bay leaf before serving.

—*Zarela Martinez, Café Marimba, New York City*

SPICY MELON RELISH

This distinctive relish make a lovely accompaniment to grilled fish, chicken or duck.

MAKES ABOUT 3 CUPS

1 large cucumber—peeled, seeded and cut into ¼-inch dice
½ medium cantaloupe—peeled, seeded and cut into ¼-inch dice
¼ medium honeydew melon—peeled, seeded and cut into ¼-inch dice
1 tablespoon vegetable oil
1 small onion, finely chopped
¼ cup chopped fresh coriander
3 fresh red jalapeño peppers, minced
1 fresh green jalapeño pepper, minced
2 tablespoons fresh lime juice
½ teaspoon salt
Pinch of freshly ground black pepper

1. In a large bowl, toss together the cucumber, cantaloupe and honeydew melon.
2. In a small skillet, heat the oil. Add the onion and cook over moderate heat, stirring constantly, until softened but not browned, about 1 minute. Add to melon mixture.
3. Add the coriander, red and green jalapeño peppers, the lime juice, salt and black pepper. Cover and refrigerate overnight to blend the flavors.

—*Anne Lindsay Greer*

CRANBERRY-BOURBON RELISH

This tangy cranberry relish makes a good accompaniment to any pâté or cold or smoked meat. It is also quite at home beside turkey and stuffing.

10 TO 12 SERVINGS

1 cup bourbon
¼ cup minced shallots
Grated zest of 1 orange
1 package (12 ounces) fresh cranberries, rinsed and picked over
1 cup sugar
1 teaspoon freshly ground pepper

1. In a small noncorrodible saucepan, combine the bourbon, shallots and orange zest. Bring to a boil over moderate heat, lower the heat and simmer, stirring occasionally, until the bourbon is reduced to a syrupy glaze on the bottom of the pan, about 10 minutes.
2. Add the cranberries and sugar, stirring well, until the sugar dissolves. Reduce the heat slightly and simmer, uncovered, until most of the cranberries have burst, about 10 minutes.
3. Remove from the heat and stir in the pepper. Transfer to a bowl, let cool to room temperature, cover and refrigerate. **(This can be prepared several days in advance of serving.)**

—*Michael McLaughlin*

PINEAPPLE CHUTNEY

I like this chutney for entertaining because it is so bright—in color and in flavor. Its sweet-sour pungency beautifully complements the saltiness of baked ham, which is one of my favorite meats for a large gathering. The pair makes an excellent centerpiece for a buffet meal, accompanied, perhaps, with a casserole of macaroni and cheese in winter (or a creamy pasta salad in summer), a green vegetable and hot jalapeño corn bread. Begin with a tureen of fresh cream of mushroom soup, dressed up with some wild mushrooms if you like. A flaming bowl of café brûlot could be fun for dessert, with a selection of store-bought pastries.

MAKES ABOUT 1 QUART

1 large ripe pineapple
1 large red bell pepper, cut into ½-inch squares
1 large green bell pepper, cut into ½-inch squares
2 medium onions, cut into ½-inch dice
3 large garlic cloves, chopped
¾ cup (packed) raisins
¼ cup chopped fresh ginger
¾ cup (packed) light brown sugar
1 cup cider vinegar
2 teaspoons salt
2 cinnamon sticks, broken in half
½ teaspoon whole coriander seeds
¼ teaspoon black peppercorns
8 cloves
2 small dried hot red peppers

1. Trim off the top of the pineapple. With a large, sharp stainless steel knife, cut down the sides of the pineapple to remove the skin and the "eyes." Trim off the bottom. Cut the pineapple into ½-inch dice.
2. In a large noncorrodible pot, combine the pineapple, red and green bell peppers, onions, garlic, raisins, ginger, brown sugar, vinegar and salt. Tie the cinnamon sticks, coriander seeds, peppercorns, cloves and hot peppers in a cheesecloth bag; add to the pot.
3. Bring to a boil and cook over moderately low heat, stirring occa-

sionally, until the liquid is reduced to a thick syrup that binds the fruits and vegetables. Remove from the heat and let cool. Remove the spice bag. Cover and refrigerate overnight or for up to 1 week before serving.

—*Susan Wyler*

SPICED TOMATO CHUTNEY

There is no cooking involved in this refreshing chutney. Flavored with orange, mint and fresh coriander, it makes a tasty relish for charcoal-grilled hamburgers or steaks and is also good on sandwiches.

MAKES ABOUT 1½ CUPS

¼ cup minced fresh mint
¼ cup minced fresh coriander
2 tablespoons minced onion
½ teaspoon salt
¼ teaspoon freshly ground pepper
2 tablespoons tomato paste
¼ cup fresh orange juice
2 medium tomatoes (about ¾ pound), cut into ½-inch dice

In a medium bowl, combine the mint, coriander, onion, salt and pepper. With a wooden spoon or a pestle, lightly pound the mixture to bruise the herbs and extract some moisture. Blend in the tomato paste and orange juice. Stir in the tomato. Cover and refrigerate for at least 1 hour before serving.

—*Jim Fobel*

MANGO CHUTNEY

For a change, try this rich chutney on hot biscuits with cream cheese.

MAKES ABOUT 2 CUPS

¼ cup packed light or dark brown sugar
¼ cup distilled white vinegar
¼ cup light or dark raisins
5 whole cloves
½ teaspoon freshly grated nutmeg
¼ teaspoon cinnamon
¼ teaspoon salt
1 small onion, finely chopped
1 large or 2 medium firm-ripe mangoes, coarsely chopped (about 2 cups)
2 tablespoons fresh lime juice

1. In a heavy medium noncorrodible saucepan, combine the brown sugar, vinegar, raisins, cloves, nutmeg, cinnamon, salt and onion. Bring to a boil over moderate heat. Reduce the heat and simmer for 5 minutes.

2. Add the chopped mango and 2 tablespoons of water and simmer, stirring frequently, until thickened, about 5 minutes. Remove from the heat and stir in the lime juice. Let cool to room temperature. Cover and refrigerate for at least 2 hours or up to 1 week. Serve the chutney chilled or at room temperature.

—*Jim Fobel*

PEACH-PECAN CHUTNEY

This fresh chutney is delicious with Chinese egg rolls or noodle dishes as well as with pork and duck. It is also a perfect accompaniment to curried lamb.

MAKES ABOUT 1 CUP

3 medium firm-ripe peaches, coarsely chopped (about 2 cups)
¼ cup honey
2 tablespoons plus 1 teaspoon minced fresh ginger
1 cinnamon stick
2 tablespoons fresh lemon juice
¼ cup chopped pecans
⅛ teaspoon almond extract

1. In a heavy medium noncorrodible saucepan, combine the peaches, honey, 2 tablespoons of the ginger, the cinnamon stick and lemon juice. Bring to a boil over moderate heat. Reduce the heat and simmer, stirring frequently, until the syrup is reduced and has thickened slightly, about 10 minutes.

2. Remove from the heat and stir in the pecans, almond extract and remaining 1 teaspoon ginger. Let cool to room temperature. Cover and refrigerate for several hours or up to 3 days. Serve the chutney chilled or at room temperature.

—*Jim Fobel*

PINEAPPLE-RUM CHUTNEY

With a flavor that works well with ham, poultry or roast pork, this clove-scented chutney also makes a nice topping for biscuits or pound or coconut cake.

MAKES ABOUT 1½ CUPS

¼ cup packed light or dark brown sugar
3 tablespoons distilled white vinegar
3 tablespoons dark rum
8 whole cloves
Half of a large ripe pineapple, coarsely chopped (about 2 cups)

1. In a heavy medium noncorrodible saucepan, combine the brown sugar, vinegar, 2 tablespoons of the rum and the cloves. Bring to a boil over moderate heat. Reduce the heat and simmer for 5 minutes. Add the pineapple and cook, stirring frequently, until the syrup is slightly reduced, about 10 minutes.

2. Remove from the heat and stir in the remaining 1 tablespoon rum. Let

cool to room temperature. Cover and refrigerate for a minimum of 24 hours or up to 1 week. Serve the chutney chilled or at room temperature.

—*Jim Fobel*

PLUM NUT CHUTNEY

Serve this textured chutney with any roasted meat, curries, vegetarian dishes and Chinese dishes, especially fried wontons.

MAKES ABOUT 1½ CUPS

⅓ cup cider vinegar
¼ cup dry Madeira
2 tablespoons light unsulphured molasses
2 tablespoons sugar
1 teaspoon powdered mustard
¼ teaspoon freshly grated nutmeg
¼ teaspoon cayenne pepper
1 garlic clove, minced
6 medium firm-ripe red plums, coarsely chopped (about 2½ cups)
¼ cup whole blanched almonds
¼ teaspoon almond extract

1. In a heavy medium noncorrodible saucepan, combine the vinegar, Madeira, molasses, sugar, mustard, nutmeg, cayenne pepper and garlic. Bring to a boil over moderate heat. Reduce the heat and simmer for 5 minutes.
2. Add the plums and simmer, stirring frequently, until the mixture thickens and reduces to 1½ cups, 15 to 20 minutes.
3. Meanwhile, in an ungreased medium skillet, cook the almonds over moderate heat, tossing frequently, until lightly toasted, about 3 minutes. Let cool; then finely chop.
4. Remove the plum mixture from the heat and stir in the almonds and almond extract. Let cool to room temperature. Cover and refrigerate for at least 3 hours or up to 1 week. Serve chilled or at room temperature.

—*Jim Fobel*

CHUNKY APPLE CHUTNEY

Although wonderful cold, this chutney makes a tangy side dish when served hot or warm. It is especially good with pork chops.

MAKES ABOUT 1½ CUPS

½ cup dry sherry
¼ cup sugar
3 tablespoons fresh lemon juice
1 cinnamon stick
8 whole cloves
¼ cup minced onion
1 garlic clove, minced
¼ teaspoon salt
2 medium, tart green apples—peeled, cored and coarsely chopped

1. In a heavy medium noncorrodible saucepan, combine the sherry, sugar, lemon juice, cinnamon stick, cloves, onion, garlic and salt. Bring to a boil over moderate heat. Reduce the heat and simmer for 5 minutes.
2. Add the apples and 2 tablespoons of water. Simmer, stirring frequently, until the chutney is thick but the apples still chunky, about 5 minutes. Serve warm or let cool to room temperature, cover and refrigerate for up to 3 days.

—*Jim Fobel*

CONCORD GRAPE JAM

This tart, flavorful jam contains very little sugar. Double or triple the recipe if you wish. This jam will keep in clean jars for up to two weeks in the refrigerator.

MAKES ABOUT 1⅓ CUPS

2 pounds Concord grapes, stemmed (about 6 cups)
½ cup sugar

1. In a large noncorrodible saucepan, combine the grapes with ½ cup of water and bring to a boil. Reduce the heat to moderately low, cover and simmer until the grapes are completely collapsed and exude their juice, about 10 minutes.
2. Press through a sieve with a wooden spoon; discard the solids in the sieve. There will be about 2½ cups of juice and puree.
3. Return this mixture to a clean saucepan. Add the sugar and stir until dissolved. Bring to a boil over moderately high heat and boil until reduced to 1⅓ cups, about 20 minutes. Stir constantly during the last 5 minutes of cooking, lowering the heat if necessary to prevent scorching. Let cool and store, covered, in the refrigerator.

—*Diana Sturgis*

QUINCE MARMALADE WITH LEMON AND GINGER

I think it is always worthwhile to make a healthy amount of any preserve, but you can easily halve this recipe if you prefer. The quince mixture sits for 12 hours or so before canning, so plan accordingly.

MAKES 12 HALF-PINT JARS

3 pounds quinces
2 lemons

Large chunk of fresh ginger (about 5 inches long), coarsely grated
About 10 cups sugar

1. Peel and core the quinces. Place the cores in a small saucepan; discard the peels. Coarsely shred the quinces, or cut them into fine julienne strips. In a large heavy noncorrodible pot, combine the quince with water to almost cover.

2. Halve the lemons lengthwise. If there are any seeds, add them to the small saucepan with the quince cores.

3. Thinly slice the lemons and add to the shredded quince. Add the ginger and bring the shredded quince mixture to a boil. Boil gently for 15 minutes and remove from the heat.

4. Cover the lemon seeds and quince cores by a few inches with water; boil gently for 30 minutes, adding water to keep the seeds well covered. Strain this pectin-rich liquid into the shredded quince mixture, reserving the seeds and cores. Cover the seeds and cores with water again and boil gently for another 30 minutes to extract more pectin. Strain this into the quince mixture and discard the solids. Cover the pot with a towel and let stand for about 12 hours.

5. Measure the mixture and divide it evenly between two heavy noncorrodible pots. Add the same amount of sugar as there is fruit to each pot (about 10 cups total). Bring to a boil, stirring often. Boil, stirring often, until the mixture begins to get sticky and thick. Then continue to boil, stirring constantly to prevent scorching, until the mixture reaches the jelly stage (220°, or 8° above the boiling point of water at your altitude).

6. Ladle into hot, clean half-pint jelly jars. Clean the rims with a towel dipped into boiling water. Screw sterilized lids on and process in a hot water bath for 10 minutes. Set the jars on a towel. Do not disturb until cooled.

—Elizabeth Schneider

POMEGRANATE SYRUP

This brilliant ruby homemade grenadine will last indefinitely and will add color, sweetness and a slight pomegranate taste to drinks, fruit mixtures (cooked or raw) and sauces. Sharpen the naturally delicate flavor with lemon or lime juice if you wish.

MAKES ABOUT 2 CUPS

2 cups pomegranate seeds (from 2 large pomegranates)
2 cups sugar

1. In a noncorrodible saucepan, combine the pomegranate seeds with the sugar. Stir to blend, crushing the seeds until you have a wet mass. Cover and let stand at room temperature for 12 to 24 hours.

2. Bring to a boil over moderate heat, stirring constantly. Reduce the heat and simmer for 2 minutes. Strain out the seeds, pushing down hard to extract all the juice. Pour the syrup into a clean jar, cool, then cap tightly and refrigerate.

—Elizabeth Schneider

GINGER SYRUP

This tasty but not too sweet syrup is wonderful drizzled over vanilla ice cream. It can also add an intriguing flavor to applesauce, stewed pears or chunks of fresh melon or pineapple.

If the ginger is shiny, unwrinkled and firm, there is no need to peel it. If you are dubious, increase the ginger to 5 ounces, to allow for the loss of weight and flavor, and peel it. This also yields a slightly clearer syrup.

MAKES 1½ CUPS

4 ounces fresh ginger, washed and cut into ½-inch pieces.
1 cup sugar

1. Place the ginger in a food processor and process, stopping to scrape down the sides once or twice, until minced, about 1 minute.

2. Scrape the ginger into a small noncorrodible saucepan, add 2 cups of water and bring to a boil over moderate heat. Boil for 5 minutes. Cover and set aside at room temperature for at least 12 hours or overnight.

3. Strain into a bowl through a sieve lined with a double layer of dampened cheesecloth. Gather the cheesecloth together and twist and squeeze to extract as much liquid as possible. Discard the solids.

4. Return the ginger liquid to the saucepan, add the sugar, stirring to dissolve, and boil until reduced to 1½ cups, 5 to 8 minutes. Set aside to cool. Refrigerate, tightly covered, in a jar for up to 3 weeks.

—Diana Sturgis

INDEX

A

B

C

D-E

F

G

H

I-J-K

L

M

N-O

P

Q-R

S

T-U-V

W-X-Y-Z

CONTRIBUTORS

In addition to the recipes developed by Diana Sturgis, John Robert Massie and Anne Disrude in *Food & Wine's* test kitchen, we are pleased to include recipes from the following contributors to the magazine:

Nancy Verde Barr, a cooking teacher with a concentration on Italian cooking, is executive chef to Julia Child on a number of projects, including a column in *Parade* magazine, and is executive chef for all cooking segments on the "Good Morning America" show.
Rose Levy Beranbaum, food writer, consultant and author of *Romantic and Classic Cakes* (Irena Chalmers), is currently working on a book on cakes to be published in 1987 by William Morrow.
Jane Butel is the author of seven cookbooks, including the *Woman's Day Book of New Mexican Cooking* (Pocket Books), and is the founder of the Pecos Valley Spice Company.
Penelope Casas is a food and travel writer, cooking teacher and author of *The Foods and Wines of Spain* (Knopf) and *Tapas: The Little Dishes of Spain* (Knopf).
Bernard Clayton, Jr. is the author of *The Complete Book of Breads* (Simon & Schuster), *The Breads of France* (Bobbs-Merrill), *The Complete Book of Pastries* (Simon & Schuster) and *The Complete Book of Soups and Stews* (Simon & Schuster)—each of which has won an R. T. French Tastemaker Award.
Jeanette Ferrary and Louise Fiszer are the co-authors of *California-American Cookbook, Innovations on American Regional Dishes* (Simon & Schuster). Ferrary is a freelance writer and restaurant critic and Fiszer is the director of Louise's Pantry Cooking School in Menlo Park, California.
Jim Fobel is an artist, food writer, cookbook author and food stylist whose most recent book is *Beautiful Food* (Van Nostrand Reinhold).
Lila Gault is a Seattle-area wine and food writer. She is the wine editor for *Country Living* magazine and is a partner in Vintage Northwest, a wine sales and marketing company.
Richard Grausman is a cooking teacher and the United States representative of Le Cordon Bleu.
Dorie Greenspan is a freelance food writer currently at work on a dessert cookbook.
Anne Lindsay Greer is the author of *Cuisine of the American Southwest* (Harper & Row) and *Creative Mexican Cooking: Recipes from Great Texas Chefs* (Texas Monthly Press) and is a consultant to Dallas's Nana Grill.
Susan Grodnick is a freelance food writer who has just completed work on *Seppi Renggli's Four Seasons Spa Cuisine* (Simon & Schuster) and is co-author with Ed Edelman of *Ideal Cheese Book,* to be published in late 1986 by Harper & Row.
Jane Helsel Joseph is a freelance food writer.
Thorvald G. Lauritsen, using his professional name, Ted Larson, is a radio announcer with WBZ in Boston who writes two syndicated cooking columns. He is currently at work on a seasonal sampler cookbook due to be published in 1987.
Tom Maresca and Diane Darrow write frequently on the wine and food of southern Europe. Maresca is the author of *Mastering Wine* (Bantam).
Copeland Marks is a food historian and cookbook author whose most recent book is *False Tongues & Sunday Bread, A Guatemalan and Mayan Cookbook* (M. Evans & Co.). He is presently working on an Indian cookbook due in early 1986 and a Burmese cookbook due in late 1986.
Lydie Marshall is a cooking teacher, food writer and consultant whose most recent book is *Cooking with Lydie Marshall* (Knopf).
Michael McLaughlin is a food writer and co-author of *The Silver Palate Cookbook* (Workman). He owns and operates a restaurant, The Manhattan Chili Co., in New York City.
Perla Meyers is a cooking teacher and the author of *The Seasonal Kitchen* (Vintage), *The Peasant Kitchen* (Harper & Row) and *From Market to Kitchen* (Harper & Row).
Molly O'Neill, freelance writer and chef, is *Food & Wine's* "Simply Splendid" columnist.
Elizabeth Schneider is a food journalist, the author of *Ready When You Are: Made-Ahead Meals for Entertaining* (Crown) and co-author of *Better Than Store-Bought* (Harper

& Row). Her new book, *A Commonsense Guide to Uncommon Fruits and Vegetables* (Harper & Row) will be published in early 1986.
Barbara Tropp is the author of *The Modern Art of Chinese Cooking* (Morrow) and the chef/owner of China Moon, a Chinese bistro in San Francisco. She was named one of the "Great Chefs of San Francisco" in the PBS series of the same name.
Patricia Wells is the Paris-based restaurant critic for the *International Herald-Tribune* and author of *The Food Lover's Guide to Paris* (Workman).
Gayle Henderson Wilson and Jim Dodge: Jim Dodge is the pastry chef at the Stanford Court in San Francisco, and Gayle Henderson Wilson is a Bay area food consultant.
Paula Wolfert is a food writer, cooking teacher and the author of *The Cooking of South-West France* (Dial Press), *Mediterranean Cooking* (Quadrangle) and *Couscous and Other Good Food from Morocco* (Harper & Row).

We would also like to thank the following restaurants and individuals for their contributions to *Food & Wine* and to this cookbook:

John Ash, John Ash & Co., Santa Rosa, California; **Ambassador Grill,** New York, New York; **American Festival Cafe,** New York, New York; **Lauren Berdy; Cindy Black,** Sheppard's, San Diego, California; **Patrice Boely,** The Polo, New York, New York; **Brennan's of Houston,** Houston, Texas; **Cafe Fortuna,** Beverly Hills, California; **Mark Carozza,** Cafe Renni, Lambertville, New Jersey; **Christian Chavanne,** Sonoma Mission Inn, Boyes Hot Springs, California; **Steven Christianson,** The Lion's Rock, New York, New York; **Patrick Clark,** Cafe Luxembourg, New York, New York; **Jean Cooper; Creative Seafood Restaurant,** Tampa, Florida; **Sanford D'Amato,** John Byron, Milwaukee, Wisconsin; **Robert Del Grande,** Cafe Annie, Houston, Texas; **Christian Delouvrier,** The Maurice, New York, New York; **Marcel Desaulniers,** The Trellis, Williamsburg, Virginia; **Eleanor and Ferris Dove,** Dovecrest Restaurant, Exeter, Rhode Island; **John Downey,** Downey's, Santa Barbara, California; **Jackie Etcheber,** Jackie's, Chicago, Illinois; **Leona Foote; Bruce Frankel,** Panache Restaurant, Cambridge, Massachusetts; **Joyce Goldstein,** Square One, San Francisco, California; **Silva Hendricks; Chef Hubert,** Le Bistro d'Hubert, Paris, France; **Jimmy's Place,** Chicago, Illinois; **David Jordan,** Virginia Museum of Fine Arts, Richmond, Virginia; **Emeril Lagasse,** Commander's Palace, New Orleans, Louisiana; **Jack Leone,** Cafe Giovanni, Denver, Colorado; **Jennifer Marshall; Zarela Martinez,** Cafe Marimba, New York, New York; **Tom J. McCombie,** Chez T. J., Mountain View, California; **Marc Meneau,** l'Espérance, Vézelay, France; **Mark Miller,** Berkeley, California; **Mrs. Simpson's,** Washington, D.C.; **Piret Munger,** Piret's, San Diego, California; **La Normande,** Pittsburgh, Pennsylvania; **Claire Owens,** Les Survivants, Annapolis, Maryland; **Jean-Louis Palladin,** Jean-Louis, Washington, D.C.; **Cindy Pawlcyn,** Mustards Grill, Napa, California; **Nell Picower; Ritz-Carlton Hotel,** Chicago, Illinois; **Charlene Rollins,** New Boonville Hotel, Boonville, California; **Rowe Inn,** Ellsworth, Michigan; **Tim Ryan,** American Bounty, Hyde Park, New York; **Alain Sailhac,** Le Cirque, New York, New York; **Keo Sananikone,** Keo's Thai Cuisine, Honolulu, Hawaii; **Stephen Schimoler,** Terrace Restaurant, Locust Valley, New York; **Sally Scoville,** Le Cherche-Midi, New York, New York; **John Sedlar,** St. Estéphe, Manhattan Beach, California; **Stephanie Sidell and Bob Sasse,** Sidell & Sasse, Brookline, Massachusetts; **Marlena Spieler; St. Botolph,** Boston, Massachusetts; **Diana Steinberg; Leo Steiner,** Carnegie Deli, New York, New York; **Emile Tabourdiau,** Le Bristol, Paris, France; **Massachusetts Bay Company,** Boston, Massachusetts; **Jane K.L. Thomas; Véronique,** Brookline, Massachusetts; **John Virella,** Villa Virella, Blakeslee, Pennsylvania; **Barry Wine,** The Quilted Giraffe, New York, New York; **Second Avenue Kosher Deli,** New York, New York.

PHOTO CREDITS
Page 33: Frank Spinelli. **Pages 34-35:** Ralph Bogertman. **Page 35:** George Obremski. **Page 36:** Peter Johansky. **Page 69:** Ron Schwerin. **Page 70:** Irene Stern. **Page 71:** Ron Schwerin. **Pages 72 and 73:** Peter Johansky. **Pages 74-75:** Thom de Santo. **Page 76:** Marc David Cohen. **Page 109:** Matthew Klein. **Pages 110-111:** Rudy Muller. **Page 111:** Neil Rice. **Page 112:** Bruce Wolf. **Page 145:** Thomas Lindley. **Pages 146-147:** Artie Goldstein. **Page 148:** John Bechtold. **Page 181:** Ron Schwerin. **Pages 182-183:** Dick Frank. **Page 184:** Thomas Lindley. **Page 185:** Peter Johansky. **Page 186:** Thomas Lindley. **Pages 186-187:** Dick Frank. **Page 188:** Larry Couzens. **Page 221:** John Bechtold. **Page 222:** Larry Couzens. **Page 223:** Michael Molkenthin. **Page 224:** Thom de Santo.

Cover Photograph: Peter Johansky